DEPARTMENT OF INDUSTRY

The economics of industrial subsidies

Edited by Alan Whiting

Papers and Proceedings of the Conference
on the Economics of Industrial Subsidies
held at the Civil Service College, Sunningdale,
February 1975

LONDON
HER MAJESTY'S STATIONERY OFFICE

ISBN 0 11 511638 9

Contents

Foreword

The papers printed in this volume were presented at a conference on the economics of industrial subsidies which was held at the Civil Service College, Sunningdale, over the week-end 7 to 9 February 1975. The conference was arranged by the Economics and Statistics Divisions (which provide a common service to the Departments of Industry, Trade and Prices and Consumer Protection) in order to review current thinking on the economic analysis of the various forms of subsidies offered to industry and which could be of relevance to policy divisions. It was attended not only by researchers currently engaged on economic and econometric studies, including Government as well as academic economists, but also senior officials with a close knowledge of the problems encountered in translating economic advice into policy recommendations. In the event, the Department of Industry, H M Treasury, the Department of Employment, the Central Policy Review Staff and the Scottish Office were represented. A full list of participants is given.

In order to focus the attention of the contributors on problems primarily of interest to the Department of Industry contributors were supplied with background papers by government economists and officials which offered an account of how subsidy policy had evolved in the UK, how it was administered, and how it compared with policy abroad. These papers represent a contribution in their own right, and should form as useful a background to the rest of the proceedings for the reader of this volume as they did for the outside contributors.

The areas covered by the conference may be classified as (a) the rationale of subsidies to industry as viewed by the economists, the politician and the official; (b) the economic analysis of subsidies to labour, capital, and research and development; (c) the problems of quantitative estimation of the effects of industrial subsidies. The papers are published subject to some revisions made in the light of the lively discussion which they engendered, together with the comments of those who were asked to introduce them. It will be agreed, I am sure, that they offer a unique record of the current state of knowledge of an important and perplexing problem and one which merits much further investigation.

The conference was opened by Mr P W Carey, CB, Second Permanent Secretary in the Department of Industry. Mr A Whiting, an Economic Adviser in the Department has undertaken the onerous task of preparing the papers for publication as well as offering a contribution of his own. Mr J A Banfield, a Senior Economic Assistant in the Department prepared a record of the discussion for circulation to participants. I have been responsible for the choice of subjects and invitations to speakers.

Alan Peacock
Chief Economic Adviser

Participants

J A Banfield   Senior Economic Assistant   Department of Industry
Professor C Blake   University of Dundee
Professor A J Brown, CBE   University of Leeds
I C R Byatt   Under Secretary, Economics   H M Treasury
P W Carey, CB   Secretary (Industry)   Department of Industry
T F Cripps   Department of Applied Economics, University of Cambridge and Department of Industry
Professor W Elkan   University of Durham
M J Fores   Senior Economic Adviser   Department of Industry
Professor C Freeman   University of Sussex
N K A Gardner   Senior Economic Adviser   Department of Industry
K Hartley   University of York
H C G Hawkins   Senior Economic Adviser   Central Policy Review Staff
R S Howard   Senior Economic Adviser   Department of Industry
M P Lam   Under Secretary, Computers Systems, Electronics   Department of Industry
A J Lippitt   Under Secretary, Regional Industrial Finance   Department of Industry
A Lord, CB   Deputy Secretary   Department of Industry
P J Lund   Economic Adviser   Department of Industry
R R Mackay   University of Newcastle
Sir I Maddock, CB, OBE, FRS   Chief Scientist   Department of Industry
Dr R G L McCrone   Chief Economic Adviser, Scottish Office
C L Melliss   Economic Adviser   Department of Industry
B C Moore   Department of Applied Economics, University of Cambridge
R Morley   University of Durham
Miss A E Mueller   Under Secretary, Industrial & Commercial Policy   Department of Industry
M Nonhebel   Economic Adviser   Department of Employment
K Pavitt   University of Sussex
Professor A T Peacock, DSC   Chief Economic Adviser   Department of Industry
Professor A R Prest   London School of Economics and Political Science
R F Prosser, CB, MC   Deputy Secretary   Department of Industry
M H M Reid   Under Secretary, Regional Industrial Development   Department of Industry
J Rhodes   Department of Applied Economics; University of Cambridge
R M Rumbelow   Principal, Air Division   Department of Industry
D R H Sawers   Under Secretary, Economics   Department of Industry
H Scholes   Under Secretary, Finance & Economic Appraisal   Department of Industry
M T Sumner   University of Manchester
A P Thirlwall   University of Kent
A Whiting   Economic Adviser   Department of Industry
Professor J Wiseman   University of York

The administration of industrial subsidies

G M FIELD AND P V HILLS

Introduction

This paper considers some of the administrative issues which arise when governments give subsidies for industry. It describes the arrangements which have been made to administer some of the British Government's main industrial subsidy schemes over the last 15 years or so and the difficulties or criticisms that have arisen. Being a background paper, it does not stray into the potentially controversial sphere by attempting to draw conclusions about the merits of one kind of subsidy scheme over another from an administrative point of view.

The paper falls into two parts. The first deals with general subsidy schemes under which the subsidy is administered within standard rules of procedure to determine the eligibility of applicants and within those rules is available to all comers. Examples of such schemes are accelerated depreciation allowances, Investment Grants, Regional Employment Premium. The second part deals with specific or bespoke schemes under which a tailor-made subsidy is given to a particular person or firm for a particular purpose eg for a specific project or product, or for the restructuring or re-equipment of a firm. Examples of such schemes are the assistance given to aluminium smelters under the Industrial Expansion Act, and assistance to individual firms under Section 8 of the Industry Act 1972.

The two categories are not as clear-cut as this brief and simplified description suggests. Some schemes are or have been operated in a standardised way but the subsidy is tailored to the needs of the firm and the project in question, eg assistance under the Local Employment Acts and under Section 7 of the Industry Act 1972. Nevertheless the broad distinction between the two categories is helpful and these selective but general schemes are included in the first category for the purposes of this paper.

The importance of administrative considerations is obvious. It is no good having a subsidy scheme which is theoretically ideal unless it is also practicable. 'Practicable' means meeting the following criteria:

(a) The scheme should be readily understandable and should not impose an undue administrative burden on either Government or industry.

(b) It must be possible to secure that Parliament's and Ministers' intentions are carried out, by ensuring that the subsidy goes only to those industries and for those activities for which the scheme was intended.

(c) Public money must be safeguarded as far as possible against the possibilities of fraud, of legal abuse, of failure to observe the conditions of the assistance, and of losses arising from the collapse of companies.

A further criterion applying to the general schemes is:

(d) The need to secure equity in the treatment of applicants.

A comment on terminology is appropriate before the substantive discussion in Parts I and II below of the general and specific schemes. The question of what constitutes a subsidy is one on which there has been much discussion but not a lot of agreement. This state of affairs is due to a number of factors among which are the role of subsidies in economic theory as an impediment to outcomes which market forces would dictate and their doubtful position under international agreements. There can thus often be room for considerable argument about whether a given measure constitutes 'aid' or 'assistance' rather than a 'subsidy'. This paper is not the place to pursue such a venerable will-o-the-wisp. But it should be noted that not everyone by any means would accept that every measure covered in it is 'a subsidy'. The measures covered were chosen for their importance or interest – and with an eye to not making the paper too long. Their presence in it, therefore, should not necessarily be construed an admission that any particular one is a subsidy and the expression should be read in that light.

I General schemes

General schemes have been responsible for a much bigger share of total Government spending on industrial subsidies, at least in recent years, than have specific schemes. The philosphy behind blanket subsidies of this kind is that their availability and value are readily calculable by industrialists, who can therefore take them into account in planning their activities. Such schemes thus build a weighting into the operation of market forces in favour of, for example, capital investment in industrial plant and machinery, of employment in manufacturing in the Development Areas, and so on. They are an attempt to influence industry's decisions without detailed involvement in its affairs, although this as we shall see is a matter of degree. The hope is that general schemes will be relatively straightforward, quick and inexpensive to operate, indeed if they are not then a great part of their value is lost because they will not have the desired effect on industrial decision making.

Successive governments in recent years have tended to concentrate on using general subsidy schemes because of doubts about the feasibility of 'fine tuning', of a selective, discriminatory approach in which the amount of a subsidy would be negotiated case by case and pitched at just that level, and no more, which is needed to influence the decision. Although this more specific approach has been adopted to a limited extent, it has been considered too expensive in staff costs and too difficult and time-consuming to be followed on a bigger scale.

Tax incentives

In the 1950s and the first half of the 1960s the main incentives for capital investment in industry were operated through the tax system in the form of accelerated depreciation allowances and investment allowances. The acceleration was brought about mainly by an initial allowance – that is an allowance for the first year above the normal annual writing down allowance. Another form of accelerated depreciation was the free depreciation which was given for industrial plant in Development Districts from 1963 to 1966. Accelerated depreciation did not increase the amount of the total allowances over the life of the asset, which was limited to its cost; the investment allowance however was given on top of depreciation allowances. Initial allowances, free depreciation and investment allowances were in most cases replaced by Investment Grants in 1966 but the tax system returned to the forefront of Government measures to stimulate investment in 1970: when Investment Grants were ended, depreciation allowances were increased, and the rates were biased in favour of the Development Areas. It is the need to discriminate, whether between capital and current expenditure, between different parts of the country, or between different types of assets or different industries, which presents the main administrative problems for the Inland Revenue. Problems for the Revenue produce in turn problems for industry because of the greater amount of information required to enable the Tax Inspector to do his job, the greater amount of policing which is necessary, and the delays which result from the greater complication. These considerations mean that the tax system can only be a blunt instrument when used for incentive purposes. One result of using the tax system is that the full benefits go only to firms who are making enough profits, so there is a built-in element of discrimination in this sense. There are of course differing views about the extent to which this form of discrimination is desirable: the benefit of the incentive is delayed, particularly for new firms which take some time to produce profits, and even where ample profits are available there is a relatively long interval – compared with a system of grants – between the incurring of the expenditure and the receipt of the benefit in cash terms when the reduced tax is due for payment.

Under the investment allowances system, firms not only had the full cost of their qualifying capital investment deducted from gross profits before tax was calculated, but also an additional premium of 30 per cent of the cost of the investment. The allowance was thus a kind of grant except that it was paid in the form of a deduction from tax liability, not as cash payment. The chief administrative problem of this system was that it gave firms an incentive to claim that current expenditure – which is deducted 100 per cent before taxable profits are arrived at – was capital expenditure and thus eligible to be deducted 130 per cent. The distinction between capital and current expenditure is very difficult to draw at the margin, and while the Revenue adopts as a rule of thumb that capital assets last for at least two years, there is no statutory backing for this. Firms began to claim that all kinds of expenditure which had previously been regarded as current, such as the canteen cutlery, was in fact capital and Tax Inspectors were involved in a great deal of work preparing for appeals against their decisions before the Tax Commissioners.

Between 1970 and 1972 capital investment on new plant and machinery in the Development Areas qualified for a 100 per cent first year allowance, as against 60 per cent and later 80 per cent in the rest of the country. This differentiation involved two sets of calculations in assessing the value of allowances and a need or policing to ensure that assests said to be used in the Development Areas were indeed used there. The policing of the tax incentives is done locally by Inspectors of Taxes under the same procedure as for other tax allowances.

With the Finance Act 1972 the 100 per cent first year allowance, hitherto confined to the Development Areas, was extended to the whole of the country. A new system of Regional Development Grants was introduced but the value of grants received was not to be deducted from the cost of assets in calculating tax allowances. For the Revenue, this system is in a number of respects much simpler to administer than its predecessors for the following reasons:
   (a) There is no regional differentiation in the tax system.
   (b) The distinction between current and capital expenditure, while still necessary, does not have the significance which it had under the investment allowances system and there is little incentive for firms to attempt to blur the distinction for tax purposes.
   (c) The fact that the receipt of Regional Development Grants, unlike Investment Grants, has no effect on tax allowances removes the need for the Revenue to check the extent to which firms have received grants in respect of the investment for which allowances are being claimed.
   (d) All expenditure on plant not written off in the first year or carried back against profits of previous years has to be written off at a single rate of 25 per cent (reducing balance method). All expenditure on buildings has to be written off, apart from the first year allowances, at the rate of 4 per cent (straight line method).

3

Thus apart from the distinction between plant and buildings, there is no differentiation of depreciation rates and all expenditure can be put into a single pool for the purpose of calculating allowances.

The present arrangements for plant are often referred to as 'free depreciation' but in fact under a system of true free depreciation firms are allowed to write off their capital expenditure against tax liabilities in whatever way they like. There has been some pressure for such a system, which operated in the Development Districts from 1963 to 1966, to be reintroduced on a national level. The objection to this has been that the yield of Corporation Tax would be more unpredictable and this is unacceptable from a budgetary standpoint; and that in any case the present arrangements are very little less generous than true free depreciation would be.

Investment Grants

Investment Grants (IGs) were introduced under the Industrial Development Act 1966 as cash grants towards capital expenditure on new plant and machinery in the manufacturing and construction industries, and on mining works, computers, ships and hovercraft. These paragraphs are concerned chiefly with the issues arising in the area of manufacturing industry. The scheme covered the whole of Great Britain but with a higher rate of grant applying in the Development Areas, the rates being 20 and 40 per cent except for expenditure incurred in the calendar years 1967 and 1968 when they were increased to 25 and 45 per cent.

The object of the system was to encourage investment in general but to concentrate the assistance in those sectors of industry and those areas of the country where the Government particularly wished to bring about additional investment. They regarded the previous system of investment allowances as too widely dispersed to be fully effective. Two fundamental principles of the scheme are worthy of note. First, the eligibility of assets was determined by whether they were used for a qualifying process. Second, payment of grant was permissive, not mandatory. The reasoning behind these provisions was that an entirely new line was being drawn between eligible and ineligible assets in order to exclude all assets of service industries and some assets (eg vehicles) of manufacturing industries. This new discrimination would create many anomalies and give rise to numerous difficult borderline decisions. In the last resort it was therefore regarded as essential to leave it to the Department concerned to decide, within the limits of the legislation, whether or not to pay grant in a particular case. There was no provision for appeal either to the courts or to any special tribunal, because decisions of the courts were considered to have frustrated Government policy in the case of the mandatory investment allowances. There was no question of the Department discriminating between firms arbitrarily; it could discriminate only according to the type of process carried out or item of plant used. Certain categories of plant were systematically excluded in this way, notably office machinery and furniture, canteen equipment, loose tools, small and short-lived items, and all items below the specified minimum value of £25. The Department published guidance notes to help firms to know to what extent their investment expenditure was likely to be admissible for grant. Nevertheless the element of discretion was strongly opposed by industry at first and certainly detracted somewhat from the automaticity which was reckoned to be one of the basic qualities of the scheme. One effect was to produce representations against the Department's decisions through other channels such as Parliamentary Questions, letters to Ministers, and complaints to the Parliamentary Commissioner for Administration (Ombudsman). Nevertheless, considering that nearly 700,000 claims were dealt with between 1966 and 1974, the volume of such representations was remarkably small.

Investment allowances had been administered by the Inland Revenue as part of the general consideration of a company's tax liability, with no special staffing structure. The Revenue had to consider only whether the investment expenditure was of a capital nature and whether it was on plant and machinery – not that either of these tests was necessarily simple, as we have seen. On the other hand for the purposes of IG, the Department had to decide in addition whether the asset was eligible and being used in a qualifying process. It was also necessary to determine the rate of grant to be applied and whether the enterprise was carrying on business in Great Britain, quite apart from a wide variety of special problems concerning computers, hired assets, ships and so on. Applications had therefore to be presented in some detail and to be examined by staff of a level capable of interpreting the provisions of the Act and the administrative policies decided upon. Some indication of the size of the task is that in the peak years, 1969 to 1970 and 1970 to 1971, around 140,000 applications were received and £587m paid out in grant each year.

The system was administered by five IG offices situated in Glasgow, Cardiff, Billingham, Bootle and Southend, involving a total staff of 1,000 at an estimated initial cost of £2m a year. The decision to administer the scheme on a regional basis was taken for both practical and policy reasons. It would have been inconsistent with the policy of dispersal to establish a single unit in London, the only place where there was a reasonable chance of assembling and accommodating the required number of staff in the time available. Moreover industry expressed a strong preference for local decisions, while from the Department's standpoint the need to inspect assets to determine eligibility and the subsequent policing of grant payments reinforced the case for area offices. On the other hand decentralisation creates a need to secure consistency of treatment between the different offices, and inter-office consultation, particularly by Office Directors in committee, was a feature of the organisation. The role of the IG Division at HQ was to provide policy directions, to provide forecasts and reports of expenditure for Treasury and Parliamentary purposes, to review the scheme, and to deal with Ministers' cases and Parliamentary Questions. General guidance on examination procedures was given to the IG offices and supplemented by instructions on particular matters raised by individual cases as experience of the scheme was gained. Over the lifetime of IGs 632 such instructions were issued. The real world being too complex for any set of administrative rules, there was a continuing need for difficult cases to be submitted to HQ and for additional instructions to be issued.

In applying for grant, firms had to describe the assets in question, the process in which they were to be used, and the expenditure incurred. Applications had to be signed by a director of the company and by an independent accountant, this method of certification being preferred to the direct examination of invoices and receipts by the Department. The accountant's report was checked by confirming that the signatory was qualified and also by confirming with him independently that he had in fact signed the particular report. The *bona fides* of applicants was checked against a business register and with the Inland Revenue. Apart from this, the test of examination consisted in ascertaining, from the material supplied on the specially designed application forms and from questions to the applicant where necessary, whether the asset was admissible under the agreed policies, eg was plant and not part of a building. Inevitably the administrative system took some time to settle down but by 1970 a check of a proportion of claims passed for payment found errors which would have led to overpayment of about £15,000, or 0·04 per cent of the total grant payable in the sample, and underpayments of £3,000 (0·01 per cent). The cost of applying the check was £16,000.

Since the grants were in the main to be given towards expenditure on assets to be used for certain purposes, it was essential, in order to safeguard the public purse, for the Government to be able to recover grant if the assets ceased to serve these purposes. The Department therefore imposed conditions which allowed them to recover the grant in certain circumstances, notably where an asset ceased to be used for a qualifying process or was disposed of, and recipients of grant had a commitment to notify the Department of such events. Inspection teams were set up in each of the grant offices whose job was to visit firms to see if the conditions were being complied with and also to check whether the facts as stated on the application form were correct. The rate of inspection enabled the inspectors to get round all recipients of grant within about five years. In the period to the end of September 1973, 112,000 establishments were visited, and 766,000 assets were inspected of which 52,000 revealed apparent irregularities. Recovery of grant, in whole or in part, was usually effected by deduction from future payments. Over the six years 1967–68 to 1972–73, £950,000 of grant was written off, of which £712,000 was due to liquidations, the rest being overpayments or cases involving breach of conditions where for various reasons the grant could not be recovered. During this period some £2,800m of grant was paid out. In only five cases were firms or individuals prosecuted for fraud.

Three particular problems which arose on the IG scheme are worthy of note. First, the fact that the test of eligibility for grant depended on plant being used in a qualifying process meant that the purpose for which a piece of plant was being acquired had to be clearly stated in each case and frequently the process had to be examined by the IG office. This was perhaps the greatest single source of difficulty in administering the scheme. Second, the termination arrangements introduced in the Investment and Building Grants Act 1971 provided that grant could be paid on expenditure incurred after 26 October 1970 (the date of the announcement of the end of the scheme) only if the expenditure was due under a contract made on or before that date. The intention was to combine a degree of fairness to firms who had committed themselves to expenditure in the expectation of receiving grant with the maximum saving to the Exchequer and the prevention of 'forestalling' ie the bringing forward of expenditure for the purpose of receiving grant. In practice this provision gave rise to a great deal of dispute because firms claimed that in many cases it was not their practice to use formal contract procedures and thus that much capital expenditure was in reality committed but unreasonably excluded from grant. Ministers recognized that there was a strong element of rough justice about this approach but in presenting the legislation they stuck to the view that the contract test was the most generous arrangement which they could allow. Much time and effort was devoted to this issue by both industry and the Department because substantial supporting documentation was called for in many cases and there was also a good deal of misunderstanding about what legally constituted a contract. The winding up of the IG scheme was substantially delayed as a result. Third, expenditure on IGs proved very hard to forecast. The scheme was entirely new and was open-ended in that grant was payable on all valid applications, however many there were. The amount of grant payable in a given year depended on the level of capital expenditure by the industries concerned, the proportion of it incurred on eligible assets, its distribution between DAs and non-DAs, the timing of applications, and in the early years the extent to which firms opted to claim allowances rather than grants. The following table compares the original estimate of expenditure with the final out-turn year by year:

	Original estimate £m	Final out-turn £m.
1967–68	166	315
1968–69	380	475
1969–70	460	587
1970–71	600	587
1971–72	620	492
1972–73	390	337
Totals	2616	2793

To some extent the disparities were the result of deliberate Government decisions, eg to speed up the payment of grant, after the estimates were made. Nevertheless the figures indicate the substantial problems which the scheme caused to those whose task was to forecast public expenditure for budgetary and other purposes.

Regional Development Grants

Regional Development Grants (RDGs), introduced under Part I of the Industry Act 1972, are very similar in concept to IGs but there are a few important differences. Again RDGs are cash grants towards approved capital expenditure already incurred by the applicant and the main qualifying industries – manufacturing, mining and construction – are much the same as for IGs. The chief differences are:

(a) RDGs are payable on assets for use in the Assisted Areas only;

(b) The test of eligibility is that assets should be used on qualifying premises, not in qualifying processes. Thus once premises are classed as qualifying, subject to some re-checking of marginal cases, grant may be paid virtually automatically for assets which are to be used there. To qualify, premises have to be used wholly or mainly for qualifying activities. The normal test is whether more than half of the employees are occupied in qualifying activities, but other tests, eg the activities in which most of the capital equipment is used, may be adopted if the employee test is considered to give an unreal result. If premises are classed as qualifying, all capital equipment to be used there, whether or not it is to be used for qualifying activities, is eligible for grant. By the same token, if premises are not classed as qualifying, then none of the equipment is eligible for grant. The use of this criterion greatly simplifies the administration of grant, though it has an element of rough justice about it;

(c) RDGs are payable on buildings, as well as plant and machinery. This removes the need to distinguish between plant and buildings except in the Intermediate Areas where only buildings qualify;

(d) As noted above, RDGs are not deducted from the cost of an asset in computing tax allowances.

As with IGs, RDGs are administered by RDG offices – at Billingham, Bootle, Cardiff and Glasgow – and by a policy division at HQ. Because of the limited geographical coverage and the simplifications which have been introduced compared with the IG scheme, the number of staff involved is being cut by several hundreds as the IG scheme is being wound up. As far as forecasts of expenditure are concerned, the scheme was slower to build up than expected but for the current year the Vote Estimate of £225m is expected to be near the actual result.

Assistance under the Local Employment Acts (LEAs)

Various forms of assistance were available to industry in the Assisted Areas under the LEAs of 1960, 1963 and 1970, the Industrial Development Act 1966 and the Investment and Building Grants Act 1971 (referred to collectively for this purpose as the LEAs). The provisions were consolidated in the LEA 1972 but the forms of assistance referred to below were then superseded by the Industry Act 1972. The main forms of assistance were loans on favourable terms, Building Grants, Plant and Machinery Grants (1963 to 1966 only), Removal Grants and Operational Grants. Unlike IGs and RDGs, LEA assistance was mainly project based, negotiated case by case, and linked to the provision of new employment, or in some cases, the maintenance of existing employment. The grants were standardised in the sense that the rates of grants were fixed by statute or administrative decision (although from 1966 Building Grants were subject to a maximum cost per job) and the qualifications laid down, but in some cases, notably the higher rate of Building Grant and the Operational Grants, the qualifications were very narrowly drawn and complex to administer. Loans were more flexible, being tailored to the circumstances of the individual case although within certain broad restraints in the form of cost per job limits and a limit on the proportion of the cost of the project

7

which could be met from public sources. Where more than one form of LEA assistance was afforded to a single project there was an overriding cost per job limitation on the assistance.

The administrative machinery for handling LEA assistance on the Government side consisted of three elements: the Department's HQ and Regional Offices and an advisory committee called successively the Board of Trade Advisory Committee (BOTAC), the Ministry of Technology Advisory Committee (MOTAC), and the Local Employment Acts Financial Advisory Committee (LEAFAC), and hereinafter referred to as LEAFAC. Broadly speaking it was the role of HQ to lay down policy, to give guidance to Regional Offices, and to handle casework; the Regional Offices dealt with firms' initial inquiries in the light of the HQ guidance, made an initial vetting of applications for eligibility, and carried out an initial investigation of the project paying particular attention to the plausibility of employment forecasts; LEAFAC carried out a financial appraisal and advised the Minister whether assistance should be given and if so (except for the standardised grants) how much and on what terms and conditions. The Regional Offices had no devolved authority to approve assistance even in small cases. Thus the system was centralised and standardised.

The Acts provided that assistance was to be directed towards the provision of employment. Firms were required to estimate the number of new jobs which would be created as a result of the investment they were proposing so that LEAFAC and/or the Department could judge whether the amount of assistance being requested was justified. Some applicants found it difficult to make such forecasts, which in many cases were not part of their own investment planning, and there were varying degrees of realism in the forecasts provided. The Regional Offices had to assess the plausibility of the forecasts on the basis of their experience of other establishments in similar lines of business and past dealings with the firm, and LEAFAC and/or HQ took full account of this assessment. Once an offer had been made, however, generally speaking there was no effort to reduce the assistance paid or to claw it back because employment targets were not reached, unless this was the result of significant changes in the nature of the project itself. On the other hand the committee's attitude to further applications from the same company might be influenced if job forecasts in the past had proved to be over-optimistic.

Following a recommendation of the Estimates Committee, regular sample checks were made of the number of jobs actually created as a result of assistance offered. These checks revealed that the number of jobs created was around 85 to 90 per cent of the number expected to arise at the time the assistance was approved. The Department has no reason to think that the requirement to forecast jobs arising deterred many firms from applying for LEA assistance, or that the employment link caused any significant degree of distortion in firms' plans purely in the interests of receiving more assistance.

The role and composition of LEAFAC are worth attention. The committee, which met once a month or more often if the need arose, consisted of about six members, one of whom was appointed chairman by the Minister. The members were drawn from industry, banking, accountancy and the trade unions and held their positions as individuals and not in any sense as delegates. The practice was always to have a Scot, a Welshman, and a member from one of the English Assisted Areas. The committee was served by a Secretariat of up to 40 people seconded from the Department. The committee's independence from the Minister and from any outside pressures was jealously guarded and it was not required to give reasons for its decisions. It was given general policy guidelines by the Department, eg that the security for loans advanced should be the best available in the circumstances, that the purpose for which a loan was recommended should be specified, that loans should only exceptionally be recommended for longer than a ten year term, and that

Removal Grants should only cover a certain proportion of certain specified costs. For Building Grants it was required to advise whether the business and financial structure of the undertaking was such as to give reasonable assurance that the project would provide continuing employment. Except for Building Grants after 1968, assistance could not under the terms of the legislation be given without the committee's recommendation and even in the case of Building Grants the committee's advice was in practice sought in all but the small cases and never overridden. Although the committee was described as advisory, therefore, its role was plainly very powerful. When the circumstances of a case changed after the committee had made its recommendation on a loan, Removal Grant or Operational Grant, the Secretariat had discretion to agree to minor variations in the terms of the assistance but any substantial variation had to be referred back to the committee. Building Grants were referred back by the Department for a further opinion if project costs increased by more than a certain proportion before the grant was offered; some such references back were settled by the Secretariat.

The drawbacks of the LEAFAC system were a certain slowness in the processing of cases – largely because of the amount of information which had to be provided and assessed – and the lack of a strong regional representation in their assessment. The benefits were a greater degree of selectivity compared with the 'automatic' grant schemes, a consistent approach as between different cases and different parts of the country, and a strong safeguard for public money because of the independent and unbiased check which the committee provided. Some idea of the scale of the operation is given by the fact that at the maximum some 600 firms were in receipt of loans approved by LEAFAC and its predecessors. In 1969–70, the committee considered 353 cases involving loans, Removal Grants, Operational Grants and associated Building Grants, and 713 separate Building Grant cases.

The procedure was for a firm to submit its application to the Regional Office and, for applications other than for Building Grants only, at the same time to have informal meetings with members of the LEAFAC Secretariat who made regular visits (called 'clinics') to the regions advising on the criteria followed by the committee and on the processing of applications, though without any commitment. Some hopeless applications were 'talked out' to avoid wasting everybody's time. Once the Regional Office and HQ had both satisfied themselves as to the application's eligibility, a submission was prepared by the LEAFAC Secretariat, together usually with a report from the Accountancy Services Division of the Department acting for the committee and a technical report from an Advisory Officer, and put to the committee. This took the form of a factual description and comments on the soundness of the firm and the project, but there was no recommendation, as such, to the committee. In the case of loan applications, the committee decided, within the Department's guidelines, on the interest rate and other terms of the loans recommended; the rate was usually between 2 and 4 percentage points below commercial rates and applied to all loans approved at any one time. Variations in the subsidy value of loans were effected by the differing interest free periods sometimes given. Loans were typically for five to seven years. The committee gave its advice to the Minister, who was free to accept or reject the advice *in toto,* not amend it, though he could ask for it to be reconsidered. If the decision was taken to give assistance, an offer letter was sent to the applicant by the Department, and provided the offer was accepted and the conditions met, the assistance was paid.

Loan applications tended to be more complex than grant cases because of the need to safeguard and provide for repayment of the Government's money. (This was inevitable but perhaps paradoxical, because of course grants provide a greater degree of subsidy.) Consequently a wide range of supporting information was required from applicants by LEAFAC, covering trading history, forecasts of future trading, project costs and financing, management including financial control,

9

labour requirements and the security available for a loan. Cases invariably involved investigation by the Department's accountants and by the Advisory Officers, although the latter could be dispensed with where big and well-established companies were concerned. Extensive and mainly standard conditions were attached to loan offers, although the Department tried to be flexible where firms subsequently asked for particular conditions to be waived. The committee's general approach was regarded as rather unadventurous. Their good judgment and their caution are illustrated by the fact that by 1970 only £850,000, or 0.72 per cent of all loans advanced up to that time, had had to be written off. The after-care work on LEA loans was the Department's responsibility, discharged in practice by those officials who formed the LEAFAC Secretariat. In later years the committee was asked increasingly by the Department for advice on substantial issues which arose in the course of after-care work, eg requests for the postponement of capital or interest payments on loans. In this work the Department's and LEAFAC's twin concerns were to protect the company and preserve the employment whenever possible, provided this did not unduly put at risk the public money at stake.

Building Grants were available at first to a wide spread of industry, but from 1968 service industries were assisted only in respect of projects which would provide at least 50 additional jobs and which were not designed principally to serve local needs. Applications were submitted to the Regional Office, which was responsible for preliminary investigation and assessment of the employment targets; the company's forecasts had to be offset by any consequential job losses arising elsewhere in the Assisted Areas as a result of the project. The application and report was then sent to HQ and arrangements were made by the Regional Office for the necessary financial information to be sent by the applicant to LEAFAC. Building Grants, like all other LEA assistance had to be applied for in advance, thus differing from the current RDGs for buildings. Applications had to be submitted before the building work was completed or the building occupied (or part occupied) whichever was the earlier. Because of the large numbers of these applications, LEAFAC dealt with them by three two-man sub-committees. Applicants had to submit details of their project, including trading history, future trading figures and requirements and resources figures. Unless it was a new company, a report from the Department's accountants and from an Advisory Officer was not required, except where the sub-committee thought the application likely to be rejected, in which case reports would be obtained. The sub-committee's decisions were submitted to the full committee each month for ratification but only the full committee could reject applications.

Offers of grant were based on the estimates of expenditure (after vetting by LEAFAC), though a maximum figure could be stipulated on cost per job grounds. HQ also had to be satisfied that the company had security of tenure in the building concerned for at least ten years, in order to be able to meet the requirement of providing continuing employment. Plans and specifications were called for in all cases until 1971, when they were dispensed with in cases where estimated costs were not more than £50,000 and a detailed description of the work accepted instead. All plans and specifications were examined in detail by the professional staff of the Department of the Environment, who advised whether the building was reasonably suitable for its intended purpose and whether the estimated costs were reasonable. The amount of grant paid was calculated on a percentage of the actual eligible costs (except where scaled down on cost per job grounds), subject to production of an architect's or accountant's certificate. In cases where costs exceeded £20,000 two progress payments could be made on certification respectively of one-third and two-thirds of costs. Building Grants were offered subject to certain conditions, such as the continuation of the enterprise within the grant-aided building, and if these conditions were breached within a specified period of five years the Department could reclaim the whole or part of the grant. After-care activity to see that the conditions were met was handled by the Department's HQ and Regional Offices and consisted of postal checks with the company plus two visits to the site in the five year period.

One element of LEA assistance worthy of note is that in some cases a distinction was drawn between firms already existing in an Assisted Area and incoming firms. Thus a higher rate of Building Grant – at first 35 per cent of eligible costs rather than the usual 25, and subsequently 45 rather than 35 – was available to incoming firms, while Operational Grants were available only to incoming firms in Special Development Areas. Firms were only classed as 'incoming' if there were no associated enterprises within a 30 mile range of the new project on which the firm might be able to draw for resources, particularly managerial. At first Operational Grants took the form of a payment of 10 per cent of the cumulative expenditure, net of grants, on new buildings and plant and machinery, in each of the first three years of operation of the project; but this was subsequently changed to 30 per cent of the eligible wage and salary costs of the project during the first three years of operation. Again the grant offer was based on the estimated expenditure on wages, subject to overall cost per job limitation; if less was spent in the event, less grant was paid, but if the estimates proved too low there was no increase in the grant. There was no provision for Operational Grants to be reclaimed but if circumstances changed materially future payments might not be made. The theory behind this favourable treatment of incoming firms was that higher costs would be incurred than with an existing firm, but in practice the scheme proved very complicated to administer, led to lengthy disputes with applicants about whether or not they qualified, and was also felt to be unfair to existing firms who might be in direct competition with the newcomer. This form of discrimination has been dropped under Industry Act forms of assistance.

The procedure for the investigation of Operational Grant and Removal Grant applications was similar to that described for loans, which were often also involved.

Assistance under Section 7 of the Industry Act 1972

Just as the RDG scheme follows closely the precedent of the IG scheme but with certain important differences, so the experience of administering LEA assistance has been drawn on in establishing the procedures for selective financial assistance under Section 7 of the Industry Act 1972. In this case, however, the differences are perhaps more striking than the similarities. The powers are wider, in that they enable the Secretary of State to give assistance in virtually any form and in virtually any circumstances where the assistance is likely to provide, maintain or safeguard employment in the Assisted Areas and is for one of the purposes, such as the creation of productive capacity in an industry, which are listed in Section 7(2) of the Act. Administrative rules (guidelines) have been drawn up to define the circumstances in which assistance will normally be given and the main forms of assistance which are to be used. The guidelines have been published (see Appendix D in the Annual Report on the Industry Act 1972 for the year ended 31 March 1974). As under the LEA the main use of the powers is to help firms with projects providing new jobs, and loans and removal grants are still among the main forms of assistance. The third main form, Interest Relief Grants, is new however and offers substantial advantages. By assisting with the interest cost of loans raised from private sources, the Department can give the subsidy equivalent of a concessionary loan with less call on public expenditure and without the full vetting procedure which is needed to safeguard public money when a loan is given. On grounds of both policy and administration, no attempt is made to restrict assistance to projects which would not go ahead without it: it would not be practicable to distinguish fairly between projects on this basis.

The most striking feature of the administrative system which has been set up is the extent of devolution to the Department's Regional Offices. Within guidelines laid down by HQ in consultation with the Treasury, the Regional Offices have authority to approve assistance in individual cases of up to £1m in loans and the equivalent in Interest Relief Grants. Only cases above this limit or which fall outside the guidelines (and these are very much the minority) have to be referred to HQ. Regional Offices seek advice (except on small clear-cut cases) from the Regional Industrial Development Board, an advisory body consisting of people with experience of working in industry, the trade unions, commerce and the professions within the region. Cases are assessed by the staff of the Regional Offices who submit reports and recommendations to the Boards. The Boards are non-statutory so their approval is not mandatory but in practice their view is rarely set aside.

The advantage of this system of regional devolution is that cases can be dealt with quickly and by people who are familiar with the region and can take account of the region's needs, as well as the circumstances of the application, in reaching decisions. The danger is that undue inconsistencies of approach may arise between regions. A major purpose of the guidelines, which have been supplemented by detailed operating guidelines for internal use, is to minimise the risk of inconsistencies between regions. Nonetheless the guidelines leave Regional Offices and Boards a significant degree of freedom to tailor the assistance to the circumstances of each case, by choosing between loans and Interest Relief Grants, by offering interest free periods of varying length and by varying the requirements for the repayment of principal.

Cases outside the guidelines or outside the Regional Offices' delegated financial authority are decided at HQ, generally after consultation with the Industrial Development Advisory Board (IDAB). The divisions concerned at HQ are Regional Industrial Finance Division which is responsible for policy, guidelines and the handling of big and exceptional cases; the Industrial Development Unit which includes staff recruited temporarily from eg the banking and accountancy professions as well as career Civil Servants; and the industry sponsoring divisions.

Regional Employment Premium (REP)

The statutory provisions governing REP are complicated by the fact that the scheme was tacked on to the system for refund of Selective Employment Tax, which together with the SET additional payment was known as Selective Employment Premium. Thus REP, which was introduced in the Finance Act 1967, was made payable in respect of those employees for whom Selective Employment Premium was payable (under the Selective Employment Payments Act 1966) and who worked in an establishment in the Development Areas. Even now that SET and the related structure of refunds and premiums have been abolished, the provisions governing eligibility for REP are still based on that system. From September 1967 to 4 August 1974 REP was payable at the rate of £1.50 per male employee with lower rates for women, boys and girls. The rates were doubled from 5 August 1974.

To claim REP, an employer has to submit an application to be registered by the Secretary of State for Employment for the purposes of the scheme. Entitlement to be registered depends on four conditions being satisfied:

(a) The establishment is engaged wholly or partly in any of the eligible activities. Basically these are the activities listed in Orders III to XIX of the Standard Industrial Classification (SIC Rev 1968) and in scientific research or training relating to those activities.

(b) More than half of the persons employed in or from the establishment are employed wholly or mainly in connection with those activities.

(c) Not more than half are employed wholly or mainly in activities carried on for office purposes or transport or by way of the sale of goods.

(d) The establishment is situated within a Development Area.

The first three of these conditions are laid down in the Selective Employment Payments Act 1966; the fourth in the Finance Act 1967. The effect of condition (c) is that if more than half of the workforce is employed in connection with the eligible activities referred to at (a) but more than half of the total workforce is engaged in the non-qualifying activities of office work, sales or transport, then the establishment fails to qualify for registration. In most cases it is clear that an establishment satisfies, or fails to satisfy, the conditions, but borderline cases may cause a great deal of difficulty. Difficulty may arise in a number of ways; where there is doubt as to whether the activities are eligible (the SIC is not a legal document and presents problems of interpretation); in defining an establishment in the case of sites; where several activities, some eligible and some not, are carried on at a single establishment; where individual employees spend part of their time in eligible activities and part in ineligible activities. Nor is a decision, once reached, necessarily valid for a long period of time. Boarderline cases may swing in and out according to seasonal or other fluctuations in the workforce and in the extreme case an establishment may cease to qualify if a single employee is paid off. Since payments are calculated on a weekly basis, the test of eligibility has to be satisfied every week. If an establishment qualifies, even by a single employee, payments are made in respect of the entire workforce; and by the same token if it fails to qualify no payments are made even though a substantial number of the employees may be involved in eligible activities. This 'all or nothing' approach recalls the rule covering qualifying premises under the RDG scheme; and as in that case, it lays a great deal of importance on the marginal decisions. (In certain circumstances, however, the Department can divide the eligible activities in an establishment from the ineligible ones so that an employer can claim REP for the eligible activities as if they formed a separate establishment. In other cases, separate premises where the same eligible activities are carried on may be aggregated so that an employer can claim REP as if the separate premises formed one establishment.) Half rates of REP are paid in respect of employees who work less than 21 hours per week, unless they are normally contracted to work at least 21 hours.

Applications for registration are processed by the relevant local office of the Department of Employment: there are 22 offices which handle this work. If an application is approved, a certificate of registration is sent to the firm. At the same time the office notifies the Department's SEP Office at Runcorn where the details of the establishment are incorporated on computer records, and a claim form is sent to the employer. Employers are advised to submit claims as soon as possible after a claim period, lasting 13 weeks, is completed, but there is no limit to the time lag within which claims are accepted as long as records are available to substantiate them. Claims are dealt with by the computer and in straightforward cases payment is made within two to three weeks. A claim form for the next period is then issued to the employer. The premium is payable only in respect of employees for whom the Class 1 National Insurance contribution has been paid (SET used to be collected as part of NI contributions). Any attempt to claim for employees for whom this contribution has not been paid is illegal. From April 1975, when NI cards are withdrawn, REP at full or half rates as appropriate is to be paid in respect of all employees who are paid for at least eight hours employment in a week.

Procedures have been established to vet both original applications for registration and subsequent claims to prevent fraud and mistakes. Originally applications for registration were approved purely on the basis of the completed application, where everything appeared satisfactory, but many mistakes were found and visits to establishments are now made in all cases by the Authorised Officers of the Department. The officers have the right to inspect wage records and to satisfy themselves as to the nature of the activities being carried on. Checks are made on all claims going back more than a year. Checks are also built in to the computer programme so that claims can be investigated where something unusual arises. Payment is stopped automatically where it is known that the employer has gone into liquidation or when information from the Department of Health and Social Security reveals that the employer is in arrears with the payment of NI contributions. Random checks are also made on a small proportion of all claims. Notwithstanding these arrangements, the system relies to a considerable extent on the honesty of employers, who are required to notify the Department of material changes in their circumstances. The majority of prosecutions for fraud are linked with prosecution by the DHSS for non-compliance with NI contributions.

Employers have a right of appeal against the Secretary of State's refusal to register an establishment or where there is disagreement about the date of registration or the amount due to be paid. Appeals are made to Industrial Tribunals whose decision is final except that appeal may be made to the High Court (in Scotland the Court of Session) on a point of law only. The Department's view is that there is no right of appeal against a refusal by the Secretary of State to exercise his discretionary powers to aggregate or divide establishments.

II Specific schemes

Specific schemes (leaving aside the special case of Concorde) account for a relatively small proportion of Government spending on industrial subsidies. This part of the paper consists of brief descriptions of some schemes of assistance provided to individual organisations on a basis tailor-made to the particular circumstances. The following paragraphs set out the objectives of the schemes concerned and where appropriate say something about the way in which the particular circumstances of the case were appraised. It should be borne in mind that wide considerations of the national interest (eg maintaining employment, sustaining high technology) mean that the traditional forms of investment appraisal have been only a part of the Government's approach. These paragraphs also describe the terms on which the assistance is provided and the way in which the schemes are monitored. Such monitoring necessarily varies according to the circumstances of the case. It is also a developing art as Government Departments gain experience both generally and of particular cases.

Assistance to Cammell Laird Shipbuilders Ltd and Govan Shipbuilders Ltd

Objectives
The Department's principal objective in these two situations is to secure continuing employment in an efficient shipbuilding firm. This is not the same as making an investment in a major project; recently the scale of the Government's involvement in shipbuilding has been determined almost entirely by regional employment considerations although previously the objective was to promote the ability of the industry to compete in world markets. The shipyard managements have been given the task of achieving the best commercial operating performance which can be obtained within the constraints imposed by the Government's policy; this includes a budgetary constraint.

Approach to appraisal and monitoring
Both Govan and Cammell Laird are required to submit a formal long range corporate plan to be used by them and by the Department as a basic monitoring instrument. This sets out in detail what the management are trying to achieve from the use of the resources – financial, material and labour – under their control during the next four years. The more important elements of their overall planning strategy will be:

(a) market and product strategy;

(b) pricing strategy;

(c) capital redevelopment strategy;

(d) productivity improvement and industrial relations strategy,

(e) transitional problems (including, in particular, how best to phase in new capital redevelopment with the minimum of disruption to production).

It is the responsibility of the shipyard managements to find the right mix of these elements and to put the results into financial terms. The Department's job is to monitor the quality of their planning and decision making. The corporate plan – and hence the whole planning process – is updated annually.

Shorter term information

It would be less than adequate to rely on an annual updating if the Department are effectively to monitor each company's operating performance. Supplementary financial and other information is therefore required at more frequent intervals of which the following are the most important:

Monthly

Short Term cash forecast for the following three months.
Trading (Profit and Loss) Account for the previous month.

Quarterly

Trading Account and Balance Sheet for previous quarter.

Annually

Operating Forecast for current year and next two years. (This includes trading forecasts, balance sheet projections and cash flow forecasts for two years ahead and the projected financial outcome of the then current shipbuilding programme.) In each case particular regard is paid to the detailed assumptions on which financial projections have been based by the companies.

The combination of these financial and physical indicators helps the monitoring of the overall performance of the companies against their forecasts. But it has been found necessary to supplement the companies' monthly returns by regular and frequent visits to the shipyards during which trends which are noted from the returns and possible corrective action are discussed with senior managements. In addition we receive information monthly about the physical progress of the current shipbuilding programmes and the physical progress of capital redevelopment programmes.

The form of assistance – Cammell Laird

Early in 1970 Cammell Laird & Co (now called the Laird Group) faced serious financial difficulties as the result of the Group's shipbuilding subsidiary having accepted a number of loss making ship contracts at fixed prices. The then Government asked the former IRC to examine the Group's affairs. As part of complex financial arrangements, the shipbuilding undertaking ceased to be a subsidiary of the Laird Group; and the Government provided finance for the acquisition of 1½m £1 shares being 50 per cent of its ordinary share capital (now held by the Public Trustee on behalf of the Secretary of State). The Laird Group continued to hold the other 50 per cent on an 'investment' basis and agreed to provide for the foreseeable losses on the shipyard's order book up to a maximum of £7.2m with the assistance of loans totalling about £2.6m from the IRC and £0.675m from interested shipowners. The Laird Group has now repaid these loans.

In August 1971 the shareholders dismissed the then managing director and financial director from the Board of the shipbuilding company, and required the then Chairman to stand down. A new management was subsequently appointed by the Laird Group and Her Majesty's Government. After the new management had carried out a thorough examination of the company's affairs and presented plans for their future the Government announced in September 1972 that it would provide financial assitance to the company. This would amount to £20m in all, under Section 7 of the Industry Act, 1972, to enable the company to carry through this substantial programme of modernisation and to strengthen their position. It is estimated that the company will be entitled to receive a further £7m under the Act in the form of regional development grants and ship construction grants.

The scale of the Government's financial assistance dwarfs the company's present capital structure, and it will be necessary to reconstruct the capital of the company as part of the Government's public ownership plans. In the meantime, the Government has agreed to provide £9m to the company in the form of a temporary interest free loan – which is secured by a floating charge against all the assets of the company. The loan agreement which governs this loan gives the Secretary of State the power to prevent the company from altering an agreed capital redevelopment scheme; from borrowing money; from making a dividend distribution; from issuing new capital; or from selling its assets.

The form of assistance – Govan Shipbuilders

Following on the collapse of Upper Clyde Shipbuilders Ltd in June 1971, the Government commissioned Hill Samuel & Co to advise them about the future of shipbuilding on the Upper Clyde. In the view of the consultants a new shipbuilding entity could be established – based on three of the former UCS yards at Govan, Linthouse and Scotstoun – and under certain conditions would be capable of becoming viable. The Government accepted the consultants' report – published and laid before Parliament as Cmnd 4982 – and its recommendations form the basis of the financial funding arrangements of the new Company. The report estimated that the Company would require about £35m (at 1972 prices) from Government funds spread over a period of four to five years to enable the Company to modernise the facilities at the yards in order to bring them up to the best European standard, to fund losses and to replace working capital in the Company's early years.

On 30 June 1972 the then Secretary of State announced to the House that the Government would provide adequate financial support for the Company for a period of five years or until the Company attains commercial viability, whichever is the lesser period. This undertaking is conditional on agreements on working practices being respected by both sides of industry and the taking of ship contracts on terms acceptable to the Government. The new Company – Govan Shipbuilders Ltd – is wholly Government owned and funded. It commenced trading on 1 July 1972 and became fully operational on 18 September 1972. To date the Government has purchased £10m of equity (10 million £1 shares) and under a working capital agreement drawn up between the Department and the Company has made advances totalling £9.75m for working capital purposes. In addition, a further sum of £8.6m has been paid to the Company to meet the losses incurred by the Company to 27 December 1974.

International Computers Limited

Nature of support and background

International Computers Limited (ICL) was brought into existence in 1968 by the Government sponsored merger of the computer interests of English Electric and ICT. The merger was facilitated by the provision of £13.5m in Government grants towards the merged company's R and D programme. Her Majesty's Government also purchased 10 per cent of the equity of the new company.

On 4 July 1973 the Government announced its decision to provide ICL with financial support of £40m in all as launching aid for the development of a new range of computers (now known as the 2900 Series). The first £14.2m had already been announced in July 1972 and the remainder was to be made available during the period up to September 1976.

Objectives

The objective of support was to maintain the development of an indigenous capability in computer systems. This, together with the fact that the support is being provided for ICL's R & D programme as a whole (although principally aimed at launching the new range of computers) has made it necessary to include the Company's overall financial and marketing performance as well as R & D progress in the appraisal and monitoring processes.

Appraisal

An extensive appraisal exercise was undertaken following ICL's request for support in 1971. Essentially their case was that the heavy burden of their R & D programme during a period when they were hoping to launch a new range of computers, fell at a time when their Profit and Loss account would not have recovered from the world wide recession which the computer industry was at that time experiencing. At the Department's request the company provided outline forecasts and detailed projections for the period 1970-71 to 1975-76.

Merchant banking advice was sought and a team of officials and management consultants worked intensively on material provided by the company and discussed this with ICL's relevant departments. The Department concluded that on ICL's sales assumptions their forecasts were satisfactory and agreed to supply the support described above.

Terms

The £40m is to be recovered by means of a levy on pre-tax profits during the seven year period starting in October 1977. In each year ICL will pay to Her Majesty's Government any profit before tax in excess of 7.5 per cent of turnover up to a maximum of 25 per cent of the profit before tax, but subject to an overall limit which in effect means that the Government's recovery will not exceed the equivalent of £40m at a discounted cash flow rate of return of 10 per cent per annum.

Monitoring

Monitoring of the R and D programme and of ICL's financial performance generally has been accepted by the company as a necessary obligation during the period of support. The aim has been, as far as possible, not to require information for monitoring purposes which the company does not produce for its own management use.

The Department's CSE division is responsible for monitoring with the assistance of a firm of management consultants on the financial side. Payment of the instalments of the aid is to be conditional upon the Department being satisfied that the progress of the R & D programme and the financial and general state of the company are reasonably consistent with the expectation of commercial success; that the company is providing a reasonable contribution to the R and D programme from its own resources, and that it does not without the consent of the Secretary of State pay more than a minimum dividend.

17

Financial support for Kearney and Trecker Marwin (KTM)

Objective

The objective is to maintain and secure a continuing capability in the design, manufacture and sale of numerically controlled and special purpose machine tools.

Appraisal

The continued viability of KTM was considered an essential contribution to the above objective. It was decided that this could be secured by means of reorganisation of the company's capital structure, an injection of funds and strengthening of management.

Terms

It was therefore agreed to provide up to £3.5m in financial assistance, mainly in the form of preference shares, through a new holding company in which the Government hold half the equity. Vickers Ltd also agreed to provide a loan and to undertake the management of the newly reconstructed firm, with an option to purchase a controlling interest by the end of April 1976.

Monitoring

The terms of the agreement provide the Government with reasonable access to all relevant information. Within this framework detailed monitoring arrangements have been set up and include the preparation of an action plan by the company to improve its performance in key areas and the monitoring of this plan against set targets using appropriate financial and management accounting data.

Aluminium Smelters

Introduction

Following the announcement of Special Electricity Arrangements in October 1967 the Government agreed in the following year to assist the establishment of primary smelters to be operated by British Aluminium Company Ltd (BACO) and Anglesey Aluminium Metals Ltd (AAM) under the Industrial Expansion Act 1968. The smelter companies would receive their very large power requirements at charges determined by reference to the capital and operating costs of the most advanced generating capacity currently being installed. To secure this benefit they entered into firm long-term contracts with the generating boards. The power contracts are confidential commercial agreements but under them the two companies pay a capital charge in respect of the cost of the capacity required to supply their requirements and in addition they make an annual payment to cover the operating costs of the specified generating capacity plus the cost of any marginal supplies from the grids. The Government agreed to provide loans to cover the capital contributions up to a maximum of £30m for BACO and £33m for AAM repayable over approximately 30 years. The loans are at a fixed rate of interest of 7 per cent. In addition the smelter companies were eligible to apply for grants under the prevailing regional development legislation.

Objectives

The objectives (in 1967) of promoting the establishment of primary aluminium smelters, a new industry within the UK, were national economic benefits in the form of import saving and employment in development areas.

Monitoring

Monitoring is in accordance with the provisions laid down in the relevant Agreements: books of account must be kept and made available for inspection; two copies of every Annual Balance Sheet, Profit and Loss Account and Directors'

Report presented or issued to its shareholders must be supplied plus any other information relating to the project which is required.

Pre-Production Order scheme

Introduction

The Pre-Production Order (PPO) scheme provides for:

(a) Purchase by the Department of, eg a machine tool already developed to the prototype stage but in advance of its being put into production;

(b) loan of the tool to user firms, free, their obligation being to put it into use under normal production conditions and to report on its performance in detail at regular intervals;

(c) eventual sale of the tool (depreciated) or lease where possible to the user;

(d) since early 1972, re-imbursement of outgoings by a levy on the manufacturer's subsequent sales (which are assumed to have been assisted by the free trial at the Department's and user's expense).

Note: In April 1969 the PPO scheme was extended beyond the field of machine tools to include other types of manufacturing equipment. However the comments and data given below are restricted to the scheme's application to machine tool development.

Objective

The purpose of this scheme is to accelerate the introduction into productive use of more efficient equipment. The gains to the economy which are sought are the more efficient use of resources by users, the more rapid release of the manufacturer's resources for further investment, import-saving and export potential.

Appraisal

The criteria for selection of equipment appropriate to the PPO scheme have been somewhat amended since the scheme's inception in 1965. Originally machines were required to embody a significant advance in performance and to include a relatively high degree of innovation. From 1967 the absolute requirement of outstanding technical advance was relaxed but tools were still to be genuine new models with significant improvements in overall performance. Since 1969 there has again been some tightening of the technical criteria.

The Department also has to be satisfied that the users selected and the market survey in each case are such that the objective is likely to be achieved.

Scale of the scheme

To date the Department has entered into more than 60 contracts worth about £5.5m.

Recovery

As mentioned above recovery of the Department's outgoings (less the proceeds of sales of machines under trial) is now by way of levy. The levy terms are calculated on the basis of the Department recovering its outgoings, currently on a 10 per cent dcf basis, in successful cases. (In very successful cases a greater return is achieved; in unsuccessful cases they may be no return.) The levy terms are not calculated on a constant price basis but since sales receipts are affected by changes in price levels it is assumed that recovery will approximate to real terms.

Monitoring

User companies are required to supply monthly technical and financial reports and a final report on completion of the Agreement. The 'Project Officer' examines these reports and also keeps in touch with progress on the projects by visits to the

Manufacturer's and User companies' premises, and by discussion with their representatives. He is also responsible for bringing to the notice of the Manufacturers and Users any aspects of the work on the project on which he considers that their proposals or actions are not sufficient to secure the timely achievement of the project objective.

Aircraft launching aid

Introduction

Launching aid for civil aircraft has been a policy of successive Governments since the war; current procedures date from 1960. In brief, launching aid is an investment by the Government towards costs of launching civil aircraft or aero-engine projects: this investment is recoverable by a levy on sales. Launching costs comprise the cost of design and development, production jigs and tools, and 'learning costs' (ie the higher manufacturing costs incurred in the early production stages whilst workers are learning their jobs). The Government's contribution is an agreed proportion of the launching costs as estimated at the outset, normally not more than 50 per cent. Under the normal procedure launching aid is not increased if the estimate is exceeded, except to take account of inflation. In return, the Government receives as a levy on sales of aircraft/engines and spare parts a share of the margin, either forecast or actual, between the selling price and the manufacturing cost. This margin, and the Government share, is normally fixed at the outset (subject to review arrangements in some cases). The intention behind the arrangement is that production risks, as well as the risks of a cost over-run on development should lie with the manufacturer, so that for example, if manufacturing costs exceed estimates and erode the actual margin, the margin sharing recovery formula will protect the Government levy. Risk and the possibility of profit should thus remain with the manufacturer and provide a commercial incentive and a spur to exercise commercial judgement.

Objectives

The objective of this form of financial assistance is to maintain a strong and efficient aircraft industry in the UK with an advanced technological base.

Appraisal

To some extent the approach to appraisal varies from case to case to take into account wider policy considerations, the non-financial contribution of the firm, and the extent of risk born by them. In recent cases the basic 'yardstick' has been whether on central predictions of sales, cost and price the project could be expected to achieve a rate of return of 10 per cent in real terms. When cases have been supported which have not fully met this test wider considerations of policy have been involved.

Monitoring

Monitoring of civil aircraft projects falls under two heads: monitoring the project which is largely technical; and monitoring the company which is largely financial. In the former sense the Ministry of Defence (Procurement Executive) (MOD/PE) manage civil aircraft projects on behalf of the Department. This means that the Government can deploy on civil aircraft projects more powerful resources for technical appraisal and monitoring than are available in other sectors.

On the financial side, when possible, there are built-in incentives to the firm to make a success of the project, and it is hoped to limit monitoring to what is needed to give early warning that either the firm or the project are running into trouble.

Flexibility

Contracts normally contain 'break' clauses and agreed arrangements for dealing with changes in technical requirements.

Return

As was pointed out above this is typically obtained via levy on sales and other commercial receipts from the aircraft. The arrangements for the HS 146 for example very broadly provided for the sharing of the profit margin on sales and leases of aircraft and spares. These provisions were expected to permit the Government to recover its investment in real terms at 10 per cent DCF.

Parliamentary scrutiny

With all subsidy schemes, Ministers and Departments have to account to Parliament for the exercise of the statutory powers and for the control they exercise over the public funds which are made available to them. This accountability is operated in various ways:

(a) *Parliamentary debate*. Areas of policy, elements of Government expenditure and particular statutory powers may all be the subject of debate on the floor of the House of Commons and Ministers have to explain, justify and defend their actions and those of their Departments. Specific opportunities for debate arise on the annual Estimates when debate tends typically to be on policy and not just figures; sometimes on the Annual Reports which are required to be made to Parliament on some subsidy schemes, eg the Industry Act Annual Report; and sometimes on the reports of Parliamentary committees.

(b) *The Public Accounts Committee*. Officials of the Exchequer and Audit Department (E & AD) have access to Departmental files and officials in carrying out their regular checks not only on propriety in the expenditure of public money but also the general efficiency and effectiveness with which it is administered – ie the 'value for money'. On the basis of briefing provided by E & AD, the Public Accounts Committee summons officials to its hearings to explain and defend their Departments' general systems and their actions in specific cases; for example, of the measures described in this paper Investment Grants and assistance to shipbuilding have received a fair amount of attention from the PAC. The Committee's reports are often important in influencing Departments' practices and procedures.

(c) *The Expenditure Committee*. While having no separate Department to service it and no automatic access to Departmental files, the Expenditure Committee and its sub-committees – particularly for this purpose the Trade and Industry Sub-Committee – have the right of Parliamentary Select Committees to call for persons, papers and records, ie to summon Ministers and officials to their hearings and to receive written evidence from elsewhere. The Expenditure Committee roams fairly widely over policy matters – the justification for and results obtained from expenditure – and is less concerned with investigating narrower questions such as whether statutory provisions are being properly observed (though this should not be regarded as implying that the PAC restrict themselves to such issues).

(d) *Parliamentary Questions*. Ministers have to be ready to answer oral and written questions about the powers they exercise.

(e) *The Parliamentary Commissioner for Administration* (PCA). The PCA or Ombudsman is empowered, if so requested by an MP, to investigate complaints by members of the public claiming to have suffered injustice as a result of maladministration by Government Departments. He too has access to Departmental files in pursuit of his enquiries.

The existence of these different forms of scrutiny has considerable implications for administration. They require information systems to be devised to provide the necessary data for Annual Reports, for Parliamentary answers, for Ministers' use in debates, and for the appearances of both Ministers and officials before Parliamentary committees. Hitherto the information has been of a statistical nature: amounts of grant spent broken down by region and by industry, jobs created by selective assistance and so on. Information on individual cases has been regarded as confidential, although Parliamentary committees have a right to such information and have in some cases published the names of individual firms. From this year, however, lists of the major payments of RDG and offers of selective assistance under Section 7 of the Industry Act 1972 to individual firms are to be published quarterly since the present Government believe that Parliament and the public are entitled to this information. On the other hand information about the tax affairs of individual companies will continue to be kept strictly confidential by the Inland Revenue. Quite apart from the need to produce systematic data on subsidies, Parliamentary controls occupy a great deal of administrative time in other ways. It is hoped that the benefits in the form of the continuing pressure on Departments to examine and justify their actions amply repay the cost of the time involved.

Conclusion

Successive governments in recent years have taken the view that the use of general schemes of Government financial support and subsidy of the kind described in Part I of this paper is the only practicable way of doing things on a large scale. Action directed towards increasing investment throughout the country, or towards helping employment throughout the Assisted Areas can only be taken in a standardised way. The specific approach is adopted where the general approach is inadequate and where the Government have more specific objectives in view. Thus the Government had to step in with tailor-made packages of assistance when the availability of general subsidies proved insufficient to preserve the big shipbuilding companies on the Clyde and the Mersey. The specific approach has also been adopted in cases where the Government is interested in promoting the product of an industry or a firm rather than in general objectives of promoting investment and employment *per se*. Examples of this category are the aid to aluminium smelters and to ICL; launching aid; and Kearney and Trecker Marwin. These are often industries where the starting costs of new projects are high and the financial return slow to come in; and where the Government are concerned to retain or promote advanced technologies. In some cases the creation or protection of employment is an additional objective.

The present Government's proposals for a new Industry Bill, and the use which they have already made of the selective assistance powers in Sections 7 and 8 of the 1972 Industry Act suggest that there will be more concentration on the specific approach to the subsidisation of industry. At the same time the retention of the 100 per cent first year depreciation allowance for industrial plant and machinery, of Regional Development Grants and of the Regional Employment Premium indicate that general subsidy schemes will continue to play a very important part in the Government's policies towards industry.

Value of investment incentives for manufacturing industry 1946 to 1974

C L MELLISS AND P W RICHARDSON

The authors are grateful for helpful comments on an earlier draft from a number of colleagues, but claim responsibility for all remaining errors and omissions

[1]The statistics do not distinguish between expenditure on industrial buildings and commercial buildings but the latter are assumed to be a small proportion of the total.

[2]There have been two instances, in 1966 and 1971, where it was announced that changes in incentives would be of a known limited duration. It has been assumed in the analysis that these changes would last throughout the life of the asset.

Introduction

The purpose of this paper is to describe and evaluate the various systems of tax allowances and grants that have been available for capital expenditure by firms in manufacturing industry in the period since 1946. These incentives have applied to expenditure on plant and machinery and industrial building which together probably accounted for over 90 per cent of total fixed capital formation by manufacturing industry in 1972[1]. Thus the schemes considered here have excluded expenditure by manufacturing industry on vehicles, ships and aircraft and commercial buildings.

The analysis focuses on the value of the incentive as seen from the position of the firm undertaking an investment appraisal. No attempt has been made to examine the effectiveness of the schemes on the overall level or on the allocation of investment. The costs to the Exchequer of the schemes also lie outside the scope of the paper. However one may note that giving tax allowances and grants lowers the effective rate of tax that a company undertaking investment bears. Since the rate of company taxation and the level of incentives are probably not unrelated, the Exchequer costs are not simply the value of tax revenue foregone by giving allowances and these costs would therefore need to be evaluated within the general tax-expenditure framework. The value of the incentive to the firm has been calculated in discounted cash flow terms for both types of asset and when relevant at both national and assisted area rates. In evaluating the various schemes and rates of incentive that have been in operation since 1946 the general strategy has been to consider the expected value offered rather than the actual benefit received. This has the advantage of being in line with the spirit of investment appraisal and avoids the very considerable problems of evaluation on any other basis. Thus it is assumed that a particular scheme will operate unchanged throughout the life of the asset. While this implies that a firm's expectations as to the level and type of incentives are myopic there appears to be no suitable alternative to this assumption. Also consistent with the decision to focus on expected values is the use of dates for changes in allowances, grants and company taxation which relate to the time of announcement rather than the effective date of implementation[2]. This distinction is of particular significance since 1965 when changes in the rate of corporation tax have usually been announced with retrospective effect.

One may of course object to both these general methods and the more detailed assumptions which are set out in the following section on the grounds that at least for most of the period under review the typical firm was not using DCF investment appraisal methods. However a consistent set of criteria is required to make comparisons and the assumption that firms behave optimally requires that a DCF method be used.

Assumptions

I Company tax position

The financial position of a firm is important in so far as it determines the firm's ability to take full advantage of available allowances at the earliest possible occasion. The present value of any tax allowance on capital expenditure will vary according to the level of gross company income currently available for tax purposes. Thus a firm with a current gross income equal to or in excess of available allowances will, in a given year, be able to take full and immediate advantage of them, the so called 'full tax' case. One with gross income less than available allowances may obtain the full allowance but subject to some distributed lag time delays. In so far as the analysis of benefits subjects them to discounting over time, the net present value of an allowance used up immediately will be greater than if it were claimed over a period of years. Hence for a given incentive scheme there are an unlimited number of alternative valuations depending on the time profile of gross company income relative to that of available allowances, ranging from the 'full tax' case, to the 'no tax' case where a firm has accumulated sufficient allowances to entirely offset all future tax payments. In this paper we consider the valuation of incentives for the 'full tax' case, noting that it provides a maximum estimate of the schemes' present values. Gardner and Richardson (1973) examine this topic in more depth in the context of the shipping industry.

II Discount rates

There is little empirical evidence as to the discount rate that firms might have used for investment appraisal. In principle three alternative concepts of the discount rate were envisaged. Firstly the case where the benefits are evaluated independently of the rate of inflation can be considered by applying a positive constant discount rate which relates to the real opportunity cost of capital. This concept enables one to examine the effects of changes in the incentive regimes independently of actual money interest rate effects. For this constant real rate a figure of 10 per cent was used. The second discount rate that might be considered is a money rate of interest corresponding to that which a firm might have to pay on long term external borrowing. Discounting by this rate implies an underlying real discount which varies through time. For this the discount rate on long dated British Government stock was used; Table 4 shows the path of this rate (r_m) since 1946. A third possibility is that firms evaluate incentives on the basis of a constant real rate of interest (which one might assume to be zero) while making allowance for the general rate of inflation by discounting at the prevailing rate of price inflation. This constant purchasing power rate could be taken either from a general price deflator or a price deflator for capital goods thus measuring the incentives in terms of the replacement cost of capital goods. In practice because of the considerable year to year fluctuations in the GDP deflator and because of the limited availability of the manufacturing capital goods price index it has not been found possible to make a worthwhile evaluation using this concept. In using the money rate of interest it has been assumed, in accord with the treatment of a particular incentive scheme described in the introduction, that the discount rate prevailing at the time of announcement of the scheme remains constant throughout the life of that scheme. This implies that firms have static expectations about the money rate of interest.

III Rate of taxation

For much of the post war period the rate of taxation on distributed and retained profits has differed. Table 1 shows the rates of taxation; from 1947 to 1956 the rate of distributed profits tax was higher than that on retained earnings while the corporation tax regimes before the imputation system also entailed a higher rate of tax on distributed profits. However in calculating the tax variable relevant to the evaluation of investment incentives it has been assumed that the firm

24

disregards the level of taxation borne by shareholders and views allowances as offsetting tax on retained earnings. The 'company' tax rate resulting from this assumption is shown as column 7 of Table 1. Under the corporation tax regime the receipt of investment allowances and grants left unchanged the tax liability on distributed profits. However prior to 1956 the rate of profits tax on both distributed and undistributed profits tax was affected by the receipt of allowances. For this period it is therefore possible to envisage a tax variable consisting of a weighted average of the two rates of profits tax in addition to income tax. However because distributed earnings were a relatively small proportion of total profits and the amount of profits distributed may have been based on accounting measures of profits and therefore unaffected by tax allowances, such a tax variable has not been used here. The view of King (1972) that the tax variable in investment appraisal is most appropriately that on retained earning lends weight to this choice.

IV Methods of Finance

The DCF analysis has been carried out in terms of the value of an incentive scheme per unit of capital cost; a unit of capital expenditure will attract tax allowances and grants, the net present value of which is some proportion of that unit. This presentation abstracts from the method of finance of the investment and is equivalent to assuming that investment is paid for out of retained earnings or equity. In so far as capital expenditure is financed from loan capital, account would need to be taken in the DCF evaluation of the tax treatment of interest payments as well as the effect of inflation on the real terms of such methods of finance.

The incentive schemes and the method of evaluation

Provision for accelerated depreciation was first introduced in the United Kingdom in 1945 so that the period under study covers virtually the whole of the operation of policy aimed at encouraging investment in manufacturing industry through fiscal means. Since 1945 there have been a large number of schemes each involving different arrangements and fairly frequent changes in rates. Thus, for investment in plant and machinery there have since 1945 been sixteen changes excluding those brought about through taxation in the national incentive scheme, an average of about one every two years. For industrial buildings the number of changes has been twelve over the same period. The precise details of the schemes are given in Tables 2 and 3; here a more general outline of the schemes and the method by which they are evaluated is given.

I Expenditure on plant and machinery

From 1945 to 1966 incentives for plant and machinery took the form of allowances against tax. For most of the period a scheme of initial allowances which in effect accelerated the depreciation provided for by the normal writing down allowances was in operation. Investment allowances representing a net addition to the sum allowable for depreciation against tax over and above the cost of the capital good were substituted for initial allowances from 1954 to 1956 and supplemented initial allowances from 1959 to 1966. The precise details of the timing and the rates of these allowances is shown in Table 2. For tax purposes depreciation on plant and machinery expenditure is on a reducing balance basis. Following the basic approach of Merrett and Sykes (1973) the net present value per unit of capital cost over an asset life of N years is given by:

$$NPV = \frac{T}{(1+r)^L}\left[(V+R+d) + \frac{d(1-d-R)}{(1+r)} + \frac{d(1-d)\,(1-d-R)}{(1+r)^2} + \cdots\right]$$

$$= \frac{T}{(1+r)^L}\left[(V+R+d) + \frac{d(1-d-R)}{(1+r)} \sum_{i=0}^{N}\left(\frac{1-d}{1+r}\right)^i\right]$$

25

Where N is infinite this equals:

$$\frac{T}{(1+r)^L}\left[(V+R+d) + \frac{d(1-d-R)}{r+d}\right] \qquad (1)$$

Where

T = tax rate

R = initial allowance

V = investment allowance

d = statutory annual reducing balance writing down allowance (constant percentage of the balance outstanding at the end of each year)

r = rate of discount

L = lag in tax payment (years)

For values of N likely to be encountered (1) is a valid approximation.

In 1963 the first regional incentives for plant and machinery were introduced in development districts. These took the form of an initial allowance of 100 per cent free depreciation in addition to the investment allowance available nationally plus a grant discretionary on the creation of additional employment and deductible from the capital sum available for depreciation. The corresponding net present value is:

$$NPV = \frac{T}{(1+r)^L}\left[(1+V).(1-G)\right] + \frac{G}{(1+r)^g} \qquad (2)$$

From 1966 to 1970 investment grants were in operation both nationally and regionally for plant and machinery. The capital available to offset against corporation tax was correspondingly reduced by the value of the investment grants. The present value of incentives under this scheme is given by:

$$NPV = \frac{G}{(1+r)^g} + \frac{T}{(1+r)^L}\left[d(1-G) + \frac{d(1-G)(1-d)}{(1+r)} + \cdots\right]$$

$$= \frac{G}{(1+r)^g} + \frac{T}{(1+r)^L}\cdot\frac{d(1-G)}{(r+d)} \qquad (3)$$

Where G = Investment Grant (percentage of capital costs)

g = grant payment lag (years)

The White Paper of October 1970 reintroduced a system based on initial allowances. This is evaluated in the same way as for the pre 1966 national scheme. Free depreciation was made available in assisted areas for which the value of the incentive is:

$$NPV = \frac{T}{(1+r)^L} \qquad (4)$$

In 1972 free depreciation was extended to cover all areas and Regional development grants introduced in assisted areas. These differ from the grants that were available from 1966 to 1970 in that no deduction is made from the capital sum available for free depreciation. Thus (4) becomes:

$$NPV = \frac{T}{(1+r)^L} + \frac{G}{(1+r)^g} \qquad (5)$$

26

II Expenditure on Industrial Buildings

For industrial buildings depreciation is calculated on a straight line basis. The formula, using the same general notation as for reducing balance calculations, for the present value of allowances is given by:

$$NPV = \frac{T}{(1+r)^L}\left[(V+R+d)+d\left[\frac{(1+r)^N-1}{r(1+r)^N}\right]\right] \qquad (6)$$

$$\text{Where } N = \left[\frac{1-R-d}{d}\right]$$

and d is now the annual straight line allowance in each year, a fixed percentage of the original capital sum. This formula has been applicable to expenditure on industrial building nationally throughout the period. In assisted areas grants have been available since 1963. Up to 1972 these were discretionary on the creation of additional employment and deductable from the capital sum available for depreciation. The net present value is given by:

$$NPV = \frac{G}{(1+r)^g} + \frac{T}{(1+r)^L}\left[(V+R+d)+d\left[\frac{(1+r)^N-1}{r(1+r)^N}\right]\right] \qquad (7)$$

$$\text{Where } N = \left[\frac{1-R-d-G}{d}\right]$$

The regional development grants introduced in 1972 are non deductable and

$$N = \left[\frac{1-R-d}{d}\right]$$

III The overall effect of incentive schemes and taxation

The formulae presented above evaluate the effect of an incentive scheme as a proportion, in net present value terms, of a unit of capital. To assess the overall effects of incentives in the context of a firm's decision making it is necessary to consider in addition the effect of tax rate changes on the post tax income of the project. In order to examine changes in both the value of incentive schemes and taxation (which are to some extent interdependent) the ratio of gross yield to the net of tax and incentive yield per unit of capital has been considered. This may be evaluated in the following way:

A_i is the gross return per unit of capital in year i in the absence of taxation or incentive effects.

P is the net present value of incentive schemes per unit of capital derived as in (I) and (II) above.

The cost of capital is reduced by the value of incentives so that the gross return after incentives becomes:

$$A'_i = \frac{A_i}{1-P}$$

The net of tax return to the project in year i, A^*_i is obtained by multiplying A'_i by the net of tax factor $[1-T/(1+r)^L]$ where as before r is the rate of discount and L is the tax lag:

$$A^*_i = A_i\left[\frac{1-\dfrac{T}{(1+r)^L}}{1-P}\right]$$

The ratio of gross to net yield can therefore be expressed as:

$$\frac{A_i}{A^*_i} = F = \left[\frac{1-P}{1 - \dfrac{T}{(1+r)^L}} \right]$$

Thus the ratio F shows the gross return required for a given net of tax return for year i. The interpretation of this ratio remains unchanged when the returns are discounted: denoting a_i and a^*_i as the present values of A_i and A^*_i respectively:

$$a^*_i = A^*_i(1+r)^{-i}$$

$$= A_i \left[\frac{1}{F} \right] (1+r)^{-i}$$

$$= a_i \left[\frac{1}{F} \right]$$

This ratio, considered originally by Thomas (1972), shows the present value of profits before tax required to attain a given after tax yield on a unit of capital expenditure. A fall in the ratio will indicate that the pre-tax profits required for a given post tax rate of return has fallen, there having been a reduction in net taxation (after allowances) levied on the company. Where the ratio takes a value of unity the effects of tax are precisely offset by the allowances given, this will occur under a system of free depreciation. The net yield ratio has been calculated using a constant 10 per cent discount rate and the results are presented in the following section.

Results

The full details of the variables used in calculation are set out in Tables 1 to 4 which give the tax rates, the rates of grants and allowances for plant and machinery and industrial buildings and the rates of discount used. These are followed in Tables 5 to 7 by the incentive schemes for the two assets and a mixed project derived from a weighted average of plant and machinery and industrial buildings in the ratio of four to one. Table 8 shows the gross/net yield for the two assets and mixed project at the company tax rate. In order to assist in discussing the schemes, graphs 1 to 5 highlighting the main trends and features are also presented.

Throughout the post war period the rate of tax on retained profits has lain between 40 and 60 per cent. The level of this variable appears to be associated with whether or not the tax system incorporated a differential rate between distributed and retained earnings. Graph 1 shows that, apart from the immediate post war period, peaks in the tax variable have occurred when the rates of tax on distributed and undistributed profits are the same. In so far as a trend in this variable exists it is downward, the largest falls occurring on the announcement of corporation tax in 1965.

The effect of the different interest rate variables on the DCF values is illustrated by Graph 2 which shows an evaluation of a mixed project. Since 1946 the DCF value of the incentive has risen when evaluated at a constant discount rate whereas the use of the money rate for the same mixed project leads to a slight downward trend in the value of incentives. This is because the money rate of interest has only exceeded 10 per cent in the most recent years and hence the mean value of incentives and the relative value in earlier years is higher than for a 10 per cent discount rate. Under both discount rates the direction and broad magnitude of changes in DCF values resulting from changes in the parameters of incentive schemes are similar; in the following discussion we concentrate on the constant rate in order to abstract from interest rate effects.

Measuring the DCF value of the national incentive schemes at a 10 per cent. discount rate, the time profile for both the assets and the mixed project can be seen from Graph 3. In the period to 1953 and excepting 1949 to 1951 the DCF values were only slightly greater than those that were available from the statutory writing down allowances. In April 1959 investment allowances were introduced for both assets. From November 1962, with increases in initial allowances and the doubling of writing down allowances for industrial buildings, the DCF value of incentives appears to be higher than at any other time with the exception of the present scheme for industrial buildings. The reduction in the tax rate in 1965 reduced DCF values markedly. The switch from initial and investment allowances to grants for plant and machinery at the beginning of 1966 appears to have had a negligible effect on the DCF value. The incentive regime introduced at the end of 1970 reintroduced initial allowances for plant and machinery and raised the level of initial allowance for industrial building. The overall effect of this on a mixed project was to lower the DCF value of the incentive quite considerably but subsequent changes have more than reversed this fall. The value of the incentives for a mixed project is heavily weighted toward that of plant and machinery, mainly because of the weights used but also because of the lower value of incentives for industrial buildings. Although reasons for this are unclear they may be associated with the fact that, in its early stages, tax relief for investment was related to the depreciation policy that firms were thought to use.

The justification for using the gross/net yield to obtain an overall indication of the effect of taxes and allowances together has already been discussed. Graph 4 shows the gross/net yield for assets evaluated on the same basis as Graph 3. Two clear phases can be discerned from this chart. First from 1951 to 1962 there was a reduction in the gross yield required to obtain a given net yield so that by 1962 the tax and incentive system for a mixed project was almost neutral. Since 1962 the gross/net yield ratio on a mixed project has remained comparatively stable apart from a short period during 1970 and 1971. However in contrast to the period pre 1962, when the gross/net yield ratio of both assets followed a similar pattern, there appears to have been a tendency for the ratio to fall for industrial buildings particularly as a result of the tax change in 1965 while rising slightly for plant and machinery. The ratio was at its lowest for plant and machinery with a value of 0.9 in 1967 when a higher rate of investment grant was introduced temporarily. For this asset the present system of free depreciation has a ratio of unity implying that changes in the tax rate leave unchanged the post tax return of a unit of capital.

An important aspect of the incentive schemes so far neglected is that of the additional incentive offered in assisted areas. The schemes of regional investment incentives set out in Tables 2 and 3, and used in this analysis have been confined to those which have applied as investment incentives related to the level of investment and which, with the exception of grants made under Local Employment Acts, have involved a minimum of administrative discretion. The dividing line for such a choice is inevitably arbitrary so that various other regional incentive schemes eg Special Development Area operational grants and the provision of factory buildings at special rents, have necessarily been excluded which though not strictly dependent on the level of investment made have nonetheless acted as incentives to invest and provided a substantial benefit to recipient firms. This provides an important qualification to the assessment of the levels of regional differential shown in the results presented. Since 1963 when a general element of regional differential was first introduced the area covered has steadily expanded so that perhaps about one third of manufacturing investment is now undertaken in assisted area. The value of the additional incentive in absolute terms, and the gross/net yield ratio are shown in Graphs 5 and 6 respectively. For plant and machinery, apart from two relatively short periods in 1965 and 1970 to 1972, the gross net yield ratio for regionally assisted projects has been fairly stable in contrast to the rise in non assisted areas implying an increasing regional differential. This is borne out by examining the absolute differences in incentives shown in Graph 5. Regional assistance for industrial buildings was up to 1972 given in the form of grants which were discretionary both with respect to the level and whether or not the building qualified. Thus any general statements must be treated cautiously. However it would seem that for those projects which qualified, even at a rate of grant below the maximum, the regional differential in absolute terms was substantially more than for plant and machinery. In spite of this the absolute level of incentive in assisted areas has remained below that for plant and machinery. An unusual feature of the incentive regime introduced in October 1970 was that it entailed an increase in the regional differential for industrial buildings and a reduction for plant and machinery. On both the criteria shown in Graphs 5 and 6 the current scheme is shown to be more favourable to investment in assisted areas than previous ones.

Conclusion

We have presented a factual analysis which has been designed to show how changes in the various parameters influence the value of incentive schemes. However certain features emerge which are of general interest. Firstly the values of the incentive to a firm using a discounting procedure are affected by changes in both taxes and incentives. The relative importance of these two sources of change depends to a great extent on the way in which the firm carries out the discounting procedure. If it uses a gross/net yield analysis tax changes are less significant than if the NPV value is taken. The second feature which is of importance is that although some of the major changes in the value of incentives have been associated with changes in the system, eg from investment allowances to grants, under DCF appraisal the same level of incentive can be achieved in principle within different systems of incentives. If firms are not using discounting procedures then the institutional framework might be expected to have more effect on how firms perceive the incentives.

Bibliography

B Gardner and P W Richardson. The fiscal treatment of shipping. *Journal of Industrial Economics*, December 1973.

M King. Taxation and investment incentives in a vintage investment model. *Journal of Public Economics*, April 1972.

A J Merrett and A Sykes. *Capital budgeting and company finance* 2nd Edition 1973.

R Thomas. The new fiscal incentives to invest: liquidity and profitability aspects. *Scottish Journal of Political Economy*, November 1972.

Table 1 Rates of company taxation (1945 to 1974)

Notes

[1] The date or financial year from which returns were first subject to the stated rates. Abbreviations used in this column are: IT = Income Tax PT = Profits Tax CT = Corporation Tax

[2] Calculated as the overall tax on retained corporate earnings.

*Corporation tax rate was actually fixed at 40 per cent on 3.5.66 the budget of 6.4.65 however gave 40 per cent as a possible upper limit.

Announcement date	Effective date [1]	Income tax	Profits/corporation tax			Company's tax rate [2]
			Distributed	All	Undistributed	
23.10.45	1.4.46	0.4500		0.05		0.5000
17.4.47	1.1.47	0.4500	0.1250		0.05	0.5000
12.11.47	1.1.47	0.4500	0.2500		0.10	0.5500
27.9.49	1.10.49	0.4500	0.3000		0.10	0.5500
10.4.51	(PT 1.1.51) (IT 51/52)	0.4750	0.5000		0.10	0.5750
11.3.52	1.1.52	0.4750	0.2250		0.0250	0.5000
14.4.53	53/54	0.4500	0.2250		0.0250	0.4750
19.4.55	55/56	0.4250	0.2250		0.0250	0.4500
26.10.55	1.11.55	0.4250	0.2750		0.0250	0.4500
17.4.56	1.4.56	0.4250	0.3000		0.0300	0.4550
15.4.58	1.4.58	0.4250		0.10		0.5250
7.4.59	59/60	0.3875		0.10		0.4875
4.4.60	1.4.60	0.3875		0.1250		0.5125
17.4.61	1.4.61	0.3875		0.15		0.5375
6.4.65*	65/66	0.4125		0.4000		0.4000
18.11.67	67/68	0.4125		0.4250		0.4250
15.4.69	68/69	0.4125		0.4500		0.4500
27.10.70	(CT 69/70) (IT 71/72)	0.3875		0.4250		0.4250
30.3.71	CT 70/71	0.3875		0.4000		0.4000
26.3.74	73/74	0.3000		0.5200		0.5200

Table 2 Statutory grants and allowances for plant and machinery capital expenditure by manufacturing industry (1945 to 1974)

Notes

[1] These were based on a number of rates varying according to type of asset up to 1966.

[2] No account has been taken of schemes for intermediate and special development areas or discretionary assistance made available under Section 7 of the 1972 Industry Act.

*The temporary grant increase of 1.12.66 was announced to be limited to expenditure between 1.1.67 and 31.12.68. 1.1.69 therefore refers to the date on which grants actually reverted to their previous levels.

†It was announced that this change would be of a limited duration applying to expenditure made before 1.8.73.

‡1972 Regional Development Grants do not reduce the value of capital expenditure qualifying for tax allowances.

Announcement date	National				Development areas	
	Investment allowances %	Initial allowances %	Writing [1] down allowances %	Grants %	Initial allowances %	Grants [2] %
24.4.45	0	20	15.3			
6.4.49	0	40	15.3			
10.4.51	0	0	15.3			
15.4.53	0	20	15.3			
6.4.54	20	0	15.3			
17.2.56	0	20	15.3			
15.4.58	0	25	15.3			
17.6.58	0	30	15.3			
7.4.59	20	10	15.3			
5.11.62	30	10	20			
3.4.63	30	10	20		100	10
17.1.66			20	20		40
1.12.66*			20	25		45
1.1.69*			20	20		40
27.10.70		35	25		100	
19.7.71†		55	25		100	
21.3.72		100			100	20‡

Table 3 Statutory grants and allowances for industrial buildings capital expenditure by manufacturing industry [1] (1945 to 1974)

Announcement date	National		Development areas [2]			
	Investment allowances %	Initial allowances %	Investment allowances %	Initial allowances %	% Grants [3] Lower	Higher
24.4.45	0	10				
10.4.51	0	0				
15.4.53	0	10				
6.4.54	10	0				
17.2.56	0	10				
15.4.58	0	12.5				
17.6.58	0	15				
7.4.59	10	5				
5.11.62	15	5				
3.4.63	15	5	15	5	25	
17.1.66	0	15	0	15	25	35
14.4.70*	0	30	0	40	25	35
27.10.70	0	30	0	40	35	45
21.3.72	0	40	0	40	20†	

Notes

[1] Annual writing down allowances were 2 per cent before 5.11.62 and 4 per cent thereafter on a straight line basis.

[2] No account has been taken of the schemes for intermediate and special development areas or of more discretionary assistance such as that given under the Development Districts Provisions of the 1960 Local Employment Act or Section 7 of the Industry Act 1972.

[3] Grants up to 21.3.72 paid under Local Employment Act and discretionary on creation of additional employment and its level.

* It was announced that this change would be of a limited duration applying to expenditure made before 6.4.72. On 27.10.70 it was however stated that the development area allowance would continue indefinitely.

† 1972 Regional Development Grants apply to all industrial building in Development Areas and do not reduce the value of capital expenditure qualifying for tax allowances.

Table 4 Discount rate

Notes

* r_m is the annual average per cent redemption yield on long-dated British government stocks defined as 'that rate of interest which if used to discount future dividends and the sum due at redemption makes their present value equal to the price of the stock'. Source: Bank of England Quarterly Bulletin.

† Based on January to August average yield.

Year	r_m*	Year	r_m*
1946	2.52	1961	6.28
1947	2.70	1962	6.31
1948	2.78	1963	5.42
1949	2.88	1964	5.98
1950	3.00	1965	6.56
1951	3.64	1966	6.94
1952	4.26	1967	6.81
1953	3.94	1968	7.55
1954	3.55	1969	9.06
1955	4.32	1970	9.25
1956	5.16	1971	9.10
1957	5.41	1972	8.97
1958	5.45	1973	10.78
1959	5.19	1974	14.36†
1960	5.77		

Table 5 DCF value of incentive schemes at announced rates of company taxation: plant and machinery [1]

Date	Announced company tax rate[2]	National		Development areas	
		10% fixed discount rate	r_m variable discount rate	10% fixed discount rate	r_m variable discount rate
1946	0.5000	0.3150	0.4349		
17.4.47	0.5000	0.3150	0.4310		
12.11.47	0.5500	0.3465	0.4740		
1948	0.5500	0.3465	0.4721		
6.4.49	0.5500	0.3832	0.4862		
27.9.49	0.5500	0.3832	0.4862		
1950	0.5500	0.3832	0.4840		
10.4.51	0.5750	0.3237	0.4522		
11.3.52	0.5000	0.2815	0.3790		
14.4.53	0.4750	0.2992	0.3851		
6.4.54	0.4750	0.3479	0.4650		
19.4.55	0.4500	0.3295	0.4235		
26.10.55	0.4500	0.3295	0.4235		
17.2.56	0.4500	0.2834	0.3449		
17.4.56	0.4550	0.2866	0.3487		
1957	0.4550	0.2866	0.3689		
15.4.58	0.5250	0.3395	0.4034		
17.6.58	0.5250	0.3483	0.4097		
7.4.59	0.4875	0.3733	0.4510		
4.4.60	0.5125	0.3924	0.4625		
17.4.61	0.5375	0.4116	0.4748		
5.11.62	0.5375	0.4853	0.5467		
3.4.63	0.5375	0.4853	0.5640	0.6189	0.6658
1964	0.5375	0.4853	0.5530	0.6189	0.6598
6.4.65	0.4000	0.3612	0.4034	0.4828	0.5097
17.1.66	0.4000	0.3720	0.4068	0.4957	0.5311
1.12.66	0.4000	0.4029	0.4378	0.5266	0.5622
18.11.67	0.4250	0.4145	0.4528	0.5351	0.5736
1.1.69	0.4250	0.3844	0.4130	0.5050	0.5339
15.4.69	0.4500	0.3968	0.4078	0.5143	0.5253
14.4.70	0.4500	0.3968	0.4055	0.5143	0.5231
27.10.70	0.4250	0.3186	0.3247	0.3598	0.3640
30.3.71	0.4000	0.2999	0.3068	0.3386	0.3435
19.7.71	0.4000	0.3192	0.3251	0.3386	0.3435
21.3.72	0.4000	0.3386	0.3442	0.5292	0.5358
1973	0.4000	0.3386	0.3344	0.5292	0.5244
26.3.74	0.5200	0.4401	0.4112	0.6308	0.5982

Notes
[1] Tax payment lag 1½ years; Grant lag 1½ years 1966 to 1971, ½ year 1972.

[2] From Table 1.

Table 6 DCF value of incentive schemes at announced rates of company taxation: industrial buildings [1]

Date	Announced company tax rate	National		Development areas[2]	
		10% fixed discount rate	r_m variable discount rate	10% fixed discount rate	r_m variable discount rate
1946	0.5000	0.1341	0.3013		
17.4.47	0.5000	0.1341	0.3013		
12.11.47	0.5500	0.1476	0.3315		
1948	0.5500	0.1476	0.3272		
6.4.49	0.5500	0.1476	0.3220		
27.9.49	0.5500	0.1476	0.3220		
1950	0.5500	0.1476	0.3160		
10.4.51	0.5750	0.1062	0.2557		
11.3.52	0.5000	0.0923	0.1992		
14.4.53	0.4750	0.1274	0.2375		
6.4.54	0.4750	0.1279	0.2606		
19.4.55	0.4500	0.1211	0.2193		
26.10.55	0.4500	0.1211	0.2193		
17.2.56	0.4500	0.1207	0.1917		
17.4.56	0.4550	0.1221	0.1939		
1957	0.4550	0.1221	0.2275		
15.4.58	0.5250	0.1518	0.2268		
17.6.58	0.5250	0.1627	0.2375		
7.4.59	0.4875	0.1517	0.2314		
4.4.60	0.5125	0.1595	0.2282		
17.4.61	0.5375	0.1672	0.2269		
5.11.62	0.5375	0.2703	0.3459		
3.4.63	0.5375	0.2703	0.3704	0.4701	0.5589
1964	0.5375	0.2703	0.3547	0.4701	0.5459
6.4.65	0.4000	0.2012	0.2527	0.4053	0.4549
17.1.66	0.4000	0.1801	0.2199	{ 0.3808 / 0.4579	{ 0.4185 / 0.4943
18.11.67	0.4250	0.1914	0.2358	{ 0.3910 / 0.4675	{ 0.4324 / 0.5072
1.1.69	0.4250	0.1914	0.2240	{ 0.3910 / 0.4675	{ 0.4219 / 0.4973
15.4.69	0.4500	0.2026	0.2147	{ 0.4013 / 0.4772	{ 0.4130 / 0.4885
14.4.70	0.4500	0.2503	0.2591	{ 0.4638 / 0.5309	{ 0.4712 / 0.5380
27.10.70	0.4250	0.2364	0.2446	{ 0.5183 / 0.5815	{ 0.5252 / 0.5883
30.3.71	0.4000	0.2225	0.2319	{ 0.5057 / 0.5702	{ 0.5137 / 0.5782
21.3.72	0.4000	0.2488	0.2588	0.4394	0.4505
1973	0.4000	0.2488	0.2417	0.4394	0.4316
26.3.74	0.5200	0.3233	0.2779	0.5140	0.4650

Notes:
[1] Tax and grant lags are as in Table 5 notes.

[2] For the period 17.1.66 to 20.3.72 the regional incentive is shown for both higher and lower grant rates shown in Table 3.

Table 7 DCF value of incentive schemes at announced rates of company taxation: mixed project [1]

Notes:
[1] Mixed project values are a weighted average of the DCF values of schemes for plant and machinery and industrial buildings (in the ratio of 4 to 1 respectively) obtained from earlier tables.

Date	Announced rate of company taxation	National		Development areas	
		10% fixed discount rate	r_m variable discount rate	10% fixed discount rate	r_m variable discount rate
1946	0.5000	0.2788	0.4100		
17.4.47	0.5000	0.2788	0.4051		
12.11.47	0.5500	0.3067	0.4455		
1948	0.5500	0.3067	0.4431		
6.4.49	0.5500	0.3361	0.4534		
27.9.49	0.5500	0.3361	0.4534		
1950	0.5500	0.3361	0.4504		
10.4.51	0.5750	0.2802	0.4129		
11.3.52	0.5000	0.2436	0.3430		
14.4.53	0.4750	0.2648	0.3556		
6.4.54	0.4750	0.3039	0.4241		
19.4.55	0.4500	0.2878	0.3827		
26.10.55	0.4500	0.2878	0.3827		
17.2.56	0.4500	0.2509	0.3143		
17.4.56	0.4550	0.2537	0.3177		
1957	0.4550	0.2537	0.3406		
15.4.58	0.5250	0.3020	0.3681		
17.6.58	0.5250	0.3112	0.3753		
7.4.59	0.4875	0.3290	0.4071		
4.4.60	0.5125	0.3458	0.4156		
17.4.61	0.5375	0.3627	0.4252		
5.11.62	0.5375	0.4423	0.5065		
3.4.63	0.5375	0.4423	0.5253	0.5891	0.6442
1964	0.5375	0.4423	0.5133	0.5891	0.6370
6.4.65	0.4000	0.3292	0.3733	0.4673	0.4987
17.1.66	0.4000	0.3336	0.3694	{ 0.4727 / 0.4881	{ 0.5086 / 0.5237
1.12.66	0.4000	0.3583	0.3942	{ 0.4974 / 0.5129	{ 0.5335 / 0.5486
18.11.67	0.4250	0.3699	0.4094	{ 0.5063 / 0.5216	{ 0.5454 / 0.5603
1.1.69	0.4250	0.3458	0.3752	{ 0.4822 / 0.4975	{ 0.5115 / 0.5266
15.4.69	0.4500	0.3580	0.3692	{ 0.4917 / 0.5069	{ 0.5028 / 0.5179
14.4.70	0.4500	0.3675	0.3762	{ 0.5041 / 0.5175	{ 0.5126 / 0.5260
27.10.70	0.4230	0.3022	0.3087	{ 0.3915 / 0.4041	{ 0.3962 / 0.4089
30.3.71	0.4000	0.2844	0.2918	{ 0.3720 / 0.3849	{ 0.3775 / 0.3904
19.7.71	0.4000	0.2999	0.3065	{ 0.3720 / 0.3849	{ 0.3775 / 0.3904
21.3.72	0.4000	0.3206	0.3271	0.5112	0.5187
1973	0.4000	0.3206	0.3159	0.5112	0.5058
26.3.74	0.5200	0.4167	0.3845	0.6074	0.5716

Table 8 Gross/net yield ratio [1] at announced rates of company taxation using a fixed 10 % discount rate

Notes:

[1]The Gross/Net yield ratio is defined by:

$$F = \left[\frac{1-NPV}{1-T(1+r)-L} \right]$$

where NPV is the DCF value of incentive schemes using discount rate $r = 10\%$
T is the relevant tax rate
L is the tax payment lag 1.75 years

Date	Plant and machinery		Industrial buildings		Mixed project (4:1)	
	National	DA	National	DA	National	DA
1946	1.188		1.501		1.250	
17.4.47	1.188		1.501		1.250	
12.11.47	1.223		1.595		1.297	
1948	1.223		1.595		1.297	
6.4.49	1.154		1.595		1.242	
27.9.49	1.154		1.595		1.242	
1950	1.154		1.595		1.242	
10.4.51	1.317		1.741		1.402	
11.3.52	1.246		1.574		1.311	
14.4.53	1.172		1.459		1.229	
6.4.54	1.091		1.458		1.164	
19.4.55	1.083		1.420		1.150	
26.10.55	1.083		1.420		1.150	
17.2.56	1.157		1.420		1.209	
17.4.56	1.160		1.428		1.214	
1957	1.160		1.428		1.214	
15.4.58	1.189		1.526		1.256	
17.6.58	1.173		1.507		1.240	
7.4.59	1.067	—	1.444	—	1.142	—
4.4.60	1.073	—	1.484	—	1.155	—
17.4.61	1.079	—	1.528	—	1.169	—
5.11.62	0.944	—	1.339	—	1.023	—
3.4.63	0.944	0.700	1.339	0.972	1.023	0.754
1964	0.944	0.700	1.339	0.972	1.023	0.754
6.4.65	0.966	0.781	1.208	0.899	1.014	0.800
17.1.66	0.949	0.762	1.240	{ 0.936 / 0.820	1.007	{ 0.797 / 0.774
1.12.66	0.903	0.716	1.240	{ 0.936 / 0.820	0.970	{ 0.760 / 0.736
18.11.67	0.914	0.726	1.263	{ 0.951 / 0.832	0.984	{ 0.771 / 0.747
1.1.69	0.961	0.773	1.263	{ 0.951 / 0.832	1.022	{ 0.809 / 0.785
15.4.69	0.974	0.784	1.288	{ 0.967 / 0.844	1.037	{ 0.821 / 0.796
14.4.70	0.974	0.784	1.211	{ 0.867 / 0.758	1.022	{ 0.855 / 0.747
27.10.70	1.064	1.000	1.193	{ 0.752 / 0.654	1.090	{ 0.950 / 0.931
30.3.71	1.058	1.000	1.175	{ 0.747 / 0.650	1.082	{ 0.949 / 0.930
19.7.71	1.029	1.000	1.175	{ 0.747 / 0.650	1.058	{ 0.949 / 0.930
21.3.72	1.000	0.712	1.136	0.848	1.027	0.739
1973	1.000	0.712	1.136	0.848	1.027	0.739
26.3.74	1.000	0.659	1.209	0.868	1.042	0.701

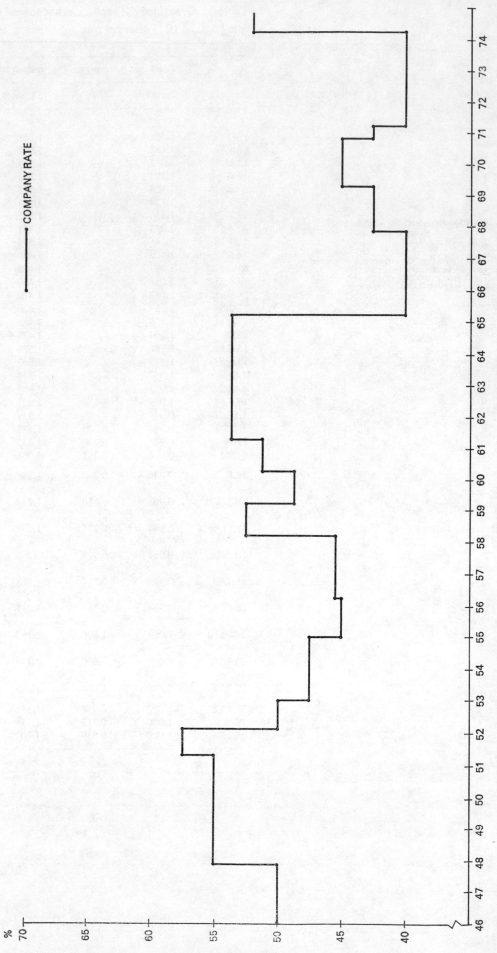

Chart 1 Announced Rates of Taxation

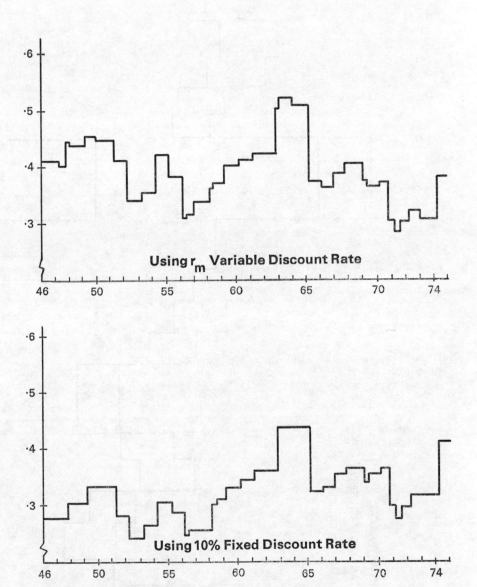

Chart 2   DCF Values for Mixed Projects

39

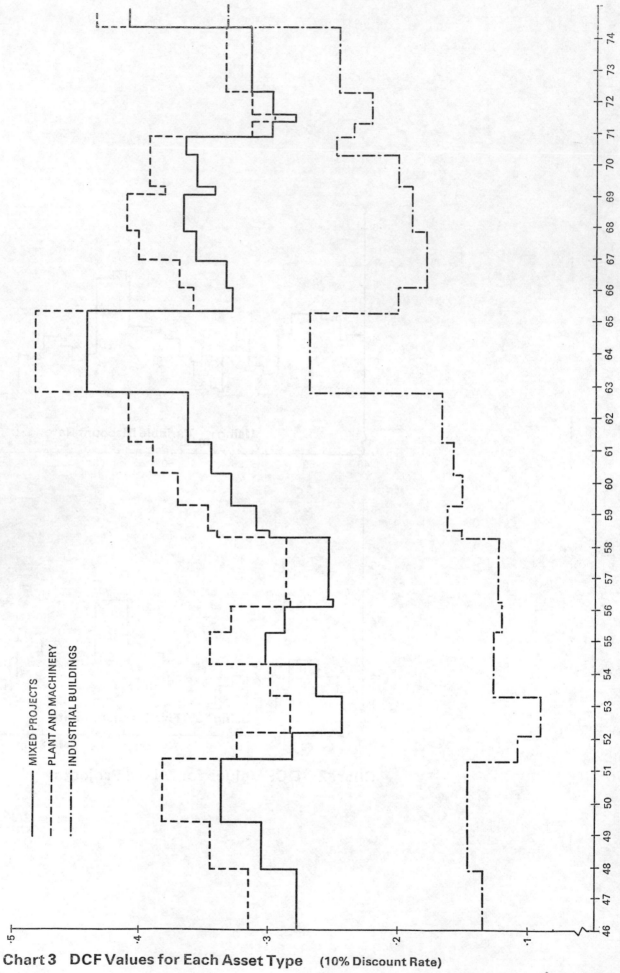

Chart 3   DCF Values for Each Asset Type   (10% Discount Rate)

MIXED PROJECTS
PLANT AND MACHINERY
INDUSTRIAL BUILDINGS

40

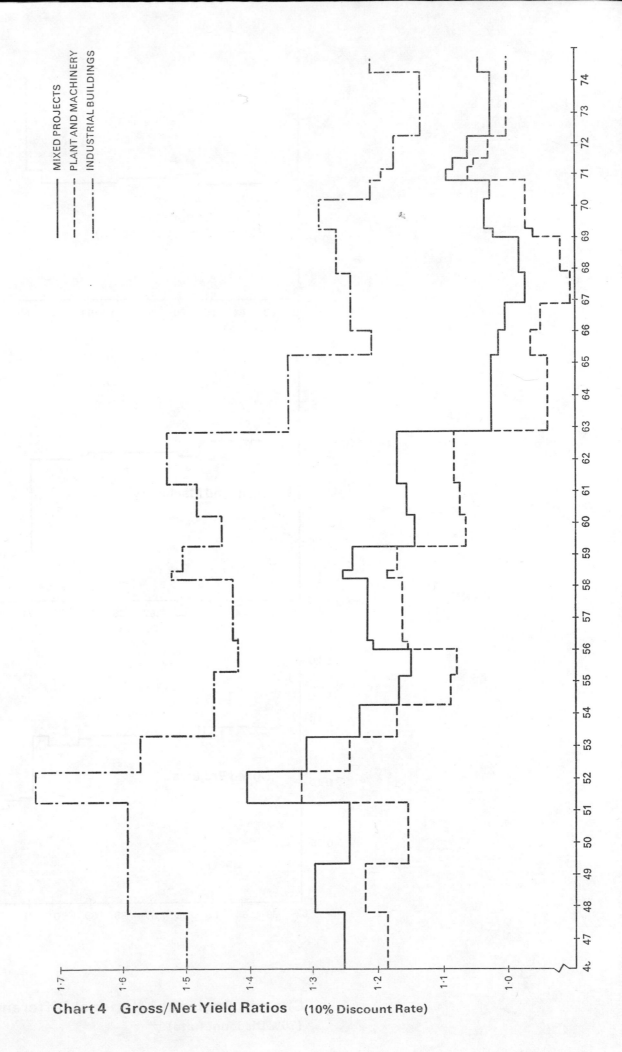

Chart 4   Gross/Net Yield Ratios   (10% Discount Rate)

MIXED PROJECTS
PLANT AND MACHINERY
INDUSTRIAL BUILDINGS

41

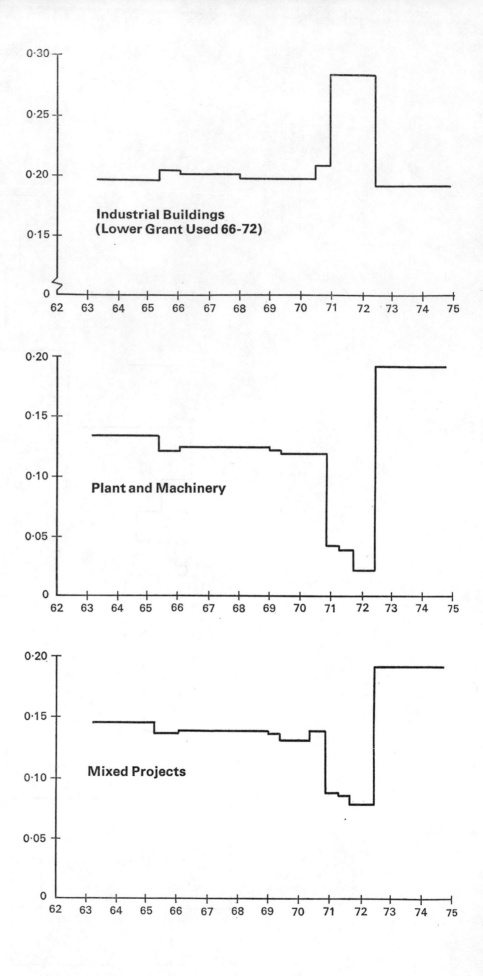

Chart 5 Regional – National Differences in DCF Values
(10% Discount Rate)

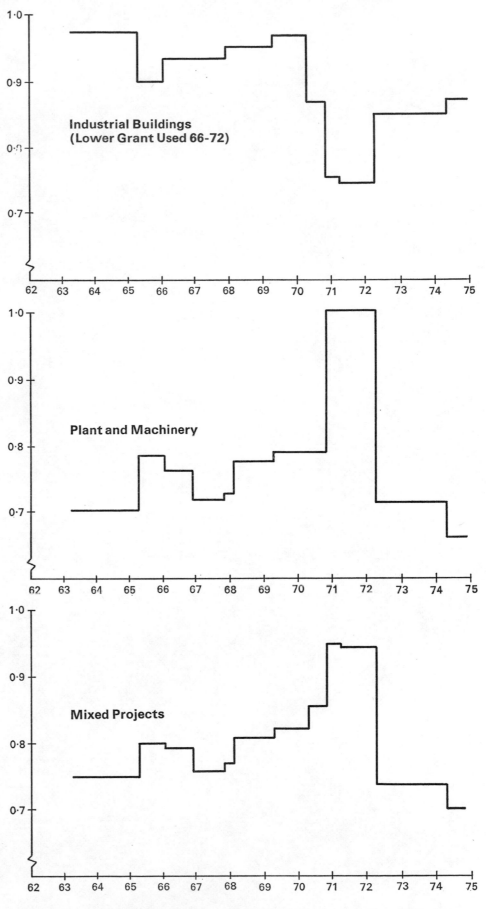

Chart 6   Gross/Net Yield Ratios for Development Areas
(10% Discount Rate)

43

Overseas experience in the use of industrial subsidies

A WHITING

I Introduction

If the purpose of this paper is achieved, it will be less controversial than its title - adopted for shorthand convenience – implies. For the aim of the paper is simply to examine government policy in six foreign countries in four fields which directly affect industry, namely investment incentives, regional development, selective intervention and research and development: the countries compared are France, Italy, Japan, Sweden, the United States and West Germany. In his recent monograph 'How Much Subsidy' Professor Prest examines the many and varied definitions of 'subsidy' and offers a definition in terms of government payments that directly affect relative prices in the private sector. On this definition all the measures listed in this paper would be classified as subsidies. Yet from the practical point of view, this definition is too broad in many cases. The subsidy clause in GATT, for example, has never worked in practice but there would be few who would regard all regional development incentives as infringing the spirit of clause 16. Most would regard regional development incentives as conforming to GATT as long as the incentive was no greater than the amount necessary to offset the additional cost of production in the development areas compared with the rest of the country. If, then, the appropriate definition of 'subsidy' to some extent depends on the purpose for which it is used, it may be more appropriate to regard this paper as a comparison of foreign industrial policies in the four areas mentioned.

The aim of this paper, then is to compare certain industrial policy measures to see if any conclusions can be drawn from foreign practice and experience which would be relevant to the UK. Two concepts nevertheless fall outside the paper's scope. On the whole no attempt is made in this paper to evaluate the degree of success of the specific measures. 'Success' can have several meanings. While a measure may achieve its immediate objective, it may not exert the desired overall effect. The desired immediate effects of industrial policies are rarely ends in themselves, so the measurement of a policy's success should involve more than the attainment of its immediate objective: lack of sufficiently detailed data has prevented the evaluation of even this latter limited measurement in most cases. Neither does the paper provide figures of government expenditure on all the measures either in absolute terms or as a percentage of gross domestic product. Such information would have been useful but was not always available. The difficulty of estimating a measure's cost to the government is difficult enough even where raw data is available, as can be seen from the analysis in the paper 'Value of investment incentives for manufacturing industry 1946 to 1974' by Melliss and Richardson.

Detailed conclusions concerning individual measures are incorporated in the text. By considering the industrial measures in total on a country basis, some interesting general observations can also be drawn.

The first general observation concerns the determination of national industrial policies. National industrial policies are determined mainly by two factors; the

45

particular set of national problems facing the governments, and the governments' assessments as to how the problems can best be overcome. Examination of the industrial problems of the countries studied reveals that the problems are much the same in all countries although their relative importance varies considerably; regional problems, for example, are far less important in West Germany than the UK, which in turn is more integrated regionally than Italy. If specific problems encountered were the main determinant of industrial policy, then these policies could be expected to be similar in the countries studied, albeit with different emphasis being placed on each measure. That this is not the case suggests that differences in economic and industrial policies are largely attributable to differences in economic and industrial philosophy. This observation is further supported by observed changes in specific national industrial policies over time although the underlying industrial problems have remained the same.

The second general observation concerns the relationship between economic growth and industrial policy. On the evidence of the countries studied, it is clear that differences in industrial policy are not capable, by themselves, of explaining the observed differences in national growth rates. Industrial policy measures must, of course, be evaluated against all their objectives which include such diverse entities as employment, regional balance and environmental considerations. Growth objectives may be a fairly minor consideration for many industrial policy measures: it is singled out here because there appears to be a tendency to believe that Britain's poor economic performance can be transformed simply by a switch in industrial policy. There may be social and other reasons why a particular type of industrial policy should be more acceptable in one country than another, but the evidence clearly shows that no one type of industrial policy can claim to be the sole generator of high economic growth. Examination of the table of growth rates (Table 1) shows that rates of growth have been achieved by countries with little central planning or public ownership (such as Germany and Sweden) as well as by those where planning and public ownership are of much greater importance (such as France and Italy). Moreover, detailed examination of industrial policy measures reveals no link between the nature and level of industrial and financial aids and the rate of economic growth: the West German economy, with little government intervention and low levels of assistance, has grown at about the same rate as France and Italy, where government intervention and financial assistance are high.

It is not surprising that differences in industrial policy are not capable in themselves, of explaining the observed differences in national growth rates. Growth is the manifestation at the aggregate level of all the changes in factor imputs and efficiency at the micro level. Growth is thus an extremely complex phenomenon and any search for a simple solution to poor growth will be self-defeating. Yet having identified the hindrances to higher growth, industrial policy measures can be vital in remedying the situation. Foreign practice and experience can be of help in formulating ideas and possible remedies, but it must be borne in mind that industrial policies are often built around and are dependent upon the social and industrial environment of the country concerned. Given different national environments, it cannot therefore be assumed that a successful policy in country X would be equally successful in country Y. UK industrial policy measures must be justified by their ability to solve the industrial problems particular to the UK, and not be based simply upon their apparent success in other industrialised countries.

II Industrial Philosophies

Before looking at individual policy measures, it is useful to outline differences in national industrial philosphy in order to put specific measures into perspective and give them a sense of proportion.

West Germany

The Germans describe their economy as a Social Market Economy, where industry is based on the 'competitive order' in which 'complete competition' prevails, not the economists' 'perfect competition' but the maximum possible competition (which may be something like 'workable competition'). The role of the state is not to stand aside, but interventions should be 'conformable', that is, they should maintain or increase competition rather than reduce it. Actions against monopolies and cartels would be conformable while subsidies would, on the whole, be non-conformable. Intervention should usually be general rather than selective (as between industries of firms), but where it is selective it should be such as to improve the working of the market system or to minimise the damage to it. Given this industrial philosophy it is not surprising that in a consideration of public ownership, it is the denationalisation of a number of publicly-owned companies that deserves mention. The most notable cases are Volkswagen and Preussag, the Prussian mining and smelting company. On the other hand, both the *Bund* and the *Länder* (Regional Governments) own shareholdings in a wide variety of companies, undertakings in which public authorities have a share accounting for 9-10 per cent of total enterprise turnover in 1973. But the shareholding is often very small, nearly always a minority shareholding. Coal mining is not publicly owned and the Federal Government involvement in the steel industry consists only of a majority holding in the third largest steel producer which accounts for about 10 per cent of national steel output. The largest shipbuilding group (Howaldtswerke-Deutsche Werft) is owned mainly by the Federal Government with a share of about 25 per cent held by the Land of Schleswig-Holstein.

Sweden

The 'Competitive order' is also fundamental in Sweden's industrial philosophy, although it is secured not so much through government intervention as through a liberal international trade policy. But the main aim of policy is undoubtedly to facilitate the adjustment of the economy to changing market forces and even sometimes to anticipate future market changes in order to avoid any conflict between the effects of economic growth and the country's main objectives. Economic growth is essential if income per head and the social services are to grow rapidly, but such growth is only acceptable if it is accompanied by full employment, a more even distribution of income and wealth and a balanced regional development (implicit in the two previous requirements). Unlike many other industrial countries, the main function of policy is therefore to help industry adapt to the changing competitive order as opposed to protecting industry from this competition. Such protection, it is held, would merely prolong the problems rather than solve them, since in the long term the industries concerned would not be able to afford the required wage level. Generally speaking, Sweden has relied on private enterprise and the invisible hand of competition to create industrial wealth; its socialist reputation stems from its policies to achieve what it is thought private enterprise cannot achieve, namely an even distribution of income and wealth between the entire population and smooth development. One would expect public ownership to be higher in countries where government intervention in industry is relatively high, but there seems no correlation between the degree of public ownership and social philosophy. Contrary to common opinion, for example, which stems from the knowledge that Sweden is a socialist country, the proportion of mining and manufacturing under public ownership in Sweden is very small by UK and West European standards. A sizeable proportion of public utilities are, however, in public hands. The proportion of publicly owned production varies sharply from sector to sector. In 1969 it was highest in iron ore mining (76 per cent.), followed by steel (12 per cent) and certain branches of the forestry industry (16 per cent. in paper and 28 per cent in fibreboard). Since 1970, all the state-owned companies working on the legal form of ordinary share companies, have been merged into one group of companies headed by a state-owned holding company, Statsföretag AB (National Swedish Enterprises in the Swedish State-Holding Co). It currently controls only about 5 per cent of Swedish manufacturing and mining. The Statsföretag is sometimes described as the IRI of Sweden, although it is by no means as large, and arguably has a different role. There is, however, a larger public participation in banking in Sweden than in Britain.

United States of America

The free enterprise system also figures foremost in the philosophy of the United States, though with foreign trade accounting for only a small proportion of its GNP, its foreign trade policy is less liberal than that of Sweden and its policy measures tend to have a nationalistic slant. Nevertheless, the Federal State and local governments intervene, to maintain the competitive order, to increase industrial efficiency and to encourage private enterprise when normal market forces are failing to produce technologies deemed necessary to society. Public ownership is virtually non-existent with even many utilities, such as the railways, privately owned.

Japan

This dichotomy between internal and external competition has also been evident in Japan, though on a much larger scale. The Japanese government has always encouraged internal competition as a means of ensuring the survival of the fittest in domestic industry, but has also given considerable help to protect infant industries from excessive foreign competition where it regards a substantial home market as a necessary springboard for overseas trading. However, for many years it was considered that excessive competition (attributable in part to an excessively large number of small firms) caused deterioration in the financial position of enterprises and obstructed the progress of rationalisation. The governments during this period, therefore encouraged cartels and mergers. In the last two years, the Fair Trade Commission has become much more vociferous and active. The government has indeed been active in influencing the direction of industry. Elaborate formal arrangements exist for forward planning on the basis of data gathered from industry which have enabled mutually agreed and reasonable targets to be drawn up industry by industry. A successful and mutually beneficial relationship has emerged between government and business based on the uniquely Japanese system of 'administrative guidance', in other words discussion, concensus and subtle use of the carrot rather than the stick. As with the United States, public ownership is very small, being almost solely confined to utilities and about a dozen financial institutions such as the Japan Development Bank and the Export-Import Bank.

France and Italy

On the other side of the coin are France and Italy who do not believe fundamentally in this philosophy of free enterprise capitalism. In the case of Italy the rejection of this philosophy appears to be based on the belief that private enterprise, left to itself, would be far too slow in achieving the changes deemed necessary to the Italian economy. For France, its rejection is based on the French conception of the role of industry which is not primarily to make profit, nor specifically to create wealth, but to make France a greater, more independent country, capable of matching others of the same size and in particular of holding its own in Europe. To ensure that French industry is capable of sustaining France in the leading European role which her political leaders conceive should be hers is the main aim of French industrial policy; it is regarded as far too important to be left to the workings of market forces. Consequently, through a host of interventionist measures and national plans, France (and to a lesser extent, Italy) has confided to the government, the role of animator, coordinator and controller of industrial development.

This industrial philosophy has required a greater degree of direct state involvement in industry, particularly in Italy, than has been evident in most other industrialised nations. The electrical industry is the only truly nationalised industry in Italy, although the three state-holding companies – IRI, ENI and EFIM – control varying proportions of the outputs of many important sectors. They have significant holdings in iron and steel, chemicals, textiles, petroleum, engineering and shipbuilding: on the basis of 1967 turnover figures they controlled 71 per cent, 65 per cent,* 40 per cent* and 25 per cent respectively of the first four of these sectors (* including Montecatini-Edison of which IRI and ENI acquired control in 1968). Together, the state holding companies account for about 40 per cent of industrial production. Public ownership is also more extensive in France than the UK, especially in the manufacturing and finance sectors where a particular feature is the existence of nationalised undertakings side by side with private companies; for example Renault, Banque Nationale de Paris. The first, second and fourth largest insurance companies are nationalised, yet the steel industry is still 100 per cent privately owned despite benefiting from substantial government aid.

III General Investment Incentives

The details of investment incentives shown at Table 2 indicate that the free depreciation of plant and machinery and the high initial allowance on buildings available in the UK are considerably more generous than the incentives available in other countries. The most common arrangement in the countries studied is for depreciation allowances for tax purposes to be related to asset life. This is the norm in France, Italy, West Germany, Japan and the United States. In West Germany depreciation for tax purposes requires a minimum asset life of six years. While in Japan, depreciation is in general based on asset life, the government has been looked to for tax concessions such as corporate tax reductions for high priority industries, and special depreciation rates on new plant and equipment required for modernisation. Until 1973, special depreciation write-offs granted to some priority industries permitted as much as 50 per cent of the cost of new plant to be deducted in the first year, with the remainder being spread equally over the useful life of the asset. However, in the last few years, government statements on tax policy revision are in line with other policy statements in calling for further expenditure to increase the quality of life and reduced emphasis on industrial investment. Among other things, the special depreciation measures were reduced to 25 per cent in 1973 and the tax reform plans for reduction, in equal instalments to zero by 1976. Tax incentives are now offered to encourage investment mainly on pollution control devices.

In the United States also, some industries, eg oil and natural gas extraction and ship building, benefit significantly from tax arrangements designed to make investment in those areas more profitable. But the main fiscal policies affecting investment are the Depreciation Guide-Lines and Investment Tax Credits. The Asset Depreciation Range (ADR) has formed the Depreciation Guide Lines in the US since 1970. It is based on broad industry classes of assets. For each asset guidance class, a range of years corresponding to the estimated average actual life of all assets in the group is prescribed by the revenue authorities. For each asset in an asset depreciation class, the tax payer selects a period within the asset depreciation range prescribed for that class. A tax payer using this method does not have to justify retirement and replacement policies, but he cannot change the depreciation period he has chosen for an asset after the initial choice. The Investment Tax Credits scheme has been used to influence the investment cycle, though its effectiveness has been the subject of considerable and inconclusive academic discussion. The scheme allows a 7 per cent credit against Federal income tax on all property with a useful life of over seven years. The credit was originally introduced in 1962, was suspended for most of 1967, repealed in 1969 and subsequently re-introduced with effect from March 1971.

In keeping with the belief in the operation of market forces and hence the inappropriateness in general of subsidies, the shortest fiscal period of depreciation for machinery and equipment in Sweden is five years; stocks-in-trade can be written off to 35 to 40 per cent of their value. For industrial buildings the depreciation allowance is up to 3 to 5 per cent per annum. There are no non-regional investment grants or other general investment incentives of the usual form.

Certain features of foreign practice in this field are worthy of special note. First, a number of countries use their investment incentives to discriminate in favour of certain activities, and especially R & D (see R & D section below). Leaving on one side the question of whether R & D should in fact receive special support, it is doubtful whether this is the best method of R & D support. Because there are serious difficulties in defining R & D, tax incentives will probably involve support for rather doubtful activities and may encourage firms to devote resources to finding ways of increasing their tax allowances by reclassifying their activities. Moreover, since tax incentives relate solely to capital expenditure, they would appear to introduce a bias in favour of capital intensity in R & D whereas much development work is labour intensive. Finally, given an almost total ignorance of the elasticity of the R & D function, there must be considerable doubt about the effectiveness of this sort of general measure in stimulating sufficient additional R & D to offset the support to R & D that would have been done in any case.

Another feature of interest, and one which might horrify a UK audience, is the recent 11 per cent. investment tax introduced in Germany (using the VAT system) on contra cyclical grounds[1]. During the post-war period, Sweden has also employed an investment tax (of similar magnitude) in some periods of inflation (1951 to 1953 and 1955 to 1957). One would certainly expect a tax rate of this magnitude to have some effect on the timing of investment over the cycle, provided that the tax was not thought likely to be retained for very long.

Sweden has also experimented with another device for reducing the instability of the investment cycle – the Investment Funds Scheme, whose day to day running is the responsibility of the Labour Market Board. The Investment Funds Scheme is not regarded as a method of industrial subsidisation or even as a means of stimulating investment that otherwise would not take place. Rather, its main purpose is to even out cyclical variations in production and employment by making it both profitable and possible for private industry to maintain a stable level of employment, even in periods of slack, for 'eligible construction works, to produce or procure necessary machinery and equipment, and, to some extent, to produce goods to be used when business prospects improved'. Briefly, the system is designed to distribute investment evenly over the whole business cycle in order to eradicate cyclical unemployment.

The Investment Funds System was inaugurated in 1938 and has formally existed as an integral part of Swedish contra-cyclical policy for over 35 years. The basic mechanics of the system are simple. In years when business is flourishing, firms may (the scheme is completely voluntary) set aside a certain share of their gross profits free of tax to an Investment Fund, thus helping to curtail current investment. Conversely, during periods of recession, the funds can be released by the Board or the Government to secure a net increase in the level of employment. The success of the mechanics rests on the benefits of released Investment Funds being sufficiently attractive to induce firms to comply with stipulations concerning especially the timing of investment projects. To make the system attractive, each firm is allowed annually to set aside to an Investment Fund a maximum of 40 per cent of its pre-tax profits. Of this 40 per cent, 46 per cent has to be deposited in a blocked Central Bank account, this figure – 46 per cent – being set a little below the company taxation rate in order to make Investment Fund appropriations more advantageous than

[1] West Germany has, subsequent to the writing of this paper, introduced a contra-cyclical investment bonus of 7.5% on approved orders for capital equipment placed between 1 December 1974 and 30 June 1975.

taxation. The accumulated Investment Funds can be released in three different ways:

(a)   Five years from appropriation, 30 per cent of the appropriation may be used freely by the firm for purposes specified by the legislation;

(b)   Firms can be required to use their funds in a specified way;

(c)   Firms can be granted permission to use their funds on application, provided that certain requirements from the labour market authorities are, or will be fulfilled. Moreover, Investment Funds can be released generally or limited to specific sectors of the economy or geographical areas (special releases). The permissible uses of released funds mentioned under (a) comprise:

(i)   investment in construction work

(ii) in machinery and equipment

(iii) a temporary increase in inventories.

With an additional reduction of taxable income (investment deduction) amounting to 10 per cent of funds actually used in compliance with the conditions stipulated by the labour market authorities, the Investment Funds System is equivalent to free depreciation plus a 10 per cent investment allowance. In order for the system to operate in the UK, which operates free depreciation generally, therefore, further incentives would need to be given to make it attractive to firms.

The Swedes believe the Scheme has functioned effectively. No detailed analysis of its effectiveness has been carried out by the Department of Industry but the favourable Swedish comments are given support by some work the Department has recently completed on the instability of the business cycle. Measuring the instability of the business cycle by the average percentage deviation per quarter of actual manufacturing output from trend, the study showed Sweden to have one of the most stable cycles of all the major industrialised countries.

IV   Regional development

Regional problems differ both in severity and in nature between countries. Italian policies, for instance, have had to devise ways of developing the southern half of the country, which is an area with many of the characteristics of an underdeveloped country. In West Germany regional problems have arisen in certain rural areas and in the peripheral areas along the border with East Germany. Neither of these countries has suffered to any great extent from structural problems of an industrial kind, which have been among the main causes of Sweden's and especially the UK's regional problems.

It is hardly surprising, therefore, that Tables 3 and 4 reveal considerable differences between the intensiveness of the regional policies of the countries under study. A glance at these tables should be enough to demonstrate that the European countries (and particularly the UK and Italy) are much more active than others in this area. US regional policy has been extremely limited. The great bulk of federal development appropriations goes in grants-in-aid to State and Local Governments for improving the infrastructure (education, road building, hospitals etc) to make the the problem areas more attractive to industry. The amount of federal development funds used specifically for business loans is very small. Some additional help has been given through manpower retraining and also through public procurement. Japan, until recently very inactive, has been increasing its regional support fairly rapidly. Her regional problems stem basically from the imbalance created by great concentration of population and economic activity in the Pacific Coast belt.

Of those countries with fairly active regional promotional policies, Japan and Sweden appear to place the greatest reliance on non-discretionary measures, assistance in Japan being selective only in the sense that specific criteria on employment and investment have to be met in order to receive support in the form of cheap loans and favourable tax treatment. In the UK too the emphasis is on non-discretionary measures which account for about three-quarters of our expenditure on industrial incentives. Similarly for Sweden. In Italy and France the balance seems to be in favour of discretionary measures, as it also is in Germany where expenditure on discretionary measures is about two-thirds of the total. There are some grounds for thinking that discretionary measures may be more cost-effective since they concentrate support on marginal activities.

Among the non-discretionary measures, accelerated or special depreciation are fairly common. France operates a 50 per cent first year depreciation while West Germany, in the zonal border area only and in addition to normal depreciation, allows 50 per cent. depreciation for movables and 30 per cent for immovables in the first five years. Special depreciation is also automatic in Japan. In Sweden depreciation loans are provided for investment in buildings and machinery. Investment grants, of the form operated in the UK, form part of the regional policy of West Germany and Sweden, although the level of grants is much lower. In Germany, tax-free investment grants are paid at a rate of 10 per cent. (reduced to 7.5 per cent under the stabilisation law) for investment for the establishment or enlargement of industrial plants in the border, rural and Saar coal mining areas, provided that these investments meet certain specified criteria, the most important of which is that sales should be mainly outside the region. In Sweden investment grants are subject to a maximum two-thirds of total investment costs.

There are a host of other non-discretionary measures including cheap loans and exemption from certain taxes in Japan, reductions in labour costs through reduced social security payments in Italy, and grants to local authorities to improve infrastructure in the USA and Japan. Sweden, in particular, offers a multitude of non-discretionary measures to firms undertaking industrial or related activities or to firms providing services for industry. Location grants or location loans are provided for investments in buildings and machinery. Location grants are fixed at a maximum of 35 per cent (50 per cent in special cases) of the total investment cost in the Outer Aid Area, and in the Inner Aid Area can be increased to 65 per cent in exceptional cases. Government guarantees are provided on loans for operating capital for regional development purposes, equal to 50 per cent of the liquid assets required during the initial stage of a new or intended enterprise. In addition, the government grants reimbursement of certain costs connected with the transfer of operations to the development areas, such as the removal of machinery. Since January 1971, a transport subsidy is available in the form of a freight discount up to 35 per cent of the costs of transporting certain types of finished product to their markets; the discount varies with distance and location. Assistance is also provided towards the training of new employees. During the first six months a new employee's training grant of Kr 5 per hour per employee is paid; or, as an alternative, Kr 10 per hour can be paid over one year to a concern provided that the firm undertakes to provide training of the same type and quality as that available at the Training Centres. In the Inner Support Area only, employment premia are payable on condition that firms abide by collective wage agreements. An employment grant is given for each worker employed for a whole year where this represents an increase in employment over the previous year. The amount payable for the first year is Kr 7,000, and if the increase is maintained, grants of Kr 7,000 and Kr 3,500 respectively are paid in the second and third years.

It should be noted that there is some tendency, although not perhaps a very marked one, for non-discretionary measures to have rather more selectivity built into them in some other countries than in the UK.

Turning to discretionary measures, it is noteworthy that discretionary industrial assistance is not given in the USA, Japan and Sweden but is a very prominent feature of Italian and German regional policy. The Industry Act gives wide powers in this respect in the UK but projected expenditure is relatively small in relation both to RDG's and to German expenditure from GA funds. The Germans, and to a lesser extent the Italians focus their expenditure on growth centres: in Germany there are over 300 of these and, with policy having been fairly successful in stimulating their industrial development, the intention of the Federal government is now to select new centres in the older industrial areas where the decline of traditional industries is now posing some problems similar to those faced by the regions in the UK. Discretionary assistance usually takes the form of grants. The maximum assistance permissible from public funds varies, with the category of the growth centre, from 9 per cent to 22.5 per cent of investment costs.

In Italy a wide range of discretionary incentives is offered to industry to invest in the Mezzogiorno. These incentives include:
    (a)   a 10 year income and profits tax holiday;
    (b)   a 50 per cent reduction in turnover tax on the purchase of capital goods and building equipment;
    (c)   capital grants for 7 per cent to 35 per cent of the total (plant, machinery and building) cost of the project, depending on the type of project and size of firm;
    (d)   cheap long-term loans for 35 per cent to 50 per cent of plant, equipment, building and inventory costs, with provision for a further 10 per cent for equipment produced in the Mezzogiorno;
    (e)   reductions (50 per cent) in railway and sea freight rates and a 50 per cent reduction in the tax on electricity consumption;
    (f)   a 10 per cent reduction in company social security contributions. (This saving amounts to about 1 per cent of the wage and salary bill.)

Probably the most important of Italian discriminationary measures, however, is the obligation imposed on the Instituto per la Riconstruzione Industriale (IRI) to place high proportions of their new (80 per cent) and total (60 per cent) investments in the Mezzogiorno. The ability to use the state enterprises in this way may well be one of the main advantages of this type of organisation. While no assessment of the effectiveness of Italy's regional policy can be made here, the conditions imposed upon IRI seem to have been fairly effective. It is true that the ratio of per capita income in the South to that in the North has remained at around three to five throughout the post-war period. But this constancy does not necessarily indicate failure: given Italy's rapid post-war growth, it is quite conceivable that without extensive support the South would have fared much worse. A factor helping to maintain per capita income in the South has been the substantial rate of emigration – averaging around a quarter of a million per annum during the 1960s. There has also been a tendency for development in the South to be rather capital intensive, and improvements in transportation have subjected some local industries to strong competition from firms outside the Mezzogiorno with the result that many smaller firms have found themselves in difficulties. But the economy of the Mezzogiorno has become increasingly diversified and certain centres (especially Taranto) have witnessed considerable industrial growth.

Dispersal policies are operated in several countries, although the UK IDC system is probably the most comprehensive of the instruments available in the countries studied. The Japanese Government can only exercise legal control over industrial building in certain metropolitan areas, although they are contemplating levying new taxes on firms remaining in urban areas. In the Permis de Construire, France possesses a similar instrument to the IDC's and can levy taxes on new building in the Paris area. In Italy there are provisions for fines where investment is made in congested areas: in practice, however, it is virtually impossible to invest without the approval of CIPE, the Interministerial Committee for Economic Planning.

One of the most interesting aspects of foreign regional development policy is the stringent conditions laid down by many countries which must be met to qualify for regional assistance. This is in marked contrast to the more 'informal' approach adopted in the UK. In Sweden, for example, assistance is only given to projects that are expected to lead to permanent employment and a sufficient level of profitalility. Employment grants are restricted to workers employed for a whole year where this represents an increase in employment over the previous year. In Japan, specific criteria on employment and investment have to be met in order to qualify for assistance. In Germany, grants are only available if the project fulfils specified criteria, the most significant of which is that the resulting output should be sold primarily outside the region. This seems a very sensible criterion since it means that support is not likely to be given to projects which merely reallocate local employment between competing firms.

V Selective intervention

Table 6 shows that there is widespread government support for the so-called advanced technology industries, with support especially heavy for the space and nuclear industries in virtually all countries. The aircraft and computer industries receive rather more support in the EEC than in the non-EEC countries shown in the table. The methods of support do not vary significantly between countries, and the motives also appear to be much the same. The Germans, for instance, see these industries as 'key sectors of decisive significance for the whole of the economy'. It is argued that German companies cannot afford the development costs or bear the risks without support from public funds. Aerospace yields substantial spin off and computers and nuclear energy have, or will have, important effects on productivity in other sectors. (The last of these arguments entails the common confusion between gains from production and use). As in the UK, it seems unlikely that the benefits can justify the high support costs that have been incurred in some of the countries under study.

Comparisons of support for other industries cannot be taken very far on a sectoral basis without much more information than is available since such intervention generally consists of action to deal with specific problems – a firm's insolvency, for instance – rather than action of an industry-wide character. Table 7 gives some details of non-AT assistance.

A sector that has received support in many countries is the shipbuilding industry. Subsidised export credit is provided in most countries and is the subject of an OECD agreement. Some countries such as the UK and Germany also provide assistance for modernisation, rationalisation etc. Taking all the quantifiable measures together, the UK appears to be among the countries offering the greatest support in relation to output. The scale of support is also high in France and Italy, while in the USA, Sweden, Germany and Japan, support is less.

Among the other industries receiving support, German assistance to the oil industry is noteworthy since this is a somewhat unusual sector for a Government to assist. The support, which appears to be given on security of supply grounds, is intended to assist the small and somewhat fragmented oil industry to develop its own sources of supply of crude oil so as to increase its competitive strength. To this end support has been provided in the form of loans for collaborative oil field exploration (on a no-oil no-repayment basis) and grants for up to 30 per cent of the cost of obtaining concessions or participating in joint enterprises. These measures have not resulted in any commercially exploitable discoveries to date. The Japanese oil industry is supported in a rather similar way.

Otherwise, it is more illuminating to compare selective intervention in terms of differences in the institutional arrangements and in the methods of support adopted; there are interesting contrasts in these respects. In the UK, USA and Sweden, the preference has been for direct state involvement in selective assistance, although the picture may be changing somewhat in Sweden with the creation of Statsföretag. In France and Italy, on the other hand, para-statal organisations have been the main instrument of intervention. Another interesting Italian institution is GEPI which was formed in 1971 to take over and transform companies believed to be viable in the longer term but suffering from acute short-term difficulties. The intention is that GEPI should sell off its holding once its task of transformation has been completed. Although it is too early to attempt an evaluation of GEPI's operations, the performance of GEPI's fifty or so companies is said to be improving in most cases and a few have already been returned to private ownership.

In France there is the IDI (Institut de Développement Industriel), set up in 1970 along the lines of the former IRC in the UK. It is endowed with a mixture of government and private sector funds to enable it to provide capital to efficient companies whose expansion is being inhibited by difficulties in financing, and to promote restructuring in sectors of particular concern to government, eg machine tools. Additionally, IDI is occasionally called upon to find a 'French solution' when an unwanted foreign takeover bid is made for a French company.

A major difference in the methods of selective intervention in the countries studied is the greater emphasis placed on assisting small and meduim sized firms in some countries compared with the UK. This is the responsibility specifically charged to the IDI in France and to KFW (a state banking institution) in Germany. In Italy it is an important aspect of the activities of GEPI and of IMI, which is responsible for administering a fund for industrial restructuring. Although the Bolton Report's conclusion that in the UK small firms do not suffer from inadequate sources of finance, might be used as an argument against any special measures to support them in this country, it can also be argued that postwar increases in concentration pose a threat to competition (though increased international competition works in the opposite direction) and that a substantial small firms sector is a useful counter weight to the market power of the larger firms. One might thus regard support for small and medium sized firms as being a part of competition policy.

VI   Technical development and scientific research

'Research and development' as it is commonly referred to, comprises a set of heterogenous activities, which unfortunately are traditionally grouped together. Separate examination of each activity type would perhaps lead to a better understanding of this form of government assistance. The classification of R & D activities varies between countries and even between firms. But market and behavioural research is not included in R & D support, although they may be of greater importance to growth than pure and so-called applied research.

The case for supporting R & D is far from clear cut. Some proponents of R & D support, argue that R & D output has certain good public characteristics and frequently suffers from limited appropriability. Hence, while society requires maximum use of R & D results, the incentive to private investment in R & D depends on the ability of the investor to retain control over their use. Varying degrees of opposition to R & D support can be discerned. At the mild end of the opposition scale, it is pointed out that the results of R & D will in some cases not be of use to others (eg because of product differentiation) and there will be other cases where R & D may yield results of private but not social value. Arguments for supporting R & D from public funds should therefore rest on a view that the good public characteristics outweigh the private benefits; but there is no way of demonstrating that this is, in fact, the case. This mild opposition argument seems very weak on several grounds. First it is possible in many countries to separate support given for pure research, the results of which become available to everyone, and support for technical development, the benefits of which are confined primarily to the firm undertaking the development work; (the status of so-called 'applied research' is obscure). But second and more important, does it matter if the 'private' benefits outweigh the purely social? If R & D is deemed to be a catalyst to economic growth there would be strong grounds for support in cases of insufficient private R & D activity: this line of argument has been behind the policy of investment grants and incentives.

The strongest argument against the support of R & D is that it does not stimulate economic growth. There is ample evidence to show that the performance of UK high technology industries receiving government support for R & D has not been any better than such industries not receiving this support. On reflection, it is not surprising that R & D expenditure and economic growth are not closely correlated. R & D is supposed to exert its impact on economic growth through technical change yet there is little direct connection between individual acts of invention and advance in scientific knowledge brought about through research. Activities which produce natural science and those which produce useful industrial hardware are very different one from the other. There is, after all, a very substantial difference between knowing how to do something and being able to put it to a commercial use and then to be able to do it at an appropriate cost. This would suggest that effort should be concentrated on technical development rather than pure research, as is the case in Sweden. Even so, this technical development must be geared to viable commercial projects; thus suggesting that support for development work would benefit from greater selectivity. Finally, it should be remembered that R & D is not the only basic work done to produce new products. Design and market research are often vital and are normally not included in R & D spending.

Nevertheless, support for R & D is general in the countries studied (see table 5), although the amounts of assistance vary considerably. Total expenditure on R & D in Sweden is fairly low, only 1.6 per cent of GNP in 1971 compared with 2.6 per cent for the USA, 2.3 per cent for the UK, 2.1 per cent for Germany and the Netherlands, 1.7 per cent for France and 1.5 per cent for Japan. Government expenditure on R & D as a percentage of GNP in 1969 was highest in the USA, 1.6 per cent, followed by the UK, 1.2 per cent, France, 0.9 per cent, Germany, 0.7 per cent, Sweden, 0.5 per cent, and Japan, 0.2 per cent. The high US figure is accounted for by R & D support to advanced technology industries which is the most important form of government assistance to industry in the USA. The similarities of R & D policy are greater than the differences, eg special tax treatment of R & D expenditure, but the differences are not without interest. Of particular interest are the NEDC, the IMI fund in Italy and the French tax treatment of profits from licenses.

Favourable tax treatment of R & D expenditure is operated in France, West Germany, Japan and the USA. In France 50 per cent first year depreciation is allowed. Special allowances are available for investment expenditure incurred exclusively for R & D in Germany. In addition to the standard allowance, firms may write off in the first year 50 per cent and 30 per cent of machinery and building costs respectively. The remainder would then be depreciated on a linear basis over the asset's standard life. In addition there is a 10 per cent investment subsidy available for all investment for R & D qualifying for accelerated depreciation. Favourable tax treatment is the government's main method of helping private sector R & D in Japan. Total R & D costs can be deducted for the year in which they are incurred, there is 95 per cent depreciation in the first year for equipment for research, and subject to approval, one third of the cost of equipment purchased for putting the results of research to use can be written off in the first year. In line with the recently increasing emphasis on pollution control in Japan, the Ministry of Finance has instituted a pollution tax reserve which entitles manufacturing firms and utilities to defer taxes for three years on 3-6 per cent of current sales revenues, if invested in qualifying pollution control equipment. This reserve becomes a permanent source of cash for a growing firm. In addition the government permits immediate write-off of 95 per cent of R & D expenditure on pollution control. In the United States, R & D expenditure is deductible in the year incurred.

Of the differences in R & D policy, the NRDC has the longest history and has been adopted in some respects by Japan in its National Research and Development Programme. The NRDC was set up as a public corporation in 1949 with the function of developing and exploiting inventions made in the public sector (Independent Research Establishments, Universities etc) and of promoting the commercial exploitation of worthwhile inventions made by private individuals or companies. Although much activity was expected to stem from this institution, its scale of operation has in fact been rather modest suggesting that there are very few commercially viable inventions that are not carried through to the development stage because of a lack of finance. This impression is strengthened by the record of those inventions which NRDC has supported, which, overall, seems rather poor. This is true both of private sector and public sector inventions. Among the latter only Cephalosporin has been a significant revenue earner.

The Italian IMI fund seems in some respects rather similar to NRDC in objectives and methods in that it too was established to provide finance (mainly in the form of cheap loans) for private sector R & D. IMI is a public sector bank but the majority of its business is nevertheless on a strictly commercial basis. It therefore has considerable financial expertise with which to back up its non-commercial activities, such as the state-funded R & D lending. IMI, however, cannot take the final decision on spending from the fund; it can only make recommendations to CIPE. It therefore seems likely that IMI's R & D activities are both more commercially orientated and more politically controlled than NRDC activities. One of the requirements imposed on IMI for administering the fund is that 40 per cent of its lending should be for projects in the south of Italy.

Finally, a method not apparently tried in other countries for encouraging the dissemination of the results of R & D is the French exemption from tax on profits from licenses.

Table 1 Industrial growth rates 1955 to 1973 (% per annum)

	West Germany	UK	USA	France	Italy	Sweden	Japan	Belgium	Holland
Total industrial production	5.9	2.8	4.4	6.1	7.1	5.7	13.8	4.3	7.1
Mining & quarrying	2.4	1.3	2.5	2.2	4.7	5.7	6.2	0.8	7.5
Manufacturing	6.1	2.9	4.3	6.4	7.2	5.6	14.2	4.9	6.7
Food, Drink, Tobacco	5.8	2.9	3.9	na	5.6	3.9	9.9	3.9	6.0
Basic Metals	4.1	1.3	2.9	4.7	6.8	6.3	14.5	4.0	8.9
Iron & Steel	4.0	0.9	2.1	4.3	7.2	6.4	14.4	na	na
Non-ferrous metals	5.4	2.3	4.5	5.9	4.1	6.2	14.7	na	na
Metal Products	6.0	2.9	4.4	7.0	7.3	6.7	17.4	5.2	6.4
Transport equipment	7.2	na	3.8	7.5	9.0	6.6	17.2	na	na
Textiles, clothing & leather	4.8	2.0	3.6	4.7	4.9	3.8	9.6	3.9ᴬ	4.5
Chemicals, Rubber, Coal & Petroleum Products	8.6	4.7†	6.3	7.4	9.1	6.4	14.3	6.3	8.9
Other manufacturing	5.8	3.5	4.2	6.0	7.6	5.6	13.0	4.9	6.7
Gas, Electricity & Water	7.3*	4.6	6.1*	7.2*	6.7*	na	12.6*	6.2‡	9.4

* Excludes water
† Excludes rubber – included in other manufacturing
‡ Excludes gas
ᴬ For period 1958 to 1973
na Not available

Source: OECD Industrial Production

Table 2 Non-regional investment incentives (non-discretionary)

	Depreciation	Grants	Other	Remarks
UK	Plant and machinery: 100% first year. Buildings etc: 40% initial allowance	–	–	
France	Based on asset life; in some cases on reducing balance method	–	–	Accelerated depreciation for assets used in R & D or pollution control
West Germany	Based on asset life; (option of reducing balance method on moveables currently suspended)	10% (now 7.5%) for investment for R & D purposes	[1]Currently an investment tax: VAT (11%) not 'reclaimable'	Accelerated depreciation for particular types of asset (ships, aircraft) or particular uses (R & D, pollution control): 50% (moveables), 30% (immoveables) freely in first five years, in addition to normal depreciation
Italy	–	–	–	
Sweden	Shortest fixed period of depreciation is 5 years for machinery and equipment. For buildings maximum allowance of 5% per annum. Stocks in trade can be written off to max. of 40% of value	–	Counter-cyclical Investment Funds Scheme	Discretion as to timing of general IF releases, which are equivalent to free depreciation and usually accompanied by a 10% investment allowance
USA	Based on asset life	–	–	Capital expenditure for R & D may be written off in first year
Japan	Based on asset life	–	–	Accelerated depreciation for enterprises deriving income from overseas transactions

[1] See footnote on page 50

Table 3   Non-discretionary regional investment and other incentives (differences from national)

	Depreciation	Investment grants	Other	Remarks
UK	–	RDGs (20% for mining manufacturing and construction)	REP – (Expenditure 1972/73 £101m)	1 RDGs – 22% in special development areas 2 RDGs 1973/4 expenditure £225m
France	Accelerated (50% first year)	–	–	
West Germany	Accelerated depreciation in zonal border area only: 50% (moveables) 30% (immoveables) freely in first five years, in addition to normal depreciation	10% but reduced to 7.5% for cyclical reasons (Expenditure £50m)	A small amount of assistance with transport costs in zonal border area (at £5 million pa)	1 Special measures for West Berlin 2 Grants only available on certain carefully specified criteria, the most the most important of which is that sales should be primarily outside the region
Italy	–	–	1 10 year tax holiday 2 Reduction in transport costs 3 Reductions in social security contributions	
Sweden	Depreciation loans for buildings and machinery	Location grants of max of 35% or 50% depending on area of total investment costs. Investment grants and loans may not exceed ⅔ of total investment costs	Transport subsidy equal to 15%-35% freight discount. Assistance towards training of employees. Govt guarantees loans for operating capital	Employment premiums in inner development area if firms abide by collective wage agreements
USA	–	–	–	1 Main regional measure is infrastructure support 2 There are taxation and other differences between States, but these are thought not to be very great
Japan	Special depreciation	–	Cheap (but not very cheap) loans; some preferential tax treatment	Assistance is automatic provided that criteria as to investment and employment are met

Table 4 Discretionary regional assistance

	Forms and rates of industrial assistance	Provisions to limit investment in congested areas	Other measures	Remarks
UK	Industry act offers great flexibility (1973/74 estimate £35m)	IDC System	LEA aids: Advance factories Training grants (Estimated 1973/74 cost £55m)	Assistance to shipbuilding (£32m in 1972/73) is mainly on regional grounds
France	Tax concessions, four rates 12-25% depending on region	Taxes in Paris area. Permis de Construire, like the IDC's	Funds made available from FDES, IDI and FIAT through the Societes de development regionale. Also direct persuasion of large firms	
West Germany	1 GA funds, (90m per annum) up to 10%–25% (reduced to 9%–22½%) depending on location, but investment grant, if taken is deducted from these limits. 2 Some Länder aids (£15m pa). 3 Some cheap ERP loans	–	–	1 Five categories of growth centres for GA funds. 2 Upper limit to amount of support and cost per job limit, in addition to specific appraisal criteria.
Italy	Grants or cheap loans for up to 50% of capital expenditure depending on size of enterprise and area of Mezzogiorno	Fines for job-creating investment in certain congested areas. Power of CIPE to veto investment projects	Support to State enterprises in return for obligation to make 80% of new investment (and 70% of total) in the South	1 Growth centre policy 2 Numerous smaller incentives also available eg exemption from stamp duty
Sweden	–	–	Special releases from IF funds	
USA	No significant direct assistance	–	Some support for retraining and through public procurement	
Japan	–	Legal control on industrial building in certain metropolitan areas, but no proper dispersal system	–	

Table 5   Support for R & D

	Support to cooperative research	State research for industry	Favourable tax treatment	Project support	Other	Remarks
UK	Grant to RAs	IREs	–	Mainly for advanced technology NRDC	–	Cost 1973/4 AT £174m other £23m
France	'Enveloppe recherche' ie grants to laboratories out of the the budget	–	50% first year depreciation	Development aid through direct govt. financing of firms	Tax exemption of profits from licences Special programmes such as the 'Plan Calcul'	
West Germany	Grants	–	Accelerated depreciation (see table)	AT support	10% (now 7.5%) grant for investment qualifying for accelerated depreciation	Also some aids from Länder
Italy	State participation in research societies (eg marine technology, housing technology) of which currently 4	Experimental laboratories mainly for traditional sectors	–	Cheap loans from IMI fund, repayable if success. Little AT support	–	IMI Fund c. £100m and is to be raised ⅔
Sweden	Financial support to industrial research associations	–	–	Support to technical R & D Grants for technical research. Also interest bearing loans		
USA	Some support from National Science Foundation	Federal installations and laboratories	Capital expenditure may be written off in first year	AT industries		Increasing emphasis on Civilian rather than military technologies
Japan	Selected projects financed by govt. Joint research endeavour— National Research and Development Programme	15 institutes and laboratories concentrate on basic research	95% first year depreciation, and discretionary accelerated depreciation for investment make use of research results	Little AT support Cheap loans to finance, applications of new technologies £12m per annum)	Tax deferment of three years or 3-6% of current sales revenues for investment in qualifying polution control equipment	

Table 6 Selective intervention – advanced technology industries

	Aircraft	Space	Nuclear	Computers	Remarks
UK	Concord development + production Rolls Royce RB211 etc. Other R & D support	National satellite programme; FSRO	Reactor R & D by AEA; loans to British Nuclear Fuels	Support to ICL for new range, and assistance through procurement policy	KEY: Subsidy-output ratios *—0–5% **—5–10% ***—10–25% ****—25–100% *****—over 100%
	***	****	****	***	
France	***	****	****	**	
West Germany	Launching aid; credit guarantees for production finance; aid with sales finance	ELDO, ESRO and a national programme	Grants mainly to industry and assistance to electricity supply industry for demonstration plants	R & D Support	Also grants (on small scale) for advanced electronics R & D
	***	****	*****		
Italy	No special measures	ELDO and ERSO	No significant industry	No support	
	***	****			
Sweden	*	No significant industry	***	Unsubsidised	
USA	*	****	**	**	
Japan	Loans for R & D and to airlines for purchase of new and domestic aircraft	Scientific and Applications Satellite Programmes	Preferential tax treatment cheap loans and some payments for R & D work	Grants for R & D and soft loans	Cheap loans are from Japan Development Bank. Also assistance for some electronics projects (grants for R & D, cheap loans and special depreciation)
	*	****	****	**	

Table 7   Selective intervention – other industries

	General approach of State	*Non—A T sectors supported*	*Institutions*
UK	Interventionist	1 Shipbuilding—considerable support through export credit, construction grants, aids to UCS etc 2 (Industry Act powers)	IDU within DTI
France	Interventionist	Particularly iron and steel, chemicals, textiles, electrical and electronics	IDI
West Germany	Strongly non-interventionist	1 Shipbuilding, (export credit and ERP aids for modernisation) 2 Oil (assistance because of high risks for exploration etc) In both cases assistance is relatively low.	1 KFW—a credit institution the major part of whose activities involves lending from ERI funds. The main industrial recipients, except for export credit, are small and medium sized companies. 2 RKW—Some state assistance for consultancy to small firms.
Italy	Interventionist, but not sectorally	Difficult to know extent of cross-subsidisation in state enterprises, but IRI certainly maintaining some uneconomic operations (eg loss-making shipyards, loans for restructuring of textile industry) (fund of £135m)	1 State enterprises (IRI, EN I, EFIM) operate in competition with private sector on fairly equal basis. 2 GEPI—recently founded to take over and transform 'lame ducks' into viable companies. 3 IMI—cheap loans for industrial restructuring (where management is sound) Total fund < £30 million
Sweden	Non-interventionist	Shipbuilding, textiles, craft glass industries	Statsforetag
USA	Non-interventionist	1 Mainly aids to avert liquidation- eg Lockheed, and Penn Central Railway. 2 Chemical industry, benefits from American Selling Price system of import valuation for tariff purposes	
Japan	Interventionist/consensual	Oil-assistance to finance prospecting etc. Mechanical engineering financial aid for development and modernisation of various sectors. Textiles—aid for modernisation	Japan Development Bank (cheap loans for industrial restructuring, new industries and technologies and on regional grounds)

The economic rationale of subsidies to industry

A R PREST

[1] A R Prest *How Much Subsidy?* (Institute of Economic Affairs, Research Monograph 32, London 1974).

[2] It is assumed that one is interested here in payments to public commercial undertakings such as nationalised industries but that one is not interested in payments from the central government to public non-commercial organisations, such as local authorities.

[3] 'Tax expenditures' in the terminology of Stanley S Surrey. See his *Pathways to Tax Reform,* Harvard University Press, Cambridge, Mass 1973.

[4] See, for example, A Whiting 'Overseas Experience in the Use of Industrial Subsidies', page 45.

[5] As in J A Pechman and B A Okner 'Individual Income Tax Erosion' in *The Economics of Federal Subsidy Programs* (Joint Economic Committee, Washington, DC (1972 to 1973). As in my earlier paper, I shall draw very heavily on this compendium.

I Introduction

I shall start by considering how to interpret the brief which has been given to me and then I shall set out the way in which the discussion will be organised in the remainder of the paper.

As I have very recently put forward some views on the meaning of public sector subsidiaries[1] it may be in order to recapitulate these ideas very briefly. The following seem to be the main characteristics of subsidies:

(1) There is no neat and tidy single all-purpose definition.

(2) The least unsatisfactory one is: payments which directly affect relative prices in the commercial sector, broadly defined[2].

(3) A distinction should be drawn between transfers in the form of subsidies and government purchases of goods and services, even though it may be difficult sometimes to say whether the government does receive a *quid pro quo* for its outpayment (eg R & D); and even though subsidies may frequently be substitutes for governmental provision without charge.

(4) There is a further distinction, albeit sometimes hazy, between those transfers which affect relative prices through substitution effects as well as income effects and those (eg a universal social dividend) where there are only effects of the latter sort.

(5) Although it is too *simpliste* to think of subsidies as negative taxes, the dividing line between subsidies and differentially favourable taxes is arbitrary (eg with a two-tier VAT, is the higher rate an extra tax or the lower rate a subsidy?).

(6) Subsidies can take many different forms. The main ones are: direct cash transfers, tax concessions[3], provision of cheap credit, 'benefit-in-kind' subsidies (sales by government at lower-than-market prices), purchase subsidies (purchases by government at higher-than-market prices), and regulatory subsidies (when regulatory powers are used to subsidise particular groups, such as tenants of houses in the UK).

(7) It is immaterial whether a subsidy is paid to a buyer or a seller in a transaction.

(8) Subsidies may affect relative prices in either goods markets or factor markets.

(9) Some subsidies are implicit rather than explicit; and there is no case for the exclusion of some payments on the grounds that they are of a capital nature.

(10) The total of subsidy payments in any one economy at any one time depends on the degree of disaggregation envisaged, in so far as there is cross-subsidisation within sectors.

It is possible to criticize this concept of subsidies both on the grounds that it is too wide[4] and that it is too narrow (eg in not counting the differences between income tax rates and capital gains tax rates as subsidies)[5]. I shall take the usual cowardly line that one may not be all that far wrong if one is liable to criticism from both sides simultaneously. In any event it is open to anyone who disagrees to extend or limit the definition as he thinks fit.

Does the phrase 'subsidies to industry' need examination? There are in fact two issues here. First, we have to decide whether 'industry' is to be defined widely or narrowly; I shall assume that it comprises all private sector activity along with commercial activities of government agencies – in other words, a very wide definition rather than one, say, which is confined to the sector covered by the Department of Industry. Second, I shall interpret 'to industry' in a wide sense too eg by including those subsidies which are paid to purchasers of goods and services or to suppliers of factors as well as those to producers of goods and services and purchasers of factors. Once again, anyone who is more interested in a subset of such payments can adjust accordingly.

As for 'economic rationale', it is assumed that this is meant to draw a dividing line between economic costs and benefits and political or social ones. Indeed, this is made clear in the briefing[6]. There is no need to dwell on the shakiness of any such distinction. But presumably it does mean that we are somewhat more interested in the resource allocation than the income distribution effects of subsidies. And that we are not here considering such economically non-sensical acts as the subsidy payments to the Central Wales railway line[7].

The final point of interpretation is that one must be explicit about the exact accompaniment to a subsidy programme. I shall assume, for better or worse, any given subsidy payment is accompanied by an identical addition to the tax take in money terms. This means that any benefits (net of administrative costs) from a subsidy have to be matched against the economic and administrative costs of the tax needed to finance it. In other words, we confine ourselves to the balanced-budget, rather than the differential expenditure, approach to use Musgrave's terminology. Needless to say, the macro-economic effects of the revenue raising and the spending operations may not be identical.

So much for interpreting the brief. We shall now apply these guidelines in considering different types of subsidy, dealing successively with those which have a broad base such as a national aggregate, an intermediate base such as an industry and a narrow base (a single firm). Obviously, there are many ways in which one could differentiate between subsidies. One might, for instance, group them according to their likely effects rather than according to the basis on which payment is made. This would not give the same classification in that, for example, a broad-base subsidy may have differential consequences for particular firms or industries, whereas a narrow base subsidy may have effects at the macro-level. We shall come to more specific illustrations of these general propositions later.

The very last proposition in this lengthy introduction is the increasing importance of subsidies in the UK economy. In the previous study, it was argued that a minimum estimate of the total for 1972 or thereabouts was around £3,000m compared with the £1,000m or so of the official figures. Since that year, there has been a sharp escalation in the official figures, reaching a total of £1,351m in 1973 and £1,123m in the first half alone of 1974[8]. So, even after allowing for inflation, we are clearly dealing with that scarce phenomenon in the UK to-day: a growth industry[9].

II Broad base subsidies

The most obvious macro-bases for subsidies are, on the incomes side, wages and profits totals, interpreting both in a wide sense; and, on the expenditure side, consumption and investment. We shall spend most of our time on these four possibilities but will examine one or two others more briefly at a later stage. We shall investigate the differing senses, if any, in which payments in respect of such money

[6] But was it a Freudian slip to posit the question: 'what economic objectives could be *saved* (my italics) by granting subsidies'?

[7] It is reported that in the course of the 1964 to 1970 Labour government the then Ministry of Transport put forward to the Cabinet what was thought to be a cast-iron case for closure. The proposals were immediately rejected on the grounds that the line ran through six marginal constituencies. Rumour has it that it would in fact be cheaper to hire taxis for the few people who use the line.

[8] *Financial Statistics*, November 1974. See also *Public Expenditure to 1978-79* (Cmnd 5879), January 1975, Table 34.

[9] See also the report in *The Times* 24 December 1974 of a sharp increase in the number of firms applying for government aid under Section 7 of the Industry Act.

[10]See N Kaldor 'A Memorandum on the Value Added Tax', *Essays on Economic Policy*, Vol 1 (Duckworth, London 1964).

[11]See J A Brittain *The Payroll Tax for Social Security* (Brookings Institution, Washington DC, 1972), The Incidence of Social Security Payroll Taxes', *American Economic Review*, March 1971; M S Feldstein 'The Incidence of the Social Security Payroll Tax: Comment,' *ibid*, Sept. 1972; J A Brittain 'The Incidence of the Social Security Payroll Tax: Reply,' *ibid*, December 1972. For a summary see G F Break 'The Incidence and Economic Effects of Taxation' p 168 ff in *The Economics of Public Finance* (Brookings Institution, Washington, DC 1974).

[12]C S Shoup *Public Finance* (Aldine, Chicago, 1969) p 266 ff.

[13]E J Mishan *21 Popular Economic Fallacies* (Allen Lane, Penguin Press London 1969); P A Samuelson 'A New Theorem on Non-Substitution' in *Collected Scientific Papers of Paul A Samuelson* (MIT Press, Cambridge, Mass, 1965, Vol 1).

[14]For relevant analysis see C S Shoup in *The Economics of Federal Subsidy Programs, op cit*, Pt 1, p 68.

[15]P Jay 'Price Stability Without Tears' *The Times*, 19 December 1974. The argument is essentially the same as that in M F Scott 'A New Way to attack Inflation' *The Banker*, April 1974.

flows can be thought of as subsidies and the varying extents to which such payments are likely to be justifiable.

In what ways would a payment proportionate to payrolls throughout the economy act as a subsidy, in the crucial sense of directly affecting relative prices? To fix our ideas more precisely, let us assume that we are considering a device which has on occasion been advocated by Professor Kaldor ie a uniform value added tax, the proceeds being used to finance a wages subsidy[10]. The first question is the exceedingly thorny one of the incidence of any such generalised outpayment. Controversy has raged for years on whether payroll taxes operate via higher prices, lower profits or lower wages and it seems a reasonable judgement to say that the controversy has hardly died down in the wake of recent work[11]. So one must expect the same degree of uncertainty to attach to general payroll subsidies as to payroll taxes. Secondly, we have the Shoup proposition[12] that there is a close affinity between a value added tax and a payroll tax, at least in an *ex-ante* sense. To that extent, one would be imposing a charge on labour costs at the same time as one is granting a subsidy towards them.

Even if it were the case that a payroll subsidy financed in this way resulted in a fall in labour costs as perceived by an entrepreneur it does not automatically follow, as is sometimes claimed, that this would result in the substitution of labour for capital. In the conventional short run, the stock of capital is given by definition; in the long run, the prices of domestically produced capital goods would, subject to well-known qualifications[13], tend to rise *pari passu* with the price of labour ie relative prices of labour and capital goods tend to remain unchanged and so in that regard the central feature of any subsidy process is missing. Further complications arise when capital goods are imported rather than domestically produced but the general conclusion remains much the same.

Another proposition is that a combination of a value added tax and a payroll subsidy would reduce domestic prices relatively to foreign ones. This clearly is possible; the usual destination basis of value added tax would not affect prices of exports whereas the payroll subsidy, on an origin basis, could be relevant. The precise effects on the size of export and import competing activities relatively to others would depend on the magnitude of the relative price changes and the usual types of elasticity assumptions[14]. And it could be a matter for prolonged debate whether such a device was preferable to exchange parity adjustments, bounties to exporters, tariff measures and the like.

There are various other ways in which a general payroll subsidy may be thought to have resource allocation effects. In so far as the subsidy does not apply, or does not apply fully, to self-employment activity we should expect to see a relative decline in such operations. It is sometimes argued (eg as with SET) that a particular fiscal device may have a 'shock effect' in the sense of acting as a catalyst to get firms to do what was already profitable anyway; but it is hard to see the precise relevance of this argument in the case of a general labour subsidy. Another context is that of anti-inflation schemes. It has been suggested[15] that a levy be imposed on increments in monthly earnings in excess of some norm and the proceeds repaid to employers on the basis of payrolls. The net result would be that prices overall would remain unchanged but with increases in those industries conceding high wage claims and with falls elsewhere, assuming that repayments to employers are reflected in prices. So the overall result is a series of changes in relative prices, though they might reasonably be ascribed to the joint operation of the tax and the subsidy rather than to the latter on its own.

A subsidy on profits and interest might at first sight seem a rather odd notion. But if one starts with the standard Haig-Simons concept of the appropriate basis for income tax, one can then argue that the sort of departure which is involved in tax-holiday schemes[16] is on all fours with the more obvious forms of subsidy arrangement. It is a well-known theoretical proposition[17] that the permanent exemption of profits and interest from income tax removes the differential against saving inherent in income taxes; and that we have a general similarity in this respect between income taxes exempting profits and dividends, expenditure taxes, value added taxes and income taxes incorporating 100 per cent initial allowances. A tax holiday for a limited period is clearly of less overall value than permanent income tax exemption to those wishing to exchange current for future consumption but the nature of the benefits it confers is usually clear enough (always assuming of course, that they are not negated by the method chosen to finance the subsidy). As we shall return shortly to the whole question of investment subsidies, we shall defer further consideration of the likely effectiveness of profits subsidisation. But it may be worth remarking at this stage on a particular point of asymmetry. Whereas subsidies on labour will tend to affect prices of capital goods and if so, cannot be expected to change labour- capital goods price ratios, the same does not apply in reverse, ie to subsidies on profits or on the price of capital goods. In other words, a policy aiming at substitution of capital for labour is likely to be more successful if concentrated on capital subsidies than on labour taxes.

There is not a great deal to be said about a uniform percentage subsidy on consumption. Indeed, it might be thought at first sight that there is nothing at all to be said. If the subsidy applies to all consumption it will not change relative prices of individual consumption goods and services; and, by analogy with the standard argument about the expenditure tax[18], one would not expect the terms of exchange between current and future consumption as a whole to be affected. This leaves out one major possibility, however: the introduction of a consumption subsidy for a strictly limited period. This could have a powerful influence in substituting present consumption for that which would have taken place in the future (after the withdrawal of the concession) and in so adding to the current pressure of demand (inventory changes apart). The analogue here is the well-known proposal made in the USA for a spendings tax for the duration of World War II. This would have applied the same general principle in reverse.

Now we come to investment subsidies in all their multifarious forms. In the space at my disposal for this subject, I cannot hope to say anything new; and in any event the whole subject is being covered by other papers. Let me state very briefly what seem to be the salient (very trite) points:

(1) We do find subsidy characteristics here. The most obvious way is in the encouragement[19] of fixed capital investment relatively to consumption[20]. Others are the relative discouragement of investment in working capital[21], the differential benefits to short and long-lived capital goods in some cases; and the differential benefits to firms paying different tax rates or borrowing at different interest rates.

(2) The usual proximate reason for the adoption of such policy instruments is the growth argument. But this in turn raises all the underlying questions about the rate of growth that is desirable or appropriate, not to mention the contribution that a higher level of investment can make towards it. Another general reason for subsidies concentrated on this variable is to offset any bias against capital investment resulting from other tax measures.

(3) The relative effectiveness of the different ways of encouraging capital investment raises many economic and administrative issues. The algebra of the evaluation of different incentives has been set out on a number of occasions[22]. Other issues are how far it is desirable to keep incentives unchanged for a longish period (a constant demand of industrialists)[23], and how far the threat of removal after a specified period can be a powerful stimulus to immediate investment[24]. Yet others are the gains and losses in public understanding and administrative costs in operating through a mechanism divorced from the tax system[25].

[16]As in much pioneer industry legislation in developing countries (cf G E Lent 'Tax Incentives for Investment in Developing Countries' *IMF Staff Papers*, July 1967; and A R Prest *Public Finance in Underdeveloped Countries*, Weidenfeld & Nicolson, London 1972). Another example of limited concessions is those given in Ireland eg in connection with the Shannon airport factories.

[17]R A Musgrave *The Theory of Public Finance*. McGraw Hill, New York, 1959 p 261.

[18]A R Prest 'The Expenditure Tax and Saving', *Economic Journal*, September 1959.

[19]Whether looked at from a liquidity or rate of return viewpoint.

[20]Note the analogy: subsidies on capital goods are more effective than labour taxes in fostering factor ratio changes they are also more effective than general taxes on consumption in changing spending patterns (leaving purely temporary changes out of account in all cases).

[21]Except in the tax holiday kind of arrangement.

[22]As in C L Melliss and P W Richardson 'Value of Investment Incentives for Manufacturing Industry 1946 to 1974'; and for accounts of US work see *The Economics of Public Finance*, op cit p 91 ff and 203 ff.

[23]See, for instance, Second Report of Expenditure Committee 1973/74 *Regional Development Incentives*, HCP 85 and 85-I, HMSO, December 1973.

[24]cf A S Blinder and R M Solow 'Analytical Foundations of Fiscal Policy' p 110 ff in *The Economics of Public Finance*, op cit, for a comparison between changes in corporation tax and investment incentive rates.

[25]cf *Regional Development Industries op cit*, Appendix 2, p 692 for the view that on administrative grounds special regional investment incentives must be in grant form rather than tax expenditure form.

[26] K Knorr and W J Baumol *What Price Economic Growth?*
Prentice Hall, Englewood Cliffs, New Jersey, 1961).

[27] A R Prest 'Sense and Nonsense in Budgetary Policy',
Economic Journal, March 1968 pp 12–13. There are many
variations on this general theme eg subsidies according to
increases in exports.

[28] With tapering relief of up to £40,000 pa.

[29] Second Report, Expenditure Committee 1973–74,
Regional Development Incentives HEP 85 and 85-I,
HMSO, December, 1973, p 26.

With such a brief summary, one is clearly not making the slightest pretence of treating this subject properly. The intention is simply to show how this type of subsidy fits into a more general framework of discussion.

It was stated earlier that the principal focus of this section on broad base subsidies would be wages, profits, consumption and investment, but that one or two other possibilities would be mentioned. One such further possibility is to revert to a suggestion made a few years ago[26] that it is desirable to subsidise firms according to the *increase* in value added in a year. This has a number of advantages, especially if a growth objective is high up on the bit of priorities but as I have examined these advantages (as well as the disadvantages) on a previous occasion[27], it is not proposed to go over them again now. Another possibility is subsidies to all firms based on turnover; but a moment's reflection enables one to see the disadvantages of any such idea. They would be the mirror image of those associated with the traditional multi-stage turnover tax; in just the same way as there was no rhyme or reason in pyramiding taxes on those industries which happened to be organised in non-integrated form, so there would be no justification for pyramiding subsidies for the same industries.

III   Intermediate base subsidies

We now consider rather more selective bases for subsidies. We shall look at the ways in which the favoured sheep may be distinguished from the unfavoured goats; the bases of payment of any assistance; the main reasons for differentiation and their relative merits; and the likely effectiveness of distributing largesse in these various ways.

Distinctions can be drawn between those to be favoured and the others in a variety of ways. Very broad distinctions can be drawn between development areas and the rest; between public sector commercial activities and others; or between whole groups of industry (eg manufacturing industry as under the original form of SET with the premium refund) and others. Finer distinctions arise when attempting to differentiate between individual industries (as, say, classified under the Standard Industrial Classification) or between groups of firms (eg small businesses and the rest) or between different categories of development areas. We may also have double threshold systems whereby two tests have to be passed. Thus, REP, has only been paid to manufacturing industry and only if in development areas.

Selective assistance may have a whole range of bases but a convenient form of classification is that by buyers and sellers and by goods and factor markets. Taking buyers in goods markets first, one very obvious example is selective treatment of purchasers of capital goods. This can take any of the well-known forms of accelerated depreciation, investment allowances, investment subsidies and the like. It may make general distinction between classes of assets (eg between buildings and machinery); more refined distinctions may also be made according to the specific type of asset within a class (eg different allowances for cars and commercial vehicles) or according to the purchaser (eg a higher total of grants and allowances if in a development area). Another example of favourable treatment of buyers of particular goods is the whole range of subsidies available to house purchasers.

Sellers of goods may also be favoured. One example relating to some sellers of all goods is the reduced rate of corporation tax and capital gains tax payable by businesses with less than £25,000 profits per annum[28]. Another example is the system of favouring development areas when government purchases are made, whether under a general or special preference scheme[29]. This is a case of special treatment of some sellers of some goods. Another possibility is that of all sellers of some goods: the food subsidies currently being paid in the UK are an example here, though in this case the main objective seems to be an income distribution one which calls more for price than for quantity re-actions to the subsidy.

When we turn to subsidies related to factor purchases there is no shortage of examples. One, extremely important in the post-war period, is the way in which interest costs of loans have been reduced by one means or another – whether in the form of the provision of public funds at less than market rates both to public and private commercial undertakings or in the form of writing down large sums of capital, as has happened repeatedly with the nationalised industries. Another example is the subsidy on labour usage emanating from REP. Yet another is relief of import duty on shipbuilding supplies. By comparison, subsidies to sellers of factors are less frequent, but grants to people willing to undertake re-training are one example.

Reasons for selective assistance are not hard to find, even though, or perhaps because, they follow the old principle that the weaker the case the longer the statement in favour of it. The standard public finance arguments for government intervention to secure better resource allocation are:
(1) The likelihood that public goods, strictly defined, will be under-provided by the private sector.
(2) Merit and demerit wants.
(3) Lack of competition.
(4) Increasing returns industries need public help if they are to follow marginal cost pricing rules.
(5) Externalities may necessitate public intervention to expand or contract the size of an industry.

It seems reasonable to argue[30] that subsidy payments have little role to play in (1) where it is more a matter of public provision. And in so far as lack of competition springs from monopolistic restriction of entry the role of subsidies is again limited. But the remaining arguments can all be readily put forward as justification for subsidies differentiating between different industries.

Other standard reasons include the second best principle, whether in the sense of counteracting defects in market structure or in public sector financial arrangements eg the proposition that public urban transport should be subsidised because of the failure to levy congestion taxes on private urban transport. Social reasons, such as income redistribution or the need to moderate the rate of decline of jobs in an industry or an area, or both, are never lacking. Finally, there are always macro-economic reasons such as the need to encourage particular industries thought necessary for the growth process or for the exigencies of prices and incomes policies; and the need to hold down prices of particular commodities which are judged to be excessively sensitive in wage negotiations and the like.

If one is unwilling or unable to put much emphasis on general economic principles in this context, one can always cite fears of consequences of other countries' practices as a justification for one's own subsidies. It is not without significance that the great majority of OECD countries were found to be subsidising shipbuilding at the end of the 1960s[31]; and that there was a vast array of methods. (16 were distinguished in all[32] and some countries used as many as 12 of them). In other words, there was no shortage of countries to emulate or methods to use.

Any one set of policies may indeed have a large number of strands to it, as the literature on regional policy demonstrates. Simply taking the arguments in one recent statement[33] and no others, one finds an amalgam of macro and micro propositions such that regional policy is conceived of as a means of compensating

[30] *The Economics of Federal Subsidy Programs, op cit,* p 45, The rather different view expressed by K Pavitt *The Choice of Targets and Instruments for Government Support of Scientific Research,* p 7 seems to be based on a somewhat different notion of public goods to that envisaged here.

[31] OECD, *Inflation*, December 1970, p 104.

[32] The main groupings were: protection of the national market, direct cash payments, tax expenditures, finance for investment and research, facilities for financing shipyard operations, export credit facilities and assistance to purchasers (*ibid*).

[33] cf B Moore and J Rhodes in Expenditure Committee (Trade and Industry Sub-Committee) *Economic and Exchequer Implications of Regional Policy* Session 1972–73 (HCP 42-XVI, HMSO, May 1973).

for the failure of wage settlement processes to secure sufficient geographical differentials in pay and sufficient migration from declining to expanding regions[34]; and yet withal this failure can be remedied without any burdens on the rest of the economy if appropriate expansionary macro policies are followed.

In evaluating the likely effectiveness of differing intermediate base subsidies one needs to ask two separate questions: which objectives make sense and which methods of reaching any one objective make sense.

Taking objectives first, it would require not just a fervent but a fanatical belief in the efficiency of the operation of a market economy to deny that there are circumstances in which government financial assistance can improve the allocation of resources, whether as between different industries, different geographical regions or different end-uses of GNP. But having made this general point, one must immediately set down the caveats.

It is all too easy to think up plausible arguments based on externalities, merit wants and the like for subsidisation of this, that and every industry. Thus an infant industry can be said to need a subsidy because it is growing; and an elderly industry can be said to need a subsidy because it is declining. It is all too easy to get into a situation where a large number of industries are being subsidised, each against one another. Furthermore, the danger that subsidies, once introduced, become irremovable whether because of potential producer, consumer or administrator reactions is too well-known to need emphasising here[35].

The use of selective subsidies as a means of redistributing income is even more questionable. It may not be easy to disentangle the effects of such subsidies on the prices of final products or the factors of production making them. And there may be many side-effects, whether due to the subsidies themselves or to the finance of the subsidies, which need to be taken into account before reaching a final conclusion about income distribution effects[36]. So unless there are very particular reasons for attaching importance to price changes of very particular commodities, one cannot look with complete favour on this argument for subsidisation. Similarly, one can be more than mildly sceptical about selective subsidisation of particular goods and services, whether they be products of private or public enterprise, as a means of holding down the rate of inflation, irrespective of whether the context is one of statutory or voluntary incomes policies. Recent experiences will be sufficiently fresh in everyone's mind to need no recollecting here.

In forming any judgment about the methods of subsidisation which make sense, the first question is: how do we appraise the results of any particular subsidy? Some people have tried to set up grand all-embracing tests, taking account of income distribution as well as resource allocation effects[37] but there are well-known reasons why many such efforts do not commend themselves to most observers. It seems better to start in a more modest way and recognise that there are inherent limitations to what one can hope to do. Thus the Joint Economic Committee Report[38] sets out the differing principles for computing and comparing all relevant benefits and costs in connection with resource allocation, growth stimulation and income redistribution goals. Even these principles may be very difficult to live up to in practice (eg choice of appropriate discount rates) and so one may be forced to make judgments of an *ex-cathedra* nature about the likely effectiveness of different methods of achieving particular goals. For instance, there is a great deal to be said for arranging subsidies in an open rather than a concealed manner, so that the task of appraisal is not made needlessly difficult. This implies that an outright subsidy, identified as such in the government accounts, is likely to get higher marks than a tax-expenditure, the true implications of which may be very hard to unravel and assess[39], but in so far as one has outright subsidies, there is a lot to be said for

[34]It was Adam Smith who observed that 'man is of all forms of luggage the most difficult to be transported'.

[35]cf A R Prest *How Much Subsidy?* *op cit*, P 35 ff.

[36]cf G F Break *The Economics of Public Finance op cit*, p 125 'No longer can the established proposition that consumption of particular products tends to decline as a percentage of income as family income increases be used to demonstrate regressivity in the vertical pattern of excise tax burdens. Instead, consumption of taxed products must be shown to decline more rapidly than consumption of non-taxed products'.

[37]See, for example, D A Weisbrod 'Income Redistribution Effects and Benefit-Cost Analysis' in S B Chase Jnr (ed) *Problems in Public Expenditure Analysis* (Brookings Institution, Washington 1968).

[38]R A Musgrave, 'Cost-Benefit Analysis and the Theory of Social Goods', *Journal of Economic Literature*, September 1969 *op cit*, Staff Study, p 80.

[39]*Ibid*, Staff Study, p 72 ff and Pt 1, pp 72–73, shows how computations can be made in simple cases.

[40]S J Nickell, 'On Expectations, Government Policy and the Rate of Investment', *Economica*, August 1974.

[41]cf *Regional Development Incentives, op cit*, p 11 ff. At the same time one must be careful about the argument of Dr S Holland (*ibid* p 689) that if government assistance is marginal to industrialists then continuity of policy is unimportant. It may be precisely because continuity is suspect that incentives are only marginally effective.

[42]cf A O Hirschman, 'Industrial Development in the Brazilian North-East', *Journal of Development Studies*, 1968. The mechanics were that special corporation tax relief was given in respect of profits invested in the North-East whether directly or via equity participation in other firms operating there.

[43]See S Brittan, *Financial Times*, 13 December 1974, for a list of government aid to individual companies in recent years under Section 8 of the Industry Act, ie where the national interest is involved and financial assistance cannotbe obtainedotherwise.And also the *Financial Times* 24 December 1974, for an account of the increase in the number of firms seeking selective assistance under Section 7 of the Industry Act, ie for maintaining or safeguarding employment in Assisted Areas, when finance is not otherwise obtainable. It was reported that the offers of financial assistance totalled £80m since January 1974, roughly three times the level for 1973; and 40 per cent of applications received had still to be processed.

choosing a form which is relatively easy to comprehend (eg regular interest rate subsidies rather than occasional capital write-offs). To secure a reasonable degree of cost-effectiveness, outpayments need to be based, whenever possible, on a marginal principle, ie one needs to avoid paying people for what they would do anyway. It is not easy to determine that a firm would have a certain capital stock or labour force in any event but it is an obvious criticism of such measures as REP that substantial payments may be 'wasted' in financing intra-marginal employment. Another general proposition is that the maximum use should be made of incentives operating for a limited period of time ahead. Thus it seems to be generally agreed that the special temporary hotel-building subsidy at the beginning of the 70s was particularly effective.[40] Obviously, there are limitations to this technique. A series of short-lived incentives implies a large number of changes, and as anyone knows who is at all conversant with the views of industrialists, frequent changes rankle deeply and may indeed be counter-productive, in the sense of discouraging businesses from taking full account of incentives[41]. A series of temporary measures can only be expected to work tolerably well if there is a fair degree of certainty about the length of time for which they will operate. This in turn leads to a more general proposition; in so far as uncertainty of the outcomes of decisions weighs heavily on business men, there is a lot to be said for devices aimed at reducing the dispersion around the expected yield of a business venture. In other words, one needs measures which take part of any loss away from an investor's shoulders and not simply ones which ensure a higher return if profits are made. It would seem that Brazil has had some considerable success with a policy of this sort in the North-Eastern part of the country[42].

IV Narrow base subsidies

Whereas intermediate base subsidies apply to industry or regions, narrow base subsidies typically apply to individual firms or towns. If an industry is monopolised and there is literally only one firm in it, the distinction disappears; and, so far, subsidies tailored to individual towns in the UK have usually been in compensation for some natural disaster or similar untoward event. Nevertheless, there has been a perceptible quickening of pace with narrow base subsidies in recent years. Before the 1972 Industry Act, there were a few isolated examples especially in shipbuilding, machine tools, aerospace and the car industry. Since that date, and especially during 1974, there has been a marked tendency to expand the scope and coverage of such operations. And it must be expected that the process will go further with the prospective National Enterprise Board and the system of planning agreements[43].

Whereas broad and intermediate base subsidies were found to take a number of different forms, the variation with narrow base subsidies is much less. The typical form of government aid is the provision of capital at preferential rights – whether by grant, loan, loan guarantee or equity participation – usually in return for acceptance of government conditions on some key matters. Whilst this is not the only form of assistance imaginable (eg there could be a special subsidy on a firm's turnover), other methods available at a more aggregated level would not be appropriate here. Thus it would be much more difficult to devise satisfactory schemes for subsidising consumers of products or suppliers of factors, when only a single firm is involved rather than a whole industry.

A number of reasons have been advanced for this degree of subsidy differentiation. One is that to achieve maximum effect it is necessary to operate at firm level rather than at industry or economy-wide level. This is partly the belief that a firm is likely to take more notice of individualised subsidies; and partly that more effective use can be made of any given supply of funds by concentrating the relief at a limited number of points – in other words, an attempt to apply the marginal principle mentioned earlier. More specific propositions relate to the need to improve productivity by concentrating on particular firms; international ramifications (Burmah Oil); or the preservation of designated jobs in designated firms or areas (journalists in Glasgow). Finally, just in case people are not sufficiently convinced by these arguments, reference is made to the allegedly beneficial effects of detailed government intervention in France and Italy[44].

It is not difficult to point to gaps in some of these arguments and to dangers which lie in wait for those advocating such policies. First of all, the job preservation argument must be looked at with some suspicion. It is one thing to attempt to slow down the loss of jobs in a whole industry or region; it is a very different one to apply the same principle to an individual firm. Not event the handloom weavers went as far in their claims. Now should one accept the particular interpretation of the marginal principle as it stands. Concentration of assistance on marginal activities might call for a thinly spread subsidy throughout an industry rather than one wholly concentrated on a particular firm.

The dangers of this type of policy are apparent enough. The first is that one may lose even the limited guidance which tax theory and practice have to offer, in that taxes are normally related to wider bases than activities or financial needs of individual firms. We are now playing in a different ball-game with the authorities responding as best as they can. This can be seen from the recent report of the Industrial Development Advisory Board on its reason for opposing a grant to a Liverpool workers' co-operative[45].
They were as follows:
  (a) No prospect of generating a positive cash flow
  (b) Doubts about managerial capacity
  (c) Poor market possibilities for the major products
  (d) Over-manning
  (e) Over-capacity.

It can be seen straightaway that these are the sort of criteria which are relevant when a subsidy is considered for an individual firm – but they are a far cry from the externalities, or merit wants arguments of traditional tax theory or from the standard techniques of cost-benefit analysis. There may be some cases in which these latter techniques are still applicable (eg cost-benefit analysis of Concorde) but they are likely to be infrequent.

It is not difficult to glimpse many other problems. One is that there is a strong presumption that firms which apply for cost aid of this kind must be in a pretty desperate position. So the chances are that aid is likely to be on a permanent rather than a temporary basis, unless they are to be allowed to go bankrupt later. In other words, we have an intervention-breeding system[46]. Another is that the selection basis for aid is likely to be such that larger companies rather than small unincorporated firms are the recipients, with obvious repercussions on the structure of industry. Another danger is exemplified by the simultaneous announcement in December 1974 that British Leyland were to receive a large amount of government aid and that a £16 a week wage claim was being lodged by employees. A highly specific form of assistance geared to a particular firm is indeed more of an open invitation to high wage claims than a more generalised form of assistance to an industry as a whole. Perhaps a new significance can now be attached to John Bright's famous remark about 'A gigantic system of outdoor relief for the aristocracy of Great Britain'[47].

[44] cf Dr S Holland 'Multi-national Companies and a Selective Regional Policy' in *Regional Development Incentives*, op cit, p 690: 'in the British case there would be a strong argument in favour of making regional assistance conditional on the fulfilment of strategic requirements of government policy.'

[45] *Financial Times*, 21 December 1974.

[46] See the apt quotation from Sir Richard Clarke on the degrading effects on individual firms of continuing government assistance (cited by K Pavitt, *op cit*, p 20n). There may also be degrading effects on the authorities concerned.

[47] G M Trevelyan *Life of John Bright* (Constable, 1913), p 274.

V Conclusions

The main points of the paper are as follows:

(1) The central notion of a subsidy is a government outpayment which directly affects relative prices; but there is plenty of scope for disagreement about any more precise definition.

(2) In discussing the economic rationale of subsidies to industry, one should not confine oneself solely to direct payments from government to business firms; and one must always ask what is the source of finance of a subsidy, or more generally, what is the relevant budgetary alternative.

(3) Broad base or macro-subsidies can be envisaged on payrolls, property income, consumption or investment. The principal effects of each of these subsidies were considered. Another possibility is the increment in value added but subsidies based on turnover do not commend themselves.

(4) Intermediate base subsidies can be arranged in a variety of ways according to whether one wishes to differentiate between industries, activities and regions on a broader or narrower grouping. The actual basis of payment may vary between buyers and sellers and as between goods and factor markets. Reasons for intermediate base subsidies range from traditional resource allocation deficiencies of market economies to second-best arguments, distributional considerations, prices and incomes policies and so on. In evaluating the likely effectiveness of such policies, one has to distinguish between the appropriateness of the objectives hand and the methods used to achieve them. But it is utopian to think that there is some all-embracing test incorporating all possible criteria and suitable for use in all contexts.

(5) Narrow base subsidies are focused on individual firms and towns rather than industries and regions. These have become much more important in the UK very recently. They differ from intermediate base or broad base subsidies in many ways: the basis on which they are typically paid, the reasons for such payments and the economic and political dangers encountered.

The economic rationale of subsidies to industry
A R PREST

[1]See also Professor Wiseman's paper, *An Economic Analysis of the Expenditure Committee Report on Public Money in the Private Sector*.

[2]Public Expenditure and Economic Management. Treasury evidence to the Expenditure Committee (Public Expenditure (General) Sub-Committee Session 1971-72. 15 February 1972.

[3]ie GDP at some pre-determined pressure of demand

Comments by I C R Byatt

I would like to draw out three points from Professor Prest's valuable and interesting paper:

(a) expenditure on industrial subsidies is rising;

(b) the effectiveness, let alone the efficiency, of many types of subsidies to industry have often not been adequately measured; and

(c) the motivation for subsidies has often not been of the traditional kind discussed by economists, ie designed to improve the efficiency of markets but of an ad hoc interventionist kind.

The general economic policy conclusion I draw is that there is an urgent need to consider what constitutes a par or base line situation. Should we take the situation where industry operates according to its own rules – maximising what entrepreneurs are alleged to maximise – as the baseline from which we are to consider government intervention designed to remedy specific shortcomings in the market economy, eg tendency to monopoly, failure to take account of externalities, market imperfections, etc? Or is the baseline position one where the Government is constantly involved in the affairs of industry – as is said to be the case in France – and is itself operating as an entrepreneur? The UK seems to be shifting from the first to the second. This, given the growth in the content of what are thought to be the appropriate objectives of the State, may be the right thing to do[1]. But if so, the need to develop appropriate general criteria for government assistance to industry, and in particular to develop them in a way which ensures that success and failure can be monitored, becomes more important than ever. Unless objectives can be reasonably clearly set out and policies monitored so that their effectiveness known, policy is at the mercy of whatever plausible arguments hold the scene. And as Professor Prest shows us, we are perilously close to this state of affairs.

My second comment is rather more technical. Professor Prest advocates a balanced budget approach, ie that any benefits from a subsidy have to be matched against the costs of the tax needed to finance it. The Treasury has tended to adopt a rather different approach, namely a 'demand effect' approach whereby any change in subsidy would have to be balanced by a change in taxation such as maintains an appropriate internal pressure of demand and balance of payments[2]. This admittedly involves a prior decision on macro-economic policy objectives. But it has the merit of bringing out, for example, the inconsistency involved in, say, pursuing a policy of subsidies designed to prevent the redundancies which are implied, inter alia, by the level of unemployment associated with achieving macro economic policy objectives. It also has the merit of establishing a framework which includes the effects of subsidies on productive potential[3]. This will be of general application, but is particularly relevant for regional policy, where subsidies are designed to bring into use resources, mainly of labour, which would otherwise be idle. In such circumstances, the tax cost of such subsidies could be a small proportion of the amount of money disbursed.

75

Professor Prest presents a valuable discussion of the state of the art in relation to the subsidies which have been suggested for a wide range of purposes. As he goes through his list and indicates how little we know about them, one is left wondering more and more why, if their effects are so uncertain, so much ingenuity goes into devising new suggestions for using even more scarce public money in this way.

An economic analysis of the Expenditure Committee reports[1] on public money in the private sector

J WISEMAN

[1] *Public Money in the Private Sector*, Sixth Report from the Expenditure Committee, Session 1971-72: Volume I, Report, and Volume II, Minutes of Evidence and Appendices (HMSO)
and
Regional Development Incentives, Second Report from the Expenditure Committee, Session 1973-74 (HMSO).

I Introduction and elucidation

The more detailed description of the suggested content of this paper substituted 'subsidies' for 'public money in the private sector', and said: 'The purpose of this contribution is seen to be a critical analysis of the findings of these Reports, with particular reference to the costs and benefits of subsidies.' In deciding how to interpret my brief, I also knew that Professor Prest was writing a paper on the economic rationale of subsidies to industry, which could be relied on to cover the formal economic analysis of the problem, that regional subsidies were also to be the subject of a separate contribution, and that my own paper appeared in the part of the programme dubbed 'analytical' as distinct from 'empirical'.

In the light of this information, I have still not found it easy to decide just what questions I should be asking about the Reports. The Reports provide evidence, and conclusions from evidence, concerning the use of public money in the private sector. 'Costs and benefits' I take to mean the gains and losses to the community from subsidies being used. This suggests that the central questions are: 'Do the Reports help us to identify the policy-relevant costs and benefits?' and 'Do the Reports help us to appraise (in both a conceptual and a practical sense), the extent to which an "optimal" cost-benefit relationship is in fact achieved by public policy?'

These very general questions throw up some subsidiary ones: What is the relation between the 'traditional' economist's formulation of the subsidy question and the debate in the Reports? and: What light do the Reports throw on the efficiency of decision-making procedures (which comprehends the Select Committee procedure itself, as well as administrative ones)?

I hope that this interpretation of my task is not too remote from what was expected. I would justify it on the grounds that it seems the best way to impose an analytical structure on the Reports, that it differentiates my 'product' from the other papers I have mentioned, and that it directs discussion towards what I regard as an unduly neglected aspect of economics: namely, the translation of the recommendations deriving from formal analysis into actual decisions by way of a political process.

Since I am enjoined to discuss costs and benefits, a final introductory comment is needed to explain my interpretation of this task. In its 'pure' form, cost-benefit appraisal might be regarded as an exercise in market simulation. It is called for because of market failure (for whatever reason), and its results are a quantification of the utilities and disutilities enjoyed by the individuals affected did the relevant market arrangements in fact exist. Its conclusions are about whether (and if so, how) it would be in the community interest to find means to 'substitute' the postulated market arrangements.

In practice, of course, cost-benefit appraisal has tended to become something rather different. In the nature of things, there may often be no practical way to 'simulate' a market solution (that is frequently one reason why a market does not already exist?) and the proxy solutions involve a different kind and distribution of utilities and disutilities: the evaluation thus inevitably incorporates eg considerations of distributional equity. More important in the context of my present brief is the fact that cost-benefit studies are frequently concerned with situations in which market simulation is not (or is not alone) the relevant policy objective. This general topic is a fascinating one which I cannot treat at length: enough to point out that there is continuing disagreement between the proponents of CBA, who take the general position that any quantification of a clearly specified kind is of potential value for the efficiency of the decision-making process, and/or that the analysis can in principle be related to any set of postulated objectives, and the critics who see CBA as at best misleading and at worst a sham, because it cannot intergrate into the quantification exercise a plausibly sophisticated 'mix' of objectives.

From my immediate point of view, the matter of interest is that the Reports can be seen as concerned with the 'costs and benefits of subsidies' in two related but distinguishable ways. First, they may provide information which helps us evaluate whether or not subsidy arrangements are 'market-perfecting'. Second, they may throw light on the broader issue of the relation between policy objectives and subsidy arrangements. We shall find the Reports interesting in both contexts, and informative about the relation between the two.

I shall proceed by summarizing the specification of its task by the Sub-Committee (Section II), then commenting on the discussion and findings in the context of 'orthodox' concepts of economic analysis (Section III). This opens the way to a broader discussion of the treatment of policy objectives, and to some conclusions and suggestions.

II The Sub-Committee's specification of the problem

This Section sets out the interpretation placed by The Trade and Industry Sub-Committee of the Expenditure Committee on its remit to investigate the use of public money in the private sector. The summary, which provides the context of our subsequent discussion, is taken from Chapter 1 of the Report, supplemented by such other evidence as the character of the questions posed to witnesses (Volume 2).

The crucial decisions concerning scope and content are explained in paras 8 and 9 of the Report (p 8). The committee recognised that '. . . the question had been, and was likely to remain, a subject for argument between the political parties,' and that '. . . such broad terms of reference might rule out examination-in-depth and make much more difficult specific and detailed recommendations.' Being 'anxious to avoid as far as possible the most sensitive areas of immediate political controversy in order to make constructive suggestions of general significance', they 'took the view that in two particular respects Parliament had a duty which did not intrude upon either the prerogatives of Government or the strict merit of decisions' (whatever that means?). The first of these two respects concerned objectives: 'when public money was made available to the private sector these objectives should be stated as clearly as possible.' The second concerned control: expenditure of this kind should be strictly monitored to ensure that the nation got 'value for money from its investment'.

Thus, there are two initial restrictions of coverage. The remit itself limited the enquiry to the private sector, so excluding the whole field of nationalised industries, although no one would suggest that subsidy-type policies do not exist there, and the sub-committee itself excluded 'areas of political controversy.' To these general areas were added some specific exclusions: agriculture, computers, space, defence research and development.

Also left aside was the whole area of unselective incentives for industrial investment, including investment grants and depreciation allowances, although the sub-committee recognised, and discussed with witnesses, the fact that such general measures, and indeed tax policies in general were alternative means to similar ends to the specific policies actually given attention. (This exclusion is justified by an argument whose force escapes me: '. . . these wider incentives', they say, 'are not government intervention in the sense that we are primarily discussing in this report. One basic feature of unselective grants and allowances is that, provided certain conditions are met, Government assistance is automatically given. No question normally arises of monitoring by Government or Parliament.' But if it is accepted that unselective grants have these characteristics, then this would seem to give them an advantage over other (selective) grants, whose justification would then depend *inter alia* upon a demonstration that unselective grants could not do the job? In fact, the sub-committee, as we shall see, could not and did not maintain the distinction vigorously.)

On the other hand, the sub-committee did not restrict itself to a narrow definition of 'public money' (much less to 'subsidies' as usually defined by economists), but took under review a whole set of public policies that might bear upon the results of selective financial support by government. To illustrate, the investigation embraces the use of Industrial Development Certificates to prevent/relocate new industrial development. Witnesses made it clear that the effects of regional subsidy policies could not be understood otherwise: for example, some firms which have qualified for subsidy by investing in development areas would have preferred unsubsidised development at their existing location had this been permitted. Again, public policy towards industrial training comes under scrutiny. For the academic economist, this might appear to be a 'human resource' problem, to be dealt with by general policies concerned to remedy or offset postulated deficiences in the human capital market. But again, there turns out to be a close affinity with regional subsidy arrangements: the costs of re-location may be greatly affected by the need for, and costs to the firm of, industrial training and re-training.

Positively, the sub-committee's interpretation of its task translated into an examination of a specific set of industries and associated public policies: they investigated the civil aerospace industry, shipbuilding, and 'other industries' – primarily aluminium smelters and hotels. Regional policy was also examined, but dealt with more fully in a subsequent Report (1973-74). Beyond this, the case was examined for the use of some kind of agency arrangement to improve monitoring and control.

Subsequent sections will attempt to relate this context, and the evidence and findings, to the questions posed in Section I. In doing so, I should perhaps emphasise that my concern is with general questions of decision-making as illustrated by the material I am asked to review, and in no way with personal comment or criticism. So far as one can judge from the written word, all the actors in the play – Sub-Committee, civil service, business and 'expert' witnesses – gave excellent performances. But was it the right play in the right theatre, and did we have all the right actors in the right parts?

III   The role of 'orthodox' concepts of economic policy

This section considers the Reports from the viewpoint of what I called in Section I the 'market-perfecting' role of subsidies. It is concerned, that is, with the relation

79

between the discussion and findings of the Reports and the 'orthodox' economic analysis of subsidies.

Professor Prest is writing a paper on the economic analysis of subsidies, and I have no wish to stray too far into his territory. The propositions I wish to make, however, are both simple and orthodox. I think it unlikely that his own paper will contradict me, though it is less unlikely that his more sophisticated examination will open up lines of thought which I have neglected.

The orthodox model within which economists would examine the rationale of subsidies is concerned with consumer satisfaction: the 'optimal' use of community resources is that which promotes this satisfaction, and the purpose of subsidy is to preserve/promote that resource-allocation. This basic objective of Pareto-optimality is usually agreed to be constrained in two ways. First economic growth is admitted as a relevant objective, though there is no agreement as to whether it needs to be a distinct one, save to the extent that the government needs to influence the level of investment for reasons of stabilisation policy. Second, all resource-allocation propositions carry a distributional corollary: and an independent income-redistribution objective is generally accepted as an unavoidable part of the policy problem.

Within this framework, the reasons for (subsidy-type) government intervention relate to the shortcomings of 'market' solutions to the resource-allocation problem. That is, policy should be concerned with the correction of externalities, with the problems of resource-allocation in increasing-return industries, and with 'second-best' problems which are technical in origin, and not simply the result of the pursuit by government of objectives other than those comprehended by the model. (I confess that I find it hard to think of significant practical examples of these last two categories: but perhaps the group will be able to help me). It is also sometimes suggested that 'merit wants' constitute a further 'departure' to be corrected by policy. But insofar as these are wants that people 'should' have but in fact don't, it seems to me both more practical and more intellectually honest to treat them as a change of policy objective. However carefully the case is argued, merit wants ultimately imply that one person is a better judge of another person's welfare than is the second person himself. Since this is argued to justify the abrogation of the second person's choice by the first, the proposition is clearly incompatible with a model concerned with resource-allocation as directed solely by individual choices. The concept is the more uncomfortable in that the mode of selection of the people fitted to decide about merit wants is obscure, save that those who support the idea always seem to be part of the elect. The classic example is the proposition that the better educated are entitled to decide that the worse educated should be better educated than they want to be. (I am not here arguing that paternalistic attitudes are in some absolute sense 'wrong': only that we shall communicate better if we call things by their proper names).

Insofar as policy objectives are of the kind to which the model relates, subsidy-type intervention would of course be related in its detailed characteristics to the nature of the 'market failure' the intervention is designed to correct. In particular, quasi-permanent intervention, justified by inherent deficiencies in market arrangements, needs to be distinguished from 'corrective' intervention, designed to deal with temporary aberrations. This distinction is clear enough conceptually: practical policy is another matter.

The influence of this 'orthodox' economic analysis upon the Reports is interesting in a number of ways: First, the focus of the economic analysis is the consumer: the prime objective illuminated by the model is that of want-satisfaction. But this would hardly be the apparent concern of the Reports as interpreted by an intelligent lay reader. The 'interest groups' giving evidence included civil servants responsible for implementing relevant policies, businessmen as actual or potential beneficiaries, representatives of workers, and various technical 'experts', none of them concerned with consumer welfare save indirectly. It might reasonably be claimed that this comment is unfair, in that eg both the members of the Parliamentary Sub-Committee conducting the enquiries, and the civil servants giving evidence, saw themselves as guardians of the consumer interest: the fact that that interest is for the most part only implicit in their arguments does not mean, it might be said, that it is not pervasive. As James Thurber might have said, implicit is what it is. I have not read the Reports so carefully that I am willing to say that consumers are not mentioned. But they don't make the list of possible reasons for intervention given in *Public Money in the Private Sector* (Chapter 2), and I am sure that even the most conscientious reader of the Reports would not become bored by the number of references to them. Simply, the constitution of the Sub-Committee, and the nature of the witnesses appearing before it, focussed the discussion on the mechanics of the system rather than directly on outcomes. Thus, it is apparent both from Volume I of the Report (Ch 2), and from the actual evidence, that both civil servants and businessmen placed great emphasis on the importance of market forces: 'Most of our witnesses' said the Sub-Committee, 'accepted the principle that, as far as possible, industry should stand on its own two feet.' DTI witnesses interpreted the Department's task in carrying out government policy as the establishment of a 'general framework' within which 'firms could operate as freely as possible to their own individual advantage'. The business community were generally opposed to government intervention 'in principle': Sir Ronald Edwards perhaps expressed the philosophy most forcefully: 'we should rely as strongly as we could on market forces, and if these forces were working badly, we should try to find out why and make them work better.' Even the TUC made market efficiency an important part of their case for intervention: their evidence attaches great weight to the alleged inefficiency of the private capital market.

At the same time, it would be misleading to suggest that the model provides an adequate framework for a critical (cost-benefit) appraisal of the discussion and findings of the Reports, even if we interpret the desire to preserve unsubsidised competitive markets as being motivated exclusively by a concern for consumer welfare. There are four areas of differences:

(1) The interest in 'lame ducks'. An important aspect of the enquiry was concerned with the question of how to discover which ducks are likely to go lame, how to decide whether to kill them off or try to save them, how to decide whether they are getting better, and how to know when further treatment is unnecessary. (In particular, this is the kind of context in which the various suggestions for public agencies, and considerations of monitoring and control, were discussed).

Viewed in isolation, this formulation is quite compatible with orthodox economic analysis: the enquiry is concerned with procedures for the identification and correction of particular kinds of externality in a competitive environment characterised by uncertainty. (The business witnesses would put it more simply: are there any special reasons why a failing business might be worth saving?). But in fact, examination of this question tended to merge with the other considerations at (3) and (4).

(2) Problems arise in relating the discussion of policy concerned with specific problems/industries to the more general technical and policy context.

Again, there is no necessary divergence between the formal analysis and the concentration of the Reports on specific situations: conceptually this might be thought of as the 'policy' reflection of the analytical distinction between partial and general equilibrium questions. But, as we pointed out in Part I, the enquiry excluded important general policies which must in many contexts be regarded as possible substitutes for/influences upon the specific measures. The business witnesses in particular persisted in drawing attention to this kind of question and (eg) to the difficulties it creates for the evaluation of the consequences of the more specific measures. Certainly, I myself found it difficult in reading the Reports to relate the discussion of specific policies/proposals to the alternative possibilities that different general policy situations might throw up for consideration. The Sub-Committee itself experienced some difficulty with this question, which no doubt contributed eg to their conclusion that 'far too little information is available to government on the effectiveness of regional incentives' (para 265). (The question of information is further discussed below).

Perhaps the most instructive illustration of the nature of the problem is provided by the discussion of the subsidisation of aluminium smelters. While this venture was undoubtedly influenced by the pursuit of 'intermediate' objectives (discussed below), it was also affected by a particular interpretation of the market environment Specifically, a 'viable' development required the availability of cheap electricity, which was precluded by the pricing policies of the (nationalised) electricity authority. Thus, an important argument for Government intervention is the need to offset in this case the consequences of the general behaviour of a state body. But there is no way of knowing, as Sir Ronald Edwards pointed out, that this specific action will be more 'efficient' (in the context of our model) than would be a smaller reduction in the price of electricity to a wider range of industries.

(3) Despite general approval of a competitive market philosophy, all witnesses, says the Sub-Committee (para 19) 'recognised' that 'certain situations might require government intervention': they quote DTI to the effect that 'there are cases where any government finds it necessary to put in money in support of various kinds of industry.'

More, witnesses' lists of reasons for intervention 'coincided fairly closely': the need to maintain international competitiveness; defence requirements; the balance of payments; the maintenance of an industry considered nationally essential; the special difficulties of advanced-technology industries or projects; and social needs, especially the need to maintain employment.

No one would deny the practical importance of such matters: the difficult problem is to relate them to an analytical context which enables some kind of consistent appraisal. Failing such a context (and I do not think that the Reports provide one), there is an ever-present danger that propositions concerned with one aspect of public policy will be countered by assertions relating to another.

The list could be regarded, of course, as being simply an iteration of important ways in which the economy is likely to diverge from Pareto-optimality in the absence of intervention. (For example, economists have argued the case for the 'shadow pricing' of foreign exchange to offset domestic market imperfections). But this interpretation is not very plausible. We shall see, eg, that the Reports treat the balance of payments and employment-maintenance as objectives in their own right (see 4): and what concrete meaning is to be given, in such a context, to such phrases as 'an industry considered nationally essential'? Considered essential by whom? For what?

In fact, these 'reasons for intervention' are clearly seen not simply as 'market imperfections' within what I have called the 'orthodox' economic policy context, but also as reasons for widening that context. Thus, the need to sustain a competitive market prevails unless one or more of these other considerations is thought relevant, in which case the two must be weighed one against the other. It is the weighing procedure, and how it is to be distinguished from special pleading, that I find obscure. Who exactly is expected to gain from the special support of advanced-technology industries, and why? Why precisely should the availability of cheap subsidised foreign goods require countervailing subsidies here? (the Sub-Committee grappled heroically with that one): and so on.

(4) Finally, and indeed implicit in (3), the Reports are never constrained to the discussion of only those general objectives (resource allocation by consumer preference, perhaps economic growth, and income-distribution) to which the 'orthodox' model is relevant. To this extent, the value of that model in appraising the arguments and conclusions of the Reports is itself restricted.

The next section examines this broader context.

IV The broader context: the treatment of policy objectives

Although I had always been interested in subsidies from an analytical point of view, my own first awareness of the special relevance of policy objectives to an understanding of the problem came from the coincidence of this interest in subsidies with another, in the cotton textile industry. The Cotton Industry Act of 1959 provided for the subsidised destruction of textile manufacturing machinery. Owners were paid a specified sum for destroying unused machinery in unused plants, a larger sum for destroying machines not in use in operating plants, and a still larger sum for destroying machines that were actually being used. Cotton manufacturers not being daft, the Act stimulated requests for a definition of destruction. It meant, they were told, that '. . . it must have the hammer put through it'.

Viewed within the context of the economist's traditional models, the Act appeared to undertake to pay people more, the more harm they promised to do to the potential growth of community output. Unwilling to believe this to be the aim (I was pretty young) I sought other justifications. There were two possible ones: the disappointment of expectations because the industry was denied the tariff protection it had been led to expect, and the much greater disappointment of the expectations which had been created by the government-stimulated expansion of the cotton textile industry after the Second World War. But neither of these reasons was prominent in the official justification, nor could they be argued to lead to the kind of subsidy arrangements contained in the Act. Its purpose was said to be the elimination of 'weak selling' – the evil practice of producers with old equipment, of selling at lower prices than producers with more 'modern' equipment, so inhibiting technological progress. This seemed – and seems – to me to be of the same order of plausibility as the proposition that it is better to walk than to ride in a second-hand car[2].

In any case, it led me to the conclusion, which I have since found no reason to change, that there is a very considerable gap between the objectives postulated, or illuminated, by the models habitually used by economists, and the objectives which commonly underlie public policy decisions. It seems to me that failure to recognise this is responsible for a good deal of misunderstanding at the policy-making level. Nor is the confusion restricted to the academic 'experts': as these Reports demonstrate, it pervades the whole debate.

Economists as well as others are of course aware that politicians have objectives different from those illuminated by Pareto-type models, and that market transactions are only one of many possible voting systems that can be used to allocate resources between uses. Indeed, they have begun to develop models concerned with the outcomes of other methods of voting, and these recognise (eg) that politicians are in the business of 'trading policies for votes'. This implies, among other things, that politicians will not only have objectives in mind other than satisfying the wants of consumers, but that they may also see no particular benefit in specifying those other objectives explicitly. Thus, it should come as no surprise either to find that the Sub-Committee was concerned with broader objectives, or to discover that those objectives are neither easy to identify with precision nor to relate to the economist's technical apparatus discussed above. It is in the nature of the game.

Nevertheless, an examination of the actual treatment of objectives in the Report is not without practical interest. It was pointed out in Section I that the committee set out to avoid 'sensitive areas of political controversy', but nevertheless wished to concern itself with the twin problems of objectives and control. The Committee

[2]See Cmnd 744 (May 1959), and J Wiseman, *The Reorganization of the Cotton Industry*, London & Cambridge Economic Service, September 1959.

83

squared this circle by interpreting their interest in objectives as one of specification: it emphasised that adequate discussion of public policy must begin from a clear statement of the Government's aims, whatever they might be. But it did not really face up to the question of how to bring this about. Members of the community no doubt have an interest in such clarity of statement. It is less clear that politicians do: and the reports are concerned essentially with a political decision process. We are still waiting for the Committee's recommended 'clear-headed decisions by government openly explained, adequate monitoring and control thereafter, and a system of reporting regularly and fully to Parliament.' (para 261). I suspect we will wait a long time.

In any case, the sub-committee was too intelligent to stay within its own restrictions. It did in fact enter into at least restricted debate about objectives, not least because witnesses made this unavoidable, and concluded that the evidence 'gives a convincing picture of the confusion of objectives and the shortcomings of control that have too often characterised the inadequacies of government.' They also expressed some dissatisfaction with Treasury control and with the general administration of policy. It is my impression that this dissatisfaction derives at least in part from an inadequate recognition of the relevance of governmental objectives to official behaviour. Summarily, the official witnesses paid the appropriate homage to the strong competitive economy, and then talked of other social goals. But they were never very specific about these: they saw themselves as using informed judgment to interpret the wishes of the Government. It is clearly frustrating to bowl at this kind of dead bat, but it has to be recognised that it is in the nature of the exercise: officials responsible for implementing policy cannot be expected to specify objectives more precisely than will the responsible government.

Although the Sub-Committee did pay some attention to objectives, it remains true that the Reports avoid any discussion of fundamental differences of view, and this must be considered a limitation. For if the objectives of policy are fundamentally different, then it follows that the cost-benefit appraisal (evaluation of efficiency) must also be quite different, as must the case for and against particular sorts of agency, monitoring arrangements, etc. The point is a simple one, but its importance can hardly be over-emphasised. From his public statements, it is arguable that the Minister presently responsible for industrial subsidy policy is some kind of syndicalist: his concern is less with consumer satisfaction from buying motor cycles than with worker-satisfaction from making them whether anyone wants to buy them or not. It is possible that he may be right: it is certain that a practical appraisal of his policies must take such objectives into account. (The Sub-Committee reported in 1972: I find it fascinating to speculate as to what they would produce if re-convened now.)

As a corollary to this argument, it is interesting to return to the evidence of the TUC. Although this emphasised the alleged imperfections of the private capital market, it did not suggest measures specifically to improve them. Rather, the concern was for such things as the provision of information to workers and for general and ongoing intervention by government, motivated by considerations not relevant to private decision-makers. These issues were not pursued in detail: they quite clearly reflect markedly different objectives and (perhaps) a different interpretation of the facts from those held by other witnesses.

To conclude this section, some comment on 'intermediate' objectives is needed. In addition to differences in objective that derive essentially from differences in political philosophy, we saw in the last section that policy also tends to be influenced by 'intermediate' objectives. These are particular aims which might plausibly be regarded as 'inputs' to the attainment of Pareto-type objectives (hence the label 'intermediate'), but which in fact somehow acquire an independent end-content of their own. Two which receive a good deal of attention in the Reports are export-stimulation and employment-creation. I have already explained the difficulties these cause for policy evaluation. The Sub-Committee had problems with them, and this is one area in which economists outside government might be of some help, in elucidating the policy-relevant end-means relationships.

V Concluding comments

I should reiterate that I do not intend this review to be interpreted simply critically. The committee brought out much useful evidence and made valuable proposals about practical policy matters. But my obligation to evaluate the reports in what was called a cost-benefit context has forced me to the conclusion that this is (or was treated as) the wrong forum for the discussion of the fundamental policy issues, which inevitably incorporate questions of objectives. It follows that the organisational discussion and proposals (concerning eg the establishment of agencies to administer subsidies) can be of only limited value. I am sceptical of the suggestion that there are proposals of this kind which can transcend the political debate about objectives, at least when that debate reveals divisions as deep as those now before us.

In the same way, while I sympathise with the sub-committee's dissatisfaction with the actual information available to it on the results of subsidy etc. policy, and its plea for more attempts at quantification, I also think it important to recognise that this question is itself not unrelated to the difficulties about objectives which I have emphasised. No one would doubt that better information about the employment-generating consequences of regional policies is of practical importance. But its significance relative to other possible enquiries depends upon the extent to which employment-creation is seen as the sole or predominant aim of regional policy. Thus, the official initiative in encouraging or undertaking research in these areas, which the sub-committee urges, must clearly originate in the specification by government of its attitudes to objectives. How to improve the flow of such information about objectives thus seems to me to be the most crucial practical question thrown up by the reports: but I don't pretend that I know how to answer it, any more than they did.

An economic analysis of the Expenditure Committee reports on public money in the private sector

J WISEMAN

Comments by A Lord

Professor Wiseman's paper is of great importance both for its analysis of the role of the Expenditure Committee; and secondly for its wider implications as to whether economists are in a position to make a sensible contribution to policy on account of the break between conventional economic analysis and public policy.

Professor Wiseman's central criticism of the Expenditure Committee relates to its inability to develop the broader objectives of government policy. In the absence of a clear statement of objectives, and of any weighting being applied to each of the objectives, the cost-benefit analysis of the economist, he suggests, becomes inapplicable. In part, however, this failure to develop further the objectives of policy might stem from the specific nature of the Parliamentary Committee system in the UK context. It is in the nature of the UK parliamentary system that political parties are predominant, with parliamentary careers centred on political parties and parliamentary work subordinate to wider party interests and wider political conflicts. Parliamentary Committees therefore are unlikely to assume the importance in the British political system that they assume, for example, in the US, or the same role in the formulation of policy. One effect of this, it has often been claimed, is that even within the sphere of work they are able to undertake, some attitudes may tend to be directed by wider political requirements, aiming for example at 'scoring political points'. A more important consequence of the predominance of party conflict, is the limitation of the scope of the work Parliamentary Committees can undertake. In order for committees to function, the *a priori* and political areas have to be explicitly excluded. The development therefore of a more comprehensive function for parliamentary committees in determining the allocation of expenditure or, as Professor Wiseman suggests, defining the broader objectives of policy may be unlikely.

Professor Wiseman proceeds to suggest that without any such statement of the wider objectives of government, either by the Expenditure Committee or directly by Ministers themselves, economists generally may be as constrained as the Expenditure Committee to making only a limited critique of the efficiency of policy, and only a limited contribution to its formation. Professor Wiseman's aspiration appears to be that, given a clear definition of the various objectives of government, with fixed weights attached to each objective, it may be possible to incorporate objectives previously regarded as outside the 'orthodox' economic policy context nto the more conventional cost-benefit analysis, and only then to be able to make any evaluation of the efficiency of policy. It is doubtful however whether such a clear definition of objectives could be achieved. Few actions have a pure and simple objective; and which of the several objectives is prior changes over time. This applies both to micro and to macro policies, for example the arguments for free depreciation. This lack of clear policy objectives does, as Professor Wiseman suggests, limit the amount of economic analysis one can do and the scope of economists in contribution to the formation of policy in an analytical way or in monitoring performance; but considerable scope for analysis and criticism remains. In a multiple objective situation, for example, economic analysis may allow the implication of any policy on each of the objectives to be defined, and suggest the economic costs of pursuing 'non-economic' objectives; it may therefore itself contribute to the weighting of different political objectives. Additionally, *post-hoc* analysis of previous objectives and performance may help to improve subsequent performance in meeting the future requirement of Ministers. Such analyses can still provide a significant input into the decision-making process.

In summary, Professor Wiseman's paper raises several important issues. The inability of the Expenditure Committee to define the broader context of policy objectives, and therefore to adapt a more formal cost-benefit approach may be in part ascribed to the limitations under which Parliamentary Committees operate. Though, as Professor Wiseman suggests, the changing and ill-defined political objectives of policy raise difficulties for and limit the scope of economic analysis, economic analysis may still have an extensive role to play in the formulation and criticism of policy.

Some economics of investment grants and allowances

C BLAKE

Introduction

In this paper I have set myself the fairly limited aim of summarising what can be said, in the abstract, about investment incentives: in particular, about how they may work as a regional subsidy. This provides at best a necesssary, but scarcely a sufficient, background to the policy debate.

Fixed investment by industrial concerns – ie, the gross total of outlays on new assets acquired by them during some time period – breaks down into capital replacement, capital widening and capital deepening, although any actual project may contain elements of all three. These categories can be distinguished according to whether (1) the new acquisition allows existing capital to be retired, (2) capacity is extended using existing technique, or (3) the ratio of capital to labour and to output is increased. Provided that the price of capital goods, and the wage rate, do not change relative to each other, or to the price of output, the first component depends on the age-structure of the capital stock and the rate of innovation, given the need to maintain current levels of output. With the same proviso the second component depends on a change in the rate of output. The third depends on a change in the price of capital relative to labour when both prices are expressed in output terms.

Investment grants and allowances alter relative factor prices, and so influence the level of gross investment by creating an extra capital deepening effect. However, the rate at which they can do this depends on the other two components, of capital replacement and widening respectively. Investment is subject also to constraints imposed by cash flow and the availability of credit; and by strengthening the post-investment liquidity position of the firm, grants and allowances also tend to loosen that constraint. But the extent to which they do so is likely to be small compared with (say) the impact of monetary policy, the application of price controls, or even marginal adjustments to the rate or timing of corporation tax.

Fiscal inducements to invest can have several objectives. They may be directed at the timing of investment, at its composition by asset type or by investing industry, or at its location: or they may simply be aimed at raising the gross rate of capital expenditures – a blunt instrument for improving the quantity or quality of the stock. Whatever their purpose, they are presumably offered in the belief that the social return on subsidy-induced investment exceeds the return available to the capitalist before subsidy. In the United Kingdom, influencing the timing of investment seems to have been of negligible importance in the application of grants and allowances, compared with a longer-term restructing of some sort.

Recent policy in this country has subsidised manufacturing investment against non-manufacturing, with differential rates for plant and buildings, and has simultaneously favoured some locations over others. We should therefore want to distinguish analytically between subsidy-created and subsidy-diverted expenditures.

89

As a working assumption, we may assume that non-manufacturing investment is unaffected by subsidy-induced changes in the manufacturing sector. Similarly, any substitution between types of asset (eg, between plant and building) within manufacture, because of discrimination, can be dismissed.

The distinction however is highly relevant to the phenomenon of subsidy-induced inter-regional shifts. Yet we lack any theory of the relevant response functions, so that (for a given two-tier differential subsidy) we can predict neither the pace nor the scale at which relocation would take place, although intuitively we believe that it must occur. Our problem arises from the impossibility of defining 'regional cost advantage'. The investment subsidy works, as an engine of relocation, presumably by posing a counterweight to the advantages of preferred locations as seen by the investing firms. But these advantages need not correlate with any objective, observable features of the choice.

Hence, while an investment subsidy will in general tend to increase the capital intensity of production, by an amount which is (at least in principle) calculable, a differential subsidy may concurrently displace investment between regions by an unpredictable amount. Thus, even if the nature of the potential social costs and benefits of the latter process were fairly clear, their assessment is beyond our reach.

I Subsidy-created investment

The following analysis takes some inevitable liberties with the complexity of real affairs. For instance firms are assumed to assess their cost of capital on an after-tax basis, in spite of evidence that this is scarcely universal practice. They are regarded as counting that cost with no allowance for risk or for the possibility of yet another policy change. Although tax reliefs or grants, available after the investment has been made, are assumed to be discounted back to the moment of decision itself, the firm is otherwise assumed to make its decision in a 'timeless' context: ie, where capital has an inaugural cost but no maintenance costs; and where wage rates do not change relative to those costs during the asset's lifetime. (For an alternative approach, see Harcourt (1968).). Finally rational (cost-minimising) behaviour is assumed to underlie the revealed structure of production, and to govern changes in that structure made in response to subsidy in any form.

The phrase 'investment subsidy' is intended to include both cash grants or tax credits against completed expenditures, and a variety of relaxations to the rules governing the depreciation chargeable against taxable profit. (The forms of subsidy adopted in the United Kingdom since 1945 are described in the background paper prepared for the conference by Melliss and Richardson.) Such measures may, on appropriate assumptions, be expressed as a proportionate reduction in the cost of an asset, ie, as a present value to the recipient at the moment of capital expenditure. This value depends on:
   (a) The rate of company taxation
   (b) The incidence of tax benefit (eg, whether liability is reduced or deferred, and whether there are currently profits to be taxed)
   (c) The rate for discounting future tax reliefs or cash receipts
   (d) Time lags in the payment of grants
   (e) The ratios in which buildings are combined with plant and machinery in investment projects

In principle, it is possible to express the incentive effect of any policy – assuming where necessary some average 'mix' of buildings and plant – as a net (present value) reduction per £ of required investment outlay. Where the policy package includes regionally differentiated subsidies, it is possible also to express the additional incentive in this way. A figure so obtained (defined by Melliss and Richardson as P=the net present value of incentive schemes per unit of capital) may then be inserted in a definition of capital rental, or user cost. For this, the firm is thought of as acquiring assets in order to provide capital services for itself, for which it charges itself an implicit rent. We may then define (Boatwright and Eaton, 1973) the user cost of capital (c) in any period by:

$$c = (q(1-P)(\delta+r))/(1-u) \tag{1}$$

where

q = the price of capital goods
δ = the (proportional) rate of physical depreciation
r = a discount rate
u = the rate of corporation tax,

and P is the present value of the incentive provided by subsidy. Thus the term $q(1-P)$ is to be interpreted as the effective price of assets, provided that their market price remains constant whenever the value of the investment incentive is changed.

This effective asset price – the price as seen by the investor – is then translated into a capital cost, per period, over the life of the asset by the factor $(\delta+r)$, wherein δ represents the *ex ante* rate at which the capital stock is expected to wear out (ie, a notional loss of value, not the realised incidence of maintenance and repair), and r (and externally given rate of return) the fact that capital services involve waiting, and thus incur an opportunity cost. Then after dividing this capital cost per period by $(1-u)$, ie, the complement of the tax rate, we are left with the 'user cost': the implicit rental for services obtained from an asset, charged by the firm to itself; or, what it must earn from the use of capital to pay off the inaugural costs.

If we now make the usual neo-classical assumptions about goods and factor markets being perfectly competitive, and about constant returns to scale, and postulate also that the flow of capital services is proportional to the capital stock, the optimal (or equilibrium) level of capital for the firm can be deduced from the conditions that its marginal product should equal its rental price. Assuming, further, a constant elasticity of substitution (δ) between capital (K) and labour (L), we define the curvature of the isoquant such that, for a given output, following a 1 per cent change in the marginal rate of substitution there will be a σ per cent change in the ratio between capital and labour (K/L) in the factor mix. Since the marginal rate of substitution is the ratio between marginal products (Q_L/Q_K), and since under competitive conditions the latter is supposed to be equal to the ratio of factor prices (P_L/P_K) expressed in 'output' terms, we have:

$$\sigma = \frac{\text{relative change in } K/L}{\text{relative change in } P_L/P_K}$$

If we then assume P_L to be constant, it follows that a 1 per cent fall in the user cost of capital $(c = P_K)$ will bring about a σ per cent rise in the equilibrium capital stock; in other words, σ measures the elasticity of the desired capital stock with respect to a change in the cost of capital relative to wages, such as might be brought about by a subsidy to investment as defined above.

But to the extent that the subsidy is paid to manufacturing investment alone, not only is capital now relatively cheaper than before for manufacture compared to labour, but capital and labour in combination are relatively cheaper compared to output. Thus we have an 'income' as well as a 'substitution' effect: subsidised firms, besides moving around the isoquant for their present output, are able to move simultaneously to a higher isoquant for the same outlay. Provided that competitive conditions prevail, there will therefore appear a number of hitherto-submarginal plants, or projects, which are now viable at going prices. In the extreme

91

case (ie, extreme in theory – it may be fairly prevalent in practice) where there exists only one technique, or factor mix, for producing a commodity – so that the substitution elasticity for the corresponding industry is zero – the whole effect of the subsidy will show itself in a downward shift in the industry supply curve. Since, however, the relative size of that shift will depend on the capital cost component in the prevailing technique, the amount of market expansion will be relatively greater for more capital-intensive industries, so tending still to increase generally the use of capital relative to labour in manufacturing as a whole.

This then is the way that the neo-classical theory of production establishes a connection between investment subsidies and equilibrium capital stocks. However we have not yet arrived at a rate of investment corresponding to any specified level of incentive. If we leave on one side the possibility of short-run 'illiquidity' frictions, and of reaction lags in adjusting expenditures to a change in desired capital, what is the maximum attainable rate of adjustment? For an extreme position on this issue consider Eisner and Nadiri (1968): '. . . along with the "neo-classical model" involving relative prices, it may be appropriate to utilize a "putty-clay" hypothesis which would distinguish between the response of investment to changes in relative prices and the response to change in output. If new capital can be moulded into any shape (putty) but once installed is not malleable (clay), . . . changes in the equilibrium stock of capital . . . would be effected to a large extent only as the older capital . . . wore out' (p377).

Now this does not seem quite right. In the first place, 'replacement' is not simply a matter of waiting for some palpable moment when physical decay has made it no longer postponable; it is also a positive response to technological change. In the second place, where additional capital is created in response to a change in output, it will presumably be of the desired new 'deeper' variety required to bring the actual stock closer to the ideal. A more acceptable interpretation is that the gross investment rate – an observable phenomenon – and not some notional net rate, determines the speed of adjustment. Once the equilibrium capital-labour ratio has been altered by subsidy it is altered for every project undertaken from that time forward. Thus the question of how much difference a subsidy will make to the processes of modernising and extending capacity is answerable only when we know how quickly these processes take place.

Now if we know the elasticity of the capital stock with respect to a change in its (relative) price, and if we also know the extent of the effective (subsidised) change, then it is theoretically possible to say *ex post* how much of any recorded flow of new capital goods, in any industry, represents deepening due to subsidy, rather than either replacement, or extension, or that degree of deepening which (with technical progress but in the absence of intervention) would in any case have occurred. But this is a less ambitious programme than seeking to predict *ex anté* how much gross investment would result from a subsidy. For that we need some estimate of an expected unsubsidised rate of investment: hence of depreciation (or, rather, obsolescence) rates, of technical progress, and of the accelerator mechanism, industry by industry. There seems to be no reason to doubt that, in principle, the job can be done.

II   Subsidy-diverted investment

So far, we have tried to articulate a chain of deduction, from some given form of investment grant or allowance to its consequence in a flow of incremental expenditures intended to change the capital inputs into production. We have now to recall that investment incentives usually serve also as regional subsidies, through

92

differentiating the levels of allowance or grant. When we consider how such differentials may work, we have to recognise that the chain of deduction comes to an end.

Suppose that only two rates of subsidy are offered, when the present value of the saving on a unit of capital outlay in the favoured region (however defined) is some multiple of that available elsewhere. Then, if we knew the substitution elasticities involved, once again we should be able to say *ex post* how much more capital deepening would have been undertaken by firms already located in the favoured region than if there had been no discrimination. But this is only a part of the 'regional shift' effect. For some proportion of the investment by firms outside the favoured region will presumably have been displaced towards it. By definition this will have occurred among relatively 'footloose' industries: a category which is fairly well defined on past records of mobility. More important, intuitively it should occur more readily in those industries for which the capital coefficient in new projects is relatively large and inflexible; so that, for these industries, a reduction in the user cost of capital is a substantial offset to the disturbance costs, and subsequent external diseconomies, of the move.

Now it seems that there is no way by which the economist may put any measuring-rod on the strength of this displacement effect. Perhaps he can do no more than refuse to accept two extreme possibilities: either that a differential subsidy to capital generates no regional shift in capacity; or that the presence of a differential effectively removes all incentive from the lower-rated region, causing the entire subsidy-induced effect to take place in the other. Reluctance to consider either of these as a realistic possibility is due, partly, to the many-sided nature of the investment decision: in particular, to the different considerations governing spatial mobility among the replacement, enlargement and improvement components respectively, of investment, Any one of these categories may be indifferent as between regions for a single firm, or it may be wholly specific to one region; but the degree of mobility – ie, the elasticity of relocation with respect to subsidy – will vary between firms in an essentially unclassifiable way.

The full effect on the favoured region will not however be limited to either increasing capital intensity among indigenous firms, or causing an influx of migrants for whom the differential subsidy is a reward for relocation. For the former, there will again be an 'income' as well as a 'substitution' effect; the higher subsidy will not only change the price-relativity between capital and labour more than in unfavoured but will also, relative to other regions, lower the cost of factors in combination by a greater amount. As a result, firms already located in the favoured region will acquire a price advantage over firms outside such that, in the absence of spatial frictions, they are in a position to obtain a larger share than before of the output of their industry nationally. Once again, the effect will be more pronounced among those firms for whom new projects have a high capital content in their costs.

Now if we had the empirical wherewithal to quantify the factor-substitution effect on indigenous firms in the favoured region, we could in principle calculate the extent to which these firms ought, at the same time, to improve their national market share. But we do not know even what further data we should need in order to make a quantitative statement about the capacity displacement effect. Certain components of locational advantage, for example transport costs, may be measurable. It might even be plausible to represent prevailing differences in labour productivity between regions as an 'index of attraction' for firms who are contemplating the private costs and benefits of subsidised removal. But no such empirical makeshift could capture the whole range of felt gains and losses for the potential migrant.

Furthermore, even if we were to postulate a given amount of output displacement (involving both residents and migrants) in one industry towards a definable region, we should not have delimited the full extent of the regional impact. There is bound to be a degree of regional preference – or even of regional specificity – in the inputs to relocated capacity, thus creating a second-round effect in the form of investment by the supplying firms. Then, the regional incomes paid out of the increased value added whether from the originally-displaced capacity or because of derived demands transferred to regional suppliers – will bring about further expansion, this time in regional consumer goods and service trades.

I shall not recapitulate here the theory of regional multipliers, which is adequately represented in the literature. But the progress now being made (or at least being made possible) in measuring regional reaction paths from a given increase in the activity of one sector suggests a potentially important contribution to policy appraisal. That is to say, the tools are being developed which will translate any predetermined vector of subsidy-induced increase in regional capacity in to a new equilibrium level of regional activity, on the assumption that the indirect, or multiplier, effects are not frustrated by regional capacity constraints. (Sadler, etc, 1973; Blake, 1973: Jones, 1974.)

However the higher subsidy whose attractions determine that vector of regional output changes will (as noted) bring about both a degree of substitution of capital for labour among firms already in the region, and a (relative) improvement in their competitive position. Thus, beside the benefit of increased employment from immigrant projects one must set conflicting pressures on employment from indigenous projects: which, as was argued above, can be inferred if we know the factor substitution and demand elasticities involved. Clearly, therefore, the extent to which a differential investment subsidy – even one whose direct and displacement effects are known – actually creates a net employment gain in a favoured region depends on the outcome of contrary mechanisms, whereby firms already established in the region increase their demand for labour in order to meet the requirements of the incomers, and of their own increased market shares, yet at the same time reduce that demand as they convert to more labour-saving techniques.

This effectively places an insuperable burden on attempts to measure the impact of regional investment subsidies through subsequent changes in employment. The same burden does not fall upon attempts using investment data; an Appendix to this paper shows what may be done in this respect for one differentially-subsidised region. But then we must recognise that the simultaneous application both of a labour subsidy (REP) and of physical controls (the IDC's), together with other inducements to relocate, confuse the historical record. Moreover the existence of regional differences in industrial structure, in the age-distribution of capital, in prices other than for capital goods, in the accessibility of finance, and in effective demand, not to mention all sorts of random disturbance, would make it almost an act of faith to attribute some part of any apparent shift to the intervention of investment allowances or grants.

III Welfare implications

So far, this paper has been concerned with the positive economics of investment subsidies. Now we turn to normative issues. We have, I think, shown that any attempt to articulate *a priori* the causal chain linking a specific subsidy to an observed increase in regional outputs or employment must break down at the stage where a spatial difference in the cost of new capital is taken into individual decisions where to locate. Are we then to conclude that economic theory has nothing to offer the appraisal of investment subsidies as a regional policy? I shall approach this question by summarising first of all one quite specific answer (Johansen, 1967; Archibald, 1974).

Let it be assumed that the regional problem exemplifies some kind of market imperfection. Due to a combination of regional labour immobility and national wage fixing, earnings do not everywhere reflect the marginal opportunity cost of employing labour, because of significant inter-regional difference in the levels of effective demand. Then, let the formal structure of inter-regional resource allocation be represented by a linear programming model, as follows.

Consider two regions A and B, each with two characteristic industrial processes which employ factors (inputs) in fixed proportions, ie, with zero elasticity of substitution; so that every change in capital-labour ratios creates a new process. Each process absorbs two region-specific factors, say labour and 'old' capital, and one common (mobile) factor, say, 'new' capital, whose allocation is assumed to take place within some frictionless planning period. The resulting system of four outputs using five inputs is subject to physical constraints on the supply of all the inputs. Given the prices of outputs, it is then possible to define an objective function for maximising the value of the sum of the four outputs, and to solve for this value within the constraints. Corresponding to such a solution in terms of physical outputs, there is always a 'dual' solution in terms of the shadow prices of inputs (expressed in units of output price).

If it is assumed that entrepreneurs will use a process only when its accounting costs to them do not exceed the value of its output, subsidies should be used to present entrepreneurs with accounting prices that will induce them to operate processes at those levels which, taken together, maximise the value of total output. If (as was assumed) labour's market price in one region exceeds its shadow price, then the required form of subsidy is one which lowers the accounting price of labour in that region. Further, since the prevailing (non-optimal) levels of activity leave some region-specific labour resources unemployed, all labour in that region has a zero shadow price. Since this holds true for all potential users of labour in that region, the subsidy should be both universal across processes and (in order to absorb all the slack) set at the full extent of the market price.

If the other factors - respectively, 'old' and 'new' capital - the former is also region-specific, but has an accounting price which is a residual after labour charges have been met and therefore presents no problems; while the latter is assumed to be fully mobile and will presumably allocate itself between regions in such a way as to maximise its contribution to total output. Hence not only is there no case for subsidising investment; there is a positive case against. In Johansen's words (p 69): 'It (the common factor) appears in the dual problem with a single price which enters the calculation in both regions. Thus the accounting price for the common factor should be the same in both regions.' Hence we have the full Johansen rule: for optimal levels of activity, common resources must bear the same accounting price in each region, whereas regional resources – even if they are physically identical between regions – should be subsidised so as to bear accounting prices which differ from region to region according to their shadow price.

Now this rule presupposes a criterion of maximising total output. Regional employment – what the real-life regional problem, after all, seems to be about – does not appear as an argument in the objective function. Nevertheless it can be shown that, provided that is even one process in either region which uses only labour and whose output appears in the optimal (putput-maximising) solution, then it is impossible to have unused labour in that solution. The inference can be put more forcibly in its negative form: 'Whenever we get unused labour in one or more regions in an optimal solution, the reason must. . . be that in every potential production process labour is complementary to some other factor which is scarce and which is more valuable in other uses even though labour inputs in the regions in question are regarded as free factors' (Johansen, p71).

So we have the general conclusion of the Johansen/Archibald analysis. If labour is under-employed in one region because institutional forces have priced it too high in that region, and it is not mobile between regions, then there will be a loss of potential output which can be removed only by counteracting those forces or subsidising this over-priced labour. Conversely, if there is an input which is fully mobile between regions, then in order to maximise output and employment no subsidy need be given. Moreover, a subsidy should not discriminate between processes in one region, so long as the subsidised factor is mobile between processes.

The same conclusion may be expressed rather less formally. If industrialists are to be bribed to employ more labour in some regions without consequently employing less in others, then they must do this by combining the hitherto-idle labour either with existing (under-utilised) capital or with new capital which otherwise would have located where labour was already fully employed. If, then, the bribe takes the form of an investment location subsidy, only one of two possible means of absorbing the idle labour will have been exploited. If, however, the bribe takes the form of a differential labour subsidy, then idle labour ought to be absorbed both by the increased use of existing, region-specific capital and by the re-location of investment in pursuit of lower labour costs. The likelihood that labour is less productive with older capital does not really matter: any output is better than none at all.

However conclusive this analysis appears, a case may be made in favour of investment subsidies as complementary to, rather than as 'third-best' substitutes for, a subsidy to labour. If there it a chronic demand deficiency in one region combined with immobility among its surplus labour, this will be so because the regional economy either makes the wrong (obsolescent) things, or makes them by high-cost (obsolescent) methods, or suffers from a 'pure' locational cost disadvantage of some sort. If it were the last of these alone, then the 'best second-best' solution would be to identify the particular form of disadvantage and to offset it directly by some appropriate fiscal device. If however (as seems likely) either, or both, of the other causes were to obtain, then while labour subsidies treated the symptoms of the regional problem – and the case for doing so is unassailable – investment subsidies might be required to effect a cure.

This would follow from either of two possibilities.

(a) Contrary to the Johansen-Archibald assumption, 'new' capital is far from being regionally mobile – possibly because of external economies and linkages – so that, in spite of a labour subsidy, depressed regions still obtain less than their proportional share of investment. In this case an investment subsidy may help overcome inertia, especially in more capital-intensive sectors.

(b) Because labour is the only subsidised input, there is a tendency for any displaced 'new' capital to be of a technically less advanced variety, making less sophisticated products, and thus perpetuating the basic structural deficiencies of the assisted regions. In this case, an investment incentive may operate simply to correct any subsidy-induced bias in the choice of technique.

IV Conclusion

The benefits which are proffered by investment subsidies remain elusive: only a lower limit may be set, at the discounted sum of net present and future gains in regional incomes due to subsidy-diverted investment after all price and output adjustments have been made, but ignoring any secondary relocation effects. The same elusiveness characterises the resource costs. This paper has earlier emphasised the difficulties of measuring the extent of subsidy-induced diversion; yet this is the quantity which (if indeed relocated firms are the best judges of their location choices) sets the upper limit on those costs. In other words it is not the whole financial outlay on grants or allowances which represents their burden on the community, but the proportion of that outlay that has sufficed to persuade firms to do what otherwise they would not have done, or have done differently. Unrequited subsidies to intra-marginal projects are merely transfers, except perhaps to the extent that they draw upon a limited Exchequer fund and therefore represent fiscal opportunities foregone. Until we know more about the actual magnitudes of costs and benefits, however, the policy problem of fixing the right level of regional discrimination remains. Clearly there is a substantial field of research here waiting to be explored.

Finally, what can be said about any gains from a general (non-discriminatory) subsidy to manufacturing investment? It may be that a certain level of subsidy is sometimes required to maintain an adequate return on exportable manufactures, which are sold in international competition with the products of subsidised capital equipment abroad. But no really firm evidence has yet been brought forward to connect our chronic low rate of growth nationally in labour productivity with a low rate of investment in manufacture. On the other hand, intuition does suggest that the private rate of return to innovation – perhaps because of imperfections in labour markets – falls well short of the stream of potential future national gains, through international trade, accruing from structural and technical change. It may simply be that any advantage from encouraging investment in the development areas, *vis-à-vis* the rest of the United Kingdom, reappears writ large when we consider the United Kingdom as a whole *vis-à-vis* the rest of the world.

Bibliography

Archibald G C (1972); On Regional Economic
Policy in the United Kingdom.
Essays in Honour of Lord Robbins (ed Peston
and Corry), London. Weidenfeld and Nicholson,
1972.

Blake C (1973); The Gains from Regional
Policy. *Cost Benefit and Cost-Effectiveness*
(ed J N Wolfe), London. George Allen and
Unwin, 1973.

Boatwright B and Eaton J (1972); The
Estimation of Investment Functions for
Manufacturing Industry in the United
Kingdom. *Economica,* November 1972,
pp 403–418.

Eisner R and Nadiri M (1968); Investment
Behaviour and the neo-Classical Theory.
Review of Economics and Statistics, August
1968, pp 369–382.

Harcourt G C (1968); Investment-decision
Criteria, Investment Incentives and the
Choice of Technique. *Economic Journal,*
March 1968, pp 77–95.

Johansen L (1967); Regional Economic
Problems elucidated by Linear Programming.
International Economic Papers No 12, London.
Macmillan and Co, 1967.

Jones T T (1974); *Regional Multipliers and the
Location of Industry*. PhD Thesis, University
of Dundee. 1974.

Sadler P, Archer B, and Owen C (1973);
Regional Income Multipliers. Bangor
Occasional Papers in Economics. University
of Wales Press, 1973.

Appendix
The effect of policy on investment in one region

[1] Begg, H M, Lythe, C M, and Sorley, R, *Expenditure in Scotland 1961 to 1971, Edinburgh.* Scottish Academic Press, 1975.

It is argued in the paper that gross investment in a development area will be affected in several ways simultaneously by discriminatory subsidy: an enhanced degree of factor substitution by indigenous firms; increased capacity among these firms to meet a larger market share (due to lower relative costs); an influx of migrant firms; and further increased capacity by indigenous firms to meet intermediate demands from the migrants. It is also conceded that the subsidy displacement effect is obscured to *a posteriori* measurement, to the extent that it is the whole regional 'package' whose consequences will be picked up.

Nevertheless, the recent compilation of Social Accounts for Scotland on an 'expenditure' basis (Begg, etc, 1975)[1], has made it possible to compare GDFCF in one region, most of which has enjoyed 'development' status, with the figure for the UK as a whole. One way of presenting the results is to compare annual actual values for GDFCF in Scotland with an expected value, being UK figures standardised to Scottish employment size and structure.

Thus,

Expected GDFCF in Scotland $= \Sigma_i I_i (e_i/n_i)$

where $I_i =$ GDFCF by industry i in the UK

$n_i =$ employees in employment in industry i (UK)

$e_i =$ employees in employment in industry i (Scotland)

The weakness of this kind of standardisation, ie, the existence of inter-regional differences in intra-industry structures, is admitted; yet the results (see Table) are sufficiently consistent with expectations to suggest that the method can not be wholly fallacious.

We can summarise these results if we divide the whole span into successive periods of 'passive' policy (1951 to 1959) and 'active' policy (1960 to 1971). During the former, there was an average annual shortfall of actual from expected investment in Scotland of about 15 per cent and in the latter an average excess of about 16 per cent. While less can be read into year-on-year movements, it may be significant that the excess proportion moved sharply up in 1966 with the announcement of investment grants and fell even more sharply with their removal in 1971.

Actual and expected gross domestic fixed capital formation by manufacturing industry in Scotland; 1951 to 1971

£ million

	1951	1952	1953	1954	1955	1956	1957	1958	1959	1960	1961
Actual (A)	40.2	38.0	39.3	41.2	54.7	75.7	69.8	72.0	73.0	94.0	115.0
Expected (E)	48.8	52.2	50.7	54.5	62.8	77.6	85.2	82.5	74.9	88.0	103.8
Ratio A:E	.824	.728	.775	.756	.870	.976	.819	.873	.974	1.069	1.107

£ million

	1962	1963	1964	1965	1966	1967	1968	1969	1970	1971
Actual (A)	115.0	97.0	103.0	129.0	156.0	135.0	162.0	192.0	220.7	178.6
Expected (E)	96.8	86.5	101.8	116.3	120.5	117.4	135.2	148.5	167.5	169.9
Ratio A:E	1.189	1.122	1.012	1.109	1.294	1.150	1.198	1.293	1.318	1.051

Some economics of investment grants and allowances
C BLAKE

Comments by A P Thirlwall

Professor Blake's paper has three main sections. The first uses neo-classical concepts to develop a model to predict the effect on investment and the capital-labour ratio of a given change in the user cost of capital from the introduction of investment subsidies. The second section discusses the difficulties of developing a model to predict the investment elasticity of regionally differentiated investment subsidies. The third section criticises the conclusions of static linear programming models applied to regional economic problems that if labour is unemployed and less mobile than capital, the optimal policy is necessarily to subsidise labour. I shall first of all make a few specific points relating to Professor Blake's paper, and then develop a few hobby horses of my own.

My first point is that there seems to me to be a doubtful presumption running through the paper, and this is certainly implicit in the model developed in the first section of the paper, that the main effect of investment subsidies is to raise the level of investment by the substitution of capital for labour as a result of a fall in the relative price of capital. Not having been born a neoclassicist, or conditioned too strongly in later life, I must confess I am not at all sympathetic to the measurement of the effect of investment incentives using the concept of the elasticity of substitution, as Blake is suggesting. In fact, it could give positively misleading results. The essence of a subsidy to investment is not primarily to induce substitution along a given production frontier, but to make profitable projects that were previously just below the margin of profitability. The new investment demand pushes the firm onto a higher production frontier which may, or may not, embody a more capital intensive technology as a result of the relative price change depending on the nature of the project and any bias in technical change. If the effect of investment subsidies was confined to factor substitution alone, not only would they cause unemployment but also we should be forced into the absurd position of having to argue that a reduction in the cost of capital is incapable of inducing more investment in a firm employing fixed coefficients of production. Since the elasticity of substitution is not a measure of the movement from one production frontier to another in response to changes in relative prices, it is not possible to measure the sensitivity of investment to investment subsidies from knowledge of the elasticity of substitution alone. Even if the elasticity of substitution could be measured with some confidence firm by firm or industry by industry, which itself is doubtful, simply multiplying the elasticities by the relative price change of capital will give distorted results.

The point can be illustrated diagrammatically. Consider figure 1 below with capital measured on the vertical axis, labour on the horizontal axis, and the quantity of output producible with capital and labour represented by successive production functions (isoquants)$0_1 0_1$, $0_2 0_2$, etc.

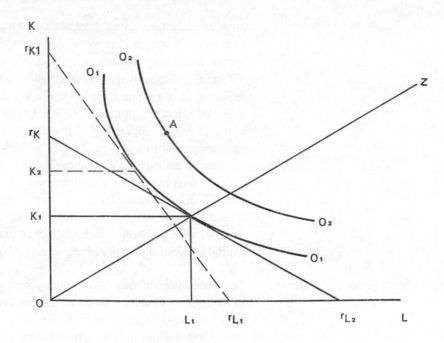

Let the relative price of capital and labour be represented by the slope of the price line (isocost curve) $r_K r_L$, giving an equilibrium capital stock of OK_1. According to Blake's model a fall in the relative price of capital (say to $r_{K1} r_{L1}$) causes a movement along the firm's production function to OK_2, the effect of which is measurable *a priori* using an estimate of the elasticity of substitution. My point is that this ignores income effects. The essence of an investment subsidy, which raises the rate of return on capital and reduces rentals, is to make previously intra-marginal projects profitable which pushes the firm onto a higher production function, say $O_2 O_2$. How much the capital stock will increase will depend on the nature of the project. Let us suppose the firm settles at point A. Since the firm has moved from one production function to another, it should be obvious that the change in the equilibrium capital stock is not measurable using the elasticity of substitution.

I see no alternative but to employ the econometric approach using multivariate analysis, with the cost of capital as one of the independent variables in the investment equation. This allows us to isolate the effects of other factors that affect investment and to capture the total effect of investment subsidies on investment, both the encouragement of more investment as well as the effect of capital-labour substitution. The assumption underlying the studies reported by Mr Lund in his excellent survey paper is that investment is a function of the rate of return, and that investment subsidies, and incentives in general, affect the rate of return calculations. To sum up my first comment on Professor Blake's paper, therefore, it seems to me that the elasticity of substitution approach that Blake suggests for analysing the effects of investment subsidies is only half of the story and probably not the half that ought to be concentrated on. Indeed, if policy makers thought only in terms of factor substitution they would have to concede that investment subsidies displaced labour when, in fact, one of the explicit intentions of investment subsidies is not only to increase investment, but also to increase output as well and to keep the demand for labour buoyant especially in particular parts of the country.

It follows from what I have said above that I cannot agree with one of the major conclusions of Professor Blake's paper (first stated on p 90) that while in principle the effect of an undifferentiated investment subsidy on the capital intensity of production is calculable (using the elasticity of substitution) the effect of a differential subsidy between regions is not calculable because differential subsidies have (unknown) displacement effects as well as substitution effects. The displacement effect between investment and consumption that may be expected to occur as a result of cheapening the cost of capital, which Professor Blake's model seems to ignore, is as tricky to measure as the displacement effect that a regionally differentiated subsidy may be expected to have of shifting investment from one region to another. The main difference between the two situations is that in the case of the undifferentiated subsidy nationally there are two effects to consider; in the case of a favoured region there are three. Nationally, there is the encouragement to investment and substitution to consider. Regionally there is the additional factor of the displacement effect due to the differential subsidy; that is, the investment which would otherwise have taken place in alternative locations which is diverted to the favoured location. If the econometric approach to measurement is adopted the difference might be reflected in an additional independent variable in the regional investment equation measuring the relative cost of capital between the favoured region and the rest of the country.

My second point concerns the employment-creating effects of investment incentives in the regions. Professor Blake recognises the conflicting forces operating, but is non-committal about the overall effect. On balance, however, the presumption must surely be that the employment creating effects of investment incentives in the regions are greater than the labour displacing effects; otherwise a regional policy which stressed investment incentives would indeed be a paradox when the heart of the regional problem, at least as conceived of by policy makers, is differences in employment opportunity. But it is important to realise (and Professor Blake's paper does not bring this out), that the employment creating effects come not only from the displacement of investment that would otherwise have taken place elsewhere in the country but also from a greater volume of investment in general than would otherwise have taken place because at the margin investment subsidies have caused substitution of investment for consumption.

Displacement investment in favoured regions essentially consists of two types therefore. Investment that would have taken place anyway but which now prefers to go to the favoured location, and investment that would not have taken place anyway, but is now just profitable in the favoured region but not elsewhere. The employment creating effects of investment incentives will be greater than the employment displacing effects the greater the labour intensity of the new investment attracted to the region and the less the possibilities of substituting capital for labour in existing plants.

A related point in this connection is that it is often said that capital subsidies in depressed regions will encourage capital intensive new industries, whereas it is labour intensive industries that the regions need. The argument is not water-tight. It is true that a capital intensive industry will have more to gain from investment subsidies than a labour intensive industry, but the essential point about any locational subsidy is that it makes all activities marginally more profitable in the favoured location. There may be as many labour intensive marginal projects as capital intensive marginal projects and labour intensive industries outside the region may have as much to gain as capital intensive industries inside the favoured region if their expansion in alternative locations is being thwarted by a shortage of labour which the favoured location does not suffer from. The statement by Moore and Rhodes in their paper (p 218) that a high proportion of investment subsidies is paid to capital intensive firms does not surprise me, but it is also interesting to note that they find no evidence that firms are more capital intensive than they would otherwise be, casting doubt on the notion that investment subsidies induce the substitution of capital for labour along existing production functions.

My overall conclusion then, contrary to that of Professor Blake, is that the factor substitution framework is as inappropriate for analysing the investment responsiveness of regionally undifferentiated subsidies as it is for analysing the investment responsiveness in regions to regionally differentiated subsidies. In both cases knowledge is required not only of substitution but also of how much investment is encouraged relative to consumption, and additionally in the case of the favoured regions, how much investment is attracted from outside. I have no theoretical framework to offer outside the standard models of the response of investment to changes in the cost of capital. But in any case, this matter is, in the last resort, an empirical one. I can think of many ways of going about the empirics if there was adequate data. Empirical work at the regional level is difficult in the absence of data on the regional capital stock. Perhaps this is an appropriate time and place for the academic researcher to make a plea to government departments to extend the range and improve the quality of regional statistics, especially those of the capital stock.

[1]For a further discussion see R Dixon and A P Thirwall, 'A Model of Regional Growth Rate Differences on Kaldorian Lines', *Oxford Economic Papers*, July 1975.

Labour subsidies

To assist high unemployment regions there now exist both capital and labour subsidies. Some critics have taken this as evidence of schizophrenia in regional policy. From Professor Blake's paper, and the discussion above, at least one simple rationalisation can be seen for the simultaneous use of labour and capital subsidies in depressed regions. It is to redress the possible labour saving bias in factor proportions introduced by capital subsidies in the course of using capital subsidies to attract more investment and demand (and hence to create more employment) than would otherwise be the case. The theoretical foundation for the use of labour subsidies for this purpose is much sounder than for the purpose of increasing regional growth by increasing exports which was the original stated purpose of the Regional Employment Premium. It is true that a perpetual wage subsidy is equivalent to a once for all currency devaluation but I know of no model of regional growth which either makes regional growth a function of the absolute level of exports, or which makes the rate of growth of exports a function of the level of export prices, either of which would be a necessary condition for a labour subsidy to raise the growth rate permanently[1].

I also agree entirely with Professor Blake's criticisms of the conclusions of static linear programming models which argue that labour subsidies are the first best policy in conditions of unemployment. As soon as we move away from the maximisation of present output as the objective function, and the dynamic effects and externalities of alternative policies are considered, labour subsidies look decidedly second best. What most depressed regions require is a massive direct boost in investment demand which will not only create employment directly but which will create an environment favourable to the continual expansion of the region. We are now witnessing on the north east coast of Scotland the dramatic effects that a sustained bout of investment demand can have on the fortunes of a regional economy. I would not want to argue that equivalent labour subsidies would have had the same effect.

Regional or industry specific subsidies?

Up to now regional investment subsidies have tended to be blanket subsidies given indiscriminately to any industry willing to establish in the favoured regions. I wonder whether the time has not come to think seriously about the possibility of relating subsidies to particular industries within regions as opposed to the regions themselves, according to the contribution that particular industries may be expected to make either directly to the regional economy or more broadly to the achievement of particular national economic objectives. I have in mind particularly the contribution that particular industries make to the national balance of payments, which at the same time would contribute to regional growth given that regional growth is primarily determined by demand from outside the region. I would like to see studies done, for example, of the income elasticity of demand for the products of different industries in both home and overseas markets, so that particular industries might be singled out for encouragement. I would also like to see studies of the matrix multiplier attached to different activities in different regions on various assumptions about where they might purchase their inputs from. Is there really any point in subsidising an activity in a depressed region which generates more direct plus indirect activity elsewhere? Since the major determinant of the multipliers will be the import coefficient attached to the industry or project, subsidies could be offered on condition that the industries bought their inputs from specific regional suppliers which would then help to contain the secondary indirect effects of subsidised expansion within the region. To make such studies possible there is again need for more data, particularly for data on inter-industry linkages within and between regions.

The economics of labour subsidies

T F CRIPPS

The case for government intervention in industry cannot readily be understood in terms of traditional economic analysis of the market economy. The purpose of this paper is to propose some alternative starting points in economic analysis which provide a more realistic basis for assessing the advantages of selective intervention in industry, taking labour subsidies as an example.

The traditional theory of competition provides an abstract, highly-simplified picture of the workings of a market economy under conditions of full employment.

This theory was developed in support of the liberal revolution against mercantilist restrictions and broadly conceives the role of the Government as that of a referee whose task it is to see that the rules of fair competition are not infringed. According to the theory of competition, selective taxes or subsidies which distort the workings of the market generally have harmful effects on efficiency and national welfare. Selective labour subsidies, in particular, would tend to reduce labour productivity below its optimum level in firms receiving subsidy – for example, by causing postponement of scrapping of obsolete plant, by encouraging the choice of a low level of mechanization in new plants, and by encouraging excessive use of overhead labour.

These arguments are only relevant to an economy in which full employment of labour can easily be maintained and where the productivity of labour is mainly determined by the rate of scrapping and the choice of techniques in new investment. They are of little relevance to the UK.

The institutional reforms which are now being introduced to provide more democratic and accountable decision-making in industry will involve the Government more and more in negotiations over specific industrial decisions of great importance to individual companies and public corporations. This will demand policies on financial assistance to industry which are consistent with actual macro-economic objectives and realistic in the specific circumstances of each individual decision. Labour subsidies, in particular, must be viewed in this context rather than in the framework of the abstract theory of competition.

I Macro-economic objectives

The UK is faced with the problem that Keynesian budgetary policy alone cannot secure an acceptable level of income and employment. The level of income and employment which can be achieved through budgetary policy is constrained by several factors:
   (a) regional imbalance in the demand for labour
   (b) lack of competitiveness in foreign trade
   (c) inadequate industrial capacity.
Each of these constraints could be tackled by a variety of types of intervention, ranging from controls and directives to general tax and subsidy measures. Each

105

provides an example of how labour subsidies, in particular, could potentially assist the achievement of macro-economic objectives by correcting imbalance or instability in the actual functioning of competitive markets.

(a) Regional imbalance

The only explicit labour subsidy at present in force – the Regional Employment Premium – was introduced to help correct the regional imbalance in the demand for labour. It was argued that if demand for labour could be redistributed away from areas of labour shortage to areas of unemployment it would be possible to allow the economy to reach a higher level of total employment and output. Under these circumstances the REP could well have been self-financing, because the stimulus to demand provided by payment of the subsidy might well have been less than the increase in demand warranted by the improved regional distribution of employment.

(b) Competitiveness in foreign trade

Since the mid-1960s the achievement of full employment has been prevented at least as much by balance of payments problems as by regional imbalance in the demand for labour. The weakness of the balance of trade largely reflects the lack of cost competitiveness of UK industry, for which labour subsidies could arguably provide a remedy.

Labour subsidies paid to manufacturing producers would reduce their production costs relative to foreign competitors and could thereby make possible a substantial increase in exports, total employment and national income. Under these circumstances they could, as was argued for the REP, be regarded as self-financing.

Consider, for example, a labour subsidy paid to manufacturers who export one-third of their output and for whom the elasticity of foreign sales with respect to unit labour costs is at least three. Then each £1 of subsidy paid will generate at least £1 of additional export sales. The ultimate effects per £1 of subsidy could be additions of roughly £2.50 to national income, and £1.00 each to exports, imports and tax revenue. The subsidy would then have increased income and employment without causing any increase in the trade deficit or in the financial deficit of the public sector.

(c) Inadequate industrial capacity

In the last two years it has appeared that the level of national income and employment has been held back, and the size of the foreign trade deficit increased, by the inadequate productive capacity of UK industry relative to the full employment level of demand. Evidence of this is provided by the slow average growth rate of the index of production from its 1969 peak to the peak in 1973, by the 'shake-out' of labour from manufacturing in 1971 which was not reversed in the recent boom, by the high rate of redundancy and plant closure following mergers over the past five years, by the low rate of investment in manufacturing industry since 1970, and by the widespread reports of bottlenecks and shortages during the 1973 boom.

Here again labour subsidies could serve a useful function, at least in the short run, as a means of delaying the closure of high-cost plants to secure the preservation of a margin of reserve capacity during recession. A policy of this kind could be justified as a stop-gap measure until the rate of investment in new capacity can be substantially increased.

In relation to national economic strategy labour subsidies can therefore potentially assist in removing major obstacles to the achievement of a high level of income and employment. The administrative feasibility and effectiveness of the REP has already been demonstrated, although it remains a crude instrument because it is applied at a uniform rate to very broad geographical areas. The SEP was introduced as a means of improving the cost competitiveness of manufacturing industry, but only at a very low rate and for a brief period, in 1966-67. No new scheme of that kind has since been devised. Finally the use of temporary labour subsidies as a means of postponing redundancies and closures has been canvassed recently but there has been no definite proposal on how such a scheme might be administered.

II Micro-economic considerations

The case for government intervention must not be regarded entirely in macro-economic terms. The traditional theory of competition is inaccurate not only in its assumption that full employment can easily be maintained but also in its description of market forces and managerial decision-taking at plant or enterprise level. Here again, a more realistic analysis will establish many reasons why intervention may be desirable.

In contemporary circumstances two particular examples come to mind:
    (a) the problems of firms trapped in a cumulative spiral of decline;
    (b) the influence of organized labour on managerial decisions.

(a) Problems of cumulative decline
In many industries the long-run prospects of individual firms tend to improve or worsen with cumulative effects. Initial success provides the opportunities for exploiting economies of scale and specialization, together with the profit and easy access to external finance needed to fund continued expansion. In this situation continued productivity improvements will follow as a result of growth from an initially advantageous position. On the other hand, initial failure results in continued slow growth, lack of finance, inability to reorganize and low productivity growth.

This analysis provides a justification for any form of subsidy which is sufficient to set a firm or industry on the path of sustained expansion. It is an argument for selective, temporary subsidies at very high rates in order to rescue industrial invalids and restore them to health – after which they should be able to survive and prosper without further aid. Since it would hardly be justifiable for shareholders to receive the profits resulting from large initial subsidies at the taxpayers' expense, this argument leads to the case for public ownership of ailing firms or industries.

The view that subsidies will tend to improve the chance of survival and raise productivity within the firms to which they are paid is probably valid and relevant to many industries. But the benefits are doubtful in the context of serious labour shortage where the survival of one plant can be a substantial impediment to the expansion of another, more successful plant. They can also be doubtful, for the same reason, in the context of industries limited to closed domestic markets.

(b) The influence of organized labour
In most manufacturing industries the freedom of managerial decision-making is in practice severely limited by the bargaining power of organized workers. The workers' demand for continuity and security of employment is often in sharp conflict with managerial desires to raise productivity, particularly in plants and industries which can only secure slow growth of demand.

On the other hand, in a labour-controlled firm fully committed to the permanent employment of its members, there is a strong incentive to raise productivity in order to increase sales revenue and earnings.

It is indeed arguable that workers can only adopt a commitment to reorganization and investment with the aim of raising labour productivity provided they are guaranteed a higher degree of continuity and security of employment than most companies are now able to afford. In this situation, only the Government can provide the greater security through selective and temporary subsidies to avert unacceptable lay-offs and redundancies. A government guarantee of greater job security for industrial workers could largely eliminate the need for restrictive practices which reduce labour productivity.

These two examples show that labour subsidies could be used to improve industrial efficiency and productivity by mitigating the damage which market forces can inflict on industrial enterprises. The case for intervention on these grounds has become increasingly strong in Britain as market forces have become increasingly destructive in their effects.

Alternative methods of intervention

None of the possible motives for government intervention discussed above are necessarily arguments for the use of labour subsidies in preference to other instruments of interventionist policy. The choice of methods of intervention involves political and administrative questions as much as economic ones.

The administrative advantage of labour subsidies as a selective policy instrument is that employment is probably the best-defined and most easily measured quantity which can be assessed on a plant-by-plant basis. Furthermore employment is already recorded in detail for National Insurance and PAYE purposes.

III Conclusion

Labour subsidies offer a convenient method for providing selective assistance to industry in pursuit of key economic objectives. Hitherto they have been little used (with the exception of the REP) because of the mistaken belief that they would cause a reduction in productivity. The administrative machinery for payment of labour subsidies on a flexible and selective basis does not yet exist but could in principle be developed in conjunction with the PAYE system.

The economics of labour subsidies
T F CRIPPS

Comments by K Hartley

Introduction

This is a short paper, for which any discussant is obviously grateful! Nevertheless, it is not at all clear what the paper really means. I've treated it as a serious contribution and, in the circumstances, I see my role as someone who is desperately seeking clarification. A set of questions (and there are lots) have to be posed, especially about the underlying analytical framework and the associated policy model. Questions which are particularly relevant in view of the current developments in industrial policy.

My remarks can be grouped around some general worries about the methodology of economic policy, at least as used in this paper. At the start we have to be quite clear about the value-judgements (whose?) which are floating around. We've also to distinguish between, on the one hand, assertions and religious passion and, on the other, logical propositions capable of being tested and refuted. I want to concentrate on three areas: first, policy objectives; second, the relevance of economic theory to policy and third, policy instruments and the 'appropriateness' of labour subsidies. The points are embarrassingly basic but nonetheless relevant.

The objectives of policy

What are the stated policy goals: what are we talking about? The first part of the paper seems to suggest that policy aims to maximise income and employment subject to constraints of regional imbalance, lack of competitiveness and inadequate industrial capacity: elements which contribute to 'imbalance or instability' in markets. Immediately, problems arise because we are never given a clear specification of what these elements might mean. What, for example, is meant by 'inadequate' industrial capacity? What is 'adequate' and how are we supposed to define and measure industrial capacity: is it physical capacity somehow defined or are we including human capital and the skills and mobility of the labour force? Also, what is 'imbalance and instability' in the functioning of competitive markets? Is there some alternative (implied to be preferred but never specified) organisation of economic activity which avoids 'imbalance and instability'?

Elsewhere in the paper, there are hints of policy objectives which embrace industrial democracy, labour controlled firms, the continuity and security of employment, public ownership and a concern with the '. . . problems of firms trapped in a cumulative spiral of decline . . .' Additional constraints appear to include the influence of organized labour and the 'perfect' immobility of labour. In other words, some clarification is required of the author's interpretation of the policy problem, a clarification which is obligatory if economists are to avoid some of the criticisms which they themselves make, for example, of policy-makers and Expenditure Committee reports (see, for example, conference paper by J Wiseman).

109

Economic theory and policy

Once we have identified the policy problem, questions arise about causes: why do we have these problems? This is where you expect to find some economic analysis. For example, if the 'problems' we are considering reflect the failure of markets, it is necessary to start by identifying the sources and causes of failure. Is it, for example, the capital market which is 'failing' to invest in an adequate amount of physical and human capital? Is this the market which is failing to invest in the Development Areas? Is this the market which is failing to reflect the preferences of workers and failing to give industrial democracy? If this is the case, we need to know whether the market failure is due to imperfections and/or externalities and the form of these deficiencies.

What, for example, are the causes of inadequate industrial capacity? Is it a supply side problem and/or a demand management problem? No model is suggested. We are simply given some 'evidence' about 'shake-out' and the closure of plants following mergers: evidence which is consistent with, say, a technical inefficiency hypothesis rather than a capacity hypothesis.

On the other hand, if we don't accept the traditional view of governments as social-welfare maximising agencies, we have to return to fundamentals and ask why governments have economic policies. Here, the paper expresses a worry about the traditional theory of competition and the role of the state as a referee enforcing the rules of fair competition. The paper then tells us that current policy 'will involve the Government more and more in negotiations over specific industrial decisions.' Why this increasing state involvement? We are never told. Is there an economics of politics behind all this in which governments are vote-maximisers, influenced by producer interest groups (management and unions) and by budget-maximising Ministries, state agencies and departments? We are never told. The alternative economic analysis which is to 'provide a more realistic basis for assessing the advantages of selective intervention in industry . . .' is conspicuous by its absence.

Policy instruments and the 'appropriateness' of labour subsidies

I'm at a loss to know how we conclude that labour subsidies are 'desirable'. For a start, it is never made clear which type of subsidies are being considered: is it solely the subsidisation of employment? If so, what about the existing state subsidies for labour mobility, industrial training, job search and labour market information? Also, how do the proposals in the paper relate to the Manpower Services Commission with its Employment and Training Services Agencies, the Industrial Training Act and the Training Boards: where, if at all, do these fit into the proposed policy framework?

Let's see if the paper suggests any consistent policy guidelines ('rules') for subsidy policy. Here, confusion arises because there appear to be at least two sets of criteria for subsidies. The first set suggests that subsidies should be given to labour employed in manufacturing firms – no other economic activity appears to have any relevance to regional balance, international competitiveness, etc. In addition, to qualify for labour subsidies, the manufacturers have to be located in Development Areas and possess both export markets and high-cost plants. But later, we are introduced to a second general set of criteria and it is not at all clear how (if at all) the two sets relate. It is suggested that the case for labour subsidies rests largely on two new considerations:

    (a)   On the recognition of the influence and the bargaining power of organised labour, which seems to suggest a trade union criterion for labour subsidies: subsidise whenever there are powerful (undefined) trade unions. What about

110

unorganised labour and their employment opportunities? Or is this once more based on the economics of politics with a vote-maximising government responding to trade union interest groups?

(b) But there is a further case for labour subsidies. This is related to something called '. . . the problems of firms trapped in a cumulative spiral of decline.' We are presented with a more realistic analysis based on 'cumulative effects'. The central hypothesis seems to be that 'initial failure results in continued slow growth, lack of finance, inability to reorganise and low productivity growth'. Sounds like those terrible markets trying to work! We are then told that 'This analysis provides a justification for any form of subsidy which is sufficient to set a firm or industry on the path of sustained expansion'. Questions are inevitable:

(a) What analysis are we being referred to?

(b) Are there any firms in the UK which would not qualify for a subsidy?

(c) How do we select firms for subsidy and are these to be open-ended (eg cost-plus Concorde) types of subsidies?

(d) We are told this justifies any form of subsidy, so some additional arguments are required for labour subsidies.

All this is most worrying but more follows. We are told that once 'industrial invalids' have been restored to 'health' 'they should be able to survive and prosper without further aid'. Now I don't know whether this is supposed to be a prediction derived from some (unspecified) model, or, is it an expression of blind faith? Are we seriously being asked to believe that governments are somehow endowed with perfect foresight? I find this hard to accept. There is also another logical point. If these industrial invalids restored to health are supposed to survive and prosper without further aid, why are subsidies required: why not loans?

Some comments on labour-controlled firms

Throughout the paper, we are never presented with a model of firm behaviour which provides predictions about the likely effects of labour subsidies. And then, without any explanation, we are suddenly introduced to the labour-managed firm (LMF). No formal model of the behaviour of a LMF is outlined. Are they maximising employment, the wage bill or some utility function (whose)? Without any reference to empirical evidence (eg foreign experience), it is suggested that subsidies to LMF's (are they a necessary condition in the policy model?) will guarantee job security and so reduce restrictive practices. Even if this happens, what if the labour is in the 'wrong' industry, the 'wrong' region and has the 'wrong' skills (where 'wrong' means non-marketable)? If this happens, won't governments be blamed rather than management, which brings us back to an economics of politics. Just how is it proposed to 'solve' the allocation and re-allocation problems? With massive subsidies, will state aid be on a fixed sum or a cost-plus basis? Will the Government in any way, concern itself with the internal efficiency of firms or will it accept as constraints the existing employment level, skill composition and manning requirements of a firm's labour force? And where a firm is subsidised, will there be state regulation of its prices (eg marginal cost pricing)? Perhaps those 'terrible markets' are not too bad after all: it's amazing the number of problems we create for ourselves when we try to replace them.

A final policy question

The proposals in this paper seem to be at variance with the Department of Industry's criteria for 'practicable' subsidy scheme (see Conference papers). The Department of Industry maintains that a practicable subsidy scheme should:

(a) Be understandable.

111

(b) 'Safeguard public money against . . . the possibility of losses arising from the collapse of companies.'

(c) Be equitable in the treatment of applicants.

(d) Not ignore transactions costs. The Department of Industry paper suggests that selective discretionary subsidies are 'too expensive in staff costs and too difficult and time-consuming to be followed on a bigger scale'.

The labour subsidies suggested in this paper seem to be in conflict with each of the points made by the Department of Industry.

Conclusion

How can we wind up? It's tempting to refer to the fallacies of the grass is always greener and of the free lunch, both of which seem abundant in this paper. A little quote from J S Mill might help. 'There are some things with which governments ought not to meddle and other things with which they ought; but whether right or wrong in itself, the interference must work for ill, if government, not understanding the subject which it meddles with, meddles to bring about a result which would be mischievous.' Can I suggest that if we accept this paper, we shall be committing a massive mischief?

The choice of targets and instruments for Government support of scientific research*

K PAVITT

*The author is indebted to his colleagues at the Science Policy Research Unit for comments, suggestions and criticisms of an earlier draft of the paper. Responsibility for this draft is, however, his own.

[1]The numbers in brackets refer to the relevant sections of the paper.

Summary

Science and industrial development

Government (or industrial) support for scientific research will not automatically result in the commercial introduction and diffusion of economically useful technology: considerable additional expenditures are required on development, tooling and marketing; the pace and direction of technical change is heavily influenced by economic factors; some innovations happen without scientific research; and others through an experimental approach to technology (II)[1].

Nonetheless, the modern chemical, electrical and electronics industries are based on scientific research, and a large number of industries use scientific research in a supportive role. Invention and innovation have increasingly, but not entirely, become specialised and professionalised activities, to which scientific research in industry, government and the universities make significant contributions. Maintaining close contacts with outside sources and users of knowledge are critical functions of this R & D system (II).

Possible reasons for government support

In our present state of knowledge, it is not possible to define the appropriate targets and instruments for government support for scientific research from calculations and comparisons of the cost and benefits of different lines of research. However, possible reasons for government intervention can be derived from imperfections in the market system. Government support for fundamental research can be justified as a public good, as can support for longer term R & D, in so far as industrial firms tend to concentrate on short-term, incremental innovations. Government R & D may also be justified in sectors (such as agriculture) where – for historical and institutional reasons – private firms cannot undertake research to put technology on a sounder scientific footing, and in sectors where social and private costs diverge. Scale factors may justify common research programmes undertaken in government laboratories in areas of peripheral importance to a number of industrial firms; but they have also been used (together with 'security of supply') to justify heavy government financial support for scientific research and related activities, as well as for full-scale commercial development, in the high technology industries (aerospace, nuclear energy, advanced electronics) (III).

Unfortunately, empirical knowledge of the nature and scope of market imperfections requiring govenrment support for industry-related R & D is very limited. So is knowledge of the effectiveness of government programmes designed to correct them, and of the effects of various economic rewards and incentives on the propensity and ability of industry to innovate (III).

Patterns of UK support

UK spending on academic research is not 'too much' by international standards, and many of the problems of university/industry links that have been assumed to be

British problems are in fact common to many countries. The one exception may be engineering, but some commentators have argued that change and improvement depends on industry more than the academic system (IVa).

The R & D activities of the former Department of Trade and Industry, are heavily weighed towards commercial development which (nuclear energy excepted) accounts for about three-quarters of the total, the remainder being spent on scientific research, exploratory development and related activities. Commercial development activities are heavily concentrated in aircraft. The justification for them in terms of scale and security of supply has been questioned by a number of economists and political scientists, some of whom argue that government expenditures should be concentrated on scientific research and exploratory development, rather than on commercial development (IVb, IVc, IVd).

As in other Western European countries, DTI expenditure on R & D are heavily concentrated in the high technology sectors. Only 15 per cent of the funds are devoted to the remainder of industry, and the industrial customer/government contractor principle has been applied more stringently to these other sectors than to the high technologies (with the exception of some of the nuclear establishments). The Research Requirements Boards (which do not cover aerospace R & D) appear to accept a Government role in financing longer-term R & D and common programmes in these other sectors. It is less clear that they accept a role in financing research with environmental and social benefits, and for the benefit of technically and managerially backward firms. Only the Research Associations devote the majority of funds to the traditional industries, and even they have not been able to reach the majority of small firms (IVe).

R & D financed by industry has grown more slowly since the beginning of the 1960s in the UK than in any other industrialised OECD country; industrial R & D in the UK is no longer high by international standards. We do not know why this is the case, or what its implications are for the competitiveness of British manufacturing industry and for government policy (IVf).

Assessment and recommendations
It has been the declared intention of successive UK governments over the past ten years to make Government-financed R & D more relevant to industry. It has failed to achieve this objective in three important respects:

(a) expenditures have been concentrated too heavily on a few high technologies, and on commercial development instead of research, exploratory development and related activities;

(b) the Government has not adopted an incremental, step-by-step approach to R & D policy or to project and programme planning. In a number of significant cases, commitments to full-scale commercial development have been too early and too big, and too little was spent on applied research and exploratory development beforehand;

(c) policy-machinery, operating procedures and public debate have often not been focussed on the critically important problems (Va).

Given these deficiencies, government expenditures on commercial development projects should be considerably reduced over the next ten years. Government-financed programmes of research, exploratory development and related activities should be such as to give sufficient support to commercial development programmes, and to technical awareness, in industry; they should also act as a reasonable insurance policy for security of supply (Vb).

At the same time, a more active policy should be followed towards research and related activities for sectors other than the high technologies. This would probably involve a revised and wider role for the NRDC, and greater funds for the organisations funded through the Requirements Boards. Any policy changes should focus on ends and means, and not on re-organisation (Vb).

Some unanswered questions

Assessments of UK policy and recommendations for change would be more firmly based if we knew more about:

(a) the history and effectiveness of UK policy towards the high technologies;

(b) the economic effectiveness of government funding of commercial development activities in industry;

(c) the economic contribution made by government-financed programmes of research, exploratory development, and related scientific and technical activities;

(d) the factors influencing the propensity and competence to innovate in UK industry;

(e) the political and sociological reasons why high technologies receive so much government support, and why governments have tried to supplement and not to complement the private market over the past ten years (Vc).

I Introduction

The subject of this paper is the choice of targets and instruments for government support of scientific research in the UK. Section II will review briefly what we know about the relationships between scientific research and industrial technology, and section III what we know about imperfections in the processes whereby industry uses science and technology, which may justify government intervention. Section IV then describes and analyses the targets and instruments of British government support for industry-related R & D. Section V concludes by making a (subjective) assessment of the present pattern of government support, by making some recommendations for change, and by identifying some unanswered questions. But it is first necessary to define what, for the purposes of this paper, we shall mean by scientific research, and then to make some assumptions about the policy objectives in relation to which support for scientific research should be evaluated.

According to the OECD definitions (37)[2], scientific research is original investigation in order to gain new scientific knowledge and understanding; such research is 'basic or applied' depending on whether or not it is directed towards any specific practical aim or application. It is different from 'experimental development' which is defined as the use of scientific knowledge in order to produce new or substantially improved materials, devices, products, processes, systems or services.

Like all definitions of social activities, the above are arbitrary and open to different interpretations: for example, what is 'basic' research to a scientist or an engineer working in a laboratory on solid state physics may be called 'applied' by the institution financing the research. Definitions must ultimately be judged according to the degree to which they help us to understand and analyse the problem under discussion. Whilst they are adequate in sections II and III for the discussions of the relationships amongst scientific research, development, innovation, technical change in industry and government policy, they are too restrictive for the examination of UK policy in sections IV and V.

Another paper at the conference will discuss the economics of 'launching aid', namely, the largest part of UK government financial support for full-scale commercial development of specific products and processes. Between such activities and basic and applied research, there is a whole range of scientific and technical activities that are or could be financed by government with the objective getting new and better technology into UK industry: for example, scientific and technical informa-

²References are given at the end of the paper.

tion services, technical and managerial advisory services, and financial support for advanced (or exploratory) development and demonstration projects designed to test and evaluate the characteristics of subsystems, prototypes and pilot plant, before going ahead to full-scale commercial development[3].

We shall discuss these intermediate activities in sections IV and V, for two reasons. First, to ensure that the totality of government-financed and industry-related R & D activities are covered at the conference. Second, because there is a debate amongst some economists about the degree to which governments should get involved in financing full-scale commercial development of industrial technology, and which has implications for UK Government support (or lack of it) for scientific research and exploratory development.

For the purposes of this paper, we shall also assume that UK welfare depends in part on the improvement of the UK balance of payments and of industrial productivity compared to other industrialised countries, and that the introduction and diffusion of new and improved technology in UK industry is a necessary condition for this to happen. This is not to assume that it is a sufficient condition. It may well be that, by comparison with its competitors, UK industry's main problem is one of organisation, management and motivation to ensure that technology and skills are used and improved efficiently. It may also be the case that even the most intelligent and far-sighted policy by the Government to provide scientific research and related activities will be in vain if the incentives and pressures on industry to innovate do not exist.

However, the existence of any such inadequacies does not justify the neglect of science and technology, either by industry or by government. Advances in economic theory over the past twenty years suggest very strongly that innovation and diffusion are essential ingredients of industrial growth and exports in the industrially advanced countries (63). Furthermore, recent OECD statistics (41) show that the UK's main industrial competitors have not been neglecting R & D expenditures that are related to industrial technology. The proportion of national resources spent on industry-financed R & D was already higher in 1971 in FR Germany, Japan, the Netherlands and Switzerland, and the British Government's expenditures on civilian R & D are no longer high by international standards. The UK no longer spends 'too much' on civilian R & D by international standards, even though the myth dies hard, and defence R & D spending remains high[4]. It is therefore relevant to ask to what extent the pattern of allocation of resources to scientific research and related activities is economically the most appropriate one. This first requires a discussion of the role of scientific research, and of government intervention, in the processes of technical change in industry.

II Scientific research and industrial development

It is wrong to assume that a greater commitment of government and industrial resources to basic and applied research will automatically lead to a greater flow of innovations and to improved economic performance. Considerable additional expenditures are required to turn knowledge into economically useful goods and to diffuse their use throughout the economy. In addition, the linear model of innovation implicit in such a policy prescription – with research leading to discovery and then to practical application and commercialisation – is misleading. Economic historians such as Mantoux (25) and economists such as Schmookler (48) have produced convincing evidence of the strong influence of economic factors on patterns and rates of technical change in the eighteenth and nineteenth centuries. More recent empirical studies of industrial innovation confirm these conclusions; most but not all contemporary innovations tend to be stimulated initially by

[3]For an attempt to categorise the programmes and institutions in the UK government that are involved in commercial development in scientific research and related activities, see Table 1 on page 123.

[4]It should not be assumed that other countries' governments' allocations of resources to R & D are the 'right' ones. Indeed, we shall argue later in this paper that some other governments have misallocated R & D resources just as has happened in the UK.

116

'economic need' rather than by 'scientific and technical opportunity, (43)' and the most important factor in the eventual commercial success of an innovation is the extent to which it has been consciously adapted to the users' needs (49).

Furthermore, many innovations take place without any direct contributions from scientific research. It is generally accepted that scientific expertise played a very small instrumental role in the wave of textile innovations which were at the heart of the industrial revolution at the end of the eighteenth century, even if an inconclusive debate continues among economic historians about the wider role of science during this period (27). In addition, many significant innovations have taken place as a result of an experimental approach to technology rather than through experimental scientific research. Bernal points out that it was improvements in the precision and reliability of metal cutting and forming, and in empirical knowledge of the knowledge of the mechanical properties of materials, that made 'design (not research) and development' possible and useful in the machinery-making industries (4); even today a high proportion of inventions in the mechanical industry are made outside formal R & D activities, and a recent Dutch study has shown that acquaintance with formal science and with formal R & D was not a significant factor in innovativeness in the materials handling sector (52).

In the iron and steel industry, experimental development predominated before scientific research:
    'The decisive break came with the radical innovations of Bessemer in discovering a way of making cast steel on a large scale. In his converter, air, blown through melted pig iron, burns away the carbon, producing enough heat to keep the resulting steel melted. This may be called a semi-scientific result, for though it lacked a theoretical foundation it was arrived at by experimentation. Bessemer was not a scientist but a typical inventor, who knew just enough and not too much science and had a little experience of metals, but not in the iron industry. It is notable that neither the ironmasters nor the professors of metallurgy never proposed any such crazy processes; they knew enough to be sure that they would not work' (4).

The emphasis on development rather than research remains a characteristic of industry today. Most R & D expenditures in industry are on development rather than research (38) and development activities make the most significant contribution to advances in useful knowledge in the period immediately preceding the commercialisation of innovations (20).

However, within this framework, the role played by scientific research in changes in industrial technology is essential and has been growing since the beginning of the industrial revolution. The modern chemical, electrical and electronics industries can truly be described as 'science-based' in that their existence has resulted from the direct application of basic discoveries made by scientists like Lavoisier and Dalton, Faraday and Hertz; today they are the industries that undertake most of the basic research performed in industry (40). One USA study has shown that discoveries resulting from basic research activities typically contribute to practical applications after a period of 20 to 30 years (20).

In addition, a larger number of industries have become 'science-related' in that they make use of scientific knowledge in a supportive role, in deepening and widening their understanding of technological processes. Just as theoretical understanding of thermodynamics which came after the invention of the steam engine in the nineteenth century and contributed to its improvement, so two recent studies have shown the important supportive role played by scientific research in commercial development of innovations (18, 20). Most large firms now have R & D laboratories, even the traditional industries.

These trends towards the professionalisation and specialisation of industrial invention and innovation were already apparent in the late eighteenth and nineteenth centuries. Adam Smith spoke of the contribution to innovation made 'philosophers or men of speculation, whose trade is not to do anything, but to observe everything; and who, upon that account, are often capable of combining together the powers of the most distant and dissimilar objects.' (50) And de Toqueville later predicted that the industrialising countries would need large numbers of applied scientists, supported by a wide range of basic research activities (51).

This tendency towards a division of labour between innovative and conventional production activities has been reinforced by the introduction of heavily interdependent and of continuous flow production methods. It has also created its own dangers and its own requirements. The main danger is the isolation of the various subsystems of the process, as they become geographically and administratively separated, and as their members adopt different professional norms of behaviour. All recent empirical studies have shown the importance in successful applications of knowledge of effective coupling – within industrial firms amongst R & D, production and marketing, and outside companies with prospective customers and prospective sources of scientific and technical knowledge (49). In particular, the studies have shown that the interaction between science and technology is mainly 'person-embodied', resulting from people meeting each other and from changing their places of work (43).

[5] The remainder of this section draws heavily on the writings of Richard Nelson and his colleagues, in particular, references 13, 33 and 34.

Finally, the professionalisation of scientific research has meant that, although basic research results are normally published, they cannot be described as a 'free good'. The ability to locate and understand research results and to translate them into practice depends itself on the ability to perform research. This is one of the main reasons why large companies and utilities undertake basic research themselves and why, for example, Philips, Eindhoven, was able to reproduce the transistor effect one week after it had been originally announced by the Bell Laboratories in the USA. And Japan's success in importing foreign technology has been based on a strong, indigenous R & D capability (41). Thus one essential function of scientific research is the monitoring of similar research being undertaken in other countries. It is important to stress it now that the UK is no longer a major power in the world's R & D activities.

III Possible reasons for government funding of scientific research

Although empirical studies have improved our knowledge of the links between scientific research and industrial technology, and although many of them show the importance of government-financed activities, they give us no basis for evaluating whether the UK (or any other) government is spending too little or too much in various areas of scientific research and related scientific and technical activities. Given that the results of any piece of scientific research may be combined with the results of other research, and then with development, tooling and marketing activities, before it is applied, the attribution of any meaningful figure of economic and social benefit to past research is very difficult (5). Given the uncertainties about cost and outcome, the *ex ante* assessment of the costs and benefits of proposed avenues of research is well-nigh impossible. Nonetheless, it is possible to identify and discuss possible market imperfections, the correction of which may require government-financed R & D activities. As a general rule government intervention may be justified when for structural or other reasons, industrial firms are not capable of using science and technology efficiently and when there is a divergence between the private interest and the general economic and social interest (28). We shall now discuss the specific cases in which this may arise[5].

(a) Basic research as a public good

Governments finance basic research for reasons in addition to those of economic growth and international competitive efficiency. Economists have argued that there will be a tendency towards private underinvestment in basic research for these economic ends. Since it is uncertain if and where a specific piece of basic research will be applied, and since it will often be applied in combination with the results of other research, the system of publishing the results of basic research increases the likelihood that practical application will be identified. At the same time however, private firms will not as a consequence be able to pre-empt all the results of basic research that they undertake, so that without government funding there will tend to be underinvestment.

(b) Risk aversion, time horizons and oligopoly

In addition, since basic research (and some applied research) is a long-term and risky activity, industrial firms will tend to underinvest in such activities to the extent that their time horizons are short and that they have an aversion to risk. And dominant firms competing under oligopolistic conditions may tend to concentrate a disproportionately high percentage of their innovative efforts on short-term improvement innovations and product differentiation to the neglect of long-term, more radical innovations. Comanor has argued that this is the case in the USA drug industry (8).

(c) Technically backward management and institutions

Industrial firms may also tend to underinvest in applied research and develop activities related to their technology, to the extent that the institutional base of the industry and its management procedures became established before the potentialities of science became apparent. It has been argued that the organisational and managerial characteristics of each industry reveal fundamental differences deriving from the fact that firms in each industry were founded at different times in the development of organisational and managerial skill and knowledge, and that further evolution is slow (43). Thus, in the USA, research financed by the Federal Government has made a considerable contribution to improving the scientific underpinning of technology in agriculture and defence (34). Furthermore, as Cox has recently shown (10), there remains many small, traditional firms with no in-house R & D, and no contacts with external sources of scientific and technical knowledge. There may therefore be a case for a government-funded programme of research and exploratory development, and technical and managerial advisory services similar to those that have been so successful in agriculture.

(d) Inappropriate economic rewards and incentives

Some economists argue that tendencies towards short-term and safe R & D in some industries, as well as general technical incompetence in others, reflect an inappropriate set of economic rewards and incentives for innovation, and can be overcome by their manipulation. However, our manipulative power is very limited given how little is known about the way in which the various rewards and incentives – competition, monopoly, patents, profits and taxes – influence the industrial firm's propensity to undertake R & D and to innovate (45). This lack of knowledge is particularly damaging in cases where a country finds that certain of its industrial sectors have a poor performance by international standards in the introduction and improvement of product and process technology. It has been argued that this is the case for parts of the UK mechanical engineering industry (56).

(e) External costs

The market mechanism may not reflect the full social costs of existing or new technologies in terms of health, safety, pollution, amenity etc. Regulations and taxes may help internalise these costs and thereby induce industry-financed R & D and innovation to reduce them. But government-funded research will still be required in order to identify and assess costs, to monitor and enforce regulations, and to improve basic understanding.

(f) Knowledge imperfections amongst buyers

Empirical studies of innovation show that sensitivity to users' needs is one of the most important factors for commercially successful innovation; the results do not confirm the Galbraithian attack on consumer sovereignty (17), quite the contrary. But most of the studies have been in producers goods where the users have, in general, been large and technically sophisticated organisations. Such is not necessarily the case for consumers goods, or for goods sold to local government authorities. Government funded R & D may therefore be justified in order to provide or reinforce countervailing technical knowledge amongst such buyers.

(g) Risks to early buyers

Empirical studies of the diffusion of innovation (31) show that early adopters of radical innovations sometimes face considerable technical and financial risk, whereas later adopters do not. It can therefore be argued that government support for full-scale demonstration projects may be justified in order to ensure the rapid diffusion of radically different technologies, that are considered economically or socially desirable.

(h) Indivisibilities

These can be of two very different kinds. First, a large number of firms may each require small amounts of knowledge in a specific area, but not on a scale to justify a number of R & D programmes. In such cases, a commonly funded programme may be necessary. There is no ecomonic justification for government funding, but neither is there any reason for excluding government laboratories from seeking such work, especially when they have spare capacity and the requisite competence.

Second, Galbraith (17) and many governments have argued that the absolute scale of effort required for the development and commercialisation of certain technologies can only be mounted with government money, in order to develop the infrastructure of fundamental knowledge and of testing facilities, and component and equipment supply, and in order to launch commercial products and processes. Such arguments have been used in certain Western European countries (including the UK) to justify government support for the aircraft, space, computers and nuclear energy sectors (the so-called 'high technologies'). The supposed inadequacies in the private capital market implicit in the justification for government support for full scale commercial development has also been used to justify the establishment of government-financed institutions like the National Research Development Corporation (NRDC) in a number of Western European countries, in order to finance commercial development outside the high technology industries.

(i) Security of supply

Heavy government support for the high technology sectors has also been justified on the grounds that they concern strategic technologies that are crucial to the functioning of the modern industrial system (and to defence), and that it is therefore economically dangerous to become critically dependent on foreign sources of supply and on foreign technology, especially when these sources are capable of exerting monopoly power. Such arguments were prevalent in Western Europe in the mid-1960s when there was concern about the 'technological gap' between the USA and Western Europe (39). They have re-emerged in the past year in the wake of the oil embargo and the higher prices of energy and raw materials.

IV Targets and instruments in the UK

Before discussing in more detail the targets and instruments of UK policy in industry-related research, it is necessary to stress the limitations of what follows. In spite of our growing knowledge of the role of scientific research in industrial development, and of the progress made by certain economists in identifying the nature of possible market imperfections requiring government action, there remain large and important areas where we are still ignorant. In particular, we have very little systematic empirical knowledge of either the nature of market imperfections justifying government support, or of the effectiveness of the various methods of government action that have been tried to correct them.

[6]The establishment by the Federal Government of the Energy R & D Agency may change the USA situation considerably in the next few years.

Certainly there are strong theoretical and empirical grounds for government support of basic research; such support is given in all countries. Similarly, the institutional inadequacies for the performance of R & D in agricultural 'firms' has been widely recognised and effectively dealt with through government-financed R & D, and related extension services. However, the terrain is much messier when it comes to government support for civilian, industry-related R & D. In practice, the extent of this support varies considerably from country to country; in aggregate, it is relatively high in the UK and France, smaller but growing rapidly in Federal Republic of Germany, and relatively low in Japan, the Netherlands, Switzerland and the USA[6] (38). Economists have recently made important contributions to the debate about government support for the high technology industries, about which we shall say more later in this section. But we are on much shakier ground when it comes to the appropriate government policies towards oligopolistic industries concentrating on short-term, incremental innovation, to traditional industries without a research base, or to industries with poor innovative performance by international standards.

Furthermore, this author does not have detailed, first-hand knowledge of UK Government support for research and related activities. This means that the following description, analysis and assessment are concerned with broad trends. If they have any value, it is that of an outsider looking in, and that of an academic critic arguing why certain policy questions should be asked, and giving his own (inevitably subjective) answer to them.

We shall concentrate mainly on the scientific research and related activities of what was until recently the Department of Trade and Industry (DTI). But we shall first say something about the universities, and end up by discussing industry's own allocation to R & D activities. Government expenditures on university research amounted to £73m in 1969/70, those of the DTI on R & D to nearly £180m and those of industry itself to nearly £410m. These expenditures made up nearly all the civilian industry-related R & D expenditure in the UK (60).

(a) Academic research

Universities perform about half the basic research undertaken in the UK, and about two-thirds of that financed by the Government. It has been argued in the past that, from the economic point of view (a) the UK spends too much on academic research, (b) the university system tends to cream off the most able students and to leave the second best for industry, (c) scientists going into industry have the wrong, 'un-industrial' mentality, (d) links between academic research and industry are not strong enough, and (e) there is something badly wrong with British engineering education. However, such factual information as exists casts doubt on some of these assertions.

(i) As we have already argued, it is impossible to calculate what would be the economically 'optimum' expenditure on academic research in the UK. All that one can say is that, by international standards, it does not appear high. Indeed as a percentage of all government expenditures on R & D it is extremely low, and as a percentage of GNP it is about the average. During the 1960s and early 1970s, the growth of government expenditure of academic research was below the OECD average (38).

(ii) The tendency for the university system to try to cream off the best scientists is well-known, and its effects are likely to be all the greater when, as in the 1960s, the university system was expanding rapidly. However, neither the tendency nor the expansion was unique to the UK. The effects are likely to be less marked now that the university system is no longer expanding.

(iii) It used to be a common assumption amongst sociologists that scientists trained in the academic ethos would (in all countries) have greater difficulty in adapting to the ethos of industry (29). Recent empirical studies in the UK show that this is not in general the case (3, 14), although there is some evidence that industrial firms do not use the skills of scientists effectively (26).

(iv) The UK is one of the few countries where a detailed study has been made of links between the universities and industry in science and technology (9). It showed that the links were stronger in large firms than in small ones, and in chemistry, physics and engineering than in mathematics and biology. However, partial evidence shows that similar patterns exist in other countries (40). A recent OECD report noted the widely held belief that university/industry links were better in the Federal Republic of Germany than in the UK, but it could not find any systematic evidence to corroborate this view. Two OCED reports (40, 43) have argued together with Gibbons and Johnston, that good university/industry links depend mainly on the initiatives of industry rather on those by the universities. However, Langrish has argued that in industrial chemistry the contribution made by university research in the UK is relatively small by international standards (24).

(v) For a long time, UK policy was based on the assumption that higher education was not training a sufficient number of engineers. However, international comparisons by the OECD have led certain authors to doubt that this is any longer the case (39). Instead Fores and others have argued that, by comparison with other W European countries, the British engineering professions do not recruit the most able students, who do not receive an appropriate education, and do not achieve high social and managerial status and high pay in industry (16). Fores argues that the best way to remedy these defects is to increase the status and pay of engineers in industry. This situation may change as the increased numbers of engineers trained in the UK since the Second World War reach higher managerial positions. But there may be resistance in those parts of the industry that have traditionally had mistrustful attitudes to university-trained engineers (2).

Thus many of the criticisms levelled against UK Government allocations to academic research appear to be misplaced. The UK does not spend 'too much' by international standards. Many of the problems that have been assumed to be uniquely British problems are in fact common to many countries, and grow out of the adoption of different professional norms of behaviour as a result of the specialisation of the innovative function (see Section II). The one exception may be engineering, but even here – as in other areas – it can be argued that the main impulsion for change and improvement must come from the industrial more than the academic system.

Finally, it is worth noting that few, if any, critics appear to have asked how effective the UK academic system is in monitoring developments elsewhere in the world system. Ben-David has argued that one of the strengths of British academic science is that it is an integral part of the world system (11). Casual observation suggests that this may be true for the USA and other English-speaking countries, but that some UK academic scientists may have underestimated the growth of academic science in Western Europe (12).

(b) Scientific research and related activities financed by the DTI[7]

The Department of Trade and Industry was the largest single institutional spender on civilian R & D activities in the UK. In 1970–71, its R & D accounted for 48 per cent of all civilian government R & D expenditures, and amounted to about 44 per cent of industry's own expenditures on R & D. During the late 1960s, the R & D activities for which it was responsible declined as a proportion of total civilian government expenditure on R & D, but remained constant as a proportion of industry's own R & D expenditures.

The activities supported by the DTI cover a very wide spectrum, from basic research to technical information and advisory services for industry, and from R & D related to supersonic flight to R & D related to laundering. Table 1 below tries to categorise the different institutions and programmes in various sectors according to whether they are for financing scientific research and related activities or full-scale commercial development[8].

Table 1   Institutions and policy instruments for civilian, industry – related R & D financed by the UK government

Sector	Type of R & D	
	Basic and applied research, exploratory development and other scientific and technical services	Commercial development
Aircraft	Royal Aircraft Establishment (RAE) National Gas Turbine Establishment (NGTE)	Launching Aid
Space	Rocket Propulsion Establishment (RPE)	?
Nuclear	Atomic Energy Authority (AEA)	AEA
Computers & Automation	**Research Requirements Boards** Computer Aided Design Centre (CADC)	Launching Aid
Other Industry	Research Associations (RA's) National Physical Laboratory (NPL) National Engineering Laboratory (NEL) Warren Springs Laboratory (WSL) Hydraulics Research Laboratory (HSL) Harwell (Non-Nuclear)	National Research Development Corporation (NRDC) Launching Aid (?)

It is difficult to distinguish from published statistics the expenditures on these two types of activity. The First Report on R & D activities by the DTI in 1972–73 (61) describes in commendable detail scientific research and related activities but, with the exception of computers, gives no information on expenditures on commercial development[9].

Nonetheless, Table 2 makes some rough estimates of the distribution of DTI's R & D expenditures between the two types of expenditure. It shows that outside nuclear energy, just over one-quarter of the expenditures were for scientific research and related activities, and the remainder for commercial development. About 45 per cent of the scientific research and related activities financed by the DTI were

[7]These activities are now financed by the Departments of Industry, of Trade, and of Energy. They are considered together in this paper because most of the information published on them was collected when the DTI was still in existence, and because they are all related to industry.

[8]The R & D activities of the nationalised industries will not be treated as a separate entity. There is no reason why they should be treated differently from other industrial firms with respect to government-financed R & D.

[9]It is difficult to understand why this information on commercial development activities is not given. The sums of money involved are considerably larger than those described in the Report, and they certainly comprise large amounts of R & D activity.

performed in industry, as presumably were all the commercial development activities. Although no figures are available, the pattern is certainly very different in nuclear energy R & D, given the design and development activities of the Atomic Energy Authority (AEA).

The relative importance of the two types of activities varies considerably amongst sectors. Commercial development took 86 per cent of R & D funds in aircraft, and 71 per cent in computers. In both space and other industrial sectors, however, 60 per cent or more of the funds were spent on scientific research. Table 2 also shows the preponderance of aircraft in total R & D expenditures by the DTI, and the overwhelming concentration of expenditures in four high technologies. Only 13 per cent of total R & D funds were concerned primarily with other sectors of manufacturing.

As Table 3 shows, similar concentrations of government expenditures on civilian R & D in the high technology sectors exist in the other main spenders on R & D in the EEC. However, there are important differences by comparison with the UK. All three governments spend relatively less than the UK on aircraft, and relatively more on nuclear and space, as do France and Federal Republic of Germany on computers and automation. Other data show that the scale of government expenditures on civilian, industry-related R & D is bigger compared to industry's own R & D expenditures in France and the UK than in the Federal Republic of Germany and the Netherlands, and that a relatively higher proportion of these funds were spent in industry in France and the UK than in the other two countries (45).

Table 2 DTI spending on civilian industry – related R & D 1972-73 (£ millions)

Sector	Type of R & D			
	Basic and applied R & D exploratory development and other STS	Commercial development	Total	Sector as percentage of grand total (inc nuclear)
Aircraft	13.9 (14)	86.9 (86)	100.8 (100)	50
Space	7.8 (66)	3.9 (34)	11.7 (100)	6
Nuclear	?	?	49.2 (100)	24
Computers and automation	3.6 (29)	8.8 (71)	12.4 (100)	6
Other industry	16.1 (60)	10.7 (40)	26.9 (100)	13
Total (excl nuclear)	41.4 (27)	100.3 (73)	151.7 (100)	100

Note: Figures in brackets are percentages of sectoral totals.
Source: Reference 61, and UK submission to EEC.

Table 3   Comparison of Government spending on civilian, industry – related R & D in four countries (1971)

Sector	Country							
	France		F R Germany		Netherlands		UK	
	MFF	%	MDM	%	MG	%	£M	%
Aircraft	500	16	198	8	23	9	95	51
Space	638	20	516	20	45	18	12	7
Nuclear	1363	42	1224	49	108	43	50	27
Computers and automation	314	10	249	10	7	3	2	*1
Other industry	390	12	330	13	69	27	26	14
Total	3205	100	2517	100	252	100	185	100

*The discrepancy between this percentage, and that in Table 2 arises because of a new Government loan to ICL in 1972/73.

Sources: Reference 15, and UK Government submission to the EEC.

Given the terms of reference of this paper, this pattern of UK Government expenditures suggests three subjects that merit more detailed discussion: first, the balance of expenditures amongst sectors; second, the balance of expenditures between research and related scientific and technical activities, on the one hand, and on commercial development, on the other; third, the allocation of resources within scientific research and related activities.

(c) The allocation of R & D resources amongst sectors

DTI's expenditures on civilian, industry-related R & D activities are, like defence R & D expenditures, heavily concentrated in a few high technology sectors, which receive a much higher proportion of government R & D funds than they contribute to employment, output or exports. There is good reason for believing that R & D allocations by government should not reflect *pro rata* the economic weight of various sectors, given the considerable variance amongst them in the opportunities to exploit science and technology. However, even compared to the skewed pattern of industry's own expenditures on R & D the government's expenditures are even more skewed. And one can argue, on the basis of Section III, that government expenditures should be skewed in the opposite direction towards traditional sectors, in order to compensate for the institutional and historical blockages to putting their technologies on a more systematic and scientific basis. But the overriding economic arguments advanced to justify government expenditures in the high technologies have already been mentioned in Section 3, namely, large scale and security of supply. It is therefore necessary to examine more closely the validity of these arguments.

The scale argument is basically that the development of certain modern technologies is so expensive that the commercial capital market cannot mobilise sufficient funds to ensure the development; sometimes a supplementary argument is added that, by their very scale and sophistication, these government programmes lead to the general upgrading of industrial technique. However, over the past four years, these arguments have been questioned by a number of economists and political scientists, in particular by Eads and Nelson in the USA (13), by Cairncross (6), Jewkes (21) and Hartley (19) in the UK, and by Zysman (65) in France. Their arguments can be summarised as follows.

First, the commercial system in industrialised countries is normally quite capable of mobilising very large sums of money for civilian commercial developments:

witness, for example, the IBM 360 series, the Boeing 747, the investments of the chemical companies in new products and large-scale processes, and of the oil companies in under-sea oil exploration and extraction. Second, if commercial money is not forthcoming for full-scale development, it is usually because entrepreneurs do not think that the technology, the market, and/or the management is such that an adequate rate of profit will be made. Third, government money invested in commercial development projects will therefore either be a substitute for industrial money, or invested in second-best projects, given that governments are not in a position to make better guesses than industrial firms about future technical and commercial prospects. Fourth, once governments invest in second-best commercial development projects, it becomes difficult to stop them, because of public commitments and of political lobbies and pressure groups. Fifth, this will lead to good money being thrown after bad, and to a degradation of the public service, which then will become an advocate of commercially questionable projects. Sixth, it will also lead to the degradation of the commercial capacity of private firms involved in such projects who devote their resources and their skills to political lobbying instead of to production and marketing[10]. Seventh, the arguments that a low commercial rate of return is compensated by 'externalities' such as exports and the general upgrading of industrial technique (which are generally invoked in the later stages of projects as they come under mounting criticism) are spurious; there is no reason to believe that industry-financed commercial developments produce such 'externalities' to a lesser degree.

(d) The balance between commercial development and research and related activities

Nonetheless, Eads and Nelson (13) conclude that government does have an important role in financing scientific and technical activities related to industrial development, when the pace of scientific and technical development may be too slow from an economic point of view. They argue that there are several possible reasons why this might happen. For historical, institutional or financial reasons, private initiatives may not enable a technology to be put on a sounder scientific basis, or sufficient attention to be given to exploratory development activities to test the broad attributes of new product or process designs; alternatively, because of market imperfections, governments may decide that a new technology needs to be developed faster than the pace established by industry. In such circumstances, governments should support applied research and exploratory development in order to speed up scientific and technical development. By comparison with commercial development activities such programmes would be relatively cheap. They would cover a broad front and should be managed on an incremental, step-by-step basis, with the purpose of reducing key scientific and technical uncertainties to a degree what private firms can use the resulting knowledge to decide when (with their own money) they should move into full-scale commercial development.

Eads and Nelson argue that this approach has been successfully followed in the USA by the Department of Agriculture, by the National Advisory Committee on Aeronautics (NACA) in the 1920s and 1930s, and by the Atomic Energy Commission (AEC) in the 1950s. It has also been followed since the Second World War by the Japanese Government in shipbuilding (1). If Eads, Nelson and the other critics are right, the allocation of resources to R & D by the UK Government needs fundamental re-appraisal. We shall return to this subject in Section V of this paper. In the meantime, it is necessary to examine the other main argument advanced for government support of high technologies, namely, security of supply.

As has already been mentioned in Section III, it was and is argued that the high technologies are of 'strategic' importance to the UK, both for industrial and military reasons. Given that there are strong elements of monopoly in foreign sources of these technologies, the UK should develop and commercialise its own indigenous technology.

[10]The same argument has been made by the Permanent Secretary of the Ministry of Technology from 1966 to 1970: 'Once the company begins to determine its policy by what it has to do in order to continue to get money from government, its national value in the widest sense is already beginning to disappear: it looks to the department for guidance and for decisions, and the top management find it easier to seek the company's income by bringing pressure to bear on the department instead of by developing the competitive power of the business.' (7).

126

The critical importance of these technologies cannot be denied. Nor can the fact of monopoly power. The US Government holds it in relation to military equipment, nuclear fuels, nuclear power reactors, and commercial application satellites. IBM holds it in computers. The oil producing countries have begun to exert it over the past year, and it is feared that other producers of primary commodities will learn from their experience. This means that policies designed to 'optimise' the UKs' contribution to new technology within the framework of a perfect world market would be wrong, even if it could be translated into operational terms. Hedging against monopoly risks must inevitably be a part of UK policy, and is likely to cost more than an 'optimum' policy.

However, these considerations do not justify continuing and complete reliance on indigenous technology. Technological autarky even in a few selected areas is bound to be expensive for a country controlling no more than 10 per cent of the world's scientific and technical resources. A decision to become or remain autarkic assumes that the risks of abuse of monopoly power are high, and are likely to remain so, once the indigenous technology has been commercialised. It also assumes that there are no intermediate policies between complete dependence and complete autarky.

Neither of these assumptions are justified. First, monopoly and other risks may be real, but just how big they are depends to a large degree on subjective judgement. And the experience of the past thirty years shows that, over the lifetime of large-scale projects, the technical, economic and political factors that led to their initiation can change considerably: see for example, the Manhattan and Apollo projects in the USA, the UK atomic energy programmes in the 1950s and 1960s, the European space programme in the 1960s, and the Concorde. This suggests at least that policy and project planning should from the beginning be an incremental, step-by-step process, with continuous review of internal progress amd external factors, rather than a long-term (seemingly) irreversible commitment with inevitable and often agonising re-appraisals when circumstances change.

Second, there are policies that can be intermediate between complete dependence and complete autarky, for example, policies supporting applied research and exploratory development, designed to have the basic technology 'on the shelf' for eventual use without going into full-scale development and production. The extent to which such a policy is realistic depends on the size of the risk, and the time delays and technical uncertainties between having the basic technology 'on the shelf', and getting it into full-scale production. But these factors must be weighed against the costs of immediate full-scale development. And there are examples of industrial companies which have consciously adopted such an intermediate policy.

Few people would deny the pervasive influence of solid state electronics and the computer in the economy in general and in the electronics and electrical equipment sectors in particular. Yet in the face of stiff competition, two large US companies (GE and RCA), and one large British company (GEC) in the electrical industry have stopped full-scale development and production in many areas of electronic components and computers. Instead, they are maintaining an in-house R & D capability in order to follow external developments, to evaluate alternative external sources of supply, to assess the implications for future products and equipment of present developments, and – if necessary – to move into production should monopoly power be exerted, or should a profitable commercial opportunity re-emerge.

To sum up, an incremental policy, treating R & D as a technical overhead or as an insurance policy instead, as the basis for full-scale commercial development may be both a cheaper and a more realistic policy[11]. Once again, it suggests a strong emphasis on research and exploratory development compared to full-scale com-

[11] For an example of such a policy in practice in the Netherlands, see reference 35.

mercial development[12]. We shall return to this point in Section V of the paper. In the meantime, we shall look in a little more detail at UK policy towards the funding of research and related activities.

(e) The allocation of resources to scientific research and related activities

To an outsider like this author, it is a puzzling but significant fact that, over the past two to three years, the procedures for reviewing recording and publicising the management and control of government-funded scientific research and development appears – with the exception of nuclear energy, – to have been much better developed outside the high technology sectors than in relation to the much higher expenditures that these technologies entail. The Rothschild Report took a cold hard look at the Agricultural and Medical Research Councils (59). The Research Requirements Boards were established in the DTI, but they do not cover aerospace, which accounts for about half of DTI's non-nuclear research and related activities (62). And the DTI's *Report on Research and Development,* 1972–73 has very detailed information on all the laboratories under its control, except those doing aerospace research (61).

Nonetheless, the information that is given shows that, by contrast with other government laboratories, those dealing with aerospace have not succeeded in generating any significant contract income from industrial firms. Presumably, it cannot be argued that these laboratories are serving technically backward clients, and this lack of income must be contrasted with the success of the Harwell laboratories in obtaining income from non-nuclear work. We shall return to this point in Section V of the paper. In the meantime, we shall examine two aspects of the DTI's research and related activities: the work of the Research Requirements Boards, and the activities of the Industrial Research Associations.

Eight Research Requirements Boards were established in the DTI in 1973, all outside the aerospace and nuclear fields. Their terms of reference are: '(a) to help the Government identify those areas which will most benefit by R & D support by the Department of Industry. (b) to determine the objectives and balance of research and development programmes to support departmental policies within the broad allocation of funds available to them' (62).

The preoccupation of the Boards are reflected in many of the points raised in Sections II and III of this paper. All the Boards accept the need to develop explicit strategies and criteria for government support. The Chemicals and Minerals Board has compiled an 'output budget', in which it has categorised the expenditures for which it is responsible according to broad technical functions, and from which it concluded that insufficient attention is being devoted to scrap and waste recovery. At the same time, many Boards would like to see more rigorous cost/benefit analyses of the contribution of the proposed programmes to the national economy, and some suggest formal forecasts of future industrial and national needs towards the fulfilment of which research programmes should be directed. However, the Ship and Marine Technology Board stresses the need for flexibility in fixing priorities given that circumstances change. And the Computers, Systems and Electronics Board stresses the need to clarify 'the roles of government, the Requirements Boards and the Industrial Research Establishments in relation to R & D undertaken in industry, and to distinguish between areas of work where industry can be expected to take the necessary action and those where government action is needed, either directly or in a coordinating role' (62).

In fact, from the decisions made by the Boards, a high degree of consensus emerges in relation to two areas for government action, mentioned in Section III above. First, they all accept the 'indivisibilities' argument for research in government establishments in areas where a large number of firms can each benefit a little from a

[12]It is sometimes argued that government support for civilian, industry-related R & D should be given in order to enable industrial companies to profit from, or to amortise, the capability to development and produce sophisticated defence equipment. Three objections can be raised against such an argument. First, if civilian developments are being financed for defence purposes, they should be financed through the Ministry of Defence. Second, it is far from certain that diversification from defence to civilian markets is either necessary or practicable: SAAB in Sweden and Dassault in France have successfully concentrated on military aircraft; indeed Dassault is now in difficulties because of an unsuccessful diversification into large civil aircraft; and US aerospace companies did not succeed in building good high-speed trains. Third, it can be argued that a capability to produce military equipment can be maintained even if industry's R & D is concentrated mainly on civilian goods. In 1940, little military R & D was performed in the USA, yet it quickly became the 'arsenal of democracy' and in five years developed the atomic bomb. And today nobody doubts Japan's technical ability to produce nuclear weapons, even though the level of government support for military R & D is small.

common research programme. They also believe that the government programme will be more responsive to user needs if the users have to pay themselves. Furthermore, one Board encourages the association of foreign firms with the programme; this seems a desirable policy, since it would increase revenue, and could provide a means of assessing the degree of technical awareness of UK companies by comparison with their foreign counterparts.

Second, many Boards accept explicitly the Government's role in financing research beyond the time horizons for commercial decisions of industrial firms. However, one Board was concerned about financing scientifically interesting work, the precise industrial significance of which was hard to assess, and many Boards seemed anxious to ensure that long-term projects did not continue beyond the point where industry should take over responsibility for further developments.

In relation to two further reasons for government intervention, mentioned in **Section III** of the paper, the Boards' positions are far less clear. Some Boards accept responsibilities for dealing with programmes contributing to objectives other than economic growth and international competitiveness (eg scrap and waste recovery, marine safety), whereas others do not (eg desalination, dental tribology). In addition, the Boards gave very little attention to sectors or firms where, for institutional or historical reasons, the technical awareness of management needs to be improved.

To what extent to the activities of the research associations (the RA's)[13] compensate for these deficiencies? Their expenditures amount to about 2 per cent of industry's total expenditures on R & D, and about one third of their money comes from Government. This Government contribution amounts to about 7 per cent of all DTI's expenditures on non-nuclear research and related activities, and about 18 per cent of such expenditures outside aerospace and computers.

Unlike the remainder of government-financed, industry-related R & D, the research associations' activities are not overwhelmingly concentrated in the high technology industries or, more generally, the research intensive industries: 80 per cent of their expenditures are in sectors other than aerospace, electrical and chemical. Johnson has recently shown that the relative importance of the RA's in an industry's total R & D increases as the R & D intensity of the sector decreases (22).

Similarly, unlike the remainder of government financed R & D, the RA's are not heavily weighted towards development activities: 80 per cent of their R & D is basic and applied research, and all of them spend a significant proportion of their resources on information and advisory services, and on user education (22). As might be expected from such a pattern, their main contribution is not to the commercial development of new products, but to understanding, improving and upgrading process technology, to improving the technical awareness of management, to diffusing known technology to a wider number of firms, and in certain cases to health and safety (22). Over the past ten years, the purely cooperative aspect of their activities has declined relative to contract research done for specific clients. It can be argued that such a trend reflects the success of RA's in improving the level of understanding of industrial technology, and in making themselves useful to clients in technically backward industries.

If this is the case, it can be argued that government should encourage the RA's in new directions: more fundamental understanding of industrial technology of the one hand, and the testing of new design and development concepts, on the other – in other words, a diversification out of applied research into basic research and into exploratory development.

13 The research associations have been established over the past fifty years. Their purpose is to perform research and related activities relevant to a whole industry (eg textiles), or to techniques relevant to a number of industries (eg welding). They are financed partly by the DTI and partly by industry and other sources. Their activities now fall formally within the remit of the Requirements Boards.

129

On the other hand, the RA's membership covers a higher proportion of large and medium-sized than of small firms (42). They have not in general been able to respond to the needs of the small, technically and managerially backward firms, that are not even members of RA's that are unable to use the information coming out of the RA's and that get little technical and managerial assistance from suppliers and customers. Clearly not all small firms fall into this category; some are scientifically and technically aware and highly innovative. Nonetheless, as Cox's study of firms with less than 200 employees has shown, they exist in large numbers. (10). The economic justification of government assistance to them is strong in theory, and Sir Richard Clarke has suggested an annual expenditure on technical information and advisory services of £10m. This is about 60 per cent of what the RA's spent in 1970, and more than three times the DTI's annual contribution to them (7).

(f) R & D and innovation in industry

Government-financed scientific research and related activities cannot replace the R & D and innovative activities of industrial firms; they can only reinforce and complement them. Their usefulness ultimately depends on the scientific and technical and managerial competence of industrial firms, and their propensity to innovate. There is room for doubting that the competence and propensity in British industry is satisfactory. Britain's relative decline in the export of capital goods is well known. In addition, UK industry has the slowest rate of growth of industry-financed R & D in the industrialised OECD area in the 1960s and early 1970s. By 1971, UK industry's expenditures on R & D as a percentage of GNP was 1.0, as against 1.1 in the Federal Republic of Germany and the Netherlands, 1.2 in Japan and 1.6 in Switzerland (41). Even if one assumes that R & D costs in the Federal Republic of Germany are double those of the UK at today's exchange rates, German industry's expenditures were already 40 per cent more than those of the UK in 1971-72.

It is important to understand the reasons behind this relative decline. Does it simply reflect the overall relative decline in the efficiency and volume of UK industry's output, given that industrial firms tend to plough back a fixed percentage of their sales into R & D? Or the fact that UK industry is leading the world in weeding out and cutting back on wasteful, prestigious expenditures before industries in other countries do? Or the misplaced application of the accountant's criteria to long-term and risky activities? Or the technical and managerial incompetence of UK industry? Or its lack of cash? Or insufficient pressures of foreign competition? We do not know the answers to these questions, even though an effective government policy towards industrial R & D and innovation cannot be formulated without them.

V Conclusions

Nonetheless, policy assessment, like policy decisions, have to be made, even with incomplete knowledge. We shall now make such an assessment, and some policy recommendations. Given the imperfect state of knowledge, both are bound to be subjective. Their purpose is to provoke m ore discussion and debate, and (hopefully) to increase our understanding of the problem. Some of the areas where more knowledge would be useful are mentioned at the end of the section.

(a) An assessment

Britain's main problems in developing a policy for industrial R & D and innovation has been the same as in other key areas, such as defence, the role of the £ sterling, and foreign policy, namely, that of adjusting both ends and means from those of an imperial world power to those of a medium-sized European power. The main aspiration of Government policy towards R & D over the past ten years has been to put the R & D that it finances on an economically sounder, more 'businesslike' footing, of greater relevance and use to industry. To what extent has this objective been achieved?

In order to begin to answer this question, it is worth setting out how industry itself is 'businesslike' about R& D:

'... the typical R & D strategy of the business firm is to avoid major financial commitments to untried ideas; rather, it seeks to obtain knowledge and thus to reduce the uncertainty surrounding the idea by investing relatively small sums in additional research. At each state in the process, the company spends money to generate the knowledge necessary for deciding whether to proceed or retrench. As the idea proceeds from design concept to laboratory experimentation to prototype construction to production of limited batches, the investment becomes larger, and is undertaken only if the evidence increasingly points to the probability of profitable production' (34).

'decision making tends to be sequential, ... and the key criteria in project evaluation change in importance as the project progresses. On the one hand, exploratory projects requiring few resources are decided between the researcher and his immediate superviser, and the key criterion tends to be "chance of technical success". On the other hand, decisions involving large expenditures are made by the firm's top management after obtaining information from the firm's marketing, financial, manufacturing and R & D departments' (45).

Obviously it is wrong to make too close a comparison between industry and government. Government is concerned with national economic performance and with political intangibles rather than with making a profit; and it is not operationally responsible for the commercial application of technology, whereas industry is. Nonetheless, there are three principles of good management of industrial R & D that can also be applied to government.

First R & D activities should be evaluated carefully in the light of the overall objectives of the organisation that is financing them. Second, programmes and projects should be funded incrementally, and the amount of money allocated at each step should increase as the technical and commercial uncertainties are reduced, and as time horizons become shorter. Third, decision-makers' attention should be concentrated on the important problems, and this will often mean the expensive decisions. It is this author's opinion that the targets and instruments of UK Government policy towards R & D has failed to adhere to these principles in the following significant ways.

(i) The objectives of UK Government policy have been wrong in two respects: they have concentrated spending on a few high technologies, and on commercial development activities instead of research and related activities
The UK experience over the past 25 years shows that the UK no longer has any comparative advantage in the high technology sectors. This results partly from bad management (for example, the UK aircraft industry's inattention to the factors governing airlines' decisions to buy new aircraft, see reference 30), and partly from the misallocation of resources by the Government (for example, to the Fast Breeder Reactor by comparison to the High Temperature Reactor, see below). But there are also important factors over which neither UK industry nor the UK Government have any control. For the past 20 years, the UK has had neither the technical nor the financial resources (nor the geopolitical ambitions) to keep up with the much higher volume of expenditures in these technologies in the USA; nor does it appear to have any pressing or unique needs or opportunities which justify on economic grounds any government support of commercial development of British technology in these sectors.

There is no reason to believe that a reduced government commitment in these high technologies will harm Britain's long-term economic performance, or the strength of its industrial technology. The experience of other industrialised countries shows no correlation between the scale of commitment to high technology and any measures of economic performance or technological quality. Indeed, a comparison between Japan, Federal Republic of Germany, Netherlands and Switzerland, on the one hand, and the UK on the other, suggests the contrary. One can argue that the opportunity cost of the UK commitment to high technology has been and is considerable, and that more attention and resources should have been devoted to improving industry's performance in the other innovation-intensive sectors of the economy, which have been the basis of most of our competitors' growing industrial strength over the past twenty years.

14 The evidence presented elsewhere in this book by N Gardner on Launching Aid supports this conclusion.

In addition, as Eads and Nelson, Jewkes and others have argued, the concentration of government resources on commercial development activities has not, on the whole, led to commercially successful innovations or to noteworthy external benefits. There have been specific successes but, as far as one can gather from the published information, no government programmes have sustained a commercially viable rate of return[14]. This appears to be the case not only in the high technology sectors, but also amongst the development activities of the NRDC. At the same time, promising projects outside the high technology sectors have faced considerable difficulties in getting Government money for relatively inexpensive applied research and exploratory development: witness the experience of British Rail with the Advanced Passenger Train (23).

Finally, the government-funded commercial development activities in the high technologies have not been very effective in ensuring 'security of supply'. In aircraft, nuclear energy and advanced electronics, many commercial development programmes have been abandoned or curtailed, with the net result of increasing dependence on foreign technology. Yet only with regard to commercial application satellites does the UK Government appear from published information to have given up the pretension of technological autarky, and to have concentrated available resources on sustaining an R & D capability (see Table 2, and reference 56).

(ii) The UK Government has not adopted an incremental, step-by-step approach to R & D policy and to project and programme planning
Clearly, R & D projects and programmes must be conceived within longterm perspectives, and within the framework of a long-term strategy. However, given inevitable technical, economic and political uncertainties about the longer-term future, there are considerable dangers in rigid and seemingly irreversible long-term commitments. For example, the full-scale commercial development of Concorde was agreed before reliable information became available on the economically critical lift/drag ratio of the full-scale delta wing in supersonic flight. The RB 211 was launched before the properties of carbon fibre blades were fully understood and tested. Similarly, long-term, ambitious programmes for the Magnox and Advanced Gas-cooled Reactors were launched, and both had to be revised drastically in the light of changing economic and technical circumstances. In some cases, it can be argued that the commitments to full-scale commercial development were too early and too big; and in some cases it can be argued that too little had been spent on applied research and exploratory development beforehand. The recently stated UK policy towards nuclear reactor choices shows a welcome trend towards incremental, step-by-step policy making. However, according to the principle practiced in industry that R & D expenditures should be smaller on longer-term and riskier projects, it is difficult to understand why the Fast Breeder Reactor is being funded at 12 times the level of the High Temperature Reactor (57).

(iii) To an outsider it appears that policy-making machinery, operating procedures and public debate have not been focussed sufficiently on the critically important problems

The Rothschild Report, entitled *A Framework for Government Research and Development* in fact concentrated its attention on the activities of the Research Councils, and specifically on the re-allocation of responsibility for 4 per cent of total government expenditure in R & D, whilst saying nothing about the rest. Two of the changes resulting from the Rothschild Report have been the obligation to publish annual reports on Departmental R & D expenditures, and the establishment of the Research Requirements Boards. Yet information on most of the commercial development activities are not included in the former, and aerospace activities are excluded from the latter. Furthermore, the customer/contractor principle appears to have been applied with far greater stringency to government laboratories outside the high technology sectors than to those within them. The RA's, which are mainly concerned with traditional industry, get one-third of their income from government sources. For the other government laboratories related to industry, over 90 per cent of income comes from government, and those concerned with aerospace earn much less in contract income relative to their total expenditure than the other laboratories do (61). It is difficult to find any economic justification for this pattern of government involvement in different sectors.

Certainly there have been significant attempts to analyse and debate publicly such major problems as the aircraft industry (54), technological innovation in British industry (56), and the organisation of the nuclear industry and the nuclear laboratories (58). Yet little appears to have been made to convert the aerospace laboratories to the customer/contractor principle. Little attention appears to have been given to government support services for R & D and innovation outside the high technology industries. And relatively few resources continue to be devoted to these sectors.

(b) Some recommendations
Given these apparent shortcomings in the targets and instruments of UK Government support for scientific research and related activities, the following changes are proposed.

(i) Government expenditures on commercial development projects should be considerably reduced over the next ten years. At the same time, programmes of scientific research and related activities should be reviewed to ensure that they give sufficient support to commercial development programmes, and to general technical and managerial awareness, in industry; and that they act as a reasonable insurance policy for security of supply. In particular, this would mean:

   (a) a considerable reduction of government support for the aircraft industry (whether private or nationalised), resulting from the reduction of funds for commercial development, and greater pressure on the aerospace establishments to seek contract research with industry, along the lines practiced at Harwell over the past six years. At the same time there may be a case for more Government support for (far less costly) exploratory development projects.

   (b) considerable reduction of government funding for commercial development in the computer industry.

   (c) a clarification of the respective roles of the AEA and of industrial consortia in the applied research, exploratory development and commercial development of nuclear reactors, leading to a clear definition of technical, financial and commercial responsibilities.

   (d) a revision of the terms of reference of the NRDC, giving it greater latitude to spend money on applied research and exploratory development, without the constraint that costs must be fully recovered from the commercial exploitation of such projects and programmes.

(ii) A more active policy should be followed towards Government-financed research and related activities directed towards sectors other than the high technologies. The nature of such a policy must depend on an appreciation of the shortcomings of present patterns of R & D, innovation and technological improvements in various parts of UK industry, and such an appreciation can emerge only from detailed review and study. Suffice to say here that promising candidates for immediate attention would be the mechanical engineering industry, and small, technically and managerially backward firms. Any revised policy would probably include:

(a) a revised and enlarged role for the NRDC, along the lines suggested above, giving increasing weight to the criteria of the technical entrepreneur and less to those of the accountant.

(b) greater government expenditures on the research associations: on longer term exploratory research and development, at one end of the spectrum, and on liaison and advisory services, at the other end.

(c) continued and eventually growing support for government laboratories outside the high technology sectors. Whilst the Requirements Boards are naturally concentrating in the initial stages on trying to ensure that the work of such laboratories is relevant to industry, it is to be hoped that their long term objectives are more than rationalisation. In particular, it is to be hoped that proper consideration will be given to longer term programmes where the specific applications of which cannot be foreseen, and to programmes likely to lead to social and environmental benefits.

(d) a reconsideration of how the Government's own purchases of equipment could be used to stimulate changes in technology which can be applied in the civilian economy.

In the course of implementing such a policy, some consideration may have to be given to the reorganisation of the government R & D support system. However, one must recommend very strongly against this being the primary objective of any revised policy. Too often in the past, there have been long and heated discussions on the reorganisation of UK Government machinery for R & D, with the result that the more important debate about objectives and resources has been neglected (53, 54, 59).

Furthermore, it is far from certain what the appropriate form of organisation should be. Should all government support services be grouped together, as proposed for the British Research and Development Corporation (BRDC), or as practised by the TNO in the Netherlands (7, 45)? The apparent advantages of such an arrangement is that it simplifies the process of government control, and that it can enable a more flexible redeployment of resources in response to changing requirements. However, strong control may mean lack of continuity in policy. It may also constrain laboratory directors to spend their energies lobbying in London instead of being of service to industrial firms. On the other hand, the flexibility of such organisations may be imaginery rather than real, if their various sub-components *de facto* remain virtually autonomous.

Alternatively, there is the Federal Republic of Germany, where there are a multitude of institutions and laboratories supporting industry: the Frauenhofer and Max-Planck Institutes, the Technical Universities, the AIF and the RKW, Government laboratories and semi-autonomous laboratories, some of which are financed by various Federal Ministries, some by Lander, some by private sources, and some by various combinations of all three (45). But although the system is apparently messy, impressionistic evidence suggests that the coupling between industry and these organisations is better than in the UK.

(iii) Decision-making and policy formation in the UK Government support for industry-related R & D should at the same time be more open and explicit, and more incremental. In particular:

(a) the excellent beginning made in the first Annual Reports on R & D in the various Government Departments – in making public information on expenditures, income, projects and decisions – should be extended to all DTI's R & D Activities, including the high technologies, as should the activities of the Requirements Boards.

(b) differences of opinion within the Government (and within Departments) on the validity and effectiveness of proposed and on-going programmes should be made known to the public, perhaps through statements to the Parliamentary Select Committee on Science and Technology.

(c) the more open debates about policy resulting from the two above changes should in itself cause decisions to become more incremental, since it will be all the more difficult to believe – or to advocate with apparent authority – that the longer term technical, economic and policies future can be foreseen with any accuracy. Such a tendency towards incrementalism should be reinforced by the Treasury's insisting that frequent reviews and 'break points' should be built into projects and programmes that involve potentially expensive and long term commitments, and results of these reviews should be published.

(c) Some unanswered questions

Many of the controversial conclusions in the above assessment and recommendations could be shown to be valid or invalid in the light of more detailed analysis on, for example:

(i) the history and effectiveness of UK Government support for the high technologies;

(ii) the economic effects of government funding of commercial development activities in industry;

(iii) the factors influencing the usefulness to industry of government-financed scientific research and related activities;

(iv) the factors influencing the propensity and competence to innovate in UK industry, particularly outside the high technology industries.

These problems are amenable to economic analysis. But there remain two important questions that remained unanswered, and where the skills of the political scientist and the sociologist, and the knowledge of inside observers, would be particularly valuable.

First, why have the high technologies consistently succeeded in pre-empting such a high proportion of government funds for industry-related R & D, not only in the UK, but also in other Western European countries, and in spite of severe and authoritative criticisms of such programmes[15]? One explanation is that high technology programmes are difficult to stop because of the slow rate of growth in the UK Lord Rothschild is attributed the remark that it is difficult to cancel Concorde with a million unemployed. Whilst it can readily be admitted that employment considerations have been, and should be, an integral part of government decisions about such programmes, and that redeployment is easier in conditions of faster growth, this explanation is not altogether convincing. Slow growth in the UK has not stopped considerable reductions in employment in the coal mines, on the railways and in the textile industry. At the same time, higher rates of growth have not stopped the emergence and maintenance of government-funded high technology programmes in other Western European countries.

An alternative explanation is the political strength and effectiveness of the high technology lobbies. But why should they be so effective? Other lobbies represent bigger constituencies, and presumably can develop the same political acumen. Why

[15]See for example, the criticism of overcommitment to aircraft R & D in the Brookings report on the UK economy (46); also the aspirations of the first Wilson Government (47).

does high technology find such resonance amongst decision-makers[16]? With their links to defence, to certain basic industrial requirements, and to exciting technical challenges, could it be – as Jewkes has suggested – that high technology is 'the last refuge of the enthusiastic nationalist'? (21) If so, does this explain why effective management and market structures have not, on the whole, emerged from past attempts at European co-operation in high technologies? (44).

A second related question is why Western European Governments seem to have become increasingly involved in supplementing the R & D activities of industrial firms, by financing commercial development activities, instead of complementing them, by financing longer-term, more speculative work. Is it because of the insidious influence of the economist, who wants 'hard' cost/benefit analysis, which inevitably leads to a concentration on short–term, low risk activities (or to spuriously accurate predictions of the long term)? Is it because of the natural tendency of the administrator to want 'concrete results' during the time span when he holds an R & D job? Is it because politicians are unwilling to admit that they cannot predict the long term future? Or is it because industrial management and the trade unions receiving Government R & D money prefer the illusion of long term security offered by big, seemingly irreversible commitments, to the initial uncertainties of incremental review and evaluation? These and many other questions remain unanswered.

[16]For a recent, brief and informative account of the French Government's involvement in high technology, see reference 64.

References

(1) W Al-Timini, 'Innovation-led Expansion: The Shipbuilding Case', *Research Policy* (forthcoming).

(2) E Ashby, *Technology and the Academics*, Macmillan, 1958.

(3) B Barnes, 'Making out in Industrial Research', *Science Studies*, Vol 1, No. 2 (April 1971).

(4) J Bernal, *Science in History*, Vol 2, Penguin, 1969.

(5) I Byatt and A Cohen, 'An Attempt to Quantify The Economic Benefits of Scientific Research', *Science Policy Studies* No 4, HMSO, 1969.

(6) A Cairncross, 'Government and Innovation', in G Worswick (Ed), *Uses of Economics*, Blackwell, 1972.

(7) R Clarke, 'Mintech in Retrospect', *Omega*, Vol 1, No 1 and 2, 1973.

(8) W Comanor, 'Market Structure, Product Differentiation and Industrial Research', *Quarterly Journal of Economics*, 1967.

(9) Confederation of British Industry, *Industry, Science and the Universities*, 1970.

(10) J Cox, *Scientific and Engineering Manpower and Research in Small Firms*, Committee of Inquiry on Small Firms, Research Report No 2, HMSO.

(11) J Ben-David, *Fundamental Research and the Universities*, OECD, 1966.

(12) L Drath, M Gibbons and J Ronayne, 'The European Molecular Biology Organisation: A Case Study of Decision-Making in Science Policy', *Research Policy* (forthcoming).

(13) G Eads and R Nelson, 'Government support of advanced civilian technology', *Public Policy*, Vol 19, No 3.

(14) N Ellis, 'The Occupation of Science', *Technology and Society*, Vol 5, No 1 (1969).

(15) European Community Statistical Office, *Etudes et Enquetês Statistiques*, No 2, 1971.

(16) M Fores, 'Engineering and the British Economic Problem', *Quest*, (Autumn 1972).

(17) J Galbraith, *The New Industrial State*, Penguin, 1969.

(18) M Gibbons and R Johnson, 'The Roles of Science in Technological Innovation', *Research Policy*, Vol 3, No 4 (1974).

(19) K Hartley, *A Market for Aircraft*, Institute for Economic Affairs, Hobert Paper 57, 1974.

(20) Illinois Institute of Technology Research Institute, *Technology in Retrospect and Critical Events in Science*, NSF, 1968.

(21) J Jewkes, *Government and High Technology*, Institute of Economic Affairs, Occasional Paper 37, 1972.

(22) P Johnson, *Co-operative Research in Industry*, Martin Robinson, 1973, also, by same author, 'The Role of Co-operative Research in British Industry', *Research Policy*, Vol 1, No 4 (December 1972).

(23) S Jones, 'High Speed Railway Running with Special Reference to the Advanced Passenger Train', *Chartered Institute of Transport Journal*, January, 1973.

(24) J Langrish, 'The Changing Relationship between Science and Technology', *Nature*, Vol 250, p 614 (1974).

(25) P Mantoux, *The Industrial Revolution in the 18th Century*, University Paperbacks.

(26) K McCormick, 'Models and Assumptions in Manpower Planning for Science and Technology', Sociological Review Monograph No 20, *The Sociology of Science*, Paul Halmof (Ed), September, 1972.

(27) P Mathias, 'Who Unbound Prometheus? Science and Technical Change, 1600-1800', in P Mathias (Ed), *Science and Society, 1600-1900*, Cambridge UP, 1972.

(28) R Matthews, 'The Contribution of Science and Technology to Economic Development', B Williams (Ed), *Science and Technology in Economic Growth*, Macmillan, 1973.

(29) R Merton, *Social Theory and Social Structure*, Free Press, 1967.

(30) R Miller and D Sawers, *The Technical Development of Modern Aviation*, Routledge and Kegan, 1968.

(31) L Nabseth and G. Ray (Eds), *The Diffusion of New Industrial Processes*, Cambridge UP, 1974.

(32) National Research Development Corporation, *25 Years of Service to Innovation*, Bulletin 41, Autumn 1974. See also, J Cain, *Stimulation of Innovation in the UK – The Role of* NRDC (mimec), paper given at Institut für Systemtechnik und Innovationsforschung, Karlsruhe, FR Germany, 15 May, 1974.

(33) R Nelson, 'The Simple Economics of Basic Scientific Research', *Journal of Political Economy*, June, 1959.

(34) R Nelson, M Peck and E Kalachek, *Technology, Economic Growth and Government Policy*, Brookings, 1967.

(35) G Nieuwland, *Choice and Balance: A Research Programme in Aerodynamics in Perspective*, The Eighth Congress of the International Council of the Aeronautical Sciences (1972), ICAS Paper, No 72-01.

(36) OECD, *The Overall Level and Structure of R & D Efforts in* OECD *Member Countries, 1963/64*, 1967.

(37) OECD, *The Measurement of Scientific and Technical Activities*, (Frascati Manual).

(38) OECD, *International Statistical Year*.

(39) OECD, *Gaps in Technology: General Report*, 1968.

(40) OECD, *The Research System,* Vol 1, 1972.
(41) OECD, *Patterns of Resources devoted to Research and Experimental Development in the* OECD *Area, 1963 to 1971,* document SPT (74) 12, 17th May, 1974.
(42) K Pavitt, *Government and Technical Innovation,* OECD, Paris, 1966.
(43) K Pavitt and S Wald, *The Conditions for Success in Technological Innovation,* OECD, 1971.
(44) K Pavitt, 'Technology in Europe's Future', *Research Policy,* Vol 1, No 3 (1972).
(45) K Pavitt and W Walker, *Government Policies towards Industrial Innovation,* The Final Report of a One-Year Feasibility Study (The Four Countries Project), mimeo, Science Policy Research Unit, November, 1974.
(46) M Peck, 'Science and Technology', in R Caves (Ed), *Britain's Economic Prospects,* Brookings, 1968.
(47) H and S Rose, *Science and Society,* Penguin, 1969.
(48) J Schmookler, *Invention and Economic Growth,* Harvard UP, 1966.
(49) Science Policy Research Unit, *Success and Failure in Industrial Innovation,* Centre for the Study of Industrial Innovation, London.
(50) A Smith, *The Wealth of Nations,* Dent, 1960.
(51) A de Tocqueville, *Democracy in America,* Oxford UP, 1946.
(52) TNO, *Innovatio Processen in de Nederlandse Industrie,* 1974.
(53) *Report of the Committee on the Management and Control of Research and Development* (Gibb/Zuckerman Report), HMSO, 1961.
(54) *Committee of Enquiry into the Organisation of Civil Science* (Trend Report), HMSO, 1963.
(55) *Committee of Enquiry into the Aircraft Industry* (Plowden Report), HMSO, 1965.
(56) UK Central Advisory Council for Science and Technology, *Technological Innovation in Britain,* HMSO, 1968.
(57) UK Atomic Energy Authority, *Annual Reports.*
(58) UK Parliamentary Select Committee on Science and Technology, various reports on nuclear energy.
(59) UK Government, *A Framework for Government Research and Development,* HMSO (Cmnd 4814).
(60) UK Government Statistical Service, *Research and Development Expenditure,* Studies in Official Statistics, No 21, 1973.
(61) UK Department of Trade and Industry, *Report on Research and Development, 1972-73,* HMSO, 1973.
(62) UK Department of Industry, *Reports of the Research Requirements Boards, 1973,* HMSO, 1974.
(63) R Vernon, 'International Investment and International Trade in the Product Cycle', *Quarterly Journal of Economics,* May 1966.
(64) N Vichney, 'Les Nouvelles Cathédrales', *Le Monde,* 5, 6 and 7 November, 1974.
(65) J Zysman, 'Between the Market and the State: Dilemmas of French Policy in the Electronics Industry', *Research Policy* (forthcoming).

The choice of targets and instruments for Government support of scientific research
K PAVITT

Comments by D R H Sawers

I agree with the basic argument of Mr Pavitt's paper: that the Government, when choosing areas for support, should seek to correct imperfections in the market system, especially by doing what the market fails to do at all. The difficulty in applying this criterion is that of judging whether the market is really failing. It is very easy to argue that the market is failing to support a project in the R & D field because it is taking too short-term a view of commercial prospects, when the project really has no commercial prospects. It is for this reason that I agree with Mr Pavitt that the Government's most appropriate role is in supporting projects which are not intended to produce commercial returns to the sponsor, but which will produce information of potential value to a number of users.

This analysis implies that present government policies for supporting research and development place too much emphasis on projects which have some commercial prospects. Mr Gardner's paper shows that much of the assistance given to such projects has been lost, perhaps because it is so difficult to judge whether the market is wrong.

It is also difficult to judge whether a project that is not intended to produce commercial returns is worth supporting for the information it would produce, so that switching policy in the way Mr Pavitt recommends does not avoid problems of judgment – about whether to support projects for which quantitative analysis is inappropriate. The decisions would have to be taken on estimates of external benefits which would be extremely uncertain, being based on judgments of the technical results of the work and of the commercial benefits which might follow. Such estimates could be little more than guesses, and could do no more than provide a framework within which the case for supporting research could be considered. Given the large numbers of individual projects which could be concerned, the scope for analysis would be very limited. Decisions would have to be taken largely for technical reasons, and therefore would be taken by the research workers and their immediate superiors. Government control over expenditure could then be only through an arbitrary budget for each research institution or area of research. There could be no objective method of establishing how much ought to be spent in each area, or on each project.

The danger of such an approach would be that the government laboratories, or other institutions undertaking research with government funds, could be inclined to adopt scientific rather than commercial objectives – as was true in the past. The danger would be lessened by setting clear objectives for the staff of government laboratories, which directed their efforts towards industrial needs; and by interchanging staff between government laboratories and industry. The criteria for success in a government laboratory should be creating knowledge that was appreciated by industry, not by other scientists.

Mr Pavitt's suggestion that the National Research and Development Corporation should be encouraged to support only the early and non-commercial stages of development raises the same problems of evaluation as would his suggestions for government support of research and development. The problems might be even greater, because the work would be nearer to the market; decisions would have to be made as to whether the market was wrong in failing to see the potential in an invention, and, if the NRDC did back the early development, as to when support should be withdrawn. If commercial support was not forthcoming, the NRDC could easily be led into starting to finance commercial development in cases where the market was right to leave the project alone. Mr Pavitt's policy would reduce both the expenditure and the expected returns of the NRDC.

Mr Pavitt's recommendations thus involve difficulties and risks for government decision takers, but have a compelling economic logic, and should reduce government expenditure for the support of research and development. While they would also reduce the likelihood of government returns, experience suggests that the projects governments support have poor commercial prospects. The actual loss might therefore be small.

Economics of launching aid

N K GARDNER

The author is indebted to his colleagues in the Department of Industry for their help in collecting data and in suggesting improvements. Responsibility for this draft is, however, his own, and the views expressed do not necessarily represent the views of the Department of Industry.

[1] the precise meaning of 'full recovery' is referred to later (pp 144-146).

Summary

This paper first considers possible *ex ante* approaches to launching aid from the viewpoints of the Exchequer and of the recipient firm, and from the stand point of national welfare. Having posed some questions which might be answered by a review of launching aid experience, it then looks at the history of UK launching aid since 1945, with particular reference to aerospace. Finally, it attempts to draw some lessons from that experience.

I Introduction – the theory of launching aid

Launching aid is a topic which sits somewhat uncomfortably in the company of a collection of learned papers on subsidies. The question of eligibility is, sooner or later, bound to arise. Historically, it is true (as I shall show) that the qualifications of the launching aid family as a whole to be recognised as subsidies are quite impressive. But there have been exceptions, and even if there had not, it would not be legitimate to assume that any particular launching aid proposal amounts to the same thing as a proposal for a subsidy. The idea of launching aid is that the Government should make a contribution toward the development of a new product, and that the contribution should be recovered in full, if the product is sufficiently successful, from the proceeds from sales. Since recovery of the contribution is conditional upon the success of the product, and since success cannot be guaranteed, some divergences between *ex ante* and *ex post* views of any particular case is only to be expected. It will be useful to start with an examination of some *ex ante* viewpoints.

The Exchequer viewpoint of a launching aid proposal might be thought of as having two dimensions:
    (a) the extent of the Exchequer's financial contribution; and
    (b) the expectation that its contribution will be fully recovered[1].

These two dimensions can be used as in Fig 1 (page 154) to define the field of possible launching aid schemes. Certainty of full recovery, which would make launching aid the equivalent of a secured loan, defines the upper boundary, and 100 per cent government finance, which would put the firm in the position of an agent, defines the right-hand boundary. The area between these boundaries and the axes of the diagram then covers all possibilities. There is a beguiling symmetry about this picture, which suggests to the mind that the central point is in some sense a neutral or desirable position. A 50 per cent government contribution has often been advanced as a recommended norm, and it has for some time been accepted that governments should not give launching aid without a 50 per cent or better chance of recovery; other than for exceptional reasons, concerning which Parliament should be informed. This simple picture of launching aid is in fact highly misleading, and the centre point of the diagram does not have the significance which has apparently been claimed for it. Since the main consideration determining the required government contribution is the financial position of the firm – a matter to which I shall return – the 50 per cent contribution line has no operational significance. And since expected value, not expectation of recovery, is the rational criterion, the horizontal dividiug line is also misleading. To illustrate this latter point, consider Project A below, for which, let us suppose, there are just three possible outcomes.

Project A

Outcome Z	Government overrecovery (+) or underrecovery (—) under outcome Z V(Z)	Probability of occurrent of outcome Z E(Z)	Product E(Z) V(Z) EV(Z)
1	+£10m	0.1	£1.0m
2	0	0.8	0
3	—£10m	0.1	—£1.0m
		ΣEV(Z):	0

For this project, it could be said, on the grounds of symmetry, that there is a 50 per cent probability of at least full recovery. Since the summation of the Bayesian products EV(Z) is zero, it can also be said that the central expectation is that the contribution will be fully recovered (neither more nor less). But for project B below, the situation is different: of it, too, it can be said that there is a 50 per cent probability of full recovery, but the mean expectation is an under-recovery of £0.2m.

Project B

Outcome Z	Over or under recovery V(Z)	Probability of Z E(Z)	EV(Z)=E(Z) V(Z)
1	£10m	0.1	£1.0m
2	£5m	0.4	£2.0m
3	—£4m	0.3	—£1.2m
4	—£10m	0.2	—£2.0m
		ΣEV (Z):	£0.2m

A sufficiently long succession of projects like project A would, if the expectations were unbiased, leave the Exchequer in balance; but if they were like project B, the Exchequer would show a loss. Project B would, *ex ante*, be a subsidy, but Project A would not. *Ex post*, the balance would depend upon the outcome which had eventuated, but it would not be possible to deduce from the *ex post* balance whether a subsidy had been intended. In relation to launching aid the term subsidy has a definable meaning only in terms of *ex ante* judgements. It exists, to coin a phrase, only in the eye of the beholder. As a policy instrument, launching aid thus has the disadvantage (or advantage?) that it is transparent only to the extent that the government view of the commercial prospects for the project in question is transparent.

Turning now to the firm's *ex ante* viewpoint, the essential feature of launching aid is the conditional nature of the repayments. If the project should go well, the firm might have to pay back more than it had received; but if it should go badly, full repayment would not be required, and if the product should turn out to be unsaleable, there would be no repayments to make. Thus the worst prospect which the firm could have to face would be the loss of its own contribution. The existence of a substantial risk of losing most, or perhaps all, of the investment in a new product does not in itself make a case for seeking launching aid, however. In some industries, notably the pharmaceutical industry, such risks are commonplace, but do not give rise to applications for launching aid. It is not the risk of loss which is relevant, but the risk of ruin. In the classical gambler's ruin problem, the risk of ruin is given by[2]

$$pr=(q/p)^{k/c} \qquad q=1-p\neq0.5$$

where q is the risk of losing one throw in a win-or-lose, winner-takes-all game in which an amount c is repeatedly staked; k is the amount with which the gambler starts; and, pr is the risk of losing it all if the game is played indefinitely.

The problem faced by a firm contemplating the launching of a new product is, of course, vastly more complicated than that postulated in this mathematical puzzle, and no such elegant solution is available. But solutions do emerge in the form of semi-intuitive rules of policy.

[2]A more sophisticated analysis appears in Chap 12 of *Executive Decisions and Operations Research* by D W Miller and M K Starr Prentice Hall.

[3]K J Arrow 'Economic Welfare and Allocation of Resources for Invention' in '*The Rate and Direction of Inventive Activity: Economic and Social Factors*' National Bureau of Economic Research, Princeton University Press 1962.

It may plausibly be supposed that such policy rules look beyond the risks entailed in launching a new project, that they are designed to be applied repeatedly without undue risk of ruin, and that they are as much concerned with the riskiness of the particular commercial environment in which the firm operates as with the riskiness of the project under consideration. The policy rule will in other words take q as given and set a limit on k/c, the ratio between the project investment and the financial resources of the firm. Under such a rule, a project which exceeds the limiting k/c cannot be financed by borrowing, it can be undertaken only if some means can be found either to reduce k or to increase c (which can conveniently be thought of as the firm's equity). Launching aid can be regarded either as a way of reducing the firm's investment k, at the expense of a reduction in its expected profit, or as a special way of obtaining a contribution to equity – special in the sense that the government takes an equity state in the project, not in the company as a whole. Whichever way it is looked at, it constitutes a service for which there is no direct private sector equivalent.

From the viewpoint of national welfare, launching aid may be regarded as providing a substitute for Arrow's 'market for commodity-options' and thus as a means of avoiding the resource misallocation which would result if firms in possession of the capacity to innovate were unable to do so because they were unable to bear the necessary risks. (It is not of course the only available substitute; risks may be shared by mergers or by project consortia, or simply by a share issue. This paper does not attempt a comparison of risk-sharing institutions.) While contributing, in principle at least, to allocative efficiency, launching aid may however reduce technical efficiency in two possible ways. The first is Arrow's 'moral factor' – the argument being that 'any device for the shifting of risks can have the effect of dulling incentives[3]. The normative corollaries to this observation could be stated as:

rule (a) the penalties to the firm of technical inefficiency should, as a proportion of the firm's investment, be the same as they would have been had there been no government contribution (and the same should be true of the rewards for efficiency); and,

rule (b) the amount of launching aid should be sufficient but no greater than is necessary to reduce the firm's risk of ruin to an acceptable level.

The second possible cause of technical inefficiencies would be the inclusion in the launching aid contract of clauses tending to motivate non-optimal decision-making. If, for example, the contract penalised the firm for cost over-runs but not for quality shortfalls, the firm's trade-off between cost and quality would be distorted. Legal obstacles to the abandonment of a deteriorating project might also distort decision-making. It is arguable that a sufficiently wide interpretation of rule (a) should avoid such distortions.

143

II Review of launching aid experience

(a) The questions

The above analysis of *ex ante* viewpoints for launching aid suggests that some of the questions to which answers might be sought from a review of the history of launching aid are:

    (i) was the intention to provide a subsidy, and if so for what purpose?

    (ii) was the amount of the government contribution necessary and sufficient to reduce the risks to the firm to an acceptable level?

    (iii) did the terms of aid tend to distort commercial trade-offs?

In asking whether launching aid is, or could be, an effective instrument for promoting economic welfare, it is convenient to take as a reference point a simplistic ideal in which the sole intention is to improve allocative efficiency by providing risk insurance, while avoiding distortions which would tend to reduce technical efficiency. If all of the cases available for review conformed to this ideal, the financial outcomes would on aggregate reflect upon the quality of judgment applied to the selection of projects. Since the real-world cases which we shall be looking at do not conform to this ideal, it will be necessary to take what account we can of what is known of departures from it. It will in any case be necessary to look at a sufficiently long run of cases to eliminate the chance variations which would be inherent in the results of any scheme of risk insurance.

(b) Aerospace launching aid: UK experience

The main source of historical information concerning launching aid is the record of government contributions to the development of civil aircraft and aero-engines.

The present-day equivalent of about £1,500 m has been contributed by post-war governments for this purpose, of which less than £150 m has so far been recovered. Table 1 (page 153) lists the 40 projects which have been supported in this way. (There could be some question whether the term 'launching aid' can legitimately be applied to the contributions to all of these projects; the term did not come into general use until the 1960s and it has not generally been applied to Concorde. However, the list has been framed to exclude grants and loans, and the projects listed have the common characteristics that recoveries by levies from sales had been provided for, and that something less than 100 per cent government funding had been contemplated – even for Concorde – when they were started. Thus, they all fall within the boundaries of Fig 1, by intention at least even if, in the case of Concorde, only marginally within.) Interpretation of the evidence provided by this list depends upon judgments concerning the policies being pursued by governments in making the contribution. In the early post-war years, for example, a convincing infant-industry case could have been made for supporting the industry, since UK civil aircraft development had ceased in 1939 but US developments had continued through the war. Projects may well have been supported during this period which were not expected to bring a commercial return. Again, in the period around 1960 the government of the day prompted a number of shot-gun marriages as a result of which 24 of the larger firms in the industry merged into four main groups. Some of the launching aid contracts awarded at this time may well have been in the nature of dowry[4]. And there is said[5] to have been a period in the 1960s when the needs of UK airlines were given priority over the prospects for sales abroad. The annotation (a) in Table 1 has been placed against all those projects for which factors other than normal commercial considerations are believed to have played an important part in the decision to give launching aid. The inclusion in this category of Concorde and its engine the Olympus 593, requires no explanation, but the two other 'international' projects the A300B and the M45H have, for somewhat less obvious reasons, been included. The annotation (b) has been placed against those projects for which the account cannot yet be closed because further receipts are expected. If the cate-

[4]This was said of the VC10 and the Trident 1 in evidence to the Committee of Public Accounts on 24 May 1971 (Q3309).

[5]This was said to be the primary objective of giving support to the BAC1-11/500 and the Trident 3B, in evidence to the same Committee.

gory (a) projects are left out of account, together with those projects for which the account cannot yet be closed, the list reduces to 14 and the balance sheet for these 14 is:

(1974 input prices)	Contributions £ million	Recoveries £ million
8 Airframe projects	78.5	38.4
6 Engine projects	76.0	52.5
Total	154.5	90.9

For projects for which there was no obvious reason for subsidy, therefore, recoveries amounted to about 60 per cent of contributions. (It is possible that this figure is biased by the exclusion of projects for which further recoveries may be expected, but unless future receipts from the three projects marked (b) but not (a) exceed £24m, the percentage will not increase.) From only one of the projects – the Viscount – has there been any substantial excess of recoveries over contributions in constant price terms, and in this case the excess was not sufficient to provide for a reasonable allowance for interest[6].

One of the reasons for the low recovery of government contributions was the formula used for recovery in launching aid contracts. In 1965 the Committee of Enquiry into the Aircraft Industry (The Plowden Committee) described the formula as follows

'Since 1960 there has been a standard formula governing the shares which the Government and the manufacturers receive from the proceeds of sales of aircraft which have been launched by joint finance. Where the estimated launching costs are shared equally between the parties (and a 50 per cent contribution from the Government is now normal) the 'margin' on each sale is distributed as follows:

(i) 75 per cent to the Company and 25 per cent to the government, until the Company's share of the margin equals their contribution to the launching costs, as estimated in the contract,

(ii) thereafter, 75 per cent to the Government and 25 per cent to the Company, until the Government's share of the margin equals its contribution to the launching costs as estimated in the contract,

(iii) thereafter, 50 per cent to each, until the Government's share of the margin equals its contribution to the launching costs as estimated in the contract plus 25 per cent,

(iv) finally, 75 per cent to the Company and 25 per cent to the Government.

(The margin in some cases a fixed sum negotiated in advance and in others a variable sum, is the difference between the production cost of the aircraft and the actual price for which it is sold.)

If launching costs are shared on other than a 50/50 basis, the recovery arrangements follow the same principle, adjusted to the ratio of the respective contributions.'

What the Plowden Committee did not remark on was that the formula operated in money terms with no corrections for inflation and that it did not provide for the payment of interest on the government contribution. The introduction in 1960 of a new policy toward launching aid had been announced to Parliament by the then Minister of Aviation.

In answer to a Parliamentary Question on 15 February he had said
'. . . Suitable arrangements will be made for the Government to participate in the proceeds from sales. The manner in which these will be shared between the Government and the firm will vary and will depend among other things upon the proportion of the risks borne by each.'

[6]For Viscount, it has been estimated that after discounting at 8 per cent pa levy payments recovered about 75 per cent of the HMG contribution.

145

Commenting on these arrangements in 1971 The Public Accounts Committee reported that

'The Ministry accepted that the sharing arrangements favoured the manufacturers . . . the decision . . . had been a deliberate act of policy to encourage them to embark on projects which otherwise they might not have embarked upon, and had taken into account that the manufacturers not only carried the risk of development costs exceeding the estimates on which launching aid had been based but also had to finance production. However, they had decided to depart from this policy and examine each future case on its merits.'

Subsequent reviews of launching aid policies have led to terms being offered which have been much less favourable to the firms. To judge from what was said[7] at the time of the decision to give launching aid for the HS146, more recent policy has been to put the Government on an equal footing with the firm so that the Government's contribution would be recovered at about the same point as the firm's.

[7]Reply by Secretary of State for Trade and Industry to a Parliamentary Question on 22 October 1973 which included the following words
'The recovery terms broadly reflect the respective contributions of the two parties'.

[8]eg Minutes of Evidence taken before the Expenditure Committee (Trade and Industry Sub Committee) Session 1971-72.

It has been a feature of most launching aid contracts that the amount of the government contribution has been fixed – calculated as a percentage of estimated, not actual, launch costs – so that any launching cost over-run has had to be borne by the firm. (Until 1972 the firm had also to bear in full any cost increases due to inflation but since then provision has been made for index-linking of government contributions.) This has been attributed partly to a Treasury aversion to 'open-ended commitments'. Levies on sales to recover the government contribution have also normally been fixed in amount – a percentage, not of realised margins, but of the margin estimated at the time of the contract – albeit with some provisions for review (here again an index-linking provision has been introduced since 1972). The government contribution has also been limited to a specified proportion of stipulated categories of expenditure: R & D, tooling and 'education' (which is the difference between the cost of, eg, the first 100 aircraft and 100 times the cost of the 100th aircraft), without any other contribution to production work-in -progress. Thus a 50 per cent government contribution has not necessarily reduced the firm's peak cash flow by 50 per cent: it could amount to more, but usually it has probably been less.

III   Analysis of aerospace launching aid – the answers to the questions

It is clear from the record that a net subsidy of over £1,300m at 1974 input prices (nearly £700m at current prices) has been given to civil aerospace projects since 1945. What is not obvious is the extent to which that subsidy was intentional, nor the extent to which it achieved its objectives. The analysis above does not conclusively answer the first of these questions since the amount of Exchequer loss on projects supported for largely non-commercial reasons may have been greater than intended; and there may, on the other hand, have been an intention to give a modest subsidy to projects supported for mainly commercial reasons. The recovery arrangements prior to 1972 certainly indicate an intention to subsidise, in that the probable outcome would, on average, have favoured the firm at the expense of the Exchequer. This and other evidence suggests that although a substantial part of the *ex post* subsidy may have been inadvertent, there was also (until 1972, at least) a substantial element of *ex ante* subsidy. Evidence given to Parliamentary Committees[8] supports this conclusion and gives some indications of the benefits which were sought in granting subsidies. Foreign exchange earnings seem to have been an important factor. These are fairly easily quantified because, except for a relatively small import content all civil aircraft sales are either exports or import savings. Since 1945, civil aerospace exports have amounted to about £4,500m (1974 prices) and there have been import savings of about £3,500m, a total of around £8,000m, of which about three-quarters came from supported projects. But the alternative position is very difficult to quantify. To quote a Treasury witness[9]

'Generally speaking, I think it is a fair assumption that in manufacturing industry, if this is what they were doing if they did not build the aircraft, the foreign exchange advantage of the resource use there would be not much less, and might be no less; but this is a very difficult question on which to make a judgment, and I do not think that there is a single answer to this one.'

And later the same witness acknowledged that as a means of saving foreign exchange launching aid had been unsuccessful:[10]

'I think it is probably right to say that the particular aircraft projects that have been supported are projects which if we were looking at them afresh we would not support – most of them, not all.'

It has frequently been said that maintenance of employment in the aerospace industry has not been a primary objective of launching aid; successive governments have accepted the Plowden Committee's recommendation that the size of the industry should reflect the amount of work it succeeded in obtaining. But in making individual decisions, account must inevitably have been taken of the transitional problems which would accompany any rapid fall in the industry's employment. The industry provides very little employment in assisted areas and experience of past redundancies shows that alternative employment has usually been obtained in a matter of months, but nevertheless the loss of output represented by unemployment and reductions of earnings (to say nothing of the social costs of unemployment and redeployment) must frequently have been a significant factor in the decision to give launching aid. Employment in the aerospace industry has fallen steadily from about 300,000 in 1961 to just over 200,000 in 1974 (an average rate of about 3 per cent a year) but the bulk of this decline seems to have been on the military side. Whatever the stated objective, it appears that launching aid can be credited (if that is the word) with maintaining a fairly stable level of civil aerospace employment. The maintenance of a civil aircraft capability in view of the expected growth of the world market has been cited as an objective, often in the context of European collaboration, but no estimates of the long-term economic benefits needed to justify this extension of the infant-industry argument have been made public. Technological spin-off has also been referred to as an unquantified benefit, but the concensus seems to be that 'there is something in this argument but it is certainly not a very decisive one[11].'

As to whether the amounts of launching aid were appropriate to the risks faced by the recipients, experience has been varied. Since 1960, three[12] aerospace firms have found themselves insolvent as the result of setbacks to projects receiving government support. After the last of these (the Rolls Royce collapse) it became accepted policy to look at the project in relation to the financial strength of the company before granting launching aid. It is difficult to say whether in other cases the amount had been too large or too small, but some light is thrown on industry attitudes to risk by a statement in 1973 by Sir Arnold Hall, Managing Director of the Hawker Siddeley group. Asked why his company had sought a 50 per cent contribution to the £80m estimated launching cost of the HS146 he replied[13]:

'. . . the company's liquidity . . . on the last report showed a £30m positive balance . . . and we have world wide facilities of over £60m which are free, and it is therefore quite right that in terms of cash the company could handle the whole lot . . . we felt that we must seek a partnership to avoid all eggs in one basket to protect the company's investment in growth in all other areas . . .'

Some two years previously, Sir Arnold had hinted[14] that he would be prepared to hazard only a third to a half of his shareholders' funds in the aerospace sector on a single project 'a hazard figure in the typically £10m region' (which amounted to only $7\frac{1}{2}$ per cent of the £130m which he attributed to the whole of the Hawker

[9]Op cit Q321.

[10]Op cit Q362.

[11]Op cit Q2489.

[12]Handley Page, Beagle and Rolls Royce.

[13]From a transcription of a Press Conference on 29 August 1973.

[14]Reference 6 Q1048.

147

[15]*Public Money in the Private Sector* Sixth Report from the Expenditure Committee. House of Commons 1972 Paragraph 264 Lesson 4.

[16]Government Observations on the Sixth Report from the Expenditure Committee House of Commons Paper 347 Session 1971-72 Page 5.

[17]this point is explained more fully in the Annex on page 155

Siddeley Group). The previously accepted norm of a 50 per cent government contribution had already been breached for Rolls Royce (the initial contribution to the RB211 had been 70 per cent of estimated launching costs) and other companies undertaking major new projects may need contributions in excess of 50 per cent. This is partly a reflection of the fact that the financial strengths of UK aerospace firms have not grown as rapidly as the costs of the projects they undertake.

Apart from any errors of judgment on the part of firms or of governments in the selection of projects, there have been a number of features of aerospace launching aid schemes which may have tended to motivate non-optimal behaviour. The favourable recovery terms of the 1960s are obviously a case in point. Taken on their own, these terms might well have persuaded firms to undertake projects which would otherwise have been commercially unattractive even if they had offered no threat of insolvency. The fixed-contribution arrangement, under which the firm alone bore the brunt of any development cost overrun may have provided a countervailing deterrent, but there is no reason to suppose that these two features worked together to motivate normal commercial behaviour. On the contrary, they might have been expected to lead to an excessive preoccupation with the immediate problems of the development programme, and a reduced regard for the saleability of the developed product. The more equitable recovery terms adopted since 1971 are free from one of these criticisms, but the principle of the fixed contribution has been retained in spite of a recommendation to the contrary by the Expenditure Committee[15], [16]. Numerous decisions have to be taken in the course of a development programme which imply a choice between restricting development cost, on the one hand, and increasing commercial attractiveness or reducing production cost on the other. The fixed-contribution system motivates non-optimality in such decisions by distorting the normal commercial trade-offs. The fixed-recovery system produces a further distortion; this time to the pricing decision. If the levy is a constant sum per sale, then a profit-maximising firm will treat it in the same way as a production cost, and price to optimise the production margin less the levy. As Fig 2 demonstrates (page 154), this will motivate the firm to increase the price from P_O to P_L and hence reduce the total profit on sales from its optimum level at AB to the reduced level at CD [17]. Other things being equal, the fixed-contribution and fixed-recovery systems might be expected to reduce the total value of the project to firm and government combined. These value-reducing distortions can only be avoided by fixing the government contribution as a percentage of realised investment and fixing the recovery levy as an equal percentage of realised sales margin.

With the benefit of hindsight and a certain amount of subjective interpretation, limited answers to the questions of Section II (a), as far as aerospace launching aid is concerned, can now be offered by way of summary:

(i) Although much of the ex post subsidy seems to have been inadvertent, there was, in the period 1946 to 1971, a substantial element of intentional subsidy. The main intention was to promote foreign exchange earnings but avoidance of transitional unemployment had an important secondary influence.

(ii) The extent of risk-alleviation was not sufficient to protect three firms from insolvency, but since the Rolls Royce collapse a much more cautious attitude is being taken.

(iii) The terms of launching aid contracts prior to 1971 provided an incentive to firms to undertake uneconomic projects. Current launching aid contracts still seem likely to motivate non optimal choices in the management of new projects.

The unstated question – 'what was the effect of launching aid on national welfare?' – is more difficult to answer because it requires a quantitative balance of a number of different effects. Taking the commercial effects first, it has to be recognised that some projects – notably the Viscount and the Dart engine – earned profits for the firms although the Exchequer took a loss. But, taking the assisted projects as a whole it seems likely that the firms also took losses. To establish a net welfare benefit for aerospace launching aid as a whole therefore, it would be necessary to find externalities sufficient to balance a total commercial loss of at least £1,300m.

On any reasonable estimate of the shadow price of foreign exchange, exports and import savings totalling around £6,000m which can be attributed to aided projects did not confer a sufficient external benefit, especially if account is taken of the foreign exchange earnings of alternative uses of the resources. But for launching aid, the losses of output due to transitional unemployment would have been greater – the employment rundown would have been perhaps twice as rapid on average and many times faster at times. But bearing in mind the numbers involved (say 100,000 over 12 years) the employment benefits do not seem likely to have been sufficient to tip the balance. It may be argued that when the future benefits of 'maintaining a technological capability' are taken into account, the policy of launching aid has been justified in welfare terms. This is, in effect, an on-going version of the infant industry argument; and it is, of its nature, not open to objective refutation. There may also have been other economic benefits, not publicly de-clared, such as the avoidance of transitional losses to the defence programme. And for some, there may have been intangible benefits relating to national morale and prestige. The overall balance must be a matter of subjective judgment, but the author of this paper is prepared to defend his belief that the net effect of aero-space launching aid has been a loss of national welfare. The evidence does not suggest, however, that a loss of economic welfare was an inevitable consequence of giving launching aid.

Projects which were supported on mainly commercial grounds resulted, as noted above, in comparatively modest financial losses (£65m in cash terms, or about £90m after discounting at 8 per cent) which might well have been justified by the external benefits obtained. But for the support given on non-commercial grounds, especially to the larger prestige projects such as Concorde and RB211, the picture would have been considerably brighter.

IV Other launching aid experience

Another major source of experience of launching aid is the National Research Development Corporation. The NRDC use the term 'joint venture' to describe a variety of different methods of financing industrial development projects, but among these the normal method is to provide a fixed contribution related to (frequently 50 per cent of) the estimated development cost, to be recovered with interest, if the project is sufficiently successful, by means of a levy on sales. Several hundreds of projects have been financed in this way, most of them during the past ten years; and over £20m (current prices) has been invested in joint ventures by NRDC, of which about £11m has so far been recovered. These figures do not of themselves indicate an *ex post* subsidy since they include projects for which further returns may be expected. Published cost information does not draw the distinction necessary for evaluation, nor does it provide estimates of future returns. All that can be said is that they indicate, on plausible assumptions, the existence of a probable *ex post* subsidy, without enabling any estimate to be made of its amount. (The NRDC is limited in its capacity to give subsidies by its statutory[18] duty 'to secure, in so far as can be done consistently with the fulfilment of their purposes, that the return to them from their activities shall be sufficient to meet their outgoings on revenue account, taking one year with another', and by the limitation to £50m of its long-term borrowing powers. But it receives a substantial licence income – £29m, current prices, over the past 25 years – from the patenting of inventions made in government establishments and universities, much of which is available for subsidies to industry, in addition to which it has accumulated a deficit of expen-

[18]Development of Inventions Act 1967 as amended by the Industrial Expansion Act 1968.

[19]Statement by M W Innes, Controller Financial and Legal Services NRDC in *25 years of service to invention* NRDC Bulletin Autumn 1974.

[20]Introduction to NRDC Annual Report 1970-71.

[21]NRDC Leaflet No 5. Finance for project development.

[22]NRDC Leaflet No 6. Information required for project assessment.

[23]Autonomics 1971.

[24]For example Rank Hovis McDougall who received a £500,000 NRDC contribution to the financing of a protein-recovery developments.

[25]*The Docksey Report:*
First Special Report from the Select Committee on Science and Technology. December 1972.

[26]'Government Support for Research and Development A Case Study' K Grossfield and J B Heath *Economic Journal* September 1966.

diture over income amounting to over £16m.) The NRDC undertakes to 'consider participation in the funding of any venture involving technological innovation, so long as the venture is deemed by the Corporation to be in the public interest and can demonstrate a reasonable prospect of commercial success'[19]. A former managing director has explained that 'A key factor is that the project should in some way be concerned with the public interest, for example by helping to promote or improve the nation's business or otherwise being of value to the community at large. Naturally the Corporation is particularly interested if part of the objective is to promote exports or to provide some product which would enable imports to be reduced'[20]. These statements convey a clear hint of an *ex ante* intention to subsidise – if only by way of a general predisposition to give technological innovation the benefit of any financial doubts – together with some indication of what are considered to be relevant externalities. In leaflets published for the guidance of applicants, NRDC makes it clear that it is interested in the financial capacity of the firm to undertake the project. Applicants are invited to state 'the reasons why the company cannot undertake the project from its own resources'[21] and the financial information sought[22] from applicants appears to provide a means of checking that the company has the resources to take its share of the risks involved. A glance over a list of firms which have accepted joint venture finance, however, seems to indicate that NRDC policy has not in this respect been entirely consistent nor consistently successful. One computer firm[23] went into receivership after receiving £500,000 from NRDC; and, on the other hand, NRDC financing of similar magnitude has gone to some firms with massive financial resources of their own[24]. One observer has reported[25], however, that 'there is no strong demand from the larger firms for government help in funding the development of particular inventions', noting also that there have been some exceptions.

The arguments used in examining the value of aerospace subsidies cannot be applied to all of the NRDC's activities. Aerospace R & D, in common with all other R & D, is in some sense concerned with the production of knowledge. But the aerospace knowledge-producer, unlike some others, is in a good position to appropriate that knowledge and to reap its benefits; an aeroplane is a very difficult thing to imitate. For some of the NRDC projects, the resulting knowledge would have been very difficult to appropriate; and since the knowledge-producer would not, without a subsidy, have had an adequate financial incentive, there would have been a misallocation of resources away from knowledge-production. The degree of appropriability – as measured by the ratio of internal to external commercial benefits is thus an important parameter in considering the case for supporting R & D projects. If the degree of appropriability is high, then the case must rest mainly upon the inability of the firm to bear the required risks on its own. If it is low, then the prospect of diffusion of benefits to other users becomes the major consideration. But if the degree of appropriability is low, launching aid is a particularly inefficient way of administering aid; in seeking to recover the contribution by sales levies, it is in danger of discouraging the diffusion of knowledge which is its prime objective. If there is a good case for supporting an R & D project solely on the grounds of the benefits obtainable from non-appropriable knowledge, then there are no rational grounds for attempting to recover the government contribution. To apply the launching aid concept in such cases amounts to making a contribution which provides more than the required incentive, and subsequently recovering some of the excess. Seen in this light, the NRDC's statutory duty to balance revenues against outgoings is clearly incompatible with a function of correcting resource misallocations by subsidising non-appropriable knowledge – and but for the fortunate 'accident' of a substantial income from the licensing of a single highly successful antibiotic, it as hard to see how it could have discharged that function.

The net welfare effects of NRDC launching aid would be very difficult to estimate. A study by Grossfield and Heath[26] showed that the benefits to farmers of a potato harvester developed with NRDC assistance (not launching aid) greatly exceeded the costs of development, even when the costs of developing an earlier unsuccessful model were included. But neither individual case studies nor year-by-year accounts of costs and revenues can provide a sufficient basis for an assessment of NRDC launching aid. What is needed is first an assessment of the *ex post* subsidy element in a wide spectrum of projects and, secondly, estimates of the benefits to manufacturers and users which resulted. Neither is at present available, but the records of NRDC should provide a rich source of material for enthusiasts of cost/benefit analysis.

The majority of other selective support to industrial projects has taken the form of grants, loans or equity participation but a number of projects have received government support in the form of launching aid or in forms akin to it. Government-guaranteed NRDC joint ventures have been used for some projects which the NRDC did not feel able to support on its own account, and direct launching aid has been given to a number of other such projects. Finance has also been provided for mineral exploitation and for ICL's new computer range on terms which made repayment conditional upon profitability. But none of the supported projects has as yet reached the stage at which an *ex post* assessment is feasible.

The lessons of experience

It seems that in most of the cases which have been reviewed, launching aid has served as risk insurance combined with some degree of subsidy, intended or inadvertent. The question of efficiency has thus been complicated by multiple, possibly conflicting, goals. Launching aid is unlikely to have been the most effective way of pursuing goals which were not specific to the supported projects – simpler and more direct instruments were available to promote foreign exchange earnings, preserve employment, or support an infant industry – but incidental benefits of this type have from time to time influenced decisions. Launching aid would have been more effective in promoting project-specific benefits, but these may not have been fully reflected in benefits to the participants in the launching aid contracts; the NRDC sponsored potato harvester yielded benefits to farmers, and the VC10 aircraft is said to have conferred benefits upon operators and passengers. It is unlikely, however, that benefits to travellers by way of reduced fares and travel times were among the goals sought in granting launching aid to aerospace projects; such subsidies to air travel must be classed as inadvertent. For aerospace projects at least, the efficiency of launching aid in attaining its intended objectives can be largely, though not entirely, related to the returns received by the participants. Correspondingly, the lessons to be learned are mainly those concerned with the effect of launching aid upon the technical or commercial efficiency of project selection and execution.

The commercial aspects of aerospace project assessment appear to have received scant regard in the early post-war years but they are nowadays given close attention. The lessons yet to be learned are probably those concerned with the handling of uncertainty, especially the uncertainties of development work and of oligopolistic competition. These problems are not peculiar to projects receiving launching aid but there is one aspect which might nevertheless be mentioned in this context. An outwardly confident and decisive attitude may be tactically advantageous, especially in an oligopolistic market, but there may be heavy penalties in carrying that attitude through into decision making for R & D work. It is in the nature of development work that the money spent on it buys information – or the reduction of uncertainty – and it can easily be demonstrated that there is much to be lost if information adverse to a project is not recognised and acted on promptly. If these penalties are to be avoided, the launching decision must be seen not as a once-for-all

151

commitment, but as one of a series of decisions whether to continue or stop. This has important implications concerning the relations between government and firm. It is important for this reason and in the interests of efficiency project management that the launching aid contract should be so drawn as to avoid creating conflicts of interest between firm and government or between firm and project. A fixed government contribution creates such a conflict and the arguments advanced for such an arrangement deserve re-examination. The argument that the firm is thus motivated to control costs should be seen as missing the point if the objective is profitability; and the argument that the Exchequer should not undertake an open-ended commitment should be seen as inconsistent with a desire to improve resource allocation by risk-sharing. Attempts to compensate for the consequently disproportionate risk-bearing during the launching phase by disproportionate margin-sharing during the selling phase merely carry this inconsistency a stage further and can lead to further conflicts of interest. This is not to say that margin-sharing must always be in the same proportion as that agreed for the sharing of investment cash-flows; if it is intended to introduce an element of subsidy then probably the most effective way of doing so is an offsetting bonus related to sales.

In many circles, launching aid has a bad name. It will be said that in view of its record this is hardly surprising. But the record does not show this to be for reasons inherent in the concept, and it can be argued that, properly applied in well-chosen circumstances, it could be an effective, if somewhat specialised, instrument for the promotion of economic efficiency. It does not appear to be an efficient instrument for the promotion of external benefits, however, and there is much to be said for a clear separation between launching aid as an instrument of risk insurance, on the one hand, and a subsidy system related directly to the achievement of specified external objectives, on the other.

Table 1

Government contributions to and receipts from the launching of civil aircraft and aero engines since 1945

(£ millions)

Type		Contributions to 31/3/74		Receipts to 31/3/74		Notes
		Current prices	At 1974 input prices	Current prices	At 1974 input prices	
Aircraft						
Shetland						
Sandringham						
Solent	1945	2.25*	11.7	n.a	n.a	(a)
Tudor						
Air Horse						
Apollo	1948	1.25	6.5	nil	nil	(a)
Brabazon	1948	6.45	32.8	nil	nil	(a)
Hermes	1949	1.3*	6.4	n.a	n.a	(a)
Comet 1 - 4	1956	10.25	38.0	4.1	12.2	
Ambassador	1951	1.85	7.6	.15	.4	(a)
Princess	1951	9.1	47.1	nil	nil	(a)
Viscount	1951	1.8	8.4	3.0	9.8	
V-1000	1955	2.35*	7.8	nil	nil	(a)
Twin Pioneer	1955	.05	.1	.05	.1	
Britannia	1955	6.4	24.8	5.1	16.0	
Rotodyne	1956	3.05	7.8	nil	nil	(a)
Argosy	1961	.1	.2	nil	nil	
Herald	1962	1.1	3.0	.05	.1	
VC 10	1963	10.25	27.1	1.05	2.1	(a)
Trident	1965	26.1	53.5	.75	1.6	(a) (b)
BAC 1-11	1965	19.05	45.3	3.3	6.1	(b)
Islander	1968	.05	.1	.05	.1	(b)
Jetstream	1968	1.2	2.4	.1	.2	
A 300 B	1968	1.15	2.2	nil	nil	(a)
H S 146	1972	1.25	1.6	nil	nil	
Concorde	1968	233.8	406.8	3.15	5.8	(a) (b)
		340.15	741.2	20.85	54.5	(c)
Engines						
Dart	1949	5.3	21.7	8.45	20.8	
Proteus	1950	19.45	72.2	3.5	9.2	(a)
Eland	1952	10.9	34.8	.05	.1	(a)
Tyne	1958	4.0	12.6	2.1	4.0	(a)
Orien	1959	4.75	14.9	nil	nil	(a)
Avon	1958	8.5	26.7	6.95	17.1	
Conway	1960	6.65*	15.9	5.85	13.4	
Spey	1965	9.9	23.7	6.6	11.2	(b)
RB 178	1967	1.3	2.8	.1	.1	
Trent (RB 203)	1968	2.5	5.1	.6	1.0	
RB 207	1968	2.0	3.8	.05	.1	
M 45 H(for VFW 614)	1973	6.6	8.6	nil	nil	(a) (b)
RB 211	1971	146.7	224.4	6.25	10.4	(a) (b)
Olympus 593 (for Concorde)	1968	178.1	297.0	nil	nil	(a) (b)
		406.65	764.2	40.5	87.4	(c)
Totals		746.8	1,505.4	61.35	141.9	

The date shown in the type column is about the mid point of the development programme.

(a) denotes a subjective judgment that motives other than the commercial success of the project in question were responsible for the contribution.

(b) denotes projects from which appreciable further receipts may accrue.

(c) The totals shown are incomplete: see text.

*Provisional estimates.

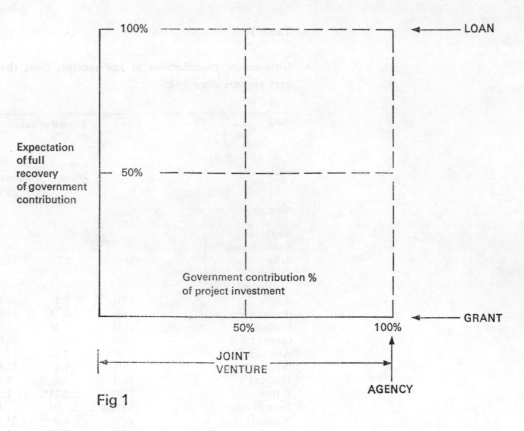

Fig 1

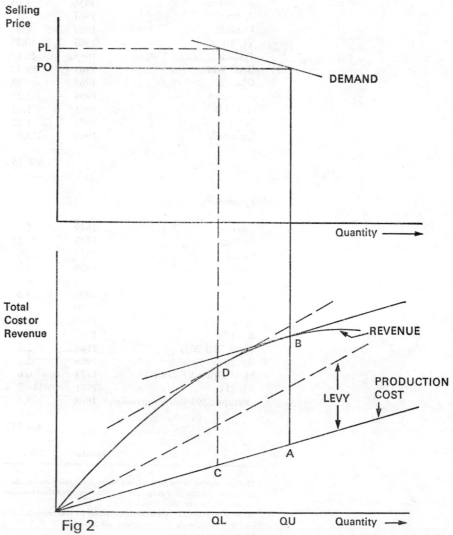

Fig 2

The assumptions underlying this construction are explained more fully on page 155.

154

Annex
The effect of sales levies on pricing

It may reasonably be assumed that a product developed with the help of launching aid will face a downward-sloping demand curve (many such products are sold in oligopolistic markets and some degree of product differentiation may in any case be expected). It can easily be shown that a downward-sloping demand curve as in the upper part of Fig. 2 will result in a convex revenue/quantity curve as in the lower part of the figure. A straight line cost/quantity curve implying constant marginal costs is assumed for convenience.

If the firm wishes to (and is able to) price its product to maximise profits, then it will choose a price which maximises the distance in the lower graph between the cost line and the revenue curve. This condition is achieved by finding the quantity Qo at which the tangent to the revenue curve is parallel to the cost line, and selecting from the upper graph the price Po which corresponds to that quantity. The effect of a levy of a constant amount per unit sold is indicated by the broken (cost-plus-levy) line in the lower graph. Profit maximising by the firm now means maximising the distance between the cost-plus-levy line and the revenue curve. The same tangency condition leads to a lower quantity QL and therefore a higher price PL. It is clear from the construction that the total of firm's-profit-plus-Exchequer-levy (denoted by CD) is lower than the firm's profit in the absence of a levy (denoted by AB). The imposition of a fixed sales levy will therefore reduce the amount available for sharing between the firm and the Exchequer. Also, since price will be increased and quantity reduced, it will reduce the consumers' surplus. This conclusion is independent of the shape of the demand curve (provided that it is downward-sloping) and of the cost line (provided that is not parallel to the revenue curve), but it is crucially dependent upon the assumption that the firm prices to maximise profit.

The alternative of a levy which is fixed, not in amount, but as a proportion of price can be explored by drawing a revenue-less-levy curve as a scaled-down replica of the total revenue curve and using the above construction to choose a price which maximises the distance between the cost line and the revenue-less-levy curve. It will be found that this type of levy also leads to a reduction in the amount available for sharing between firm and Exchequer. It is intuitively clear, in fact, that any scheme which is related solely to sales or to sales revenue will produce this effect; and that the only way to avoid it is by the sharing of sales margins (this is because margin-sharing alone avoids distortion of the cost curve or of the revenue curve as perceived by the firm). Sales-related objectives on the part of government (such as employment or exports) may justify some modification of the levy scheme, but such objectives would not be promoted by a sales levy; on the contrary a sales bonus, partly offsetting the margin-sharing scheme, would provide the appropriate incentive.

It can be argued that the profit-maximising assumption on which the above analysis is based is unrealistic; that, since under oligopolistic competition the demand curve facing a single firm is indeterminate, the concept of a profit-maximising price is non-operational; and that in any case most firms aim to maximise sales subject to a minimum-profit constraint. On the face of it, this argument greatly weakens the case against a fixed levy and in favour of margin-sharing. In practice, the disadvantage of a fixed levy scheme may not become apparent until the product approaches the end of its sales life when it may motivate the firm to cease production earlier than it would otherwise wish. Arrangements to reduce or eliminate the levy after a predetermined number of sales may avoid this disadvantage. But the risk-alleviating objective of launching aid is in any case hampered by an arrangement which leaves the firm with the residual after the Exchequer has taken a predetermined cut. Margin-sharing therefore remains the preferable method of recovery for a scheme designed primarily as risk insurance. The practical difficulty of distinguishing between those costs which are to attract an Exchequer contribution, and those costs which are to be allowed for in calculating achieved sales margins, can be overcome by arranging for the sharing in agreed proportions of all project cash flows whether inward or outward.

Economics of launching aid

N K GARDNER

[1]Peck, M J, 'Science and Technology', Ch.X, p 448-484, in *Britain's Economic Prospects* by Richard E Caves and Associates, Allen and Unwin.

[2]Maddock, Sir Ieuan, 'End of the Glorious Adventure?' *New Scientist*, Vol 65, No 936, Feb 1975.

Comments by C Freeman

Gardner's paper leaves little to be said on the experience of launching aid in the British aircraft industry, so that these comments will be mainly concerned with some of the wider implications of his analysis. The paper is an excellent factual summary of post-war experience in an important area of industrial subsidies. His data make it clear that we are dealing with subsidies and not with investment. Both the terms of recovery and the persistent tendency to neglect the market side of the process confirm this view.

The points which I wish to raise in this brief discussion are first, the wider consequences of this policy of subsidising aircraft R&D in the 50s and 60s, and secondly, the implications for industrial policy-making. Anyone who is familiar with the comparative international statistics on the industrial distribution of R&D expenditures knows that one of the most striking features of the British pattern by comparison with the German or Japanese pattern in the 50s and 60s, was the extraordinarily heavy British concentration on aircraft and the related electronics. Our R&D activities were overwhelmingly directed into products, where the principal overseas competitor was the United States. The nature of the US aerospace programmes, the size of the US military and civil markets, the scale of government subsidy and the US strategic priority made this an extraordinarily difficult area for British industry to compete in, despite the scale of subsidy revealed by Gardner's paper.

The German and Japanese R&D and related licensing programmes, on the other hand, were concentrated far more in chemicals, machinery, ships, electrical engineering and similar branches of industry, that is to say in product groups where their firms were in a strong position to compete on the world export market. The correspondence between normal commercial objectives and the relative scale of R&D activities was very much closer.

As Peck has suggested in the Brookings study of the British economy[1] and Maddock[2] has more recently argued, this suggests a wrong choice of priorities in the 50s and 60s. It is arguable in any case whether R&D subsidies are the most desirable or effective method of promoting technical improvement and efficient innovation in the private sector of industry. But leaving this point on one side (it is amply discussed in Pavitt's paper), the opportunity costs of the British policy must be taken into account. Whether or not there was a real, or only an apparent shortage of engineers and scientists in the 50s, and 60s, it is clear that a high proportion of the very best of these relatively scarce professionals were attracted in the post-war period away from the 'bread-and-butter' industries into the more glamorous aerospace and related technologies. The persistant lack of good engineers or indeed of any graduate engineers at all in some sectors of the British mechanical engineering industry in the 50s was the reverse side of the coin.

Gardner's paper does not discuss these wider aspects of aircraft launching aid and one forms the impression that at no time were they an important policy consideration. Clearly however, industrial R&D policy must be related to industrial and trade policy objectives. Perhaps the most important conclusion to be drawn from his paper is the danger of divorcing any subsidy policy from wider considerations of policy for the economy and for technology.

Unemployment, profit's share, and regional policy*

R MORLEY

*The author is grateful to colleagues at the University of Durham, particularly Professors Walter Elkan and D P O'Brien for many clarifications to the earlier draft of this paper, and to the participants in the Conference for suggestions which have been incorporated into the present version.

[1] A J Brown (1972) *The Framework of Regional Economics in the United Kingdom* Cambridge University Press, p 318

[2] Barry Moore and John Rhodes (1974) 'Regional Policy and the Scottish Economy' *Scottish Journal of Political Economy* vol XXI, No. 3, p 233

[3] North of England Development Council (1972) *The North in the Sixties* p ii

I Introduction

Regional policies in the United Kingdom have not been noticeably effective in reducing the disparity in unemployment rates between regions. Nevertheless, many students of regional policy consider that unemployment in the Assisted Areas would have been even higher without these measures. The consensus is that the policy package as a whole has been of some success[1,2,3]. Within the Assisted Areas there has been a shift in employment from primary industry to manufacturing and services, and from declining industries to the expanding ones. These changes are thought to have been encouraged by regional policies, and the problem remaining is to decide how much of this encouragement was due to investment in infrastructure, how much to Industrial Development Certificate policy, and how much to the various subsidies to industry.

It is difficult to get further in this debate without discovering what cures unemployment in the absence of regional policy. In Part II, we argue that a particular blend of investment cures unemployment. An appropriate aggregate measure of intentions to proceed with this type of investment is the share of gross profits in GNP. The predictive relationship is that an increase in gross profit's share in one year causes a decrease in unemployment the following year. A reduction in gross profit is a better predictor of increased unemployment than is a reduction in profit net of taxes and subsidies, implying that managers are as confused as the rest of us by the unreliable and complex nature of fiscal policy, so they treat taxes and subsidies as windfall losses and gains.

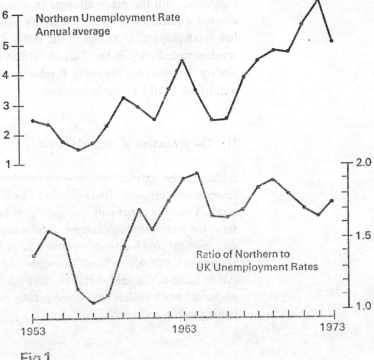

Fig 1

159

Part III extends the methods of Part II to the particular case of the North of England. This region shares with Scotland the highest unemployment rate in Britain. It has the lowest proportion of school-leavers going on to higher education, the greatest incidence of ill-health, the longest history of industrialisation, and the longest period of industrial decline. Broadly speaking, if regional policy works in the North, it will work anywhere. Figure 1 shows both the rising trend of unemployment in the region and the high ratio of Northern to UK unemployment rates.

Some regional policy measures, such as improved communications, can be expected to increase the effect of high national profit in lowering regional unemployment. Other measures, such as investment grants and Regional Employment Premiums, would be expected to reduce the effect of profit on unemployment. A comparison of the decade before the intensification of regional policy in 1963 with the decade after shows that the relationship between unemployment and profit has become closer rather than weaker, suggesting that the subsidies have been the less important part of the policy package.

In Part IV, the results of a survey of managers in the Northern Region is presented. These results illustrate the important distinction between the employment effects of investment in plant and machinery and those of investment in new buildings. Most of the managers find the regional subsidies unreliable and say that they would not have reduced investment if there had been no regional subsidies.

Part V discusses the relation between regional and national policies. An increase in gross profit's share of GNP reduces the unemployment rate in Assisted Areas by far more than in the congested areas. However, the regression lines are such that the ratio of one region's unemployment to another's stays constant. If 1969 figures are used, each increase in gross profit by £3,500 would have reduced unemployment by one person. This is the same sum of money as the estimate by Moore and Rhodes[4] of the cost per job created by REP. Since a transfer to profit is not a cost on the Exchequer, both the Exchequer and the community would have benefitted if profits had been higher and subsidies less.

The general impression is that the chopping and changing of regional policy, combined with the many changes in national policy over the last decade, have created a confusion and an instability which are not conducive to high profit and low unemployment. Although the provision by government of real goods and services to industry in the Assisted Areas seems to have been successful, the possibility remains that the main employment created by regional subsidies has been within the Civil Service in London.

II The prediction of unemployment

Although the national unemployment rate is one of the last indicators to react to economic changes, its prediction has become increasingly complex over recent years. Even for short-run forecasting, it has been found helpful to introduce a term for demographic change[5]. Explanations of longer run variations in unemployment involve female activity rates,[6] the secondary labour market,[7] the reserve price of labour[8] and attempts to estimate the number of unemployables[9]. All of these additional variables have been put forward with much important empirical work which has added greatly to our knowledge of what really is happening in the economy.

[4]Barry Moore and John Rhodes (1973) 'Evaluating the Effects of British Regional Economic Policy' *Economic Journal* March 1973, pp 87–110

[5]M J C Surrey (1971) *The Analysis and Forecasting of the British Economy* Cambridge University Press pp 66–68

[6]Barry Moore and John Rhodes (1974) *op cit*

[7]N Bosanquet and P B Doeringer (1973) 'Is there a dual labour market in Great Britain?' *Economic Journal* vol 83, no 330, June 1973 pp 421–35

[8]W W Daniel (1974) 'The Reality of Unemployment' *New Society* 19 Sept.

[9]Ministry of Labour (1962) *Gazette* February, April and September Ministry of Labour (1966) *Gazette* April and July

We now know that the length of time during which individuals remain unemployed will have a marked effect on the unemployment rate on any particular day, and this has encouraged work in the difficult field of 'search'[10]. The search theories were one of the developments from the criticisms that Clower[11] and Leijonhuvud [12] made of the 'Keynesian' paradigm: the 'Keynesians', by ignoring the effects of uncertainty on the spot market for labour and futures market for capital goods, were misinterpreting Keynes. The difficulties of measuring uncertainty in anything more complicated than a telephone line have led to its exclusion from most econometric analysis. The theoretical explanations of unemployment, as well as empirical investigation, continue to centre on some concept of excess demand.

The careful work of the Department of Employment[13] has shown that there is no consistent hard core of unemployment, merely an increasing resistance to employment as the unemployment rate declines. The various traditional categories of unemployment are ambiguous, and the numbers in each category vary with the stage of the trade cycle. It may be the case that poor schools, meagre health facilities and bad housing have created a larger proportion of unemployables in some regions than in others. In an area where the population is widely dispersed, there are more difficulties in matching redundant workers to jobs in new industries. Subsidised investment in plant and machinery may make technological unemployment a geographical phenomenon if the subsidies are confined to Assisted Areas. These are, however, possible explanations of high secular unemployment rates. They do not explain why the fluctuations in some regions are more extreme than in others.

Several hypotheses have been put forward to explain the wider cyclical swings in unemployment rates in some regions, based on the observation that regions with continuously high unemployment rates also have the widest fluctuations. Once unemployment has become high, labour hoarding can be reduced because the same man who was fired on the downswing of economic activity can be hired on the upswing. If the proportion of white-collar workers is low, as in regions like the North of England, there will be fewer workers with long term contracts of employment. Most important, some regions may have a predominance of employment in investment industries so that any variation in economic activity in the economy as a whole is accentuated in such regions.

The demand for investment goods produced by a particular region will be a national demand. Most regions still have a considerable amount of specialisation in production so will react to different extents to changes in the level of aggregate demand. However, an increase in aggregate demand may encourage both home investment and imports of finished manufactures, with increasing emphasis on the latter over the past decade.

This suggests a return to Kahn's hypothesis that home investment cures unemployment[14]. Unlike the era when the hypothesis was first put forward, there has been inflation over much of the past twenty years. The positive correlation between general price increases and general wage increases, and the negative correlation between wage increases and the rate of unemployment during the century up to 1966, led to difficult chicken-and-egg problems in the discovery of the causes of investment. The Phillips curve used unemployment as the independent variable to explain the increase of wages[15]. During the decade of work stimulated by Phillips' paper, the belief emerged that unemployment changes generally lagged behind other changes in the economy. Nevertheless, unemployment continued to be used as an independent variable as part of the explanation of inflation. As the original two-variable Phillips curve disappeared off the diagram after 1967, expectations were introduced to form a more complicated relation. Any trade-off between unemployment and inflation is now viewed as a short-run possibility

[10]E Phelps (1970) et al: *Microeconomic Foundations of Employment and Inflation Theory* W W Norton and Company

[11]R W Clower (1965) 'The Keynesian counter-revolution: a theoretical appraisal' in F H Hahn and F Brechling (editors) *The Theory of Interest Rate* pp 103–25

[12]Axel Leijonhuvud (1968) *On Keynesian Economics and the Economics of Keynes* pp 37–38

[13]*Department of Employment Gazette* (1974) 'Characteristics of the unemployed' March, pp 211–21; May, pp 385–9; June, pp 495–502

[14]R F Kahn (1931) 'The relation of home investment to employment' *Economic Journal* June 1931, pp 173–98

[15]A W Phillips (1958) 'The relation between unemployment and the rate of change of money wage rates in the United Kingdom' *Economica* Vol 25 pp 283–99

only[16]. At present, the long-run Phillips curve seems to be a vertical line moored securely on the 'natural', but unspecified unemployment rate[17].

Investment reduces unemployment, but what causes investment? A change in the aggregate of decisions to invest must involve profit, but most measures of aggregate profit have turned out to be bad explainers of investment in empirical work[18]. Nonetheless, the British economy is still largely a market economy, and firms are the prime movers of the market economy. If profit measures have not been able to predict investment, this may be because the wrong measures of profit have been used.

The individual manager will invest if he expects the rise in his revenues to exceed the rise in his costs. The expected increase in profits ensures the willingness to invest. Even if money profits increased in the last accounting period, the manager may decide not to invest because the trends in costs and revenues may be moving against him. No single price-deflator can correct money profits in a way which will reveal these conflicting trends in costs and revenues. Separate indices of movements in fuel and raw material prices, wages, and wholesale prices are still too crude to catch the way in which a particular firm is affected by movements in its costs and revenues. Each firm will be differently affected by externally set prices, and by internal decisions on quantities, efficiency and technology. Most previous studies have not shown higher profits leading to more investment because they have ignored the question of whether managers expect these higher profits to persist. If managers expect that costs are going to increase more quickly than revenues, they will not engage in capital formation.

There are severe difficulties in assessing an individual manager's expectations. The dominant cost increase may be an internationally traded commodity or wages or whatever, depending on the year and the firm's input mix. The dominant revenue increase may be due to increased quantities resulting from a recent investment, or expected price increases resulting from customers' demand. Predicting behaviour is even more difficult in times of rapid inflation, because the signals conveyed by a price-system in normal times become shrouded in static. The more rapid the inflation, the greater is the variety of price-adjustment functions between goods.

The way round this problem is to assume simple expectations on the part of managers. They expect costs and revenues next year to continue the trends that they displayed last year. However, the trends which actually were displayed last year can be measured in aggregate, because firms' costs are other incomes. In aggregate, an increase in firms' costs greater than the increase in firms' revenues means that other incomes have increased proportionately more than firms' profits, so the share of profits in national income has gone down. *Ex post,* the share of profit in national income is an indicator of the aggregate experience of managers, and it is this experience which forms the managers' expectations about the profitability of investment.

The argument is that an increase in the share of profits in national income will indicate an increase in investment, and an increase in investment will lead to a reduction of unemployment.

The next problem is to decide which expression of national income is most appropriate. Since the British economy is a money economy, the decision to invest must be backed by funds. Therefore national is more appropriate than domestic, because it gives a better indication of the funds available. Since capital consumption in the national accounts does not allow for obsolescence, gross is more appropriate than net.

[16] Dale F Mortenson (1970) 'A Theory of Wage and Employment Dynamics' in E Phelps (1970) *op cit* pp 167-211

[17] Milton Friedman (1968) 'The Role of Monetary Policy' *American Economic Review* March, pp 1-17

[18] M J C Surrey (1971) *op cit* p 34

The measurement of net profit is bedevilled by the confusion of taxes, subsidies and grants. The manager who understands these is more likely to be managing an 'investment trust' than organising real investment. The few experts who are prepared to share this understanding spend their time giving learned papers at conferences. In view of this, gross profit seems a more appropriate indicator than net profit.

If gross profit's share in GNP increases, this is an indication of the aggregate willingness of managers to invest. It is also an indication of their ability to invest because funds will be more readily available from internal financing, or will be more easily obtained from external sources. This is one reason why the gross trading surpluses of the nationalised industries should be included in gross profit's share. There is also another reason.

Gross profit's share is decided by relative prices. If more investment is desired, this has implications for optimal pricing policies in the nationalised industries. Because of the importance of flows of funds and of suitable pricing policies, the nationalised industries should be included with the company sector. This inclusion may be questioned on the grounds that government holds down the prices of the outputs of the nationalised industries when the retail price index is accelerating, so that the real value of the surplus of nationalised industries is inversely related to inflation. However, with large parts of some industries wandering back and forth between the public and private sectors, the inclusion of both sectors together has practical advantages for the analyst. The appropriate profit measure to indicate investment intensions is, therefore, the Gross Trading Profits of companies plus the Gross Trading Surpluses of nationalised industries, as a percent of GNP.

Part of the line of argument which we are developing is that an increase in gross profit's share of GNP encourages investment and hence reduces unemployment. However, there will be a time lag between the decision to invest and the consequent fall in unemployment. The decision has to be worked out in detail and orders placed. The investment industries have to discover that overtime working is not sufficient to cope with the increased orders, and that the order book is expanding by enough to justify an increase in the labour force.

When the time-path of gross profit's share is plotted alongside the time-path of UK unemployment, the lag between the peaks (troughs) of profit's share and the troughs (peaks) of unemployment is only one year. (See Figure 2, where the unemployment axis is reversed to allow comparison of peak with peak.) This seems too short a time for the effect of the investment decisions to work through into a reduction of unemployment. However, profit is reported well after the trading year has ended. Managers will recognise profitable trading, via the relative movements of costs and revenues, before the trading year is over. Although the observed lag is only one year, the actual lag will be longer than this because of delayed reporting of profit and because of managers' anticipations. The lag between the decision to invest and the creation of employment is perhaps two years. This seems reasonable.

The troughs in investment in plant and machinery lag one year behind the troughs in profit's share, but when managers seek rapid expansion of such investment, constraints on capacity cause order-books to lengthen, so the peaks lag two years behind the peaks in profit's share. Although the machinery may be used as a complement to labour for the expansion of output, it may also be used to substitute capital for labour, particularly when there is a marked increase in the relative price of labour. The main employment generated by investment in plant and machinery is therefore the labour used in the production of the machines.

163

Industrial buildings are complements to labour to a greater extent than are machines. New buildings are indicators of expansion, new processes and industrial change. Perhaps a better indicator of employment generation than investment in machinery is the per cent of GDP devoted to capital formation in non-dwelling new building and works by companies and public corporations. Although this type of investment is small, varying between 2.7 and 3.2 per cent of GDP, it is a reflection of the extent to which state and private entrepreneurs are prepared to undertake new ventures. Both the peaks and troughs of investment in new buildings lag the peaks and troughs of profit's share by one year.

An increase in profit's share is followed by a decrease in unemployment for two main reasons. Employment increases in industries which make plant and machinery, and employment increases in those establishments which invest in new buildings. Machinery investment creates cyclical employment. New industrial building does not just create cyclical employment in the building industry, but is an indicator of more permanent employment within the new buildings. (Illustrations of these different patterns of employment creation are given in Part IV.)

The hypothesis in terms of observables is that an increase in gross profit's share in one year causes a decrease in unemployment the following year. The hypothesis is tested for the years 1956 to 1972. This allows a rigorous test for autocorrelation. More important, this time span allows the testing of an alternative hypothesis.

The argument has been that taxes and subsidies are too confusing to be taken into account in investment plans, so they are ignored. An alternative hypothesis involves the more traditional measure, the share of net profit in national income. This view assumes that managers rationally, but costlessly, recalculate their plans in response to fiscal policy. Happily, the series calculated by G J Burgess and A J Webb[19] is available to test this alternative hypothesis.

[19] G J Burgess and A J Webb (1974) 'The Profits of British Industry' *Lloyds Bank Review* April 1974, p 11

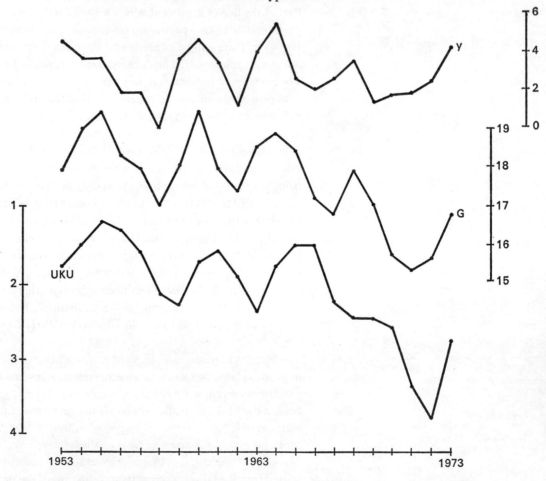

The rate of growth of real GDP (y), gross profit's share (G), and UK annual average unemployment (UKU)

Fig 2

Equation 1

G(t)   is Gross Trading Profits of companies *plus* Gross Trading Surpluses of public corporations and other public enterprises, as a percentage of GNP, in year t.[20]

UKU(t+1)   is the annual average percentage unemployment in the United Kingdom, in the following year.[21]

t   runs from 1956 to 1972

$$UKU(t+1) = 11.08 \quad - \quad 0.50 \; G(t) \qquad R^2 = 0.811$$
$$\qquad\qquad\quad (10.07) \quad (-8.03) \qquad\qquad DW = 2.12$$

[20]Source: Central Statistical Office (1974) *National Income and Expenditure 1963-73*

[21] Source: 1955 to 1961 from Department of Employment (1971) *British Labour Statistics 1886 to 1968* Table 168, 1962 to 1973 from Central Statistical Office (1974) *Abstract of Regional Statistics 1974*

[22] G J Burgess and A J Webb (1974) 'The Profits of British Industry' *Lloyds Bank Review* April 1974, p 11

The relationship explains 81 per cent of unemployment. It predicts well (the figures in parentheses are t-values). There is no autocorrelation (since the DW lies between 1.24 and 2.77, there is, unambiguously, no autocorrelation). The worst predictive performance of the equation was G(1968) for UKU (1969), and this suggests that part of the 19 per cent which is unexplained is due to the terms of trade. For most of the period, a decrease in gross profit's share by a percentage point is followed the next year by an increase of half a percentage point in the UK rate of unemployment.

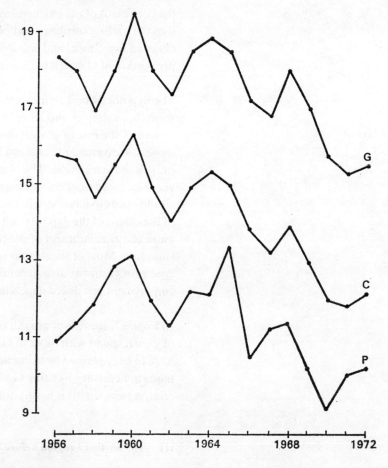

Percentage share: of GNP for G and C, of National Income for P

Fig 3

Equation 2

P(t)   is all companies UK income *less* stock appreciation, capital consumption, and taxes on income and capital, *plus* investment grants, as a percentage of National Income in year t.[22]

t   runs from 1956 to 1972

165

$$\text{UKU}(t+1) = 7.60 - 0.47 \ P(t) \qquad R^2 = 0.664$$
$$(7.70) \quad (-5.44) \qquad\qquad DW = 1.76$$

P explains less and is a worse predictor than G. Figure 3 shows that the timing of the peaks and troughs of P is not sufficiently different from those of G to justify a different lag in the relationship. The conclusion is that the explanatory power of P arises only because it is a constituent of G. Taxes, subsidies, grants and conventions for stock appreciation and capital consumption do not appear to be taken into account when decisions are made which lead to investment and the creation of employment, rather they confuse the relationship.

[23] Source: Central Statistical Office (1974) *National Income and Expenditure* 1963–73

[24] F W Paish (1968) 'The limits of incomes policy' in F W Paish and J Hennessy *Policy for Incomes* Hobart Paper 29, Institute of Economic Affairs

Equation 3

C(t)   is Gross Trading Profits of companies, as a percentage of GNP in year t.[23]

t   runs from 1956 to 1972

$$\text{UKU}(t+1) = 8.30 - 0.42 \ C(t) \qquad R^2 = 0.796$$
$$(10.48) \quad (-7.66) \qquad\qquad DW = 1.72$$

The explanatory and predictive power of C is only slightly less than G. However, the coefficient of the independent variable is smaller for C than for G. This suggests that the trading surpluses and pricing policies of nationalised industries have an effect on investment and employment which is considerable considering the small proportion of G which is accounted for by these trading surpluses.

The hypothesis that an increase in profit's share causes a decrease in unemployment seems both simpler and more fruitful than the current convention that both are caused by the rate of growth of real GDP. If real GDP accelerates, productivity increases are greater than wage increases. Because capacity is more fully utilised, profit's share increases. The GDP school argue that managers during the following year hire more workers as a lagged response to what they would have liked their employment to have been in the previous year[24]. The profit approach takes account of the extent of the gap between productivity and wage increases and provides a more accurate indicator of the resources available for investment rather than consumption. Most of the surplus is invested in fixed capital of varying types, with the type of investment also depending on relative prices, and the extent to which unemployment is reduced depending on the type of investment.

In Figure 2, the rate of growth of real GDP is labelled y. Although the turning points of y correspond with those of G, the secular trend does not. Unemployment would have to be explained by using both y and a trend variable, an inelegant complication made unnecessary by using G. We conclude that unemployment depends upon relative prices. This is hardly surprising, but the reminder can do no harm.

III   The northern region before and after regional policy

A relatively high proportion of employment in the North is in investment industries. Unemployment in the North is, therefore, more sensitive to changes in investment in the UK as a whole than is the case in other regions. If, as we are arguing, the main determinant of investment and hence employment is the share of profits in GNP, then the effect on the level of employment in the North of a change in gross profit's share, G, is likely to be greater than its effect on the level of UK employment as a whole. However, one would not expect the relationship between G and the rate of unemployment in any one region to be as precise as that previously discussed in Part II between G and unemployment in the UK as a whole.

We look first at the decade before the intensification of regional policy, 1954 to 1963, and the following equation holds few surprises.

Equation 4

G(t) is again gross trading profits and surpluses, as a percent of GNP, in year t.

NU(t+1) is the annual average unemployment rate in the Northern Region, in year t+1.[25]

t runs from 1954 to 1963

$$NU(t+1) = 17.70 - 0.82 \, G(t) \qquad R^2 = 0.514$$
$$(3.44) \quad (-2.91) \qquad\qquad DW = 0.49$$

[25] Source: 1955 to 1961 from Department of employment (1971) *British Labour Statistics* 1886 to 1968 Table 168; 1962 to 1973 from Central Statistical Office (1974) *Abstract of Regional Statistics* 1974.

In Equation 4, the coefficient on G of 0.82 is very much higher than the 0.50 for the UK as a whole, given in Equation 1. This shows that the North does react more strongly to changes in gross profit's share. However, the explanatory and predictive power of Equation 1 has been lost. More important, the relation is unstable over time. Figure 4 illustrates how higher levels of unemployment were associated with the same level for G after 1959. Throughout the decade, unemployment decreased after G increased, but after 1959 the effect of declining industries became noticeable. Between 1959 and 1963, these declining industries were not being replaced by expanding ones. Surplus funds were not moving into the region. Entrepreneurial ability was not combining with the cheap land and surplus labour. The North was isolated from the rest of the economy so far as expanding industries were concerned, although the old investment industries continued to change their employment in response to G.

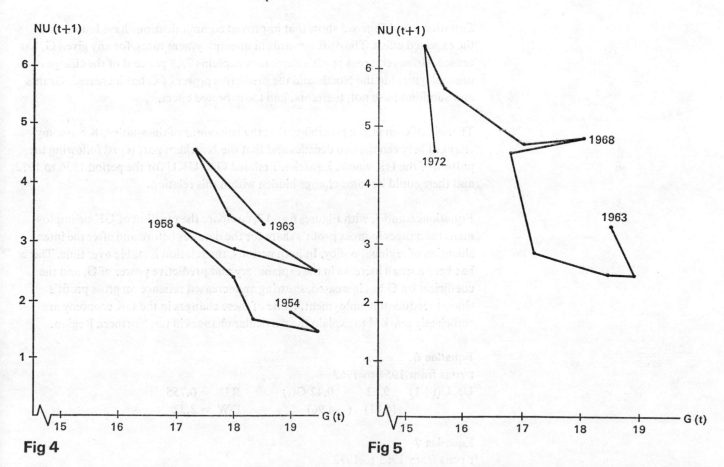

Fig 4 **Fig 5**

The intensification of regional policy in the decade 1963 to 1972 could be expected to have had three effects. First, improved communications could be expected to lead to a halt in the upward shift of unemployment rates. Firms would now be able to get to the region more easily via the motorway network, and might therefore be

167

more prepared to move to an area where labour was plentiful and land cheap. If this is right, then the relationship between G and unemployment should not display the upward zig-zag that Figure 4 showed for the earlier period.

Second, IDC policy is most effective when industry is profitable. A firm can be refused an IDC only if it is intending to expand. An IDC refusal will make managers more receptive to information about cheap sites, advanced factories, surplus labour and government training facilities in the Assisted Areas. However, the process is initiated by the managers attempting to expand in a congested area. The movement of plants is known to be due more to push factors than to pull factors,[26] and the main push factor is a desire to expand output[27]. IDC policy, combined with the provision of information services and advanced factories, is likely to increase the strength of the relationship between profit and unemployment.

[26]P M Townroe (1971) *Industrial Location Decisions* University of Birmingham Centre for Urban and Regional Studies, Occasional Paper No 15, pp 36–40

[27]House of Commons, 1973–74: 85–I, Expenditure Committee (Trade and Industry Sub-Committee) *Regional Development Incentives* Minutes of Evidence, p 534

Third, the regional incentives to industry should have a different effect from that of improved infrastructure and IDC policy. If new industry is being persuaded to move to the region by subsidies, some of the dependence on gross profit for the incentive and funds for investment should be weakened. In that case, one would expect that the equation for 1963 to 1972 would have rather less explanatory power than Equation 4, for 1954 to 1963. We now see whether improved infrastructure and industrial incentives have in fact had the effects expected of them.

Equation 5

t runs from 1963 to 1972

$$NU(t+1) = 18.68 - 0.84 G(t) \qquad R^2 = 0.758$$
$$\qquad\qquad (6.49) \quad (-5.00) \qquad DW = 1.51$$

Equation 5 and Figure 5 show that improved communications have indeed had the expected effect. The drift upwards in unemployment rates, for any given G, has ceased. However, gross profit's share now explains 75.8 per cent of the change in unemployment in the North, and the predictive power of G has increased. Grants and subsidies have not, therefore, had the expected effect.

There is, of course, the possibility that the behaviour of the whole UK economy changed between the two decades and that the Northern part is just following the pattern of the UK whole. Equation 1 related G to UKU for the period 1956 to 1972, and there could be some change hidden within this relation.

Equations 6 and 7, with Figures 6 and 7, compare the reaction of UK unemployment to changes in gross profit's share for the decades before and after the intensification of regional policy. In both periods, the relation is stable over time. There has been a small increase in the explanatory and predictive power of G, and the coefficient on G has increased, showing an increased reliance on gross profit's share to reduce unemployment. None of these changes in the UK economy are sufficiently marked to explain the particular changes in the Northern Region.

Equation 6

t runs from 1954 to 1963

$$UKU(t+1) = 9.52 - 0.42 G(t) \qquad R^2 = 0.755$$
$$\qquad\qquad (6.11) \quad (-4.96) \qquad DW = 2.32$$

Equation 7

t runs from 1963 to 1972

$$UKU(t+1) = 11.60 - 0.53 G(t) \qquad R^2 = 0.820$$
$$\qquad\qquad (7.63) \quad (-6.03) \qquad DW = 1.97$$

A comparison of Equations five and seven shows that a decrease in gross profit's share by one percentage point increases the unemployment rate in the North by 0.84 of a percentage point, but by only 0.53 for the UK as a whole. The constancy in the ratio of Northern to UK unempoyment rates from 1963 is thus consistent with the falling share of profits and lends support to the argument being developed in this paper. The rise in the ratio occurred before the intensification of regional policy.

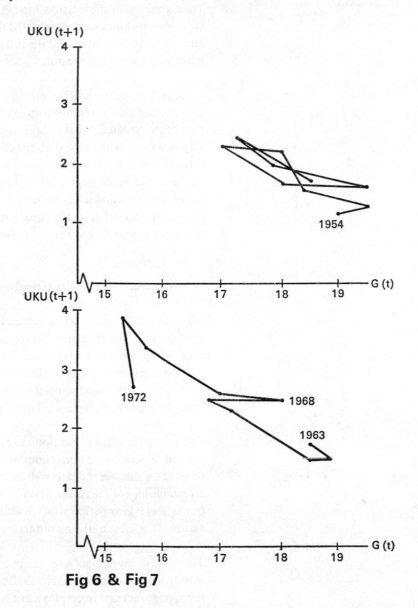

Fig 6 & Fig 7

It seems that excess demand for goods during the 1960s provided signals to wage and salary earners to buy more, but did not provide signals to managers to invest more. Managers sensed that their costs were rising more quickly than their revenues. In retrospect, the observable indicator of the aggregate of managers' expectations, at the time when they held them, is the fall in gross profit's share. The lack of investment was felt most severely in regions with a predominance of investment industry, and these reacted most to the decrease in gross profit's share. The effect of this type of excess demand was an increase in imports and an increase in unemployment in the North.

The wide gap between Northern and UK unempoyment rates is not therefore a sign of failure of regional policy, but, it is suggested, of national policy. The success of regional policy is the large amount of employment which has been created in new and expanding plants. The problem is to decide to what extent this success is due to grants, subsidies and tax allowances, and to what extent it is due to other aspects of regional policy: improved communications, particularly the motorway network, the refusal of IDCs in congested areas, the provision of information to firms wishing to expand about areas where labour is in surplus and sites are cheap and other types of central and local government services to industry which do not involve some fiscal incentive.

The tightening of the relationship between G and U in the North implies that this latter group of measures dominated the subsidies. The provision of real goods and services to industry, and the IDC policy, are clear and understandable, whereas many of the subsidies are not.

If the subsidy policy had been the most effective, one would expect to see similar changes in the G, U relationship in the other two regions which form the main part of the Assisted Areas: Wales and Scotland. In the case of Wales, the relationship was weak both in the decade before 1963 and in the decade after, although the ratio of Welsh unemployment to UK unemployment has been falling since 1966. In the case of Scotland, there is hardly any change in the G, U relationship between the two decades and it has been a fairly strong relationship throughout the twenty years. (Appendix I gives the equations for the two decades for those regions whose accounting boundaries were not changed over the period.)

IV   Managers' reactions to incentives

The results of a survey taken in the Northern region during October and November 1974 provide some evidence for the extent to which managers take subsidies into account. 117 managers were interviewed to discuss their views on regional policy. The managers were responsible for 50,000 employees in June 1974, and invested £140m during the two financial years preceding the survey. (A description of the 'sample' is given in Appendix II.)

The survey included a questionnaire sent in advance of the interview, and this yielded sufficient data about employment and investment to give some indication of what the managers did as well as what they said. The results show the effects of an establishment's investment on its employment. Since the investment occurred during a two year period which includes 1973, some increase in output can be assumed for most of the manufacturers, although no data on output were collected.

The value of investment over the two financial years ending before October 1974 was divided by employment in 1972 to give '£s invested per person employed'. The percentage increase in employment is calculated by taking the increase in numbers between June 1972 and June 1974 as a percentage of June 1972 employment. Three types of investment are distinguished: total investment, investment on plant and machinery only, and investment on buildings only. The number of observations is small in view of these data demands and is further reduced by the exclusion of those plants which opened after June 1972 and of 18 non-manufacturing establishments.

Table 1 shows that if more than £600 in total is invested over two years, per person employed, then employment within that establishment is likely to increase (using p for the probability of no relationship. p=0.007). Since new plants which might have displaced employment elsewhere are not included in this table, an increase in employment within the establishment which carried out the investment is a sufficient condition for investment to cause employment in the Northern Region.

Table 1

Change in employment	Total investment per employee		
	0–£600	over £600	row total
Constant or decrease	16	8	24
Increase up to 20%	6	11	17
Increase over 20%	5	20	25
	27	39	66 establishments

Table 2 shows that the generation of employment by investment in plant and machinery is much less likely than was the case for total investment (p has risen to 0.25).

Table 2

Change in employment	Investment in plant and machinery per employee		
	0–£600	over £600	row total
Constant or decrease	15	7	22
Increase up to 20%	10	8	18
Increase over 20%	9	15	24
	34	30	64

Table 3 shows that if more than £100 per person employed is invested in buildings, the implication from this one limited survey is that this is a sufficient condition for employment to increase by more than 5 per cent. Table 4 shows that investment on buildings of more than £100 per employee is likely to be associated with an increase of employment of over 10 per cent (p = 0.011).

Table 3

Change in employment	Investment in buldiing per employee		
	0–£100	over £100	row total
Decrease, or increase to 5%	24	0	24
Increase over 5%	11	21	32
	35	21	56

Table 4

Decrease, or increase to 10%	24	7	31
Increase over 10%	11	14	25
	35	21	56

The increase in employment occurred at the same time as the investment. Although many managers expected a slight increase in employment during the year to June 1975, there was no relation between the expected increase and investments in the preceding two years 1972 to 1974.

These findings are as expected. Investment creates employment, even within the establishment which carried out the investment. New employment and new buildings are complements. Plant and machinery are complements to labour in the main,

171

but this type of investment, which receives most subsidy, is the most likely to involve some substitution of capital for labour within a particular establishment. The total employment-generating effects within Development Areas depend on the location of the equipment manufacturers.

Given this background of what managers do, it is relevant to find out what the managers think of regional incentives, particularly since much of the previous discussion has centred on expectations and anticipations. Tables 5 to 10 refer to all the respondents, including non-manufacturing plants and recently opened plants. In some cases, there are high proportions of 'no answers'. Partly, these were servicing industry establishments, who felt that the questions did not apply to them; partly, they were personnel managers who were not sufficiently familiar with their firms' investment policies to want to answer.

Table 5 shows the large amount of uncertainty which surrounds regional policy. Half those who answered did not know how long these regional incentives would last. The General Election coincided with the survey, but there was no differences in the pattern of answers before and after the results were announced.

Table 6 shows that just over half the managers say that they take the incentives into account in their plans. The answers to the question did not differ with the year the plant started production, the type of ownership or the number of employees, provided there were more than 50. Plant with fewer than 50 employees were less inclined to take the incentives into account (p = 0.009).

Table 5
For how long do you expect the following regional incentives to remain in force? (Figures in brackets are percentages of those who answered)

	REP	Availability of loans	Availability of interest relief
Don't know	40 (47)	40 (55)	40 (54)
Up to 3 years	17 (20)	12 (16)	14 (19)
4 to 5 years	22 (26)	14 (19)	14 (19)
Over 5 years	5 (6)	6 (8)	5 (7)
	84 (100)	72 (100)	73 (100)
No answer	33	45	44

Table 6
Do you take these incentives into account in your planning?

	Yes	59	(56)
	No	47	(44)
		106	(100)
No answer		11	

It is possible that some managers who try to plan ahead in normal times had given up in despair by October 1974. The rapid increase in economic activity in 1973 was followed abruptly by the three-day week. The massive expansion in the money supply in 1972–73, and the record rise in import prices in 1973, were followed in 1974 by controls on output prices before the lagged adjustments to input prices and monetary expansion had time to work their way through the system. Many firms in the survey reported shortages of supplies and markets both at the same time. Therefore, the question on whether regional incentives are taken into account in plans may have been misinterpreted to mean 'Do you plan ahead nowadays?'

The survey contained another question on planning which yielded a useful distribution of answers: 'How far ahead do you plan your manpower policy in an approximate, "give-or-take-ten-per cent", way for each type of worker to be recruited or trained?' Table 7 gives the distribution of answers. The pattern did not vary with the size of plant.

Table 7

How far ahead do you plan your manpower requirements?

'We don't', or a fortnight	36 (33)
1 to 6 months	21 (19)
7 to 12 months	21 (19)
1 to 3 years	18 (16)
4 to 5 years	14 (13)
	110 (100)
No answer	7

As expected, those who planned ahead for recruitment and training were more likely to take regional incentives into account in their plans, but Table 8 shows that the relationship was not very strong (p = 0.011. The non-answers did not coincide, so the number of observations has shrunk.)

Table 8

Are regional incentives taken into account?

Manpower planned	No	Yes	row total
0–3 months ahead	24	14	38
4–12 months ahead	12	19	31
over 1 year ahead	8	21	29
	54	44	98

A relatively small survey of this type cannot be conclusive. So far, it has shown that investment and increased employment go together, even within the establishment which does the investing; that in times of uncertainty managers do not plan their employment very far ahead, but when they do plan in the general sense, more than half are influenced by regional incentives. Therefore it is important to find out to what extent regional incentives encourage investment.

The respondents were asked: 'By how much would you have curtailed your investment programme in the absence of government development incentives?' The distribution of answers is given in Table 9, and shows that 66 per cent of those answering would not have curtailed their investment at all. The pattern of answers did not vary with the year the plant started production, the number of employees, or the total investment per employee during 1972 to 1974.

Table 6 showed that 56 per cent did take regional incentives into account in their planning. The discrepancy between Tables 6 and 9 is puzzling. Perhaps the question in Table 9 demanded more information about the firm's decisions and so was answered by the fewer, more knowledgeable respondents, in which case more attention should be paid to Table 9 than Table 6: for two-thirds of managers, regional incentives do not encourage investment.

173

Table 9

Percentage by which investment would have been curtailed in the absence of development incentives?

No curtailment of investment	55	(66)
By up to 25%	13	(16)
By over 25%	15	(18)
	83	(100)
No answer	34	

** Roger Quince (1974) 'British Regional Policy Legislation in the Twentieth Century' Northern Region Strategy Team Occasional Paper

However, regional incentives may be taken into account in a general way and therefore encourage business optimism, but may not be taken into account in an explicit way; so, the respondent, on recollection, does not think that investment would have been reduced in their absence. Since business optimism is an encouragement to investment, this interpretation means that more attention should be paid to Table 6: for over half the managers, incentives are taken into account in planning.

On balance, Table 9 seems the more appropriate indicator of the effect of regional incentives. The package of development incentives has had at least seventeen changes in eleven years: eight changes in grants and allowances for plant and machinery, seven changes in grants and allowances for industrial buildings, and two changes in the boundaries of Special Development Areas within the Northern Region[28]. The relative importance of the development incentives depends on which particular allowances are in force nationally at a particular moment, but there were fifteen changes in the national allowances during the eleven years. The special years for regional incentives were 1964, 1965, 1968 and 1973: the years of no change. (IDC policy changed in 1965, but not incentives.)

In addition to legislated changes, all regional incentives are rapidly eroded by inflation, with the exception of the promptly paid *ad valorem* subsidy, Regional Development Grant. The *ad hominem* subsidy of Regional Employment Premium is a simple example of rapid erosion, but the more complicated tax exemptions are reduced in value by the time lag between cost being incurred and tax exemption being allowed. The preference for inflation-proof incentives is illustrated by Table 10.

Table 10

Which of the present financial incentives will, in your view, be most effective in future?

27 did not answer
of the 90 who answered, several mentioned more than one incentive:
70 mentioned RDG
21 mentioned REP
15 mentioned loans or interest relief
 4 mentioned rent relief
Of those who gave only one incentive in their answer:
48 said RDG
 8 said REP

The views of the managers on the future effectiveness of REP seems to have been influenced more by expected wage increases than by the doubling of the subsidy to £3 in July 1974. A subsidy which was 4 to 8 per cent of the wage bill in 1974 has been swamped by actual or expected wage increases of two or three times this amount.

The main surprise is the lack of curtailment of investment in the absence of incentives. When designing the questionnaire, the expectation was that most respondents would say they would have cut investment by about 25 per cent: 20–22 per cent for

174

RDG plus something for investment allowances. The result, that two-thirds of those answering felt that investment would not have been curtailed at all, seems sufficiently far from expectation to be of interest. Managers seem to trust only those incentives which are prompt and inflation-proof. Subsidies are believed only after they are in the bank.

V National and regional policies

Part II of this paper suggested that there are theoretical grounds for believing that an increase in gross profit's share encourages investment and hence creates employment. Of course, this is not because managers are carefully charting gross profit's share and then deciding what to invest. *Ex ante,* each manager notes the trends in his own firm's costs and revenues. On the basis of simple expectations, if revenues increased more quickly than costs in the immediate past, he expects profitable opportunities to be available in the future, so he wants to invest, and when surplus funds are accumulating, he is able to invest. Since the total of firms' costs are other incomes, a useful aggregate measure of all managers' opinions turns out, *ex post,* to be the share of profit in national income. Because of the confusion created by the combination of monetary and fiscal policies, gross measures are more appropriate than net.

Part III showed that the Northern Region suffered more from a decrease in profit's share than other regions. The leverage of gross profit's share on the unemployment rate in the North is greater than the leverage on the UK unemployment rate. The disparity between unemployment rates over the decade 1963 to 1973 is described by the equations:

$$NU(t+1) = 18.7 - 0.84\,G(t) \qquad \text{Equation 5}$$
$$UKU(t+1) = 11.6 - 0.53\,G(t) \qquad \text{Equation 7}$$

These equations not only show the higher rate for the North. Both the ratio between constants and the ratio between coefficients is about 1.6, which explains the rough constancy in the ratio of Northern to UK unemployment rates. Figure 1 showed that the ratio increased with the decline of employment opportunities in coal-mining and other industries after 1959. The intensification of regional policy in 1963 led to a balance between declining employment in old plants and expanding employment in new ones. The increased strength of the negative relationship between profit and unemployment suggests that the changing behaviour of the Northern Region between 1959 to 1963 and 1963 to 1973 is more likely to have been the result of improved communications, IDC policy and the provision of information, than of incentives to industry. This suggestion is supported by the greater explanatory power of the gross measures rather than the net, displayed in equations 1 and 2 of Part II. Further support is provided by the results of the survey of managers in the North, reported in Part IV.

The results of the regressions for all the UK regions are displayed in Table 11. The b column gives the coefficient on G. The U column gives the actual average unemployment rate in 1972. Comparison of these two columns shows that an increase in G reduces unemployment most in those areas where unemployment is highest, with the exception of Northern Ireland.

In view of the small number of observations used for each regression, there is some interest in investigating the pattern of the statistical relationships between the regressions. The intercept on the G-axis, a/b, is the extrapolation of the regression to give profit's share for 'zero unemployment'. For the British regions, the less is the disturbance to the relationship, the more likely is a/b to approach 20.

175

Table 11

Reactions of Regional Unemployment to Gross Profit's Share of GNP, 1963 to 1973

$U(t+1) = a - b\,G(t)$

	a	b	R^2	DW	actual U (1972)
United Kingdom	11.60	0.53	0.82	1.97	3.9
North	18.68	0.84	0.76	1.51	6.4
Yorkshire and Humberside	15.06	0.74	0.81	1.38	4.2
East Midlands	10.74	0.52	0.81	1.41	3.1
East Anglia	8.54	0.38	0.71	1.51	2.9
South-East	6.78	0.31	0.78	1.48	2.2
South-West	9.88	0.43	0.68	1.21	3.4
West Midlands	12.87	0.64	0.84	2.00	3.6
North-West	15.81	0.76	0.85	2.01	4.9
Wales	12.50	0.51	0.65	1.29	4.9
Scotland	17.82	0.80	0.77	1.67	6.5
Northern Ireland	8.59	0.10	0.23	1.20	8.1

(All the t-values for the a's are above 5.)

Table 12 shows the pattern. The lower is the t-value for b, the greater is the underestimate of b.

Table 12

	a/b	b's t-value	R^2
Wales	24.5	3.8	0.65
South-West	23.0	4.1	0.68
East Anglia	22.5	4.4	0.71
Scotland	22.3	5.2	0.77
North	22.2	5.0	0.76
South-East	21.9	5.3	0.78
North-West	20.8	6.8	0.85
East Midlands	20.7	5.8	0.81
Yorkshire and Humberside	20.4	5.9	0.81
West Midlands	20.1	6.5	0.84

Figure 8 displays what appear to be the underlying relationships. For the British regions, the relationships between G and U fan out from (G, U) = (20, 0). The North has the steepest slope and the South-East the least steep, with the other British regions in between. By similar triangles, the ratios of regional unemployment rates stay constant whatever the level of national prosperity, whether G_1 or G_2. The welfare implications, of course, are not proportionate to unemployment rates: 4 per cent unemployment is very much more than twice as unpleasant as 2 per cent.

[29]John Cornwall (1972) *Growth and Stability in a Mature Economy* Martin Robertson, p 260

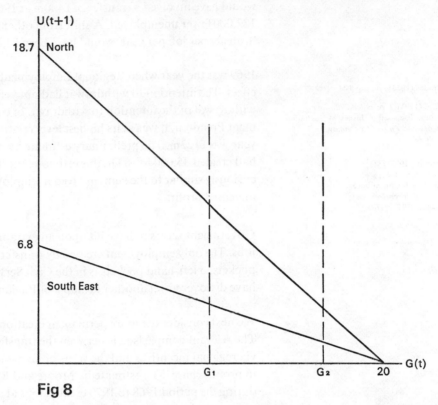

Fig 8

Any decrease in profit's share increases the absolute gap between regional unemployment rates and, though leaving relative unemployment rates constant, widens the gap in welfare between regions. Therefore, if regional policy detracts from the success of national policy, it is counter-productive. When each individual measure in the regional policy package is considered in isolation, it is usually possible to present a strong argument which demonstrates that the measure contributes to national prosperity; the relocation of industry reduces external costs in congested areas and allows unemployed people in Development Areas to become productive. However, the regional policy package as a whole may have a different effect from that of its constituent parts.

Professor Cornwall's gentle comment about fiscal policy at the national level was that 'the British authorities... have shown a willingness to implement policies with such speed and courage as to astonish economists of other countries.'[29]. The astonishment seems to be shared by British managers. When constantly changing regional incentives are added to the policies for 'fine-tuning' the result is confusion. When subsidies for employment and investment in Development Areas are added to the subsidies for commuter transport and housing in congested areas, the result is an increase in the inflationary government deficit. Uncertainty about taxes, subsidies and the rates of increase of prices is not conducive to profit, investment and the reduction of unemployment. Recently, there have been legislated reductions in the prices of outputs relative to imputs.

It is interesting to see what would have happened to unemployment if, instead of regional incentives, uncertainty and a squeeze on profits, there had been no regional incentives, more stability in policy and no profit's squeeze. We first compare the employment effects of increased profit with the employment effects of Regional Employment Premium. Since one per cent of UK unemployment involves 230,000 people, Equation 7 can be rewritten as:

The number of people unemployed in the UK in year $t+1 = 2,668,000 - 122,000$ G(t)

If gross profit's share had been greater by a percentage point in, say, 1969, this would have involved a transfer of £400m at 1969 prices. There would have been 122,000 fewer unemployed. A shift from other incomes to profit is a transfer, so the 'transfer per job per year' would have been £3,300 at 1969 prices.

1969 was the year when Regional Employment Premium was probably at its peak effect. The intention to withdraw it had not yet been announced (nor the later withdrawal of the intention to withdraw). In combination with Selective Employment Premium, it was at its highest level relative to wages. Its total amount in that year was £122m. The preliminary estimate by Moore and Rhodes[30] was that REP had created 35,000 jobs. On this estimate, the 'transfer per job per year' was £3,500, curiously similar to the sum involved in employment creation by encouraging increased profit.

Government seems to have hit upon an extraordinarily devious method of creating jobs. The only employment created by transferring sums of money from right-hand pockets to left-hand pockets is in the Civil Service, mainly in London. We seem to have discovered yet another example of Puviani's Theory of Fiscal Illusion[31].

We next consider the more permanent creation of jobs in the Development Areas. The relevant comparison is between the transfers involved in creating such jobs via regional incentives and the transfer necessary to create such jobs via an increase in profit's share. The estimate by Moore and Rhodes[32] is that regional incentives during the period 1968 to 1970 created jobs at an exchequer cost of £8,000 per permanent job created.

To simplify the comparison we make assumptions which put the case for regional subsidies in their most favourable light. All the 185,000 jobs estimated to have been created by regional policy are accepted, and none are assumed to be due to firms looking for cheap sites and surplus labour without the guilding hand of government. All the jobs are assumed to be due to subsidies and none of the provision of real goods and services to industry by government, in spite of the implications of the earlier part of this paper that the latter had the dominant effect. The jobs created are assumed to be permanent, although this assumes a strange constancy in tastes and technology. The alternative case of profit's role of employment creation is placed in its most unfavourable light by assuming that the jobs created are temporary, and that only those jobs created in Development Areas are relevant, although for every job created in a Development Area by increased profit, three are created elsewhere in the UK.

By using the equations for Scotland, Wales and the North of England, as given in Table 11, and taking the number of people represented by one percentage point of unemployment rate for each region, we can obtain an estimate of the reduction in unemployment in most of the Development Areas which would be brought about by an increase in profit's share:

The number of people unemployed in Scotland, Wales and the North of England, in year $t+1 = 747,000 - 33,000$ G(t)

Taking 1969 GNP again, as the middle year of Moore's and Rhodes' period, a rise in G by a percentage point is a rise of £400m. The jobs created in the Development Areas are 33,000. The 'transfer per job created in Development Areas per annum' is £12,000.

[30]Moore and Rhodes (1973) *op cit* p 103

[31]Amilcare Puviani (1903) *Teoria della Illusione Finanziaria* Palermo, discussed in James M Buchanan (1960) *Fiscal Theory and Political Economy* Chapel Hill, pp 59–64

[32]House of Commons, 1972-73: 327, Expenditure Committee (Trade and Industry sub-Committee) *Regional Development Incentives* Minutes of Evidence q797, p 164

178

Once a job is created, the Exchequer gains from the saving in unemployment pay, the receipts from income tax and the taxes on increased expenditure by the employed. These gains are the same whether the job is created via profit or via subsidies. The problem, therefore, is to compare the economic effects of creating a permanent job via £8,000 of subsidy with the effects of creating a job via an increase in annual profits and surplus of £12,000.

The cost to the Exchequer of increased profits is negative, since a part of profit is paid in tax. All of an increase in the gross trading surpluses of nationalised industries are a saving to the Exchequer since subsidies can be eliminated. The cost to future generations is negative, since most additional profit is used for additional investment. Comparison of Equations 1 and 2 shows clearly that the key variable is gross profit's share, not net profit's, so a particular functional distribution of income still leaves room to manoeuvre the personal distribution of income. Comparison of Equations 1 and 2 perhaps implies that the pattern of ownership is not relevant: gross trading surpluses of public corporations should be included with gross profits of private industry. The complete welfare implications depend on whether one dislikes gross profit more than one dislikes unemployment, but few outside Cambridge, England, would consider that a trade-off between two bads was involved.

Since the cost via a transfer to profit is negative but the cost via regional subsidies is positive, there is no need to use discounting techniques to convert a flow of jobs per annum into the more permanent creation of jobs. Increasing gross profit's share must be a cheaper method of reducing unemployment than regional subsidies.

Conclusions

An increase in unemployment in one year is caused by a decrease in gross profit and gross trading surplus, as a percent of GNP, in the preceding year. This relationship explains more and predicts better than net profit's share of National Income, or the rate of change of money wages, or the rate of growth or real GDP.

For each of the regions of Britain, there is a negative relationship between that region's unemployment rate in one year and the national percentage share of gross profit and surplus in the preceding year. When profit's share increases, unemployment declines most in those regions where unemployment is highest. Therefore, any regional policies which detract from the level of national profit will be counterproductive.

The relationship between unemployment and profit's share is stable for each region and is such that the ratios of unemployment rates for the regions stay fairly constant whatever the absolute levels.

The most effective aspects of the regional policy package have been those which are reliable and easy to understand. These are IDC policy, advanced factories, infrastructure and information services. The only subsidy which falls into this category is the Regional Development Grant.

Most of the regional subsidies seem to have had little effect on the Assisted Areas. Their allocative signals have been lost in the noise created by inflation and too many changes in policy. It is possible that their effects have been negated by housing and transport subsidies in congested areas. To the extent that the amount of regional subsidies has added to the inflationary government deficit, and the number of different subsidies has added to the complexity of fiscal measures, their effect will have been to increase uncertainty, and hence reduce profit, investment and employment.

Appendix I

The relation between national gross profit *plus* gross trading surplus, as a percentage of GNP, and regional unemployment rates, for the decades 1954 to 1963 and 1963 to 1972, selected regions.

$$U(t+1)=a-b\,G(t)$$

t	a	b	R^2	DW
United Kingdom				
1954 to 1963	9.52	0.42	0.76	2.32
	(6.11)	(−4.90)		
1963 to 1972	11.60	0.53	0.82	1.97
	(7.63)	(−6.03)		
Scotland				
1954 to 1963	17.36	0.76	0.72	1.90
	(5.67)	(−4.57)		
1963 to 1972	17.82	0.80	0.77	1.67
	(6.79)	(−5.23)		
Wales				
1954 to 1963	14.84	0.66	0.66	2.11
	(4.85)	(−3.93)		
1963 to 1972	12.50	0.51	0.65	1.29
	(5.41)	(−3.83)		
North				
1954 to 1963	17.70	0.82	0.51	0.49
	(3.44)	(−2.91)		
1963 to 1972	18.68	0.84	0.76	1.51
	(6.49)	(−5.00)		
South-West				
1954 to 1963	7.79	0.33	0.66	1.37
	(4.96)	(−3.90)		
1963 to 1972	9.88	0.43	0.68	1.21
	(5.49)	(−4.15)		
West Midlands				
1954 to 1963	5.49	−0.23	0.28	1.88
	(2.27)	(−1.76)		
1963 to 1972	12.87	0.64	0.84	2.00
	(7.61)	(−6.54)		
North-West				
1954 to 1963	13.48	0.62	0.79	2.72
	(6.44)	(−5.47)		
1963 to 1972	15.81	0.76	0.85	2.01
	(8.23)	(−6.83)		

Appendix II
Survey of plants in the northern region 1974

The 'sample' is really the response from a panel and a population. The panel is of 93 plants previously surveyed in 1972. The population is of 24 plants who, in 1973, announced plans to increase their labour force by at least 50 per cent and at least 50 people. The objectives of the survey were to compare problems of labour recruitment and training between plants expanding rapidly and those whose labour force stayed constant, and to compare views on regional policy.

The response rate was 84 per cent: 93 per cent from the panel, 70 per cent from the population. The main single reason for refusal was that the manager had already been surveyed several times in 1974 and could not take yet another.

A brief description of the respondents follows:

Employment:
1 – 50 employees	25	plant
51 – 200 ,,	35	,,
201 – 500 ,,	21	,,
over 500 ,,	26	,,
no answer	10	
	117	

Industry:
Manufacturing	99
Servicing	13
Construction, Mining & Quarrying	5
	117

Year production started:
before 1956	40
1956 to 1965	22
1966 to 1970	30
1970 to 1974	25
	117

Ownership:
Independent firm with no branches elsewhere	26
Independent firm with branches elsewhere	19
Subsidiary company within a larger group	42
Branch plant with head office elsewhere	30
	117

Position of respondent in company:
Managing Director	38
Other Director	21
General Manager	13
Production Manager	13
Personnel Manager	9
Other Manager	10
Owner, Partner, Chairman	5
Company Secretary	5
Accountant	3
	117

Regional aid: impressions of a decade's experience in the northern region

W ELKAN

*I would like to acknowledge the help of our Research Assistant, John Weiss, and of my colleagues Richard Morley and Joost van Doorn as also that of Mr R S Howard and Mr E Stringer of the Department of Industry

The principal aim of active regional policy since its inception following the Hailsham Report of 1963 has been to reduce male unemployment and its cyclical oscillations to the national average. During the 1940s and 1950s, the regional problem, which had first manifested itself after World War I, had seemed to have abated, since unemployment after 1940 was not very different from the national average. It was its resumed divergence from the late 1950s onwards which prompted the recognition that specific policy measures were needed and this paper, which is intended to complement Richard Morley's and which draws heavily upon the impressions I gained as a member of the Northern Planning Council until 1972, will examine some facets of the experience of a decade's active regional policy in the Northern Region.

It will argue that the specific attempts to promote industrial development have been misguided by being too much directed at the long run. A policy more immediately beamed at the short run might have been more effective in the long run by providing the additional stimulus of buoyancy associated with lower levels of unemployment in the Region. This is not incompatible with Richard Morley's conclusion that the critical determinant of the level of unemployment is the share of profits in GNP, since he points out that the divergence of the North's rate of unemployment from that of the UK as a whole is largely explained by its industrial structure, with its predominance of capital goods industries. An alternative industrial strategy would have lessened the North's dependence on a demand for capital goods.

The paper makes reference in several places to the way in which the region's problems were perceived by those charged with carrying out policy. It should be stressed that where it does so it refers to the views of officials and others within the region and that these were not necessarily always shared by Whitehall, or even unanimously held locally.

If we are to judge the success of regional policy by the extent to which it had reduced unemployment or raised incomes per head to the levels prevailing in the South or Midlands then it cannot be regarded as a great success

Table 1 shows GDP per head and unemployment in the North in relation to the UK as a whole.

183

Table 1

**GDP per head and Unemployment in the Northern Region in relation to the UK.
1963 to 1972**

	GDP per head (UK=100)	Unemployment Male and Female (UK=100)	Unemployment in the UK %
1963	na	191	2.4
1964	85.0	194	1.7
1965	na	166	1.5
1966	84.0	167	1.5
1967	84.0	170	2.3
1968	83.5	184	2.5
1969	83.6	192	2.5
1970	84.8	181	2.6
1971	85.3	171	3.4
1972	85.0	164	3.9
1973	na	174	2.7

Sources
V H Woodward, *Regional Social Accounts for the UK*
Cambridge University Press, 1970, p79
Abstract of Regional Statistics, 1974, pp136 and 90

Both continue to diverge from the UK 'norm' and therefore, by inference, even more so from income per head and unemployment in the South. It is of course true that in relation to unemployment the North faces special problems. The unemployed of the North comprise a higher proportion of men over 50 and who are either unskilled or whose skills are specific to an industry that has been declining, viz coal mining. The older industries of the North used to be notoriously profligate in their use of unskilled labour until rising wages in the 1960s forced them to economize and thereby create unemployment for a category of people for whom it is particularly difficult to find alternative jobs. This is perhaps why the decline in the divergence of the North's unemployment rate from that of the UK as a whole has been much less than has been the case in other Assisted Areas, especially Scotland and Northern Ireland.

A regional disparity in incomes is more natural. It is hardly to be expected that income per head in a country of fifty million inhabitants will be everywhere the same, and the divergence may in any case be less in real terms when differences in the cost of housing and some other components in the cost of living are taken into account. The divergence is not primarily the result of lower pay in comparable occupations. In fact, the average weekly earnings of males over 21 in manufacturing in 1973 at £40.88 were very close to the UK average of £41.52 and not much below the South East, where they were £43.21. In the case of the series that covers all industries, the disparity is even smaller. The divergence is principally attributable to three things: first, differences in the occupational mix of the working population; second, differences in unemployment and, third, differences in the female activity rate.

There are few countries in the world in which each region displays an identical occupational mix and that of the Northern region, like that of Wales, differs naturally from that of the South. In terms of the Registrar General's socio-economic categories the region is thin at the top. This has often been noted and there has been a widespread belief that the way to deal with it is to do all in one's power to promote science-based industries, in order to have more scientists and technologists, and to promote industries which will have their head offices in the region in order to have more managers. Both would then also encourage the growth of regionally-based professional services and the total effect would be to increase the numbers in the upper socio-economic groups. The object of such a policy ought, of course, to be to have more Northerners in such jobs, but it is not at all clear that this would be the result. It is true that the number of university and technical college graduates who grow up in the North exceeds the employment opportunities open to them and that this forces them to seek jobs elsewhere. But recent graduates would not necessarily be the ones whom firms would want to open up new ventures. Firms of the kind favoured by this policy are likely to have been operating in the South, and senior staff will, therefore, move to the region instead of being indigenous. This has indeed been happening and the resulting enclaves of 'expatriates' in Newcastle-upon-Tyne and Teesside bear some resemblances to their counterparts in under-developed countries overseas, and generate not dissimilar responses from the 'indigenes'!

There may also be other difficulties with such a policy. Some science-based industries are costly to establish: the type most favoured, like ICI, require a large amount of investment per job created, and whatever benefit they may bestow in generating professional and managerial employment has to be set against the greater impact on reducing unemployment which the same resources would have had in less glamourous industries. Some branches of, eg the electronics industry, are also 'science-based' and are intensive in their use of 'human' rather than of physical capital but being usually very small businesses, these were not nearly so much favoured.

In this connection, it was often argued in the region that the real choice lay between a permanent improvement in the regional economic structure and short-term 'palliatives' to unemployment, But this juxtaposition is between 'ideal types' and does not pose a realistic choice. A region that started in the 1960s with a heavy concentration of employment in three basic industries using very specific skills is really not very well poised for instant structural transformation to an economy based on the most sophisticated and capital intensive technology. One would be building a new economy over the top of the existing one, incapable, except in the very long run, of absorbing the resources that have become obsolete and unemployed. This seems a poor prescription. Nor is it at all certain that such a strategy is really optimal and that the ultimate objective may not be attained more quickly if one is prepared to do first things first. For instance, the region started in the 1960s and indeed the 1970s with far fewer and less variegated consumer goods industries than the more favoured parts of the country. That was at least in some measure due to the relatively high unemployment, which is part of the explanation for the relatively low per capita incomes which, in turn, have affected the economic structure. The reason why the region has been less attractive to consumer goods industries is the absence of a buoyant local market. It is true that if there were many more highly paid managers and professionals this would help. So would a 'palliative' policy of dealing with unemployment now, whilst leaving the long-run to look after itself.

This strategy is preferable for another reason. Part of the problem in the Northern region has been a notable lack of bounce and optimism and a singular lack of enterprise. This syndrome is both cause and outcome of the lack of a buoyant local market which in turn goes back to unemployment. Depressed areas are not very conducive to business optimism and risk taking. If that is accepted, then the 'palliative' policy of dealing with unemployment directly and at once may well engender more optimism and local enterprise, which in the long run is the only certain way of securing self-sustaining growth. The question to pose then becomes not, how to attract the right industries to the region, but rather how to create the conditions for indigenous self-sustaining growth.

In practice, there has been more success in creating new manufacturing employment than is often supposed. Table 2 shows that during a period when employment in coalmining in the North East fell by about 80,000, 269 new manufacturing establishments created just under 40,000 new jobs for men and 20,000 for women (see Table 2).

Table 2
Manufacturing firms which have located new projects in the North East 1960 to 1973: by category of output and sex of present employees

Firms Producing	Number of firms	Employees			
		Male	Female	Total	Average
1 Final consumer goods	73	9,696	11,477	21,173	290
2 Inputs into final consumer goods	64	8,008	3,596	11,604	181
3 Capital goods and inputs into capital oods	132	19,884	5,033	24,917	188
Total	269	37,588	20,106	57,694	214

Source
Computed from Information supplied by Department of Industry, Newcastle-on-Tyne Regional Office

Note:
The total of 269 firms excludes a small number that have ceased to operate, or for which no employment data were available. It also excludes firms in North Yorkshire. Had these firms been included, the total would have been 307. We ourselves classified firms into three categories on the basis of what they are said to be producing. In some cases, it was difficult to decide into which category to place a firm and we have no doubt misplaced some. But these categories seemed to us more meaningful than the only published ones, which groups firms according to the SIC.

It is interesting to note that almost one half of these plants are once again producing capital goods, albeit in many cases different in type from those – shipbuilding, marine engineering, steel and, in a sense, coal – which have dominated the industrial structure for so long. In terms of employment, the proportion working in new plants producing capital goods is not much less pronounced – 43 per cent compared with 49 per cent. It is also interesting to note the higher average number of employees per plant in the consumer goods industries. There was, unfortunately, not time to compute cost-per-workplace for the three categories of industries, but it would be surprising if it was not higher in the third category than in the first or second.

Let us now look at the third determinant of per capita income which is the female activity rate. The principal reason why the North West of England has a higher income per head is that there have always been more employment opportunities for women. When the mills stopped producing textiles, their machines were sold off and the buildings were taken over by mail order businesses which employed the same people as the textile industry: women and girls. In the North East, employment opportunities were much fewer and the female activity rate was correspondingly lower. Table 3 presents the figures: it shows employed females as a percentage of all females aged 15-59

Table 3

Female activity rates for selected regions and years

	1961 %	1965 %	1972 %
Northern region	41.8	45.0	48.7
North West	57.0	57.6	56.0
South East	55.0	58.4	58.1

Notes:
1 These are not the officially quoted rates; they take females aged 15-59 and express numbers employed as a percentage of all in that age group.
2 The 1961 figure for the South East includes East Anglia which has a lower female activity rate; the apparent increase in 1965 should, therefore, be discounted.

Source:
Abstract of Regional Statistics 1973, pp 47/8

The Table shows a significant improvement in the Northern region's female activity rate, though it is still only half way up to the rates prevailing in the North West and the South East. Continued high unemployment in the Northern region would have had a much more serious effect on average incomes per head, but for the marked improvement in the female activity rate. This has occurred despite the contraction in employment in the distributive trades which has been nationwide. It is accounted for, principally, by more jobs in offices, including central and local government offices. (SIC 25-27) The increase in female employment opportunities might have been a good deal greater if civil servants had been more welcoming to proposals to establish factories that would employ mostly females. It is not denied that many such factories were in fact established. As Table 2 shows, over a third of the employees in manufacturing firms which established new projects in the North East between 1960 and 1967 were female. But that was in spite of rather than because of official welcome. The hostility towards proposals to set up factories that would employ mainly women derived from a belief that the main object of policy must be to create more and better employment opportunities for men. This was the justification given for restricting advance factories to firms that intended to employ mainly males. It was also commonly held that factories employing mostly women would, in any case, be quite the wrong industries to encourage because they would probably not be growth industries and were more than likely to be branch factories and therefore the first to shed labour in a recession, whilst making no contribution to the great structural transformation which was thought to be the only permanent salvation of the region.

That was probably quite wrong. Our own study of 27 industrial firms which had set up plants in the North East in the mid-sixties, and the object of which was to examine the employment implications of investment in different industries, revealed, interestingly, that it was mostly those firms employing predominantly women which had expanded employment beyond the numbers anticipated when they had applied for their IDCs. These also proved to be the firms which were least affected by recessions and recovered from them soonest. Those which employed principally men tended to be in industries that were hardest hit by recession and they also proved to be the ones which were busily reducing their labour output ratios so that the prospects of reemployment after a recession were correspondingly reduced.

Nor is it true that branch plants in general are more prone to cyclical swings of employment than their parents – or indeed that they are much more prone to closure than their parents. A careful study by Diana Atkins of the Department of Industry concluded that during the years 1966 to 1971, a period of contraction in manufacturing employment, what she calls 'mature' branch plants maintained their

187

employment better than their parents and that branches in Assisted Areas were only one half per cent. more vulnerable to closure than their parents, whilst their employment actually declined much less[1].

Where regional policy has been more successful is in directing a growing proportion of total UK investment in manufacturing to the North. The North's proportion of manufacturing investment rose from 5.8 per cent in 1963 to 9.1 per cent in 1970, by which time total UK investment in manufacturing had doubled in current prices. As Richard Morley's paper argues, this may owe more to IDC policy than to fiscal inducements. Whether he is right to attach so much importance to the road improvements is more open to question. A need for improvement in the network of roads is not in dispute. What is less certain is that the very capital intensive method of building them was the optimal choice of technique. It was defended on the grounds that it was cheapest and quickest. To have used more labour intensive techniques would have made the roads more expensive and delayed the long term transformation of the regional economic structure. But no-one ever even attempted to calculate the true costs (delay) and benefits (employment) of different degrees of capital intensity in road building. Besides, it was widely believed that the unemployed could not in any case be induced to work on roads – an occupation fit only for immigrant Irishmen, who, however, earned very high wages in the process! If that were true it would, of course, raise the question of the extent to which unemployment could be described as involuntary, but there is actually no evidence that it is, as it was never put to the test.

Latterly, the emphasis has shifted and growing attention is now being paid to the differential provision in the North's social overhead capital and social services. The region lags behind others in the provision of housing, education and health services, and, it is argued, the major objective of policy ought now to be to raise standards in these respects. When that is done, appropriate industrial development will occur without any special incentives. What seems to be assumed in such reasoning is that development is a normal state of affairs and that when it does occur it must be because it had been previously constrained by barriers or obstacles. This reduces the task of development to a removal of obstacles, and makes the mechanism of development appear analogous, as Hirschman pointed out in a different context years ago, to the operation of a race course: You need only lift the starting gate and the horses will run[2]. One need not deny that development may be retarded by institutional barriers or by poor physique, poor housing or poor education to recognize that improvements in all these respects which may be a necessary condition of development is not *ipso facto* a sufficient one. Better education facilities do not guarantee that their beneficiaries will not move elsewhere, as witness the case of Scots abroad!

Should one then conclude that regional policy has been one big mistake from beginning to end? Clearly not. It is easy to draw attention to faulty analysis, errors of judgement and the mis-specification of problems. But in the end, one has to ask what could have happened had no action at all been taken to improve conditions and, given the very large run-down of employment in coal mining and the problems facing the shipbuilding and related industries, it is difficult to believe that in the absence of specific regional policy measures of one kind or another conditions now would not have been a great deal worse. A higher rate of capital formation, nationally, would have helped, but it is not clear that the reallocation of resources devoted to regional policy would have done much to raise the share of gross profits in GNP which Richard Morley's paper pinpoints as the crucial determinant of the level of employment. Meanwhile, for whatever reason, many new factories and offices have come into being and created new employment opportunities; slag heaps have been landscaped and the general appearance of the region is much less depressing than it was. Perhaps in the field of development, any action – provided it is positive and not regulatory – is better than none.

[1] Diana H W Atkins 'Employment Change in branch and parent manufacturing plants in the UK: 1966 to 1971' *Trade and Industry*, 30 August 1973 pp 437-9

[2] A O Hirschman, *Strategy of Economic Development* New Haven, 1958 p 25

Comments by A J Brown

The question behind both of these papers is, of course: Has policy been good for the North? In assessing their answers to it, I think it is useful to have in mind a particular view of the regional problem. In the North, especially, it is possible to attribute to a high reliance upon industries which have been decreasing their employment nationally – coal, shipbuilding, iron and steel – a tendency for the indigenous growth-rate of employment to fall below that of the labour-force. This has increasingly been reinforced by the relative absence there of the activities that have been showing the fastest growth-rate of employment nationally – notably the more centralised service industries. To make things worse, the North shows a high rate of natural increase of population. The result is a tendency for there to be high unemployment, or low earnings, or both, to whatever extent is necessary to promote net outward migration and inward movement of jobs to such extents as will, between them, bridge the gap between the indigenous rates of increase of jobs and of people wanting them. This state of affairs can be expected to last for a long time; apart from demographic changes, it will only cease as the industrial structure of the region is transformed by the substitution of faster-growing industries for slow-growing or declining ones. The aim of regional policy as it has operated so far has been mainly to hurry this substitution up.

Neither of the two papers attempts an assessment of the amount of incoming industry, or the effect of policy in increasing it; we get some light on these things from other papers which assess regional policy nationally. Both, however, make the points that the strain on the North increased markedly from about 1958, with the accelerated rundown of its declining industries, and that, while the line was held successfully for some years from about 1963 (which it would be natural to attribute to policy changes), there has been a deterioration recently in the North's position in the regional League table.

I am not convinced that Richard Morley's suggested reason for the deterioration – that the North is primarily an investment-goods region – is the most important. Another possible suggestion might be that it is feeling the breeze of competition from the new Intermediate Areas adjoining it. One that I would favour is that the relative position of the North has suffered from a combination of circumstances; with general economic growth and the extension of motorways the central areas of English prosperity has been creeping into Wales and north beyond the Midlands, but has not reached the North yet; meanwhile Scotland has struck oil.

This brings me to a couple of points about particular instruments of policy. I have doubts about Walter Elkan's suggestion that it would have been better to concentrate on public works in order to raise local demand and attract (or build up) local market industries. On the face of it, this is a version of the favourite developing country policy of import-substitution – or, at least, it is only through such substitution that it can have permanent effects, except in so far as it creates an *élan*

189

which primes the pump of growth generally. I am suspicious of measures that rely largely on *élan*. The second point concerns the importance attributed to roads in holding the line from 1963 onwards. The timing seems to me wrong for this argument. In 1963 – which was a year of major improvement for development areas generally – the road improvements in the North-East were still not actually to appear for years.

Richard Morley's paper, as its title says, is largely about the key part of the share of profits in promoting employment, regionally as well as nationally. This is a complex matter. I certainly would not deny that a high profit-ratio is associated with high economic activity (it results from it), nor that a high profit-ratio in turn may promote investment, which generates employment. (I have, incidentally, been very much struck by the low profit-ratio in this country generally, about half that in Japan). But I would advise caution about accepting all that Richard Morley derives from his argument, on two grounds.

First, one should be careful about accepting a lag of unemployment-changes behind other variables as evidence of the direction of causality. Unemployment notoriously tends to change some time after economic activity – hence, in part, the embarrassment of some old campaigners in the Phillips Curve jungle on finding that changes in wages-increase are apt to antedate the changes in unemployment-level to which they would like to attribute them.

Secondly, in so far as the welfare of the Northern (or any other) region depends upon a high level of national product, there are plenty of ways of influencing it by raising the latter. The point about regional policy is that it is selective (if you like it) or discriminatory (if you don't), and is for influencing the distribution of economic activity rather than the general level of it.

It is, however, perhaps part of Richard Morley's point that a high profit (and investment) ratio is good for the North because it specialises to a considerable extent on investment goods. If so, I think it is valid; though especially in view of the small size of regional multipliers in this highly integrated national economy, it is doubtful whether this regional spin-off from what would be an important change in the structure and growth of the national economy could be regarded as much of a substitute for regional policy proper, so far as the North is concerned – not to speak of other none-too-prosperous regions which are not biased in the same degree towards investment goods.

A quantitative analysis of the effects of the Regional Employment Premium and other regional policy instruments

B C MOORE AND J RHODES

This paper is a summary of some of the research carried out in the Department of Applied Economics, Cambridge, on the evaluation of British regional economic policy which has been financed by the Social Science Research Council. We are indebted to Mr W A H Godley, Mr R S Howard, Mr R R Mackay and participants to the Department of Industry Conference on Industrial Subsidies for valuable comments on an earlier draft of this paper and in particular we would like to acknowledge the encouragement and hospitality received from the Department of Industry.

Introduction

Businessmen take decisions after reviewing all the factors relevant to those decisions. Regional policy is only one of these factors and its effects are spread over a long period, during which time many of the non-policy influences may change. For this reason our basic approach to measuring the effects of regional policy was to find out what had happened in the regions and then to use statistical methods to estimate what would have happened had regional policy not been introduced or changed (ie to establish the passive policy 'alternative position'). We have had discussions with senior managers and directors of private companies affected by regional policy and with other knowledgeable people concerned with the operation of regional policies, but these discussions aimed to find out the way in which regional policy influenced decisions, rather than to assess its quantitative effects. On some aspects of regional policy we have asked companies to estimate the effects of policy, and obtained some results, but since regional policy operates as a contributory influence on most decisions, it is not meaningful or practical to ask businessmen to attribute specific decisions to policy and then add up the effects of those specific decisions.

The statistical approach is therefore the only potentially viable way of making a comprehensive evaluation of the effects of regional policy. As a statistical exercise the search for the effects of REP is very much like looking for a needle in a haystack – and, moreover, in a hay-stack which contains several other needles. Thus if we are to satisfactorily isolate the effects of REP it is also necessary to disentangle the effects of other regional policy measures which operate alongside REP. Inevitably it is an elaborate and painstaking process which ends with an attempt to judge where the balance of the evidence lies.

We have gathered together data from as many different sources as possible and used a variety of techniques of analysis. In the space of this short article we can only do three things:

    I   Describe the broad lines of our methodology.
    II Present a truncated selection of some of our results.
    III Conclude with a short discussion on the case for and against REP.

I The methodology for evaluating the effects of regional policy as a whole and the impact of individual regional policy instruments

(a) Regional policy as a whole
The central principle of our methodology is to identify the economic variables in Development Areas which ought to be affected by regional policy, to explain the movement of these variables in Development Areas relative to changes in other regions or the equivalent national series in both active and passive regional policy periods whilst making whenever possible appropriate allowance for non-policy

191

factors. Amongst the conceptual and practical difficulties which we have attempted to overcome are the following:

(i) *Measuring the changing strength of regional policy*

One important task is to identify periods of relatively active and passive regional policy. This is not a 'black and white' comparison because periods of passive policy merge into periods of active policy during a, usually short, transitional period. Complexities also arise when some policy instruments are more strongly applied whilst others are being weakened. Nevertheless, the differences in policy strength during the post war years are of a sufficient magnitude as to be able to distinguish between periods of active and passive policy, although there may be more uncertainty attached to identifying the precise limits of the shorter phases of transition from one to the other. Measuring the strength of IDC policy presents particular conceptual problems because no government expenditure is involved. Problems also arise when the geographical boundaries of the Development Areas are changed.

(ii) *The choice of indicators for measuring the effects of policy*

A priori we expect regional policy to increase the level of activity in Development Areas. We must therefore decide which indicators of economic activity will provide us with a correct picture of what regional policy has achieved. We begin with a word on the ones which ought to be rejected and why, bearing in mind that some have to be rejected in any case because of the lack of any means of measurement.

Unemployment figures are frequently adopted as a guide to how effectively policy is working. Whilst this indicator has merits for other purposes, such as measuring the seriousness of labour market imbalance in Development Areas, we believe that it is particularly unsuitable for disentangling the effects of regional policy. This is because the unemployment figures are only one manifestation of the labour market imbalance which regional policy seeks to alleviate. We have shown elsewhere[1] that an effective regional policy may have the effect of reducing the level of net outward migration from a region, or of raising activity rates, before any substantial reduction in unemployment rates is apparent.

Another indicator which could possibly be used is that of changes in total employment in Development Areas relative to national changes in total employment. This choice of indicator is not really suitable, however, because the aggregated series of total employment makes it very difficult to hold 'other things equal' whilst the effect of regional policy is isolated. Regional policies of the traditional kind in the UK work directly on only one sector of total employment, namely manufacturing industry, and employment changes in other sectors may offset and thus disguise any beneficial impact of regional policy. For example, the large coal mining industry in Development Areas maintained its employment in the passive policy period of the 1950s but suffered from a large scale run-down in manpower in the 1960s. The effect of this within the total employment series is to offset the increases in employment in the manufacturing sector brought about by the more active regional policy of the 1960s.

Since regional policy is applied directly to manufacturing industries it is clearly desirable to choose indicators which measure the performance of this sector, relative to the performance of this sector nationally, if the effects of regional policy are to be satisfactorily disentangled. However, before this exercise can be meaningful we must take account of non-regional policy factors which may intervene to distort any comparison of employment changes between Development Areas and the UK in active and passive regional policy periods. Chief amongst such factors are differences in industrial structure between Development Areas and the UK economy as a whole.

[1] B Moore and J Rhodes, *Scottish Journal of Political Economy*, November 1974.

(iii) *Taking account of differences in industrial structure*

The aim here is to eliminate the impact on employment change of the main differences in industrial composition between Development Areas and the UK. This is important because the Development Areas have traditionally had more than their fair share of those manufacturing industries which are everywhere in decline or growing only slowly. Moreover, this detrimental effect on employment growth may vary at different times and thus introduce bias into any comparisons made between relative performance in active and passive policy periods.

The technique adopted for eliminating the main effects of industrial structure is quite simple, although it involves considerable computation. We first divide the manufacturing sector into industries using the industrial order numbers within the Standard Industrial Classification. Starting with a base year (in our case 1963) we apply the UK percentage employment changes, annually and for each industry, to the Development Area employment figure at the base year. We then sum for all industries to obtain an annual series which tells us what would have happened to the pattern of employment change in the Development Area manufacturing sector had it experienced the same growth, industry by industry, as the UK manufacturing sector. We shall call this series 'expected employment'. If we compare this series with the Development Area series of actual employment we are comparing two series which have the same industrial structure – one for the UK and one for the Development Areas – at least in the base year. The main impact on employment changes of differences in industrial structure is thus eliminated. Regional practitioners will recognise this structural adjustment as deriving from a broader analytical device, sometimes referred to as 'shift-share analysis'. The use of this technique has stimulated considerable discussion in the literature particularly on its merits and limitations for different purposes[2].

A number of criticisms of the technique have been made. Tests have shown that 'shift-share' results can be influenced by the level of industrial disaggregation used, the choice of the base and terminal years adopted, and whether the standardisation is based on national or regional weighting patterns. Another criticism is that the technique fails to take account of the multiplier effects and linkages between the industrial grouping distinguished. However all these criticisms do not necessarily apply with any force to our own modified use of this technique providing we use the same method throughout the analysis. This is because we are essentially comparing the differential growth performance of the Development Areas and the UK in active and passive policy periods and the figures in both periods are affected similarly by the particular degree of disaggregation and base year adopted. The difference between the two periods is therefore not substantially affected. Whilst the method is far from ideal it is eminently preferable to making no structural adjustments at all.

(iv) *Establishing the passive policy 'alternative position' and measuring the effect of regional policy*

We can now compare changes in actual manufacturing employment in Development Areas with changes in a structurally adjusted series of manufacturing employment based on UK growth rates. Our objective is to identify the effect of regional policy by comparing the relative movements in these two series in periods of active and passive regional policy. The first task is to explore the relationship between changes in these two series in the period of passive regional policy. It is this relationship which we use as a guide as to what would have happened in later years in the absence of an active regional policy. Where the two series move closely together in the passive policy period we can use the national structurally adjusted series as our 'expected' employment in the later periods of active policy without further adjustment. In this type of case the passive policy alternative position is very conveniently established. The regional policy effect is then measured as the difference between actual

[2]Some of the main contributors to this debate are – K C Bishop and C E Simpson, Components of Change Analysis: Problems of Alternative Approaches to Industrial Structure, Regional Studies, 1972; T W Buck, Shift Share Analysis – A guide to Regional Policy, Regional Studies 1970; D I Mackay, Industrial Structure and Regional Growth: A Methodological Problem, *Scottish Journal of Political Economy*, 1968; F J B Stilwell, Further thoughts on the Shift-Share Approach, Regional Studies, 1970; A P Thirlwall, A Measure of the 'Proper Distribution of Industry', *Oxford Economic Papers*, 1967; H J Brown, Shift and Share Projections of Regional Economic Growth – An Empirical Test, *Journal of Regional Science*, 1969; E S Dunn, A Statistical and Analytical Technique for Regional Analysis, The Regional Science Association Papers and Proceedings, Vol 6, 1960; J N Randall, Shift-Share Analysis as a Guide to the Employment Performance of West Central Scotland, *Scottish Journal of Political Economy*, 1973.

and expected employment[3]. However, if the relationship between the two series is more complex in the passive policy period the estimate of expected employment in later years is less easily determined[4]. It is nonetheless crucial to identify the passive policy alternative position as clearly as possible, since this is the only potentially fruitful way of arriving at estimates of the effects of regional policy.

(v) *Confirming the regional policy effect*
Before accepting this as a true measure of the effects of regional policy it is important to seek confirmation and support from a variety of sources.

Firstly, it could be dangerous to carry out this exercise and accept its results on the basis of one single data source. This discussion has been in terms of Department of Employment data, since they are most readily available But we have carried out this analysis using two entirely independant sets of employment data and the results are entirely consistent. Moreover, we carried out the same exercise for manufacturing investment in the Development Areas and a regional policy effect, consistent with the employment results, is identified. For this reason we can conclude that what we have identified as the regional policy effect was not caused by some 'quirk' in the data (such as, for example, a change in industrial classification). Data on industrial movement can also be used to confirm the results. (See section VII).

Secondly, it is not sufficient to carry out the analysis for the Development Areas as a whole because special factors in one region might have been responsible for the entire policy effect. It is essential that the exercise is carried out in each Development Area separately. This was done and a regional policy effect was separately identifiable in each region.

In addition it is important to check that a similar effect was not to be found in the non-Development Areas which do not benefit specifically from regional policy. This test was also favourable in that the policy effect was found to be limited to Development Areas. Nor could the policy effect be satisfactorily identified in non-manufacturing sectors which did not benefit directly from regional policy measures, although indirect effects consistent with the size of the regional policy effect in the manufacturing sector were apparent.

A further factor to be checked is that the size of the policy effect in different periods bears a close relationship in terms of both magnitude and timing to relative changes in the strength of regional policy in the respective periods. This brings up the problem of time-lags. The results presented below confirm that there is a very close relationship between changes in the strength of regional policy and changes in the magnitude of the regional policy effect – and it is this evidence which finally leads us to establish the causal link in a convincing way.

Nevertheless we must still present evidence to demonstrate that other theoretically possible causes of the regional policy effect could not, in practice, have brought about the observed impact. One such factor is that of labour availability which is known to be important to firms considering new locations. For this factor to be the cause of what we term 'the regional policy effect' firms would either have to find more labour available in Development Areas relative to other areas in the 1960s compared with the 1950s or for some reason find the same amount of labour more attractive in the 1960s than they did in the 1950s. We have been unable to find any evidence to support such a contention. On the contrary the pressure of demand in the non-Development Areas was lower in the 1960s than in the earlier decade which would lead one to expect that firms would have less need to seek the spare labour resources of Development Areas. However, knowledge of the impact of variations in the pressure of demand is crucial to a meaningful evaluation of the effects of regional policy and it is to this that we now turn.

[3]For example, see B C Moore and J Rhodes, *Economic Journal*, March 1973.

[4]For example, see B C Moore and J Rhodes, SJPE November 1974.

194

(*vi*) *Taking account of variations in the pressure of demand*

Variations in the pressure of demand in the economy as a whole affect the implementation, the effectiveness and the evaluation of regional policy in a variety of subtle ways.

First, there are two ways in which variations in the pressure of demand can affect the implementation of regional policy. When the pressure of demand is high, unemployment in Development Areas falls and it then appears that the regional problem is being solved. This increases the temptation to relax regional policy. Insofar as governments are tempted to do this, as in the mid-1950s, the lagged effect of the relaxation of policy has been to reduce employment in Development Areas in the subsequent recession when the regional problem is at its worst. Variations in the pressure of demand also may have encouraged governments to treat the regional problem as a short run phenomena and diverted attention from its underlying causes which require long term policy solutions.

Secondly, where regional policy instruments take the form of administrative decisions, as in the case of the IDC policy, the detailed implementation of policy may be affected by variations in the overall pressure of demand. For example when the pressure of demand is low and there is a cyclical downturn in manufacturing investment one of the Government's national objectives might be to encourage firms to invest more. This objective may conflict with that of regional policy when considering whether to approve or refuse IDC applications outside the Development Areas. In a recession an IDC refusal may result in the firms not expanding capacity at all rather than being encouraged to divert investment to Development Areas. In this kind of situation the Government may be less inclined to refuse IDC applications for prosperous regions – this is part of the explanation as to why the pattern of the opening of new factories in Development Areas is cyclical.

But variations in the pressure of demand also affect the opening of new factories in Development Areas through the normal mechanisms of the labour market. When the pressure of demand is high, labour is particularly scarce in prosperous regions. This scarcity provides an additional incentive to establish new productive capacity in Development Areas where labour is less scarce. In a national recession, there is less need to seek to make use of unused resources in Development Areas – this is the other part of the explanation as to why the pattern of the opening of new factories in Development Areas is cyclical.

Apart from these phenomena, variations in the pressure of demand also affect the measurement of the effects of regional policy, and particularly if measured in the way outlined above. It will be recalled that our method of measuring the effects of regional policy compares actual Development Area employment with that which would have been 'expected' in the absence of an active regional policy. This method makes some allowance for variations in the pressure of demand in that both actual and expected employment series are cyclical in character and no further allowance would be necessary providing the national cycle and the Development Area cycle were identical. But there is considerable evidence to suggest that there is a differential employment cycle, even when allowance is made for the main differences in industrial structure. This differential cycle takes the form of a rather more severe recession in the Development Areas when the overall pressure of demand is low, and vice versa when the pressure of demand is high. When measuring the regional policy effect, or its change over a specific period, it is important to compare actual and expected employment at points in time when the overall pressure of demand is approximately the same. It would be meaningful, for instance, to compare the size of the regional policy effect at 1963, 1967 and 1970 because the pressure of demand in these three years was similar and therefore the differential cyclical component

195

would not distort the comparison. But if the year 1971 were chosen, the comparison would be less meaningful because of the very sharp reduction in the overall pressure of demand compared with the other three years. Indeed in 1971 there was a negative differential cyclical effect on employment in Development Areas which had the effect of more than offsetting the positive employment contribution of regional policy in that year. It is therefore essential that if the effect of regional policy is to be disentangled satisfactorily, it must be measured at a constant pressure of demand.

(vii) *The Department of Industry's record of the opening of new factories in development areas and other regions*

Further confirmation of a substantial regional policy effect can be obtained from a detailed analysis of the opening of new factories in Development Areas. This can be done using information collected by the Department of Industry on the annual number of new factories opened up in each of 50 sub-regions of the UK. Each new factory opened is recorded with its associated employment, its sub-region destination (location) and its sub-region of origin (ie where the decision was made to establish a new factory). These data build up a picture of 'industrial movement' between different regions of the UK in periods of both active and passive regional policy[5]. These data are proving to be a major step forward in securing the information which is essential to a full evaluation of regional policy and forms an integral part of our basic methodology. We show below that the volume of industrial movement to Development Areas is very closely related to the strength of regional policy and that employment associated with the policy contribution to new factory openings amounts to about two-thirds of the estimated total policy effect. There is a welcome degree of consistency between these results and the results of analysis based on actual and expected employment.

(b)   Assessing the separate effects of regional policy instruments

Disentangling the effects of individual policy instruments is so difficult that the only sensible approach is to obtain information from a wide variety of sources and carry out studies involving a variety of economic and statistical analyses to find out how consistent are the results – and whether convincing conclusions can be drawn from a careful review of all the evidence.

(i)   *The contribution of new factories distinguished from the contribution of old factories (indigenous firms) to the overall regional policy effect*

The main reason for seeking to make this distinction is that some regional policy instruments can be expected to influence primarily the building of new factories whilst others should have a bigger influence on indigenous firms. In the former category are the industrial development certificate procedures, the provision of government factories and building grants. REP on the other hand might perhaps exert its biggest influence on employment in indigenous industries which receive over 90 per cent of REP payments. The distinction between 'new' and 'old' industries should therefore throw useful light on the effects of policy instruments especially when combined with information on the timing and strength of these policy instruments through time. For example, the IDC policy and government factory building programme work mainly through the opening of new factories in Development Areas and before 1963 it was the only major regional policy instrument operating. Since the IDC policy government factory building programme was operated relatively stringently between 1945 and 1952 and between 1958 and 1963 but relatively weakly between 1952 and 1957 we can build up a fairly clear picture of how effective the new factory policy was when used by itself.

Similarly only two regional policy instruments can be expected to have much influence on employment in indigenous firms – one is the regionally differential investment grant, the other is REP. The differential investment grant was introduced in 1963 and was not supplemented by REP until late 1967. There are thus four years

[5]The first figures were published in 1968 by R S Howard *The Movement of Manufacturing Industry in the United Kingdom 1945 to 1965*, HMSO. We obtained later figures directly from the Department of Industry.

when investment incentives operated on their own and four years in which the two operated together. Notwithstanding the difficult problem of time-lags there is sufficient time to establish strong presumptions about the impact which these measures had on indigenous firms – both separately and combined.

(ii) *Investigating the time-lag problem*

On *a priori* grounds we might expect a long time lag between a change in regional policy and the eventual employment it creates in Development Areas, particularly so in the case of new factory openings in which employment starts at zero and builds up to a stable, mature labour force. In order to specify the time-lags accurately we studied the employment build-up of over 200 factories in the Northern region which were newly established between 1946 and 1970. We found that on average it took eight years for a newly opened factory to build up to its mature labour force, although nearly three-quarters of eventual employment can be expected within three years of the factory opening. This investigation on time-lags is consistent with work which has been done by the Department of Industry. Time-lags in the indigenous sector are likely to be much shorter than is the case with the employment build-up in new factories.

(iii) *Allocating the total regional policy effect between different policy instruments*

We start out with the total regional policy effect, and divide this between employment in new factories and employment in indigenous firms[6]. We then make the pressure of demand adjustment by relating annual changes in the regional policy effect (actual-expected employment) to an indicator of changes in the overall pressure of demand (the UK male unemployment rate). This allows us to estimate the regional policy effect at a constant pressure of demand.

(a) Method 1

This method has its limitations but is valuable because it enables strong presumptions to be made about the effectiveness of different policy instruments without recourse to more sophisticated econometric analysis with its more demanding requirements. To allocate the total regional policy effect between the different policy instruments we examine changes in the policy effect in periods of time when specific instruments were operating[7], making due allowance for time-lags, particularly with respect to the long employment build up in new factories.

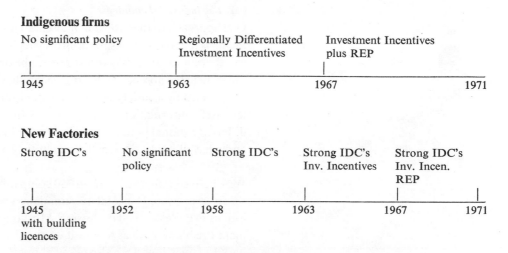

Indigenous firms

No significant policy	Regionally Differentiated Investment Incentives	Investment Incentives plus REP
1945	1963	1967	1971

New Factories

Strong IDC's	No significant policy	Strong IDC's	Strong IDC's Inv. Incentives	Strong IDC's Inv. Incen. REP
1945 with building licences	1952	1958	1963	1967	1971

This method of disentangling the effects of different policy instruments rests on the rather crude distinction between 'weak policy' and 'strong policy' for each policy instrument. Thus we establish the effects of one policy instrument in a period when this operated alone, and then assume, after adjusting for time-lags, that it would have had a similar effect in a later period had it operated alone. Thus for the indigenous firms regionally differentiated investment incentives operated alone

[6]There are several ways of doing this. For two methods see B C Moore and J Rhodes, SJPE November 1974.

[7]A detailed discussion of policy instruments and measures of changes in policy strength can be found in B C Moore and J Rhodes, *Economic Journal,* March 1973. (Appendix)

for the period 1963 to 1967, hence it is possible to isolate their effects. Moreover since we know that the investment incentives were applied at roughly the same strength in the later REP period, 1967 to 1971, we can allocate the equivalent employment (apart from differences arising from time-lags) to the latter period. The effect of REP then emerges as a residual in the latter period. The same procedure can be carried out for the new factory sector, although this is affected by more policy instruments and the problem of allowing adequately for the long employment build up can be avoided by looking at data on new factory openings rather than at the employment in new factories.

(b) Method 2

Method 2 is similar in approach to Method 1 although statistically more sophisticated. It relies on a more sensitive measurement of the changing strength of regional policy instruments which become the independent variables in regression equations. In the case of new factories the dependent variable is the number of new factory openings. In the indigenous sector annual changes in structually adjusted employment is the dependent variable.

(iv) *The input/output approach to estimating the effects of REP*

It is possible to estimate the likely effect of REP in stimulating output and employment in Development Areas with the help of input-output tables. By finding out from our industrial enquiry how firms say they have used REP we can trace the effect of REP on manufacturing prices and profits etc through the Development Area economy. Using plausible price elasticities we can then calculate the likely effect on manufacturing output. As a final step in this economic analysis we can relate changes in manufacturing output to changes in manufacturing employment in order to estimate how many new manufacturing jobs will be created as a direct consequence of REP. This approach does not tell us how many new jobs REP has in fact created, but rather the size of the REP effect which can be expected given that we know how firms have used REP and given that we know how output and employment respond to price changes.

For this exercise we were fortunate to be able to make use of an input-output table for Northern Ireland and to manipulate this using Cambridge Growth Project programmes[8].

(v) *The industrial enquiry*

One approach to the problem of disentangling the effects of regional policy instruments is to put questions to the firms which are affected by them. It is not possible to get accurate quantitative answers to the question of 'what would have been different in the absence of one regional policy instrument' since all business decisions are affected by a variety of factors of continuously changing significance. Nevertheless useful information can be gained by this method of enquiry as to how important different regional policy instruments were in influencing businessmen's decisions and what effects businessmen thought they had had on their firms.

We obtained information from 350 companies in Development Areas. In 300 cases the firms answered a postal questionnaire whilst the remaining 50 were willing to join us in quite detailed discussion. Most questions related to the Regional Employment Premium, both as to how it was used and to what effects it was thought to have had. But questions were also asked about the relevance of other regional policy instruments. In addition to the results of our own industrial enquiry it is also possible to draw on the information provided by the large ILEAG industrial survey conducted by the Department of Industry and now published. This latter survey concentrated on asking questions about regional policy instruments other than REP and that is one reason why our own industrial enquiry concentrated very much on the Regional Employment Premium. The two together contain as good a guide

[8]This approach is similar to, although a little bit more sophisticated than the back of envelope exercises carried out in the Treasury and Department of Economic Affairs prior to the launching of REP. The results are only as good as the assumptions on which they depend.

198

about the impact of regional policy as is likely to be obtained from this type of survey work. It can be used, not so much in its own right, but as valuable supporting evidence for the quantitative results of the economic and statistical analysis.

II A selection of results

(a) The regional policy effect as a whole

Taking actual and expected employment as discussed earlier, an adjustment is made for variations in the pressure of demand in order to measure the regional policy effect at a constant pressure of demand. From regression analysis it appears that each percentage point change in the UK male unemployment rate is associated with a regionally differentiated cyclical effect of up to 10,000 jobs. In estimating the policy effect the pressure of demand is held constant at a male employment rate of two per cent. In addition further work has been done to identify more accurately the passive policy 'alternative position' including a disaggregated analysis for each Development Area.

In relation to the earlier article two main conclusions follow from this extension of the analysis. Firstly a small regional policy effect can now be detected in the years 1961, 1962 and 1963, ie in the period of transition from a passive to an active regional policy. This small early effect had been offset or disguised in the interim results by the low pressure of demand prevailing in the economy in 1962 and 1963. Our analysis on industrial movement confirms that this early policy effect in the transitional period is a genuine one, and this conclusion is entirely consistent with what one would have expected from the transitional policy changes which took place between 1959 and 1963.

The second conclusion is that the total regional policy effect in the four main Development Area regions is estimated at around 200,000 manufacturing jobs between 1960 and 1971[9].

We also carried out more detailed work on the regional policy effect on Merseyside and South-West Development Areas which is estimated at about 40,000 new jobs. Allowing a further 10,000 jobs in metal manufacturing and shipbuilding industries the total regional policy effect in all manufacturing industries in all the Development Areas between 1960 and 1971 is estimated at 250,000. We ought then to add on something for the indirect multiplier effects of new jobs on employment in service industries. Using a short-term multiplier of 1.2 the additional service employment would be almost 50,000 jobs. This brings the total regional policy effect to about 300,000 jobs by 1971[10].

(b) Confirmation of a sizeable policy effect from an analysis of industrial movement

In figure 1 we show the number of openings of new manufacturing establishments in all Development Areas for 1945 to 1971. There is a close relationship between the number of moves to Development Areas and the strength of regional policy – a relationship which is unique to the Development Areas regions. Using the passive policy period 1951 to 1959 as a guide as to what would have happened in later years between 1960 and 1971 is responsible for directing about 800 new factories into Development Areas. If on average each factory builds up to mature labour force of about 200, which is roughly the figure to be expected after allowing for closures, then about 150,000 new jobs have been generated in the Development Areas in new factories alone as a direct consequence of regional policy. Employment generated in new factories in this way thus accounts for just under two-thirds of all manufacturing employment generated by regional policy in the 1960s. We return below to this series of 'moves' to Development Areas and carry out some regression analysis.

[9]This compares with our earlier estimate of 150,000 manufacturing jobs between 1963 and 1970 (shipbuilding, metal manufacture and indirect multiplier effects are excluded).

[10]This compares with the figure of 220,000 jobs in the Economic Journal article over the shorter period 1963 to 1970 without adjustment for pressure of demand. The estimate of 300,000 jobs covers the period 1960 to 1971. It should not be forgotten however that regional policy in the form of building licences, IDC's and government factory building was very active between 1945 and 1950. It is likely, that regional policy in this early posr-war period brought a further 80-100,000 jobs into Development Areas that would not otherwise have been there.

199

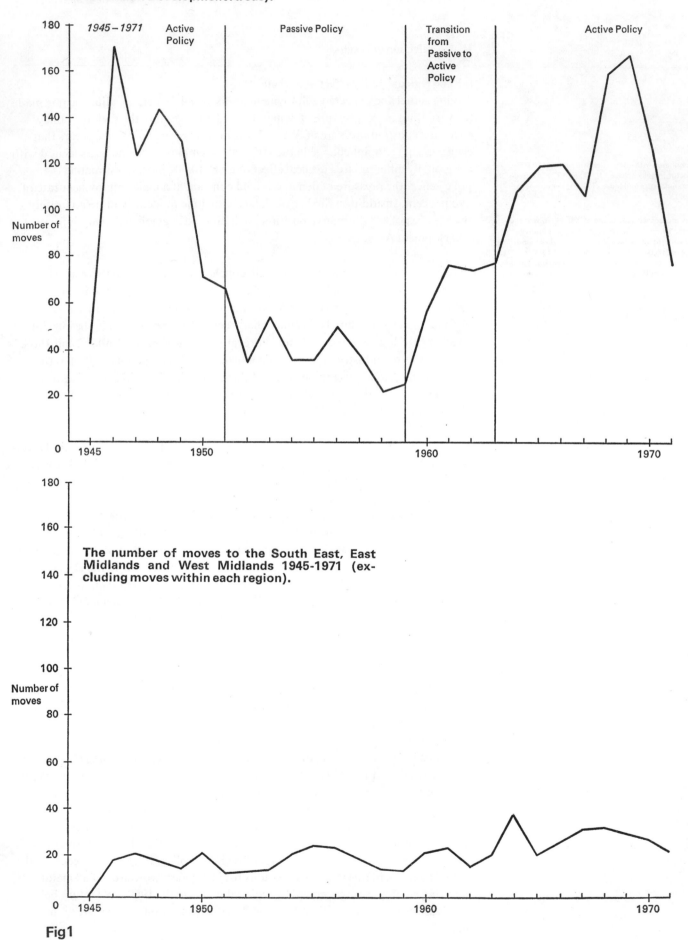

The Number of moves to Development Areas of Manufacturing Firms 1945-1971 (excluding moves within Development Areas).

The number of moves to the South East, East Midlands and West Midlands 1945-1971 (excluding moves within each region).

Fig 1

200

Before that however, in order to divide more accurately the total regional policy effect between employment generated in new factories and employment generated in indigenous manufacturing firms in Development Areas, we need a more sophisticated method of translating the number of 'moves' into employment generated by them, on an annual basis.

(c) The regional policy effect in the indigenous and new factory sectors of manufacturing industry in development areas

From an analysis of the employment build-up in 200 factories newly established in the Northern region since the war we established that, on average it takes eight years or more for new factories to reach a mature labour force. Moreover we know what percentage of their eventual labour force is likely to have been recruited in the first, second, third years and so on. Since we also have actual employment figures on all surviving moves to Development Areas at selected terminal years[11] we can construct a time series of estimated employment generated in these new factories year by year. From this cumulative time series we subtract an estimate of the non-policy employment generated in new factories again using the passive policy period 1951 to 1959 as a guide as to the alternative position.

The policy effect in new factories can then be subtracted from the total policy effect to establish the number of new jobs generated by regional policy in the 'indigenous' sector[12]. This is shown in Table 1. We do this in order to develop ways of disentangling the effects of individual regional policy instruments.

(d) Allocating the total policy-induced employment gain between different policy instruments

In this section we break-down the total regional policy effect between different policy instruments without, at this stage, worrying too much about time-lags. Our approach is to see how the total effect changes in selected time periods when the strength of regional policy was significantly different from that in other periods. The additional breakdown of the employment gain between the immigrant and 'indigenous' sectors should allow us to make presumptions about which policy instruments contributed most to the employment gain in a particular period. This may seem a rather mechanical and arbitrary approach but it should establish some rough orders of magnitude.

Table 1

The contribution of regional policy to manufacturing employment in four development areas in selected time periods (*000's jobs*)

		1960 to 1963	1963 to 1967	1967 to 1970	1967 to 1971
Total Employment Gain estimated at constant pressure of demand	Total	22.7	81.7	85.9	92.6
	Per annum	7.6	20.4	28.6	23.1
Employment gain from new factories	Total	17.9	43.8	39.8	53.0
	Per annum	5.6	10.9	13.2	13.2
Employment gain in indigenous firms	Total	4.8	37.9	46.1	39.6
	Per annum	1.6	9.5	15.4	9.9

The time periods were selected to coincide with important policy changes. The period 1960 to 1963 was the transitional phase to an active regional policy and the policy effect is small relative to later periods. The year 1963 saw the introduction of 25 per cent building grants and investment incentives which were available to all firms in Development Areas and which contained up to 1970 and beyond. The introduction of REP in 1967 clearly represented a further major change of policy which should determine the selection of time periods. Thus the years 1963 to 1967 represent an ideal choice of a pre-REP period.

[11]From the work of Mr R S Howard at the Department of Industry.

[12]The Indigenous Sector is defined as all firms in Development Areas except new factories generated by regional policy after 1959.

The choice of a suitable post-REP period is less straightforward. At first sight it would seem obvious to select the four year period 1967 to 1971 and this is indeed shown in Table 1. But there are good reasons for supposing that the year 1971 is not a wholly desirable choice as a terminal year. The first reason is that a severe weakening of regional policy occurred after the election of the Conservative Government in June 1970. The Selective Employment Premium was abolished, the IDC policy was less stringently applied and differential investment incentives were substantially reduced. In short there was in 1971 an atmosphere, in relation to the possible undermining of regional policy, which was entirely different to that in earlier years and indigenous firms could react quickly to it.

This new uncertainty which affected firms in 1971 coincided with the most severe recession which had been encountered in post-war Britain and this is the second reason why 1971 is not an ideal choice of a terminal year. We have discussed the need to estimate the effects of regional policy at a constant pressure of demand. We have attempted to make some adjustment for changes in the pressure of demand using a linear regression equation. There is a strong presumption that this method under-estimated the 'pressure of demand effect' in 1971 when unusually large numbers of redundancies in Development Areas were offsetting the beneficial effects of regional policy.

Thus in Table 1 the regional policy effect in the indigenous sector is lower in 1971 than in 1970. Some part of this fall may have been caused by the substantial weakening of regional policy in 1971. Alternatively our pressure of demand adjustment may be inadequate for years of very high unemployment because of a non-linear relationship between national/regional unemployment and the overall pressure of demand.

We have less reason to be suspicious of 1970 as the terminal year because the pressure of demand was similar to that in the other terminal years, 1963 and 1967. The period 1967 to 1970 may therefore be a preferable post-REP period to compare with the pre-REP period, 1963 to 1967.

In Table 1 we show the employment gain generated by regional policy in each selected period. In 1960 to 1963 new jobs were being generated by regional policy at the rate of about 7,600 per annum. This immediately gives some indication of the effectiveness of the IDC policy and government factory building and loans under the Local Employment Acts since these were the only policy measures in operation during this period. During this period most of the policy effect is shown to be generated in new factories which is what one would expect on *a priori* grounds from policy instruments of this type.

The regional policy package was substantially strengthened in the period 1963 to 1967. Building grants and regionally differentiated investment incentives were introduced for *all* manufacturing firms in Development Areas. The overall employment gain accelerates markedly from 7,000 to about 20,000 new jobs per annum. We cannot conclude from this acceleration that investment incentives operating alone would therefore create 13,000 per annum. What we can say is that when the investment incentives are combined with an IDC policy the result is very much more effective than when the IDC policy operates alone. In this period the overall employment gain is divided roughly equally between new factories and the expansion of indigenous firms – a conclusion which is again entirely consistent with *a priori* expectations about how the new policy instruments might work. In the indigenous sector it is clear that investment incentives had an identifiable and independent effect on employment.

The policy package strengthened again by the introduction of REP in 1967, increased in effectiveness whichever post-REP period is chosen. The increased effectiveness is most marked if the preferred period 1967 to 1970 is selected, the employment gain accelerating from about 20,000 new jobs to about 29,000 new jobs per annum.

If this acceleration could be attributed to REP it amounts to about 27,000 additional jobs[13]. Most of this gain appears in the indigenous sector which again would be consistent with *a priori* expectations because this sector receives the bulk of all REP payments. If we were to adopt 1971 as the terminal year the post-REP period still shows an improvement on 1963 to 1967 but it is much smaller at about 12,000 new jobs, most of which occur in the new factories sector. Such a conclusion would be rather odd in that it would be saying that REP of £90m per annum paid to indigenous industries in Development Areas had no effect on employment whatsoever. This would be difficult to accept if only for the reason that, even if REP was treated by firms as a windfall addition to profits, it could be expected to reduce redundancies and prevent closures of firms in financial difficulties.

But the most telling reason for prefering to measure the REP as at 1970 is as follows. In Table 1, the total regional policy effect is shown to fall in absolute terms between 1970 and 1971, the only reduction to be recorded in the entire period of active regional policy. Further it is shown that this reduction is confined to the indigenous sector. We should not expect new jobs created by investment incentives to disappear overnight nor would we expect REP to be effective in 1970 and entirely ineffective in 1971 (although it may be less effective because of the fall in its real value as wages and prices rise). We are therefore left with the only two likely explanations that the reduction in the policy effect was caused by the abolition of the Selective Employment Premium or that our adjustment for the pressure of demand is inadequate. Our interpretation is that the increase in the total policy effect occurring in 1971 was more than offset by an unpredictably large negative regionally differentiated cyclical effect.

(e) The effects of individual regional policy measures on employment in indigenous firms – a regression analysis

The hypothesis is that changes in manufacturing employment in the indigenous sector of Development Areas moves closely with UK employment in the same industries (ie after allowing for differences in industrial structure except for a regionally differentiated cyclical component and the contribution made by regional policy instruments).

The dependent variable is the first difference (annual change) in actual indigenous employment in Scotland, Wales and the North of England. This variable is derived by subtracting policy-induced employment in new factories from total actual employment in manufacturing industries (excluding shipbuilding and iron and steel).

We explain variations in this using four explanatory variables. These are a cyclical variable (MU) and the two policy variables (REP and II). The fourth variable is the annual change in expected employment derived by simply using UK industrial growth rates as a guide as to what should have happened in the Development Areas in the absence of regional policy. The basic equation to be estimated is therefore:

$$AIE = a + bMU + cEIE + dII + eREP + u$$

where[14]

AIE = the first difference (annual change) in actual indigenous employment in Scotland, Wales and North.

EIE = annual change in expected indigenous employment.

[13]Before any allowance is made for the effects of REP in Merseyside and South-West Development Areas, in shipbuilding and metal manufacturing and any indirect effects on employment in service industries.

[14]The IDC policy is not an explantory variable because its effect on indigenous firms in Development Areas is expected to be negligible.

203

MU = national male unemployment rate (%).

II = present value of regionally differentiated investment incentives in Development Areas.

REP= change in regional employment premium payments (£m in real terms).

u = a stochastic error term.

Using this formulation the equation estimated by OLS is:

$$AIE_t = 2.9 - 4.3\,MU_t + 1.08\,EIE_t + 0.7\,II_{t-1} + 0.22\,REP_{t-1} + \hat{u}t$$

$$(0.67)\,(-2.0)\quad (14.2)\quad\quad (3.8)\quad\quad (2.2)$$

$$\bar{R}^2 = 0.95 \quad DW = 2.18$$

Figures in brackets are t ratios.

Actual and predicted values for this equation are shown in Figure 2.

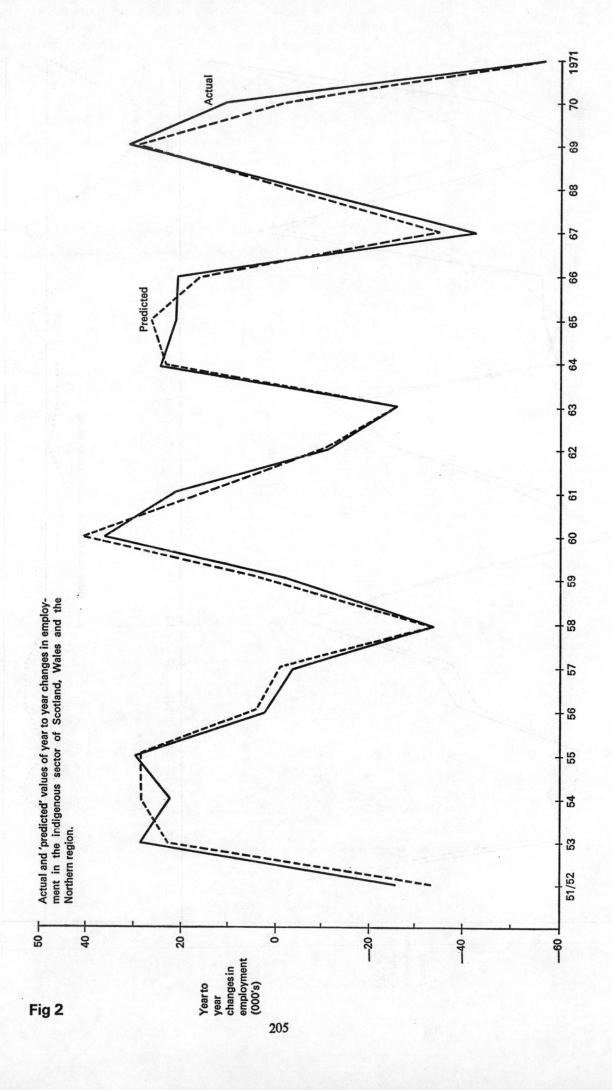

Actual and 'predicted' values of year to year changes in employment in the indigenous sector of Scotland, Wales and the
Northern region.

Fig 2

Year to
year
changes in
employment
(000's)

Actual

Predicted

50
40
20
0
−20
−40
−60

51/52   53   54   55   56   57   58   59   60   61   62   63   64   65   66   67   68   69   70   1971

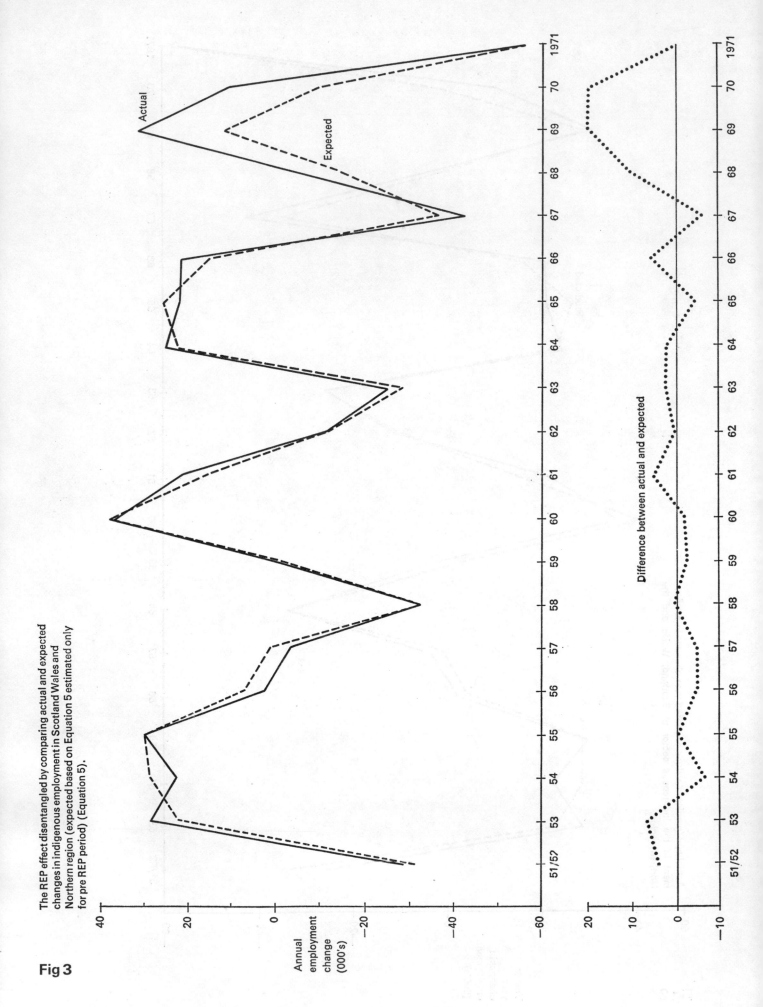

The REP effect disentangled by comparing actual and expected changes in indigenous employment in Scotland Wales and Northern region (expected based on Equation 5 estimated only for pre REP period) (Equation 5).

Fig 3

Annual employment change (000's)

Actual

Expected

Difference between actual and expected

The results are encouraging in that all the coefficients of the variables are of the 'right' sign and statistically significant (at 5 per cent) and the coefficient on the EIE variable is very close to one supporting the view that changes in manufacturing employment in Development Areas move in line with national changes after allowing for the impact of regional policy and differential regional cycle. Both policy measures are shown to be contributing to employment with a lag of about one year.

Another approach is to estimate the equation only for the pre-REP period from 1953 to 1967. Having done this the results of the equation can be used to predict what should have happened after 1967 had REP not been introduced. This expected series can then be compared with what actually happened with REP in operation. The results of this exercise were again encouraging.

The equation, run for the period prior to 1967, is as follows:

$$AIE_t = 10.5 - 8.6\ MU_t + 1.00\ EIE_t + 0.66II_{t-1}$$
$$\quad\quad\ (1.9)\quad (2.8)\quad\quad (14.8)\quad\quad (4.5)$$

$$\bar{R}^2 = 0.965 \quad\quad\quad DW = 2.28$$

This equation is then used to provide a guide as to what would have happened after 1967 in the absence of REP and this expected change in employment is compared with the actual change in employment in Figure three. In some ways this equation is to be preferred to the previous one partly because it avoids any possible collinearity between the REP and MU variables and therefore the coefficients on MU is better determined. Moreover the coefficient on EIE is now even closer to *a priori* expectations and there is further support for the conclusion that investment incentives stimulated in Development Areas when they alone were operating on the indigenous sector. This equation indicates a somewhat larger REP effect than the previous one but it does not allow for the fact that REP could well make the investment incentives more effective. For broad estimates of the effects of regional policy instruments on the indigenous sector see Tables eight and nine.

(f) The effects of individual regional policy instruments on the rate of 'movement' of new factories into development areas – a regression analysis

Because of the long time-lags relating to the build up of employment in new factories the dependent variable is the number of new factories moving to Development Areas (MDA). This is explained in terms of four independent variables.

(i) The IDC policy (IDC)

This policy is specifically designed to restrict new factory building in the more prosperous regions of the Midlands and South-East in the hope that new industrial development will be diverted to Development Areas[15]. In order to satisfactorily test for the effects of the IDC machinery on Development Areas a measure of the 'tightness' of IDC controls in the prosperous regions is required. The model could then test whether the controls on the prosperous areas were in fact diverting new factories to Development Areas. The indicator for the strength of the IDC policy is official IDC refusals (measured in terms of the expected employment involved) in the Midlands and South-East regions, expressed as a percentage of refusals plus approvals in these regions[16]. With such a measure, the expectation is of a positive sign for the coefficient indicating that the stronger is the IDC control on the prosperous regions the more moves there are likely to be to Development Areas.

(ii) Regionally differentiated investment incentives (II)

These incentives could be expected to increase the flow of new firms into Development Areas. The strength of this policy measure was estimated as the discounted present value of the regionally differentiated investment incentives per £100 of capital expenditure[17].

[15]Conceptually we regard the IDC policy as encompassing the government factory building programme in Development Areas. One arm of the policy restricts new factory building in prosperous areas – the other arm of the policy is concerned with actually building new factories in Development Areas, some in advance of known requirements. Empirically the 'carrot and stick' of this factory location policy have moved closely together in the sense that a tightening of IDC controls in prosperous regions has always been accompanied by increased factory building in Development Areas.

[16]Although we have some information on the number of involuntary withdrawals (unofficial refusals) of IDC applications in the prosperous regions there are insufficient data to incorporate them into the time series. The evidence available however suggests that unofficial refusals vary in line with official refusals.

[17]The series of present values is lower in the period of investment grants 1966 to 1970 than in the earlier period of differential investment allowances 1963 to 1965. To allow for the possibility that grants were more effective (£ for £ in present value terms) than tax allowances a dummy variable was also tried in the equation which was not lower in the grant period and therefore allowed the grants to be about 10 per cent more effective (£ for £) than tax allowances.

207

(iii) The Regional Employment Premium (REP)

Although REP was not specifically designed to encourage new factories to move into Development Areas (but rather to make existing factories more competitive) it would be surprising if it had no effect on the number of moves to Development Areas. The REP was introduced into the regression equation as an index number reflecting the changing value of the premium in real terms. The coefficient, which should also be positive, will represent the number of additional moves to Development Areas generated by REP.

(iv) The overall pressure of demand (MU)

The cyclical pattern in the volume of movement can be explained on *a priori* grounds in terms of shortages of factory space and labour in the prosperous regions whenever demand and output accelerates during the upswing of the trade cycle. On the downturn less new capacity is required and regional policy has therefore less opportunity to divert new factories to Development Areas. The male unemployment rate was used as the indicator of the overall pressure of demand. The expected sign of the coefficient is negative because when MU is decreasing (the pressure of demand is rising) the number of moves should increase.

The basic regression equation to be tested is therefore[18]:

$$MDA_1 = a_1 + a_2\,MU + a_3\,II + a_4\,IDC + a_5\,REP + u$$

where MDA_1 = the number of moves into all the Development Areas (except Northern Ireland[19]).

The Ordinary Least Squares estimates give the following equation[20]:

$$MDA_{1t} = 39.7 - 15.2\,MU_t + 1.87\,II_{t\text{-}1}\,2.14\,IDC_{t\text{-}1} + 76.31\,REP_{t\text{-}1} + \hat{u}_t \qquad (1)$$
$$\quad\ (4.26)\ \ (-3.10)\quad\ (4.10)\quad\ (4.66)\qquad\quad (5.84)$$

Figures in parenthesis are T - ratios.
$\bar{R}^2$ = .91 Durbin-Watson Statistic (D - W) = 1.29

The low value of the D - W statistic suggests serial correlation of the errors. In an attempt to allow for this the equation was re-estimated using a maximum-likelihood procedure using a second-order autoregressive error process. This brought about a significant reduction in the degree of serial correlation and resulted in the following equation[21]:

$$MDA_{1t} = 29.69 - 7.97\,MU_t + 2.01\,II_{t\text{-}1} + 2.05\,IDC_{t\text{-}1} + 52.67\,REP_{t\text{-}1} + \hat{u}_t \qquad (2)$$
$$\qquad\quad (4.28)\quad (1.81)\qquad (5.52)\qquad (5.76)\qquad\ (4.79)$$

$$\bar{R}^2 = 0.94 \qquad\qquad DW = 1.89$$

$$\hat{u}_t = 0.49\,\hat{u}_{t\text{-}1} - 0.71\,\hat{u}_{t\text{-}2} + \hat{v}_t$$

The first results are encouraging in that over 90 per cent of the variation in MDA is explained by the four independant variables, with all the policy variables significant indicating a strong presumption that all three main policy instruments have been effective in generating moves of manufacturing firms to Development Areas. Actual and predicted values for equation (2) are plotted in Figure 4. Before going on to assess the relative impact of the different policy instruments as suggested by equation (2) it is necessary to consider at least two additional factors which could have influenced the volume of movement to the Development Areas in the 1960s. These are firstly, the introduction of the Special Development Area (SDA) programme in the Autumn of 1967, and secondly the changes in the geographical designation of the Development Areas. The approach in dealing with these two difficulties is to allocate to them the maximum possible effects deemed plausible in order to find out how far such adjustments undermine the basic equation (2).

[18]The estimating period is 1951 to 1971 which excludes the period of active regional policy immediately after the war. This is because of the difficulty of obtaining a satisfactory measure of the building licence control in that period.

[19]Northern Ireland was excluded because financial inducements were given to manufacturing industry there several years before regionally differentiated financial assistance was available to British Development Areas.

[20]On a priori grounds there are good reasons for supposing that there will be a time-lag between a change in regional policy and its effect on the number of moves to Development Areas although the lag problem in the case of moves is likely to be shorter and less complex than in the case of the response of employment to a policy change.

[21]Parameters were also estimated using a maximum likelihood procedure which assumes a first order autoregressive process. The value of the log-likelihood for OLS was -49.47, for MLH first order error process -48.48 and for MLH second order process -45.84. Applying the likelihood ratio test, twice the difference between the log-likelihood is distributed as a chi-square variate. A value exceeding 3.8 is significant at the 5 per cent level. Thus the chi-squared value of MLH second order error process relative to MLH first order process is 5.29 and therefore significant at the 5 per cent level with one degree of freedom. The estimation was carried out using a programme for a small sample estimation written by M H Pesaran. The underlying statistical theory is discussed in Small Sample Estimation of Dynamic Economic Models, unpublished Ph D Cambridge 1972.

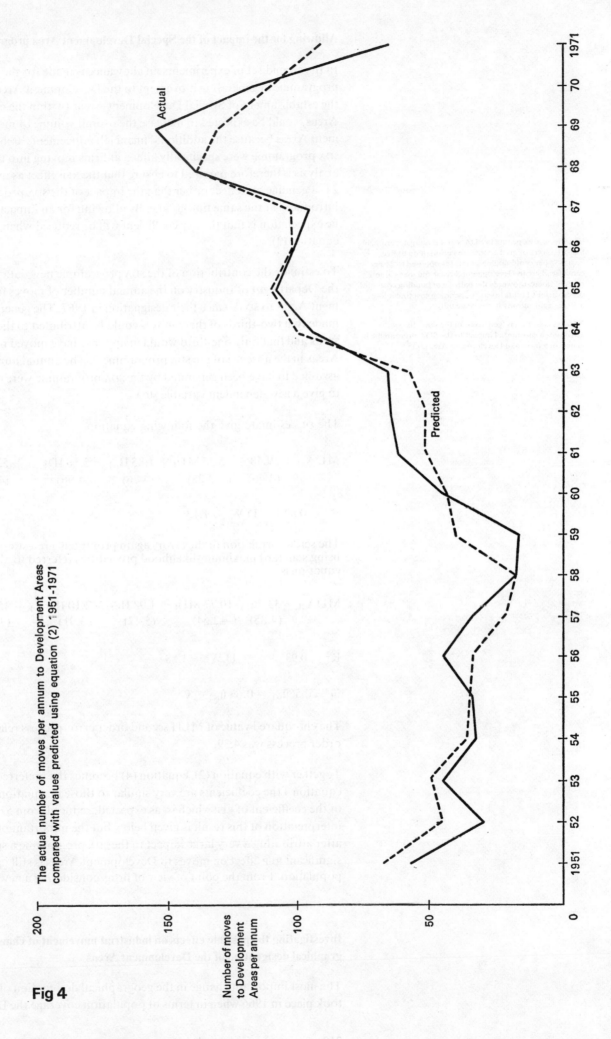

The actual number of moves per annum to Development Areas compared with values predicted using equation (2) 1951-1971

Fig 4

Allowing for the impact of the Special Development Area programme

In the second set of experiments an allowance is made for the impact of the SDA programme in generating movement to the Development Areas. On *a priori* grounds the establishment of Special Development Areas (within the existing Development Areas) could be expected to increase the overall volume of movement to Development Areas because the additional financial inducements associated with the SDA programme were specifically aimed at firms moving into these areas[22]. Further analysis is therefore required to ensure that the REP effect as measured in equation 2 is a genuine REP effect rather than the impact of the SDA programme which was introduced at the same time as REP. By allowing for an impact of SDA programme he expectation is that the REP coefficient will be reduced when compared with equation (2).

To estimate the contribution of the SDA programme new data were obtained from the Department of Industry on the annual number of moves from outside Development Areas to SDA's since their designation in 1967. The generous assumption was made that two-thirds of these moves could be attributed to the establishment of the SDA's and that only one-third would in any case have moved into the Development Areas in the absence of the SDA programme[23]. The annual number of moves thus assumed to have been generated by the SDA programme were deducted from MDA_1 to give a new dependent variable MDA_2.

The OLS estimate give the following equation:

$$MDA_{2t} = 39.48 - 15.25\,MU_t + 1.85\,II_{t-1} + 2.16\,IDC_{t-1} + 52.79\,REP_{t-1} + \hat{u}_t \quad (3$$
$$\phantom{MDA_{2t} = 39.48}(4.46)\quad(-3.28)\qquad(4.26)\qquad(4.96)\qquad(4.25)$$

$$\overline{R}^2 = 0.89 \qquad D.W. = 1.13$$

The serial correlation of the errors again prompted a re-estimation of the equation using standard maximum-likelihood procedures referred to above. The preferred equation is:

$$MDA_{2t} = 33.46 - 10.77\,MU_t + 1.98\,II_{t-1} + 2.10\,IDC_{t-1} + 35.94\,REP_{t-1} + \hat{u}_t \quad (4)$$
$$\phantom{MDA_{2t} = 33.46}(4.85)\quad(-2.54)\qquad(5.42)\qquad(5.91)\qquad(3.30)$$

$$\overline{R}^2 = 0.93 \qquad\qquad D.W. = 1.88$$

$$\hat{u}_t = 0.56\hat{u}_{t-1} - 0.63\,\hat{u}_{t-2} + \dot{v}_t$$

The chi-squared value of MLH second order error process relative to MLH first order process was 4.39.

Together with equation (2), equation (4) becomes the preferred equation. In equation 4 the coefficients are very similar to those in equation 2 with the exception of the coefficient of REP which is, as expected, reduced from 52.67 to 35.94. A full interpretation of this result is given below but the important outcome is that even after attributing a very large impact to the SDA programme a substantial and significant REP effect on moves to Development Areas is still indicated. population. From the point of view of firms considering a new location in an area

Investigating the possible effects on industrial movement of changes in the geographical designation of the Development Areas

The most important change in the geographical designation of Development Areas took place in 1966 when in terms of population coverage the Development Areas

[22]Firms newly opening in SDA's and renting government factories were offered a rent free period of up to five years, 35 per cent building grants (as opposed to 25 per cent elsewhere in Development Areas) and loans at low rates of interest towards the balance of building costs and other various grants towards operating cost (including a 30 per cent subsidy to the wage bill).

[23]The assumption is 'generous' in the sense that it attributes a substantial impact to the SDA programme in generating moves to Development Areas.

were extended by four percentage points from 16 per cent to 20 per cent of the UK where differential regional assistance will be available the main effect is to give them a wider choice of site. However since the pre-1966 Development Areas were concentrated on the main centres of population where most firms would wish to locate anyway the geographical extension of these areas may be expected to have only a limited effect on inward movement. Nevertheless a series of experiments were undertaken after adjusting the number of moves (MDA^2) by a 'geographical scaling factor' to allow for variations in the geographical designation of Development Areas. This scaling factor was constructed from a time series of unemployment statistics which indicated the proportion of the region's unemployment lying within the designated Development Area. The effect of applying this scaling factor is to substantially reduce the number of moves which could be attributed to the effect of the independent variables because the adjustment assumes that every percentage point increase in the geographical area of the Development Areas (as measured by the unemployment proportion) generates a proportionate number of moves. This is in our view much too generous an assumption but this exercise is carried out to show that, even if a very large volume of movement were to be accounted for by the geographical extension of the Development Areas, all the independent variables remain significant. The preferred equation using maximum likelihood procedures is:

$$MDA_{3t} = 48.35 - 17.26 \, MU_t + 1.13 \, II_{t-1} + 1.68 \, IDC_{t-1} + 39.42 \, REP_{t-1} + \hat{u}_t \quad (5$$
$$\qquad\quad (4.41) \quad (-4.04) \quad (2.49) \qquad (3.61) \qquad (3.52)$$

$\overline{R}^2 = 0.84$ D.W. 1.65. The chi-squared value of MLH first order error process relative to OLS was 6.91.

Where MDA$_3$ = the number of moves to Development Areas excluding the maximum possible effect of the Special Development Area programme and the geographical extension of Development Areas.

The main outcome of this third set of experiments is to confirm the significance of all the policy variables found in the earlier experiments. The coefficient of the investment incentive variable falls relative to its value in the earlier experiments. This suggests that part at least of the effect of investment incentives in the earlier equations may be due to the extension of the geographical coverage of the Development Areas. The coefficient on the IDC variable remains remarkably stable. The estimated impact of REP however clearly does not seem to depend on changes in the geographical coverage of the Development Areas.

Assuming that equations 2 and 4 come somewhere near to a satisfactory disen-entangling of the effect of individual policy instruments on the number of moves to Development Areas the results are shown in Table 2.

Table 2
Annual number of moves to Development Areas generated by individual regional policy instruments 1960 to 1971

Policy Instrument	No of years in operation between 1960 and 1971	Average annual number of moves to Development Areas derived from:	
		Equation 2	Equation 4
IDC policy	12	45	46
Investment Incentives	8	36	36
REP	4	40	26
SDA programme	4	0	20
Moves generated by non-policy factors:			
(a) at actual pressure of demand prevailing	12	11	7
(b) at constant pressure of demand (set at the 2 per cent male unemployment rate)	12	15	13

There are difficulties in relating the volume of movement attributable to the main policy instruments to the amount of employment generated. These difficulties are caused mainly by the long time lags in the build-up of employment in new factories. As a rough estimate we make use of the average job per move figures presented in Table 3.

Table 3

Average employment per move for moves to Scotland, Wales, the Northern Region and Northern Ireland

Moves taking place between	Average employment per move		
	As at Dec 1966	As at June 1970	As at June 1971
1952 to 1959	195		
1960 to 1965	190	237	
1966 to 1971			133

For moves taking place between 1960 and 1965 the average employment per move as at 1970 of 237 jobs is adopted whilst for moves taking place between 1966 and 1971 the average of 133 jobs per move is used. This latter figure is a fair reflection of the actual position as at 1971 but it must be remembered that moves in this later period will continue to generate new jobs up to 1976 and beyond whilst the earlier 1960 to 1965 moves had matured to a greater extent by 1971. These two averages are then applied to the coefficients in equation (2) and (4) to obtain the following estimates of employment creation for each policy instrument insofar as new jobs are generated through industrial movement (Table 4).

Table 4

The effect of individual policy instruments on employment generated in new factories in Development Areas

	Annual average per annum	Total in the period 1960 to 1971
(1) Additional jobs created by the IDC policy in the 1960s over and above those created in the mid-1950s (12 years)	6,250	75,000
(2) Investment Incentives (8 years)	5,875	47,000
(3) REP (4 years)	3,500–5,250	14,000–21,000
(4) Special Development Areas (4 years)	0–2,500	0–10,000
Total		143,000–146,000

(g) An input-output approach to estimating the effects of REP using information from our industrial enquiry on how firms had made use of REP

(i) How firms said they had used REP

The effects of REP may well differ according to whether firms have used it to, say, reduce prices as opposed to increasing wages or profits or doing other things such as hiring consultants, decorating the office or making a larger contribution to the sports and social club. We asked 300 Development Area firms how they thought they had used REP. Perhaps surprisingly only about one-third of companies had

212

made a formal and conscious decision as to how REP was to be used – but these firms making a conscious decision tended to be the larger ones, as they accounted for roughly half the total employment covered by the sample.

We summarise the results of this part of the industrial enquiry in Table 5.

Table 5
The proportion of REP devoted to higher profits, reduced prices or increased wages

	Number of firms	Sample Employment (000s)	% Split based on sample employment
Profits	140	48.5	38.6
Prices, sales promotion etc.	180	61.8	49.2
Wages	61	15.2	12.1

The indication from these sample results is that firms have split REP roughly as follows – profits 40 per cent, prices and sales promotion 50 per cent and wages 10 per cent[24]. This 40 : 50 : 10 was adopted as the basis for the input-output analysis.

We used this information in conjunction with two input-output models, firstly the Cambridge Growth Project on the assumption that REP was a national subsidy and secondly using an input-output table for Northern Ireland prepared in the Ministry of Finance in Belfast. The role of the input-output table is limited to that of giving us an estimate of the way REP influences prices in different categories of final demand – consumption, investment, exports etc. From then on we are forced back on to using conventional estimates of elasticities and relationships in order to estimate the likely effects of REP on employment and output. On plausible assumptions about these relationships the analysis suggest that REP should have created about 80,000 jobs[25].

(h) The effects of REP as estimated by companies
Much of our industrial enquiry was devoted to asking firms what effect they thought REP had had on such things as investment, output and employment[26]. Here we present a brief analysis of the views of senior executives in firms receiving REP.

(i) *The size and importance of REP to companies receiving it*
We wanted to know how important REP was to companies receiving it. As an indicator we asked firms to give their REP receipts expressed as a percentage of their pre-tax profits. For the sample as a whole (adding profits and losses together) REP receipts were found to be as high as the equivalent of 21 per cent of pre-tax profits. This figure is easily confirmed by national data. If we assume that one-fifth of all UK manufacturing profits are made in the Development Areas (ie in rough proportion to manufacturing employment) then total REP payments in excess of £100m would be the equivalent of about 20 per cent of Development Area profits in 1968. Clearly it would be surprising if a financial inducement of this size could be withdrawn from the Development Areas without some real adverse consequences on investment output and employment, particularly in companies in some kind of financial difficulty.

(ii) *The effect of REP on investment in Development Area plants*
At the outset REP was frequently depicted as an incentive which would be likely to make it easier for firms to increase their utilisation of spare capacity rather than an incentive that would encourage them to increase their capacity. The evidence from firms would not fully support such a supposition since over half the firms stated that REP had resulted in more investment in Development Area plants than there would otherwise have been. The textile and engineering industries in particular had tended to increase their investment as a result of REP. A higher proportion of pre-war firms tended to use REP to increase capacity than did firms established in Development Areas after 1945. Larger firms, employing more than 500 people, were more inclined to increase investment as a result of REP than were the smaller

[24]To test the reliability of this response from companies we carried out two further pieces of analysis – one on wages and one on profits. The first made use of published data on earnings by industry inside and outside Development Areas and confirmed that the REP leakage into wages was indeed small. The second made use of profits figures in two samples of quoted companies, one inside and one outside Development Areas over a 15 year period. This analysis was consistent with the enquiry result that 40 per cent of REP had been used to boost profits at least for a two year period, after which there was some indication of a switch from higher profits into lower prices.

[25]This is very similar to the results obtained by A J Brown, J Bowers and H Lind when they assumed an equal split for REP between prices, profits and wages. NIER No 40, May 1967.

[26]The questionnaire was sent to about 900 firms which were members of the Confederation of British Industry. We had 302 usable replies. The sample of firms was not selected scientifically but rather on the basis of those willing to help us. The sample firms, however, employed nearly 200,000 people, over 10 per cent of all manufacturing employees in the Development Areas.

firms employing less than 500 people. REP seems to have stimulated investment amongst parent companies (ie whose activities are concentrated in Development Areas) more than amongst companies whose Development Area activities are limited to branch plants or subsidiaries.

(iii) *The effect of REP on the volume of output*

When asked whether REP had been directly responsible for increasing output or maintaining output above what it would otherwise have been again more than half the firms (55 per cent) accounting for 58 per cent of the total sample employment said that it had. Some 41 per cent of firms said that output had definitely not been affected and the remaining 4 per cent were 'don't knows'. Of the 167 firms who claimed that output had been influenced by REP. Sixty-two said that it had been influenced 'to a large extent' and 105 firms said that it had been affected to a minor extent. In a secondary question on output we asked firms to estimate in percentage terms by how much the level of real output had been affected by REP. The results were as shown in Table 6.

Table 6

How firms replied to the question on how much output had been affected by REP

Per cent increase in output generated by REP	Number of firms	Percentage of total employment in firms which said that output was higher
0 – 2	46	25.2
2 – 4	27	19.7
4 – 6	26	15.4
6 – 8	10	1.9
over 8	39	29.0
Don't know	19	8.8

On *a priori* grounds, one might expect REP, to stimulate output, for all firms on average by perhaps 4 to 6 per cent. It is, at first sight a little surprising to find 29 per cent of the firms answering 'yes' stating that their output had been affected by more than 8 per cent. But it is less surprising when one allows for the fact that some firms may divert expansion programmes to Development Area plants as a result of REP (and this is supported by the answers on how REP influences the location of investment) and that in other firms REP may actually have been instrumental in preventing plant closures, partial plant closures and/or redundancies.

(iv) *The effect of REP on the diversion of production to Development Area factories from plants outside the Development Areas*

Those firms which had their main production plant outside the Development Areas were asked if they had diverted production to the Development Area plant as a direct consequence of REP. Some 137 firms answered this question and 43 firms (accounting for 42 per cent of employment in these firms) said that some diversion of this kind had occurred. This is a significant result because a small number of large firms with plants in many regions control such a high proportion of UK manufacturing output and the success of regional policy and the preservation of manufacturing employment in Development Areas is highly dependent on these large multi-regional firms.

(v) *The effect of REP on employment in Development Area plants*

The proportion of firms stating that REP had resulted in more employment than would otherwise have occurred was 61 per cent. These firms accounted for 60 per cent of total employment covered by the sample. Nevertheless 113 firms out of 291 answering this question maintained that employment had not been affected in any way by REP. Again this is a significant result because, whatever the a priori expectation about the effects of REP on investment or output, it was generally expected that REP should have a significant impact on manufacturing employment.

Of the 176 firms which stated that employment was higher because of REP 56 firms (accounting for 18 per cent of sample employment) said that employment was higher to a large extent and 122 firms said that employment was higher to a minor extent. These 176 firms were asked to quantify by how much employment was higher because of REP. The answers are presented in Table 7.

[27]An analysis of plant closures inside and outside Development Areas in the 1960s, using Department of Industry data, supports this conclusion that REP has prevented plant closures in Development Areas. This analysis, made difficult by the nature of data available, is not yet completed and detailed results are therefore not presented here.

Table 7

How firms replied to the question on how much employment had been affected by REP

Per cent increase in employment generated by REP	Number of firms	Percentage of total employment in firms which said that employment was higher
0–1%	31	11.0
1–2%	34	18.2
2–3%	19	3.5
over 3%	75	52.0
Don't know	17	15.3
Total	176	100.0

It is noticeable from Table 7 that REP has had a particularly significant effect on employment (ie over 3 per cent) in 75 firms which account for half the labour force in this group.

(vi) *The effect of REP on the prevention of closures and redundancies in Development Area plants*

Some 287 firms answered the question on how far REP had prevented closures and large scale redundancies. Of these 229 firms (or 80 per cent) said that REP had no effect whatsoever. These firms accounted for 71 per cent of total employment covered in the sample. Some 58 firms, however, employing 27 per cent of sample employment stated that closures had been prevented and/or redundancies had been prevented or reduced because REP had been received. The estimate of the number of jobs preserved was 7,170. This job saving represented 13 per cent of the total employment in these 58 firms.

It would be dangerous to pro-rata these sample results to obtain an estimate of the total effects of REP. Firms in which REP has been important in preventing closures had a greater incentive to reply to our questionnaire and even to exaggerate the beneficial effect of REP. We can note in passing however that when the results are pro-rated to give a figure for the Development Areas as a whole the effect of REP indicated is 72,000 manufacturing jobs, most of which come into the category of the prevention of closures and redundancies[27].

But the major conclusion of this industrial enquiry is that about half of business firms receiving REP believe that their labour force is higher than it would have been without REP. This is an important result because it has hitherto been quite commonly supposed that businessmen are in some sense 'anti-REP' and that REP has not affected important decisions relating to investment, output and employment.

(vii) *Summary of conclusions on effects of regional policy instruments*

It is difficult to summarise our results because some of the analysis relates to all Development Areas and some relates to some of the Development Areas. Moreover we stress that these are interim results and may be subject to modification as a result of further work which we are undertaking.

215

(a) Regional Employment Premium

Table 8 presents a summary of the results of the various methods of analysis.

Table 8

Provisional estimates of the effects of REP on manufacturing employment in Development Areas

	Indigenous firms estimated at		New factories estimated at		Total estimated at	
	1970	1971	1970	1971	1970	1971
'Arthmetical'[1]	20,000	2,000	8,000	10,000	28,000	12,000
Econometric	35,000*	15,000†	14,000‡	20,000‡	49,000	35,000
Input-output and 'conventional' economic analysis						80,000
Industrial Enquiry						70,000

[1] From Table 1 with pro-rata additions for Merseyside and South-West Development Areas.
* See Section 5. Includes SEP with pro-rata additions for Merseyside and South-West Development Areas.
† SEP abolished. Lower real value of REP.
‡ From Table 4 using mid-point in the range with a pro-rata addition for Northern Ireland.

A case could be made out using the survey evidence and the 'conventional' analysis, that REP had created 70-80,000 manufacturing jobs in Development Areas and therefore, allowing for multiplier effects, a total of around 100,000 jobs. However such a high figure is not supported by the statistical measurement and analysis in which we have more faith. For reasons given earlier we are also inclined to discount the low figure of 12,000 derived from the arithmetical approach. We are prepared to accept however, that the effect of REP was as low as 35,000 manufacturing jobs when its real value had been severely reduced by inflation between 1971 and 1973, and that its effect at its maximum real value was about 50,000 manufacturing jobs. These figures should be increased to the extent of any indirect effects of this additional manufacturing employment and any effects in Northern Ireland. These two additions bring the maximum REP effect up to about 60,000.

(b) Broad estimates of the impact of the major regional policy instruments

Before presenting our first estimates of the effects of individual policy instruments an important qualification has to be made about how these results should be interpretated. Regional policy has largely developed by adding one regional policy instrument to another. Therefore the results tells us how much more effective the regional policy package became when a new major policy instrument was added to it. It is not safe to presume that each policy instrument would have the same effect were it to operate on its own. Thus what we have measured is how far the regional policy package became more effective by adding, for instance, REP to the existing measures and not the effectiveness of REP operating in isolation. On this basis we suggest orders of magnitudes for the relative effects of policy instruments in Table 9.

216

Table 9

A summary of the impact of individual regional policy instruments on employment in Development Areas (1960 to 1971), as estimated at a constant pressure of demand

Provisional estimates   *(000's jobs)*

[28] In 1974 REP was restored approximately to its 1968 real value.

[29] The Green Paper on the Development Areas.

| | *Employment associated with* | | | | |
	New factory moves	*'Indigenous firms'*	*Shipbuilding and metal manufacturers*	*Indirect multiplier effects[1]*	*Total*
Industrial Development Controls and Government Factory Building	70 – 80	–	–	15	85 – 95
Investment incentives, building grants selective assistance and special DA assistance	50 – 55	75 – 85*	8	29	162 – 177
Regional Employment Premium (including SEP)	15 – 22	10 – 20	2	7	32 – 49
Total	132 – 155	85 – 105	10	51	279 – 321

[1] Using a short run multiplier of 1.2 on mid-points of the range.

* There is evidence that many of these jobs arise from expansion in the 1960s of firms diverted to Development Areas by building licences and IDC's mainly between 1945 and 1952. These building controls in the early post-war years generated about 80,000 jobs in Development Areas and these are excluded from Table 9.

III   The case for and against REP

(a) The contribution of REP to employment creation in Development Areas

One of the criteria for judging the usefulness of REP must be how effective it is in providing jobs in Development Areas. All the evidence suggests that in this respect the impact of REP is considerably less than was originally expected. When REP was at its maximum real value in 1968/69/70[28] its effect probably did not far exceed 50,000 jobs and between 1971 and 1973 when its real value was roughly halved its impact was probably no more than 20-30,000 jobs. This compares with a total regional policy effect now estimated by us at about 300,000 jobs between 1960 and 1971. Thus the REP contribution accounts for only 10-15 per cent of the total impact of regional policy on employment in Development Areas. Whilst the effects of REP on employment in Development Areas appear to be below expectations it is nonetheless a significant contribution and it is difficult on these grounds alone to justify its abolition unless there is something clearly preferable to put in its place.

(b) The costlessness of REP as adumbrated in the Green Paper[29]

One of the main points made in the case for REP as originally presented was that its real cost was very low or perhaps zero. Whilst we agree that the resource cost of REP may be near to zero we also contend that this is equally true for the other major instruments of regional policy which divert economic activity from fully-employed areas to Development Areas. Whilst it may be reasonable to argue the case for having a strong regional policy on the grounds of its low cost it seems unreasonable to argue the case for REP as against other regional policy measures on this ground.

(c) REP as a counter-balance to capital subsidiaries

One of the arguments put forward in support of REP was that regional policy before 1967 encouraged capital intensive activities in Development Areas which gave rise to relatively few jobs when what was required was encouragement to labour intensive activities. On the issue of labour and capital intensity two separate processes

217

ought to be distinguished. Firstly there is evidence that a high proportion of capital subsidies are paid to capital intensive firms and that some of these capital intensive plants have been diverted by high capital subsidies into Development Areas. Secondly it is also argued that capital subsidies promote capital substitution so that all firms are more capital intensive than they would otherwise be. We can find little evidence to support this second contention either at national or regional level – indeed evidence from other work being carried out in Cambridge suggests that a substantial part of capital subsidies finds its way, not into additional investment, but into keeping prices lower than they would otherwise be. Similarly w hilst REP has probably attracted some labour intensive firms into Development Areas we can find no evidence that REP has led to labour/capital substitution on any significant scale – indeed some Development Area firms claim to have used REP specifically to finance investment.

(d) The way in which REP and other regional policies work

Most non-REP regional policies (IDC policy, differential investment incentives, Local Employment Act Assistance and to some extent selective assistance) work principally by diverting new factories into Development Areas from more prosperous regions and there is now considerable evidence to suggest that they have been powerful in this respect (moving of the order of 1,000 factories to Development Areas and providing directly and indirectly about 200,000 jobs – some two-thirds of the total regional policy effect). Whilst REP seems to have significantly strengthened the effect of the regional policy package in this process of encouraging firms to move to Development Areas there is also evidence that REP works in other ways. Principally it is a regional policy measure which has had an identifiable (if small) effect on employment in the older indigenous and often declining firms in Development Areas. There is some evidence, for instance, that REP has preserved industrial capacity in Development Areas by reducing the rate of plant closures. Part of the case against REP as frequently expressed is that REP should not preserve existing declining industries and that regional policy should concentrate even more on attracting new firms into Development Areas, ie less productive units should be encouraged to close down. There are two problems with this kind of policy. Firstly, given the growth and performance of the British economy as a whole there are not sufficient new factories to divert to Development Areas. Secondly, if the increase in manufacturing employment in new factories is offset by the closure of less efficient plants the regional problem will not be solved and UK industrial capacity will continue to grow only very slowly. If our industrial capacity in the UK is to grow more rapidly in future there is a case for measures such as REP to help preserve existing capacity until such time as someone can get round to increasing the competitiveness of the firms concerned in other ways. Once that is done new investment will represent a genuine net increase in productive capacity.

(e) Selective assistance versus blanket subsidies

Part of the case against blanket subsidies such as REP is that they are given to all firms in Development Areas whether new or old, expanding or contracting, progressive or asleep. The implication of this criticism is that regional intervention should be more discretionary and more selective. However, there seems to be a lack of consensus as to the criteria on which selective assistance should be based. In the British context one of the problems with selective assistance may be that all firms need it. But it is also difficult to know (as with investment incentives and REP) how far selective assistance, when given to indigenous firms creates new jobs and capacity as opposed to being given to firms which would in any case have created the jobs or installed the new capacity. None of the regional policy measures, including selective assistance, operate at the margin with respect to indigenous firms. Finally, if selective assistance is not to be given to old, contracting and sleepy firms what is the justification for giving it to new, expanding and progressive companies who ought, perhaps, to be in a position to look after themselves most easily. But whichever firms are chosen to receive selective assistance there is the additional problem of inequity for those firms which do not receive it, quite apart from the problem of the time and administrative resources required to treat each firm on its merits.

(f) REP as a compensation for permanently high operating costs

Many manufacturers to whom we spoke and some giving evidence to the Expenditure Committee see the main justification for REP in terms of compensating for excess costs (mainly transport costs) of operating in a Development Area whilst excess transport costs typically represent only about one per cent of the total costs to most Development Area firms serving national markets this can represent a significant part of after tax profits.

(g) Conclusion

The case for and against REP as a major instrument of regional policy is perhaps finely balanced. In spite of its shortcomings we would not like to see it abolished unless it was to be replaced by something which was demonstrably better for the Development Areas and for the national economy.

A quantitative analysis of the effects of the Regional Employment Premium and other regional policy instruments

B MOORE AND J RHODES

Comments by R R McKay

I would like to acknowledge a considerable personal debt to John and Barry. In spite of our differences of opinion, they have given me generous assistance, we remain on rather better than speaking terms and I know that without their analysis, measurement and argument, my own attempts to identify a regional policy effect would be considerably weaker. I believe that for some years I and other researchers into the impact of regional policy will take their work as a starting point, that we will rely heavily on their evidence and techniques, but that we will then depart to our own variations in interpretation and approach. We will stray not merely because economists are naturally argumentative, but because the subject matter is complex, proof positive and beyond all doubt is extremely unlikely, and differences in opinion provide a healthy incentive to improve argument and analysis.

It may not be obvious to the casual observer, but on many issues we present a front remarkably close to united. Barry and John correctly emphasise that the important test of regional policy is the results it produces. While surveys of manufacturing industry may give useful insights on the way firms react to regional policy, they are not accurate guides to quantitative effect: added to the considerable problems involved in evaluating the importance of one of many influences there is a consistent bias introduced by the temptation to exaggerate the beneficial influence of assistance. I accept the claim that a desirable objective, reduction in unemployment differentials, will not necessarily yield an acceptable test of regional policy. In this and other areas Barry and John avoid irritating red herrings. They are correct to concentrate on manufacturing industry, it is important to allow for structural differences, the split between new factories and indigenous industry is of considerable, I would say crucial, importance. The strange Green Paper claim that the REP is self financing to a degree not shared by other regional policy measures is rejected by both sets of authors. I would agree with the important distinction made on p218 of the Moore and Rhodes paper. It is quite possible, even likely, that generous capital subsidies, will divert capital intensive plants to Development Areas, but established plants are unlikely to respond to REP by substituting labour for capital 'on any significant scale'.

I will now turn to the continuing differences of opinion that conferences are designed to draw attention to and even possibly resolve. The difference in emphasis is obvious if one compares pps40-41 of the Moore-Rhodes paper and p240 of my own.

Barry and John suggest that it is inequitable, difficult and unnecessary to distinguish between firms that wish to expand and firms that are bound to decline, firms that are established in an area and firms that are new, firms that are ambitious and firms that are content with mere survival. I stress that when assistance is scattered on the wind a high proportion will fall on stony ground. The politically convenient approach of assistance to all notably magnifies the cost of regional policy, but does not have a similar effect on achievement. Unless regional policy concentrates assistance on those most likely to respond the results are likely to be disappointing. Subsidisation,

[1] A R Prest, *The Economic Rationale of Subsidies to Industry*, p73

[2] A R Prest *Op cit* p72

[3] This is my interpretation of the move from a regional policy effect of 150,000 manufacturing jobs for 1963 to 1970 to 200,000 manufacturing jobs 1960 to 1971, after adjustment for pressure of demand. The gap between actual and expected employment is negligible for 1960 to 1963 and 1970 to 1971.

[4] The ideal series for actual indigenous employment would give employment region by region and industry by industry in firms located in a region in the base year (say 1960) and still located there in 1961, 1962 etc. In calculating expected growth in Development Area indigenous firms the performance of migrant firms would be ignored.

the transfer of responsibility from the firm to the taxpayer, is by itself no solution, but the transfer of resources from declining, low productivity industries may have a beneficial effect not only on regional, but also on national prosperity. There is a clear contrast between the firm that moves into the Development Area and the declining industry. The new firm faces obvious teething problems, but there is considerable evidence that these difficulties diminish and diminish rapidly. Assistance to mobile industry compensates for the above average costs in the early years and plays a constructive role by providing finance at the all important investment and training stage, so ensuring that the problem period is not unnecessarily extended. The region that relies on subsidisation of declining concerns builds on shifting sand. Such assistance does not improve structure and may discourage adjustment to movements in demand and to technical change. To take the example given by Professor Prest (p73), if there are poor market possibilities, doubts about managerial capacity, over-manning, over capacity, it is likely that the amount of subsidisation required to preserve a given amount of employment will rise over time[1]. The distinction between the reduction in cost disadvantage for new firms and the slide away from profitability in declining organisations is of fundamental importance.

The distinction between the revenue effect of aid and its effect in reducing the cost of adding to output is also important. A given amount of assistance will be more effective if it is sensitive to, or is allocated according to additions to employment, output or investment. In extreme circumstances where a firm is looking for 'target' profit or revenue levels a windfall gain may actually reduce employment, output and effort. The income effect of assistance is weak and not necessarily predictable in direction. Assistance that has a considerable effect on the cost of additional production provides a more obvious incentive for expansion since it notably raises the return for additional effort. The REP is the most obvious example of a regional incentive that raises revenue and therefore extends the firm's range of opportunities, but has little impact on the cost of producing additional goods. As Prest says, 'It is an obvious criticism of such measures as REP that substantial payments may be 'wasted' in financing intramarginal employment'[2].

There are good reasons for believing that the selective approach to assistance is more efficient, but the essential test is the test of experience. Barry and John concentrate on the evidence. Their statistical measure of regional policy impact compensates for the tendency for regional policy to be less effective when unemployment is high. For example, it estimates not actual regional policy effect over 1967 to 1970, but the regional policy impact if unemployment had been considerably lower. In order to calculate their hypothetical regional policy effect for 1960 to 1971 Barry and John add (1) the divergence between actual and expected employment for the four main Development Areas, 150,000 jobs, to (2) an allowance for shifts in male unemployment, 50,000 jobs,[3] plus (3) the impact of regional policy on Merseyside and the South-West 40,000 jobs, plus (4) a regional policy effect of 10,000 in metal manufacture and ship-building. I am not convinced that the ship-building and the metal industries should be treated separately. I believe that the record for these and other declining industries indicates that assistance to declining industry is an expensive way to buy time and think that the estimate of regional policy effect in Merseyside and the South-West is over optimistic. But the two part Development Areas, plus the two 'exceptional' industries are omitted from their Table 1 p201 and my really important points relate to this table.

Both sets of authors, that is Moore and Rhodes and myself, are searching for a correct or ideal split between indigenous firm employment and new firm employment, but neither set has been entirely successful[4]. This distinction is extremely important. If it is discovered that the regional policy effect is dominated by employment creation in new firms then the case for REP is extremely weak. Even if REP has an effect on industrial movement, a form of assistance which is concentrated on

221

indigenous industry (according to John and Barry 90 per cent goes to established firms),[5] is not the most effective way to encourage inter-regional transfer.

In Table 1 the really important figure, employment created in indigenous firms is derived as a residual and this essential end product relies on a number of difficult calculations with estimating procedures that are not likely to prove universally acceptable. The four essential steps are (1) calculate divergence between actual and expected employment (2) use regression analysis to calculate the effect of changes in unemployment (3) use a time series to estimate employment generated in new factories year by year and (4) allow for new firm employment creation in passive policy periods.

[5]Moore and Rhodes, p196
Moore and Rhodes, p202

The problems involved in arriving at the estimate of indigenous employment created are emphasised if one compares the statistical or arithmetic approach to employment creation with the econometric approach. In the econometric equation for indigenous employment creation (pps 203, 204 and 207) the behaviour of the co-efficient on the demand variable (national male unemployment rate) is puzzling. For the 'no-REP' period 1951 to 1967, the co-efficient implies that a one per cent increase in the unemployment rate, *ceteris paribus,* results in a loss of 8.6 thousand jobs in the Development Areas while for the equation estimated for the longer period 1951 to 1971 this job loss is only 4.3 thousand. Variation on this scale is disturbing and throws some doubt on the technique used to adjust changes in total employment gain to changes in demand pressure that is briefly described on pps 199 and 201.

The problems involved in making this adjustment are further emphasised by the firm movement econometric equations (p 208). The co-efficient on the unemployment rate suggests that eight moves per annum are lost when, *ceteris paribus,* unemployment increases by one per cent. It is difficult to turn this into an estimate of jobs lost to the Development Areas, but it is clear, that as a result of movement in one year, the level of employment in Development Areas is going to be affected several years ahead. Yet at the adjustment stage John and Barry do not worry 'too much about time-lags'. The problem of adjusting employment change to a constant pressure of demand is extremely complex.

As calculated in Table 1 there is an inbuilt tendency to exaggerate employment gain in indigenous firms. There is no allowance for the multiplier effect of new factories, a relatively unimportant point. More serious, there is an allowance for constant pressure of demand for the Total Employment Gain, but no allowance in the calculation of employment gain from new factories. This has the effect of throwing the total allowance for rise in unemployment rates on to the figures for indigenous firm employment creation in spite of the fact that change in the level of demand has a marked effect on firm movement.

John and Barry believe that 1967 to 1970 rather than 1967 to 1971 are the appropriate post-REP years. The terminal year argument would be important if one was calculating the ratio of Development Area to non-Development Area unemployment in 1967 and 1971. But if we measure what is in essence a continuous year by year regional policy effect the contrast that is important is the considerable difference between the four years 1963 to 1967 and the four years 1967 to 1971. The correct approach is to allow for differences in level of demand year by year. I can accept that particular years have an 'atmosphere'[6] and that the effect of a given rise in unemployment could be greater the higher the level of unemployment. So since I occasionally pretend to be reasonable I am willing to use both 1967 to 1970 and 1967 to 1971. If, as I believe, the contrast between REP and other regional policy instruments is marked it should show over either sets of years.

I do however find the claim that 'unusually large numbers of redundancies in Development Areas were offsetting the beneficial effects of regional policy' (p202) inconsistent with the later emphasis (p203, p213) on the importance of REP in preventing closure and cutbacks in companies faced by some kind of financial difficulty. Something strange is happening certainly, but could it possibly be that when a firm is in trouble REP makes remarkably little difference.

On p210 and p211 John and Barry allow for the change from Development Districts to Development Areas by compensating for the higher proportion of UK employment in Development Areas. On this occasion they are unnecessarily inventive. The Development Areas are more attractive not because they are larger, but because they are less likely to disappear. The considerable uncertainty involved in the Development District procedure was unlikely to encourage movement particularly if a firm had fairly definite plans for future expansion. The greater stability of expectation provided by Development Areas allows firms to move with confidence and gives regional organisations the opportunity to concentrate public expenditure on those areas which have the potential to attract industry. There is often a considerable gap between what we want to measure and what is measurable. The change to Development Areas is one example, the value of investment grants in relation to free depreciation is a second, using IDC Refusals as a proportion of IDC Applications is a third.

In spite of these and other problems the econometric approach is promising. It frees John and Barry from the assumption that the divergence between actual and expected employment is an accurate measure of regional policy impact and happily produces answers which are at least of the same rough order of magnitude as those obtained by other methods. The results help to strengthen consensus on the total effect of regional policy.

As far as the effects of individual measures are concerned there remains the possibility that running regressions between time series could provide a number of different explanations that are difficult to choose between on statistical grounds, but which have different behavioural and policy implications. A possible, but fierce, test is, will the equations fitted to the existing data continue to serve for later years? Certainly as far as REP is concerned the tests (both econometric and statistical) need more years and more observations if only to ensure that 1971 is not the only rogue year.[7]

This is an ambitious and extremely informative paper. The authors describe and give the results for four different techniques that can be used to give an idea of the employment impact of REP and other regional policy instruments. They are correct to concentrate on the results given by the more difficult, but more important measures, the econometric and statistical approaches. The Industrial enquiry and input-output measures both rely on firms' estimates of the REP effect and there is a considerable temptation to exaggerate the response to a subsidy particularly if managers are aware that the subsidy is liable to be phased out. The sheer volume of change in regional legislation, the fact that the individual measures never operate in isolation, the importance of changes in national economic conditions, the time-lag which quite probably varies according to the stage of the cycle and the type of regional assistance that is introduced, all complicate analysis. John and Barry have made a heroic attempt to solve the difficulties. But I do think that for the post REP years there are too many alterations in atmosphere, policy and economic environment to provide more than an approximate measure of the total impact of regional policy and that it is even more difficult to isolate the impact of the different parts of the regional policy package.

[7] The Premium was only introduced in September 1967. Moore and Rhodes specify a one-year lag between payment and result so the period of observation is dangerously short, especially if we ignore 1971.

223

The impact of the Regional Employment Premium

R R MACKAY

My thanks to the SSRC for giving me the opportunity to continue research into the effect of regional policy, to my wife for being the perfect secretary and to Mrs Segal for her important contribution to this paper.

[1]For women, and boys under 18, the rate was 75p, for girls under 18, 47½p.

I   Great expectations

For evidence of the 'increasing effect' of 'the intensified regional policies of recent years' the Green Paper on the Regional Employment Premium (1967) pointed to (a) 'the favourable shift in the balance between the Development Areas and the rest of the country in approvals given for industrial building', (b) the establishment of many new projects in the Development Areas and (c) the fact that 'since the government's measures of economic restraint in July 1966, the relative position of the Development Areas as reflected in the unemployment figures has not developed as unfavourably as in previous periods of restraint'. (Green Paper (GP) para 9 and 12.) Progress was regarded as unacceptably slow and the Green Paper advanced the argument for and against (mainly for) a wage subsidy as a means of accelerating improvement. The subsequent White Paper accepted the merit of a 'departure along quite different lines'. Hence REP was introduced, set at £1.50 for each man employed in manufacturing[1] and guaranteed to run for a minimum of seven years.

Until 1963 regional policy concentrated on the incoming or mobile firm. Given the importance of capital investment to the firm new to an assisted area, regionally differentiated investment subsidies (introduced in 1963) were not entirely inconsistent with the infant industry version of regional aid, but with the introduction of REP in 1967, the whole framework and philosophy of regional assistance alters. In the early years in a new location, labour costs will be an unusually low proportion of total costs while capital costs are unusually high. It therefore follows that a non selective capital subsidy will be more attractive to the new rather than to the established firm and vice versa for a wage subsidy.

Both Green and White Papers were extremely optimistic. According to the Green Paper 'the premium could, over a period of years, be expected to reduce by something like one half the average disparity between umemployment in the Development Areas and in the rest of the country, over and above the degree of success expected from existing programmes.' (See White Paper (WP) para 6 and GP para 27.) Table 1 shows that in the year prior to the introduction of REP, the unemployment differential between the Development Areas and the rest of Great Britain was 1.7 per cent. In subsequent years it rose to 2.1, 2.2, 2.2, 2.3, 3.2 and 3.4 per cent. Instead of being halved, as predicted in the Green Paper, the unemployment differential doubled. Forecasts are notoriously inaccurate, but the gap between prediction and performance is unusually large.

225

Table 1
Unemployment rates (Male and Female) for
Development Areas and the rest of Great Britain

Rounded average for 12 months ending:	Great Britain	Development areas	Rest of Great Britain	Unemployment differential between Dev Areas and rest of GB 2-3
April 1967	1.6	3.0	1.3	1.7
March 1968	2.3	3.9	1.8	2.1
,, 1969	2.4	4.1	1.9	2.2
,, 1970	2.4	4.2	2.0	2.2
,, 1971	2.6	4.5	2.2	2.3
,, 1972	3.6	6.2	3.0	3.2
,, 1973	3.5	6.2	2.8	3.4

Source:
Green Paper and Annual Reports on the Local Employment Act and Industry Act.

[2]J Callaghan, see Hansard, Vo1753, p875, 1967–68.

The most obvious criticism of the Green Paper is that it does not acknowledge that the most important prerequisite for a successful regional policy is a high level of national demand. There is little doubt that one of the main reasons for the considerable gap between prediction and performance has been the rising trend of national unemployment. The poor performance of the Development Areas in the post REP years is largely explained by the decision to raise 'the margin of unused capacity'[2]. The evidence clearly demonstrates that rising unemployment, recession and restraint, seriously reduce the impact of regional intervention. It also suggests that REP is an inappropriate and ineffective form of assistance. It supports Wilson's claim that 'a general and quite unselective subsidy' would not be as effective as assistance designed to help 'new or expanding firms during difficult periods'. (Wilson, 1967, p 11).

Neither the North West Industrial Development Association nor the Scottish Council (Development and Industry) are expected to enquire over carefully into the dentures of gift horses, but the Association argued (1969) that 'this assistance (REP) from the National Exchequer might . . . be more effectively applied in other ways', while the Council stressed (1967, para 42) that REP 'would sometimes work more to the advantage of the inefficient (rather) than the efficient company, running counter to efforts to increase productivity' and emphasised (para 3) that if REP failed 'to achieve the breakthrough in employment and growth at which it aims . . . it would create a dangerous situation in Scotland in a few years' time and our last state might be worse than our first.' There is little evidence that the Development Area 'breakthrough' has occurred and a real danger that firms given the temporary illusion of safety will face serious problems of adaptation when the Premium is eventually withdrawn.

According to the Green and White Papers (see argument pp 12 and 13 of GP), REP would achieve considerable impact without imposing any additional burden on the National Exchequer and without creating additional inflationary pressure. It is quite true that wage costs overstate the real cost of employing labour in those areas where labour is un or underemployed. It is also likely that the shift in demand from areas where resources are fully stretched to areas where there is excess capacity will reduce inflationary pressure and contribute to Exchequer receipts. But it does not follow, as the Green and White Papers imply, that a wage subsidy is in any sense ideally or uniquely suited, to either the easing of inflationary pressure, or the creation of receipts. The contribution of regional policy to the Exchequer and to a better 'regional balance' depends on the degree and direction of response. As the Green Paper suggests, one important question is will regional policy reduce 'pressure of demand for labour in the South and Midlands'? Assistance designed to encourage expansion in the Development Areas rather than the South or Midlands, or to encourage movement to the Development Areas is more relevant to the easing of inflationary pressure than a wage subsidy which has only a marginal effect on costs of expansion.

Contrary to the impression given by the Green and White Papers, the REP is not the ideal form of assistance for reducing inflationary pressure, and entirely unsuitable if the aim is to improve structure. Each employer receives a subsidy whether or not he plans to add to capacity or increase production. There is the very real possibility that such a subsidy will discourage adjustment. Altering industrial structure is a gradual, difficult process. There is no easy, simple, neat, obvious answer and there is a real conflict between the political desire to achieve results immediately and the inconvenient fact that the supply of mobile industry is limited. 'Argument about the theory of industrial mobility can give too little attention to the time scale in which change can be effected, and as a result political and social expectations may be aroused which by the nature of things cannot be quickly fulfilled. In essence the introduction of new employment into an area ... is a process which takes many years'. (EFTA 1971, p 88). An additional difficulty is that results are normally wanted when regional intervention is relatively ineffective; when national unemployment is rising the Development Area problems become exceedingly obvious, but the incentive to move to the Development Areas is reduced.

II   Quantitative analysis of the effects of regional assistance

In this paper three sets of statistics are used to show a regional policy effect, (1) Employment anticipated to result from Industrial Development Certificate (IDC) Approvals (Section III), (2) Employment created as a result of the Movement of Manufacturing Firms (Section IV) and (3) Actual Employment in the Development Areas compared with employment 'expected' if each manufacturing industry expanded at the national rate (Section V).

The Approval statistics can be related to five different phases of regional policy. The 'passive period' covers the years 1956 to 1959, the 'active period', 1960 to 1962, the 'intensive period', 1963 to 1966 and there are two REP phases, intensive plus REP (period one), 1967 to 1969, and intensive plus REP (period two), 1970 to 1972. The different phases are intended to identify major changes in the approach to the regional problem. The Local Employment Act of 1960 introduces the active period, the additional assistance provided in 1963 (Local Employment Act and Finance Act) moves the United Kingdom into the intensive years and the introduction of REP, signifies a notable change in approach and emphasis. The REP years are split into two phases to allow for (a) the effect of inflation, (b) a reduction in the value of capital assistance and (c) the steady deterioration in the national economic situation. Regional assistance was, and could be expected to be[3], more effective in phase one than in phase two.

Any firm wishing to build a factory, or factory extension, of 5,000 sq ft or over, had, in the 1960s, to apply for an Industrial Development Certificate (IDC). The Department of Trade and Industry (DTI) kept a record of the number of Approvals granted, the area of industrial building approved and the firms estimates of 'expected employment' from fully operational projects. Added to the normal problems involved in forecasting is the complication introduced by the incentive to exaggerate anticipated employment so as to satisfy the cost-per-job criterion applied to LEA assistance. In this paper the statistics have been modified to reduce anticipated employment by thirty per cent in the Development Areas. This exaggeration factor is adopted (a) because it is consistent with the experience of a group of firms interviewed by the Department of Economics at Newcastle University and (b) because it is similar to the unofficial adjustment made by DTI officials when allow-

[3]The value of the fixed grant of £1.50 per man was progressively reduced by the effect of inflation. In October 1970 a system of free depreciation, which gave Development Area firms little differential advantage over firms in other parts of the country, replaced the investment grant system. The steady deterioration in the national economic situation reduced the impact of regional policy. Relatively few firms contemplate expansion in depression conditions and those that do grow have little difficulty in finding the required labour force at their existing location.

ing for overstatement in Development Area estimates. The statistics on number of approvals granted and area of industrial building provide a check on the anticipated employment figures. The Approval figures of any given year reflect the economic climate and form of regional assistance available in that year. They are an important source of information on the timing of improvement.

New expanding industry is vitally important in regions heavily committed to sectors of decline or slow growth. The first movement figures provide information on an extremely important source of Development Area employment. They avoid one of the problems of the Approval statistics, the temptation to exaggerate future growth, by measuring actual employment. They attribute employment to the year of opening. Effective policy innovations should have a combination of a more or less immediate impact plus a delayed effect on firms openings. The rapid response involves movement into existing premises and the further delayed effects, movement to specially constructed premises which have to be completed and operational before a move is registered. This time-lag creates difficulties in attributing change to specific policy measures.

The Approval and firm movement figures provide an incomplete account of employment creation. The Approval statistics only record employment additions in factory extensions of 5,000 sq ft and over, and therefore do not detect movement into existing industrial premises, small additions to employment which involve little or no factory building, or situations where regional assistance (eg REP) helps to preserve employment. The movement statistics do not measure the effect of assistance on industry established in the Development Areas.

In theory at least the third measure provides an all embracing test for regional policy. The comparison of actual and expected employment allows for differences in industrial structure by comparing Development Area employment with the employment expected if each industry expands or contracts at the national rate. All additions to employment in existing or new factories raise actual employment, which is also influenced if regional policy helps to preserve jobs in declining industries. But, in practice, the measure gives only an approximate indication of the effect of regional intervention on manufacturing industry in the Development Areas. The measure of expected employment depends on the industrial classification adopted and, since it is impossible to separate manufacturing industry into ideal homogeneous groups of products. adjustment for the importance of differences in structure can only be approximate. Problems of interpretation are also created by the existence of a complex and variable time-lag. It takes time to build factories and to move from initial production and employment levels to the targets set by management. Thus an addition to employment in 1967 or 1968 may be a response to decisions taken in 1964 or 1965. The legislation that is relevant depends on the time-lag involved. Analysis is further complicated if one accepts that the impact of regional policy will vary according to the national economic situation.

Given the timing problem it is extremely difficult to relate the firm movement and actual-expected employment series to the five phases of regional policy (see Table 2) In this paper the two sets of statistics will be used to concentrate attention on the pre and post REP years.

In section VI the results from firm movement and the actual-expected employment analysis are combined. Where actual employment is above expected employment this may be the result of the region gaining because more (or larger) firms moved in than moved out of the region, or it may be a result of above average growth in indigenous industry. Section VI illustrates the relative contributions of mobile and indigenous firms.

The expenditure Committee Report on Regional Development Incentives lists ten 'areas of uncertainty'. The first and most important refers to 'the effectiveness of regional policy over the last 10 to 15 years in terms of increased employment . . . compared with what would have occurred otherwise'. (HMSO 1973, p 73). There are considerable problems in attempting to quantify this effect.

The first difficulty is to identify important changes in regional policy. Over the last '10 to 15 years', mentioned by the Committee, regional policy changes have been all too frequent. The sheer volume of change means that the commentator has to simplify and select in order to make a clear distinction between a limited number of policy periods where policy differs significantly. In trying to do so he may ignore changes which are of some importance.

The second difficulty is to provide an accurate account of what has happened in the different regions. Unfortunately consistent and accurate statistical series are the exception rather than the rule. Definitions of employment, unemployment, industrial building, firm movement, change over time as do industrial classifications and regional definitions. This makes comparison difficult and explanation tedious. The task of providing an account of what has happened is by no means simple, but it pales into insignificance when compared with the third problem, assessing what would have happened if regional policy had not changed. In the counter-factual situation we inevitably enter the realm of speculation. Such dependent variables as regional employment, industrial building and firm movement are strongly influenced by factors other than changes in regional policy. The strength of some of the more important relationships may be approximately measurable, but relationships change over time and even the direction of some causes and effect associations remain difficult to identify. In the real world of *non ceteris paribus* the gap between what has happened and what would have happened can only be approximately measurable. Estimates of regional policy effect are given in this paper, but they are inevitably somewhat speculative and there is considerable margin for error.

There are obvious problems in identifying a total regional policy effect, and even greater difficulties in isolating the impact of individual changes in regional policy. Regional policy measures work in concert rather than in isolation. Without IDC control, assistance to the mobile firm would be notably less effective and without assistance to cover the early settling in costs in a new location it would be more difficult to implement a steering policy. The importance of assistance in general and the relative importance of specific forms of aid varies with the economic climate and depends on the nature of the industries that are expanding or contracting. Attempting to identify the actual rather than the predicted effect of REP, the main object of this paper, is complicated by the Industrial Development Act of 1966 and the introduction of Special Development Area assistance in November 1967. The Industrial Development Act of 1966 substitutes Development Areas for Development Districts and investment grants for 'free depreciation'. The change to the larger Development Areas from the stop-check-go[4] Development District procedure assured industrialists that the area they decided to move to would continue to retain favoured area status. Such assurance could only serve to encourage movement. It is generally accepted that the 'free depreciation' system was unnecessarily complex and less attractive to industrialists than its replacement, a 20 per cent investment grant differential in favour of the Development Areas. In any case there is little doubt that the Industrial Development Act should have encouraged, rather than discouraged, movement to and expansion in the Development Areas. This is also true of Special Development Area legislation, which provided generous additional assistance in a number of mining communities within the Development Areas. The notable response to Special Development Area assistance is referred to on page 234 of this paper.

[4] If unemployment fell, or was likely to fall below 4½ per cent, the Development District could either be de-listed or stop listed (remain a Development District in name, but with no Local Employment Assistance available). The Districts were altered with alarming frequency and the approach was not consistent with a policy which emphasised potential, or proven ability, in attracting industry. Those localities most successful in attracting industry would be among those most likely to be taken off the list of eligible districts.

It is extremely difficult to isolate the effect of non REP alterations to regional policy, but it is safe to claim that they should have raised rather than lowered Development Area employment. Since it is difficult to quantify a total regional policy effect and to estimate the effect of non REP changes it is doubtful if quantification of the REP effect is a useful exercise.

Precise estimation is impossible, but we can look to the evidence to distinguish between those circumstances where the impact of change is obvious and considerable and those circumstances where it is doubtful and disappointing. This is in fact possible in the case of regional policy. The evidence shows that the policy innovations of 1960 and 1963 have had a clear and appreciable impact on Development Area employment. The impact of the Regional Employment Premium is not so obvious.

III IDC approvals

Table 2 shows the Development Area share of IDC Approvals for five distinct regional policy periods. The Development Area share is measured in terms of (1) anticipated employment (2) area of industrial building and (3) number of projects. The area and number statistics provide a check on the employment figures.

Table 2

Development Area share of E (anticipated additional employment (a), A (area of industrial building and N (number of projects) each expressed as a percentage of the Great Britain Total.

Period		E	A	N
1956 to 1959	(Weak regional policy)	18	21	16
1960 to 1962	(Active regional policy)	33	27	18
1963 to 1966	(Intensive regional policy)	44	37	24
1967 to 1969	(Intensive plus REP phase one)	38	32(b)	22
1970 to 1972	(Intensive plus REP phase two)	25	28(b)	15

(a) Anticipated additional employment has been reduced by thirty per cent in the Development Areas.
(b) The Area figures for 1967 to 1969 and 1970 to 1972 are not directly comparable with those for earlier years.
Source:
Statistics provided by DTI

All three series (*E*, *A* and *N*) rise in the years of active regional policy (1960 to 1962) and again in the intensive period (1963 to 1966). The results for the pre REP years are consistent with a strong, positive relationship between greater emphasis on regional policy and additional factory building in the Development Areas. The results for the post REP years are not. All three series fall in REP, phase one (1967 to 1969) and again in REP, phase two (1970 to 1972).

Comparing 1960 to 1962 with 1956 to 1959 the improvement in *E* (Employment) and *A* (Area) is much more pronounced than the improvement in *N* (Number). This is a natural consequence of success in steering large employers, particularly car manufacturing companies, to the assisted areas. From then on the changes in *E* *A* and *N* are of similar proportion. They are approximately one-third higher in 1963 to 1966 than they are in 1960 to 1962. Comparing 1967 to 1972 with 1963 to 1966 *E* falls by approximately one-quarter and *N* by one-fifth.

Table 3 (and Figures 1, and 2) give the year by year results and show that E, A and N reach their peak in 1965 with E at 49, A at 40 and N at 26 per cent, before falling to 20, 25 and 14 per cent in 1972. All the series improve in 1960 (Local Employment

Act) and 1963 (Local Employment Act and Finance Act). The improvements in E and A over 1959–60 and 1962–63 were greater than the change for any other two consecutive years.

Regional assistance is not the only important consideration. A high level of national demand, a seller's market for goods and labour, encourages the desirable response predicted by theory, movement of industry to, and expansion of industry in, those areas where labour is more readily available. The high and rising unemployment of the post REP years help to explain the poor repsonse to REP. In order to allow for change in the labour market situation E (Development Area share of anticipated employment) can be related to U (national male unemployment) – see Fig 2. Between 1963 and 1972 E rises whenever U falls and falls when U rises. The correlation coefficient between E and U is -0.93. In statistical terms 87 per cent of the variation in E is 'explained' by change in the level of male unemployment. The correlation co-efficient between N (Number) and U is -0.89, 80 per cent of the variation in N is 'explained' by change in U. The linear regression lines for 1963 and 1972 are $E=58.8-6.9U$ and $N=29.6-2.9U$, which implies that E falls almost 7 per cent and N by almost 3 per cent for every one per cent rise in male unemployment (between unemployment levels of 1.7 and 5.9 per cent).

It is difficult to exaggerate the importance of change in the national economic situation, but there is no indication that the introduction of REP raised E, A or N. Change in unemployment is the only clear influence from 1963 to 1972. In order to test for the effect of REP, the premium is introduced as a dummy variable with $R=0$ in the years 1963 to 1967 and $R=1$ from 1968 to 1972. The results are $E=5.67-5.7U-3.8R$ and $N=29.4-2.7U-0.6R$. The effect of R is not statistically significant in either equation, but the negative sign suggests that the relationships betwwen U and E and U and N did not move to a higher level in the post REP years.

By contrast there is clear evidence that the earlier and less ambitious innovations in regional policy notably improved the relationship between the Development Area share of factory building (E, A and N) and U. E, A and N all improve in 1960 and the marked increases over 1962–63 (E, 27–39 per cent, A, 24–31 per cent, and N, 18–22 per cent) are achieved in spite of a substantial increase in male unemployment. An indication of the shift[5] in the Development Area share of factory building is given by comparing two years with identical levels of male unemployment. In 1961 and 1965 male unemployment was 1.7 per cent but E, A and N were 30, 27 and 19 per cent in 1961 as compared with 49, 40 and 26 per cent in 1965. If the government had not operated a policy of control and inducement the Development Area share of industrial building would have been considerably lower in the 1960s.

IV Firm movement

Firm movement into the Development Areas rose absolutely and as a proportion of national movement in the late fifties and early sixties. A J Brown (1972, p 294) claims that 'from the late fifties until the middle sixties, there was a massive diversion of moves to the peripheral areas, which went on more or less continually, reached its maximum rate about 1963, and is almost certainly to be associated with the series of administrative and legislative changes of the time – each of which probably produced some effect quite quickly and further effects cumulatively over a period of two or three years'. Brown adds 'It is unfortunate that statistics of moves for more recent years are not available'. since they could be used to test the response to REP. The later movement figures are now available (see Table 4) and suggest that REP, unlike the earlier measures, cannot 'safely be regarded as effective'. (Brown, p 294).

[5]This only gives an indication of the shift resulting from the policy innovations of 1963.

231

Table 3 and Figures 2 and 3

Table 3 gives the year by year figures for **U** (national male unemployment), **E** (Development Area share of anticipated employment),(d) **A** (Development Area share of floor space) and **N** (Development Area share of number of projects). Figure 2 shows the relationship between **E** and **U** and Figure 3 the relationship between **N** and **U**

Table 3

	U	E	N	A
1956	1.2	18.4	15.3	22.6
1957	1.5	14.5	16.2	23.1
1958	2.3	17.3	15.6	20.6
1959	2.4	19.8	15.8	18.9
1960	1.8	35.1	16.7	27.2
1961	1.7	29.8	19.3	26.5
1962	2.3	26.6	17.6	24.4
1963	3.0	38.7	21.5	31.2
1964	1.9	41.2	22.6	34.3
1965	1.7	49.4	25.6	40.0
1966	1.9	46.3	24.0	38.3(c)
1967	3.0	41.8	22.3	33.0(c)
1968	3.2	41.0	22.5	34.0(c)
1969	3.3	32.2	21.9	28.5(c)
1970	3.6	27.9	15.6	30.2(c)
1971	4.8	23.8	14.1	27.1(c)
(b)1972	5.9	20.1	14.1	24.7(c)

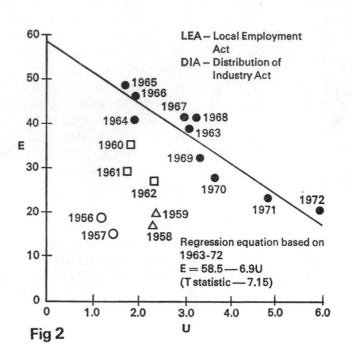

Fig 2

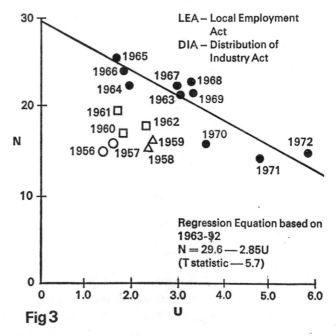

Fig 3

(a) Anticipated employment in the Development Areas has been reduced by thirty per cent.

(b) 1972 figures are for the months January to July; Approval Statistics were discontinued from July 20, 1972.

(c) The Area Statistics for 1966-72 are calculated on a different basis to those available for the earlier years. The earlier figures tend to exaggerate the Development Area share of floor space.

Source: Statistics provided by Department of Trade and Industry and Department of Employment Gazette

232

E (Development Area share of anticipated (a) employment).
A (Development Area share of floor space' and **N** (Development Area share of number of projects), each expressed as a percentage of the Great Britain (b) total.

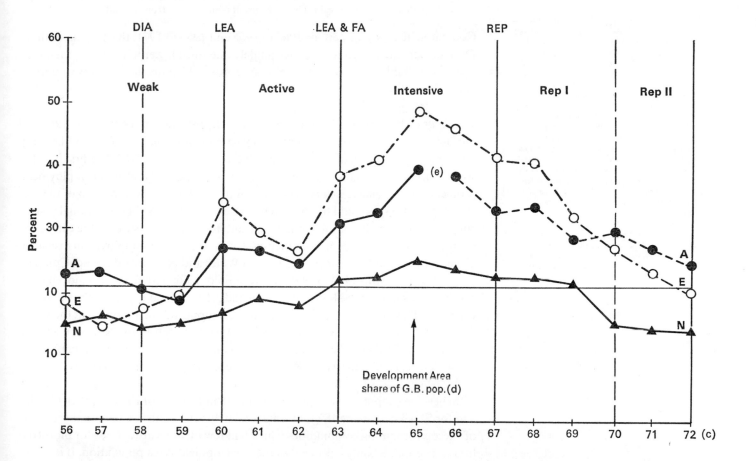

DIA – Distribution of Industry Act
LEA – Local Employment Act
FA   – Finance Act

(a) Anticipated employment in the Development Areas has been reduced by thirty percent.
(b) **There are no approval figures for Northern Ireland.**
(c) 1972 figures are for the months January to July; Approval Statistics were discontinued from July 20, 1972.
(d) As measured in 1966.
(e) The Area Statistics for 1966-72 are calculated on a different basis to those available for the earlier years. The earlier figures tend to exaggerate the Development Area share of floor space.

Source: Statistics provided by Department of Trade and Industry.

Fig1 IDC Approvals

Table 4

Inter-Regional Moves. Net gain or loss by period when moves took place (Thousands)

	Moves undertaken in:				
	1945 to 1951*	1952 to 1959*	1960 to 1965*	1966 to 1971†	1945 to 1971‡
(A) Development Area Regions[1]	+213.5	+67.0	+120.8	+80.5	+481.8
(B) Other Regions[2]	−162.7	−23.6	− 96.9	−66.5	−349.7

(*) Employment as measured at end of 1966.
(†) Employment as measured at mid 1971.
(‡) 1945 to 1965 moves measured at end of 1966: 1966 to 1971 moves measured at mid 1971.
([1]) North, Scotland, Wales, North-West, South-West and Northern Ireland.
([2]) West Midlands, East Midlands, East Anglia, South East, Yorkshire and Humberside. Taking A and B together there is a net gain. This is the result of movement from abroad.

Comparing the six year periods 1960 to 1965 and 1966 to 1971, the net gain to the Development Area regions is approximately one-third lower in the later years, when REP was available. The years of notable success are the immediate post-war years and 1960 to 1965.

The contrast between the obvious response to the innovations of 1960 and 1963 and the lack of reaction to REP would probably be even more marked if Special Develop-Area (SDA) assistance had not been introduced in November 1967. The first list of SDA's concentrated on mining communities with particularly severe unemployment problems. Additional assistance over and above that available in the rest of the Development Areas could be given to firms new to the SDA's. The additional assistance was selective, discretionary and substantially reduced costs over the early problem years of a new project[6]. Forty-two of the forty-seven employment exchanges given SDA status in November 1967 were in Wales and Northern England. Comparing 1966 to 1971 with 1960 to 1965, the net employment gain from firm movement was 7.4 thousand in the Northern Region and 5.1 thousand in Wales, the fall for the other four Development Area regions was 52.8 thousand, suggesting that the SDA measures diverted a substantial proportion of new projects to the Northern Region and Wales. A further indication of the power and importance of the original[7] SDA legislation is given in the Tenth Report on the Local Employment Act (HCP 127, 1970), which shows that the SDA's accounted for 19 per cent of employment expected from new Development Area projects in the 18 months prior to November 14, 1967, and for 50 per cent in the 18 months immediately after. This is a remarkable degree of success for mining communities which had few obvious attractions for industrialists and contained only 8 per cent of the Development Area population. It is possible, even probable, that the SDA measures had a favourable impact on total movement into the Development Areas, thus emphasising more strongly the lack of response to REP.

V Actual and expected employment

The Movement and Approval statistics suggest that REP has had remarkably little effect on firm movement and factory expansion. This is disappointing. According to the Green and White papers, the premium was expected to provide 'an additional inducement' to move to the Development Areas and 'stimulate the need for more factories'. It is, however, possible that the introduction of REP could have helped to avert decline, or could have raised employment in existing factories. Moore and Rhodes adopt the shift-scheme technique to provide a measure which comprehends 'every possible way in which REP could increase employment over and above what it would otherwise have been, including the movement of new firms into existing premises, the expansion of employment in indigenous firms within existing factories and the avoidance of contraction and closure'. (Moore and Rhodes, 1974, p 372).

[6]A complex but valuable operational grant was introduced allowing the new firm to claim, during the first three years of a project, ten per cent of the cumulative expenditure incurred each year on the acquisition of eligible building, plant and machinery. In a SDA a firm could be granted both a loan and a building grant, or a loan and a rent-free period. In an ordinary Development Area award of a building grant rendered a firm ineligible for a loan. The SDA project could be self-financing to a degree not enjoyed in other Development Areas. This proved important in a period when external finance was difficult to obtain. In an SDA a firm could be granted a rent-free period of five years, as compared with two years in an ordinary Development Area. A 'rolling programme' of advanced factory building was introduced; work on a new advance factory would start as soon as a completed factory was let. For the firm that wants to expand quickly the advance factory is often the most important and effective form of assistance.

[7]Subsequent changes in regional policy have introduced new SDA's but the Operational Grant and the 'rolling programme' of advance factory building have been withdrawn. The SDA's remain special only in name.

In order to test for the total effect of regional policy on manufacturing employment actual and expected employment can be compared. Expected employment is calculated by applying the national rate of change for each industry to actual employment for the base year and it is claimed that the changing relationship between actual and expected employment gives an indication of the impact of innovations in regional policy. Moore and Rhodes (1973) show that there is little divergence between actual and expected Development Area employment in the years 1951 to 1963, but discover a large and growing divergence in the post 1963 years. They provide convincing 'Evidence . . . to support the contention that this difference between actual and expected employment which emerged after 1963 was in fact caused by the strengthening of regional policy rather than by chance or any other factor' (p 88) and take the divergence to be an approximate measure of the direct effect of regional policy on manufacturing employment.

One of the problems of all techniques designed to allow for differences in structure is that the results depend on the industrial classification employed. Moore and Rhodes rely on Main Order Headings, even though some Order Group (eg textiles, or engineering and electrical goods) contain a considerable range of products with widely varying market prospects and employment trends. It is not possible to divide manufacturing industry into homogeneous product groups, but it is possible to move towards the Minimum List Heading classification and split industry into groups that allow for structural differences not detected at the Order level. In order to calculate expected employment manufacturing industry is split into 101 industries. (see Table 5).

In columns 1, 2 and 3 of Table 5 expected employment is calculated by applying the UK growth rate over four year periods to actual employment in 101 Development Area industries. In column 4 expected employment is calculated by applying the UK growth rates over 1963 to 1971 to actual employment in 1963.

Table 5

Actual and expected employment in manufacturing industry in the Development Areas[1] *(Thousands)*

	1 *1963* *(1959 base year)*	*2* *1967* *(1963 base year)*	*3* *1971* *(1967 base year)*	*4* *1971* *(1963 base year)*
Actual *Employment*	3332	3362	3297	3297
Expected *Employment*	3328	3274	3209	3119
Divergence	+4	+88	+88	+ 178
Index *Actual* *Expected*	100.1	102.7	102.7	105.7

[1] North, Scotland, Wales, North-West, South-West and Northern Ireland.
Source:
Employees-Employment Statistics provided by DOE

The results given in Table 5 are similar to those presented in an earlier paper. (R R MacKay, E J ,1974) This is surprising since Table 5 adds two new regions to the calculation (North-West and South-West), includes metal manufacture and shipbuilding, ommitted from the earlier calculation, and uses a finer division of industrial products. The similarity suggests that sensible variation in approach, does not notably alter the results and therefore the implications of the structure measure. The contrast between column 1 and column 2 indicates that there is a strong regional policy effect. Column 1 shows that actual employment in the Development Area regions in 1963 is marginally above expected employment. In 1967 (column 2) actual employment is 88,000 above expected employment. The results for 1959 to 1963 and 1963 to 1967 are reasonably consistent with the IDC approval and firm movement statistics. Improvement in industrial building and in firm movements occur before 1963, but it takes time before approvals and firm

235

openings notably influence actual employment. The almost identical results given in column 2 and 3, with actual employment approximately 88,000 above expected employment for both 1963 to 1967 and 1967 to 1971, suggest that there is little sign of a substantial REP effect.

This conclusion is not immediately acceptable. There are considerable problems in comparing the results for 1963 to 1967 and 1967 to 1971. Unemployment was low and generally falling over 1963 to 1967. By 1971 unemployment had risen to record levels for the post-war years. The Development Areas are extremely vulnerable in times of recession and restraint.

It is possible to argue that the difference between actual and expected employment might have been considerably smaller if REP had not been introduced. But there are two contrary arguments. Even if no additional assistance had been provided the change from Development Districts to Development Areas should have encouraged movement to and expansion in the Development Area Regions (see p 229). A more important argument, and a more difficult problem, is that the gap between actual and expected employment in 1971 does not give an accurate measure of the effect of the regional assistance available between 1967 and 1971. Employment growth may be a response to existing legislation, but it could be a reaction to previous legislation. There is an important and variable time-lag between decisions to expand and actual employment creation. A two year gap between an IDC Approval and Completion is quite usual. Even when a firm has started production a substantially above average growth rate is to be expected in the next four years (see Board of Trade, p 21). A decision to build a Development Area factory in 1963 may start contributing to employment in 1965 and substantial growth can be expected in the next few years. Additions to employment in the years 1967 to 1971 partly reflect the high levels of industrial building and firm movement in the pre REP years.

The gap between the intial response to assistance and employment creation depends partly on the nature of the assistance available. Regional assistance designed to notably reduce the cost of movement and the cost of factory expansion take time to influence employment. A specific criticism of the IDC Approval statistics is that they do not detect situations where employment growth (or preservation) involves no addition to factory capacity. The great attraction of the shift-share approach is that it could provide a total measure. Presumably, assistance designed to raise employment in existing premises should have a more or less immediate effect. Thus the results for 1967 to 1971 show the combined effect of employment gains resulting from decisions to expand taken in earlier years and the reaction to REP. This is an additional reason for believing that there was no substantial response to REP.

In order to calculate the effect of regional policy on manufacturing employment it is assumed that the change in differential shift (gap between actual and expected employment) which takes place after 1963, is entirely the result of renewed interest in regional intervention. This heroic assumption gives a regional policy effect for the six Development Area regions of 84,000 over both 1963 to 1967 and 1967 to 1971.

The heroic assumption that change in differential shift is entirely the result of change in regional policy is not defensible. The disadvantages of the shift-share approach are well known. The results are only as good as the industrial classification adopted, but even if the classification was ideal the results would only give a first indication of the importance of structure. As D I MacKay (p 135) emphasises 'The technique is based on the implicit (and unacceptable) assumption that what happens in one industry has no influence whatever on any other industry in the region'. The separation of the service from the manufacturing sector reduces the drawbacks of the technique since 'The service trades are the most obvious examples of industries, where growth, in part at least, is a function of local demand' (D I, MacKay, p 136), but this division is only a partial solution, and the technique gives a minimum rather than an accurate measure of the importance of differences in structure. Given the inherent limitations of the shift-share approach, it is impossible to provide a precise estimate of the effect of regional policy. But the change in differential shift, the turning-point which occurs around 1963, is so marked and obvious that it is reasonable to believe that the changes in regional policy had a major impact. Faith in this conclusion is strengthened by the response of both firm movement and factory building to the legislation of 1960 and 1963. The technique is more difficult to apply when there is no major change in the relationship between actual and expected employment.

[8] The difference is movement into the UK from overseas.

[9] Taking non-Development Area regions and Development Area regions together actual employment is 24,000 below expected employment. This is because the expected employment calculations include employment in firms that moved into the UK from overseas.

VI The contribution of indigenous and mobile firms compared

Above average performance (a positive differential shift) may be attributable to firms long established in a region, to firm movement, or a combination of both. In Table 6, the relative contributions are compared.

Row 1 shows that Development Area employment is approximately 94,000 above and Non-Development Area employment 94,000 below expected employment by 1966 (1960 base). Row 2 shows a net gain from firm movement of approximately 121,000 in the Development Area regions and a net loss of 97,000 in the rest of the country[8]. In Row 3 (col 1) actual and expected employment are compared for those plants located in the Development Area regions in 1960 and located anywhere in the UK in 1966. Thus when a plant moves between 1960 and 1966, the 1966 employment is attributed to the region of origin.

Table 6

Actual-expected employment and employment created by firm movement for Development area regions (a) and other parts of the UK *(Thousands)*

	1 Development Area Regions	2 Rest of the UK
1 Divergence between Actual and Expected employment in 1966 (1960 base)	+94	−94
2 Net gain or loss from firm movement (1960 to 1965)	+121	−97
3 Divergence between Actual and expected employment after allowing for firm movement.	−27	+3
4 Divergence between Actual and expected employment 1971 (1966 base)	+79	−79
5 Net gain or loss from firm movement (1966 to 1971)	+81	−67
6 Divergence between Actual and expected employment after allowing for firm movement.	−2	+12
7 Employment change 1966 to 1971 in plants that moved between regions in years 1961 to 1965.	+26	+5

(a) North, Scotland, Wales, North-West, South-West and Northern Ireland.

Source:
BOT (1968) and statistics provided by DOE and DTI

The plants located in the Development Areas in 1960 are, by 1966, 27,000 short of the standard set by applying national rate of change to employment in each industry in 1960. Those plants located in the rest of the United Kingdom, in 1960 (and located anywhere in the UK in 1966) are 2,000 above expected employment by 1966[9]. There is no indication that regional assistance had a notable effect on plants established in Development Area regions.

Rows 4 – 6 compare actual and expected employment and firm movement for 1966 to 1971. Once again firm movement is the important factor explaining differences in performance. But there is one apparently important contrast between Row 3 and Row 6. The actual-expected comparison for those plants located in Development Areas in 1966 and located anywhere in the UK in 1971 gives better results than the comparison for 1960 to 1966. At first glance it would appear as if REP had a beneficial effect on industry established in the Development Areas, but the direct comparison is misleading. Row 7 shows that the apparent 'improvement' in the performance of indigenous Development Area plants is largely explained by continued growth in employment in those firms that moved into the Development Areas between 1961 and 1965[10]. This growth cannot be attributed to REP.

The information presented in Table 6 substantiates McCrone's claim that firm movement 'seems likley to be the main explanation' of differences in differential shift (gap between actual and expected employment) 'rather than any peculiarities in the performance of those already there'. Certainly as far as the Development Areas as a group are concerned firm movement is the all important factor[11]. The major and important area of success remains the mobile firm. The attempt to encourage expansion in industry established in the Development Areas has not been notably successful.

VII Evaluation

In Policies for Regional Development (1964) T Wilson of Glasgow University stressed the importance of industrial movement and underlined the desirability of concentrating assistance on those firms that could be expected to make a positive response to assistance given. 'I shall later make a strong plea that such assistance should be on a generous scale, but this plea can be made convincing only if those to be benefited pass the test of being prepared to expand or modernise. In this way the largest gain can be derived'. In a later article (1967) Wilson states 'The regional measures previously adopted (ie before 1966) have achieved a good deal of success and it would seem too early to adandon pump-priming for permanent subvention' and predicts that 'a general and quite unselective subsidy' (ie REP) would not be as effective as assistance designed to help 'new or expanding firms during difficult periods.' M Borschette (1972) a member of the Commission of the European Community, also emphasises that 'aid must be provided where it is really needed' and claims that that is particularly important and effective when the firm is newly established in an assisted area because then 'it is most deeply affected by the handicaps which exist in certain regions' and also when the established firm has 'to meet the cost of conversion or adaptation'. Blanket subsidies, he claims are 'ineffective and often lead to the granting of further aid to eliminate or counter the difficulties caused by this very ineffectiveness'.

The evidence and argument in this paper underlines the importance of concentrating assistance on those firms that are prepared, willing and eager to respond. New industries, preferably, those with considerable growth potential, remain the most important priority, and mobile firms remain the most obvious and most important area of success. The case for assisting mobile industry has been compared to the economic argument for using tariff barriers to protect infant industry in developing countries; for firms moving to the Development Areas and the infant industry the hope is that permanent subsidisation will not be necessary and that movement towards profitable unsubsidised production will be rapid.

In comparing REP with capital incentives the Green Paper (para 28) emphasises the danger that investment incentives 'will tend to tip the balance in favour of locating capital intensive projects in areas of labour surplus'. More important than the capital-

[10]The results for 1960 to 1965 would be better, but are not available.

[11]In a criticism of earlier applications of shift-share McCrone suggests that it is extremely difficult to use the technique 'to assess the significance of locational disadvantage' when above average growth is largely the result of firm movement. By allowing for firm movement it may be possible to resurrect the technique as a guide to performance in different locations, but the history of shift-share, its changing role over the years, the problems in allowing for time-lags, indicate that the technique should be applied with extreme discretion. McCrone 1969, p177.

labour dichotomy are the distinctions between (a) assistance to mobile and to established firms and (b) between assistance designed to encourage expansion and adaptation and automatic subsidy. When a firm is persuaded or encouraged to move to a Development Area there are two forces serving to increase employment. There is first of all a displacement effect: employment is created in the Development Area instead of in the firm's established location. Secondly, there is an acceleration[12] effect. As a result of the firm receiving assistance it may be encouraged to expand more quickly and to a greater extent than it would otherwise have done. The area receiving a new firm would benefit both as the result of the displacement and the acceleration effects,[13] but it is likely that the former would be more important than the latter. Once a firm has moved to a Development Area, the natural tendency to expand in or close to a known location should have a cumulative effect, the area receiving benefit not only from the initial move but also from subsequent expansion. Growth should be appreciable since a process of natural selection is likely to favour those areas receiving mobile firms with the growth sectors of industry. Firms expand, build new factories, move to new areas in response to market opportunities and the desire for expansion is likely to be greater in those sectors where employment is growing. 'The significance of employment mobility . . is further enhanced by the fact that . . . at least as far as manufacturing industry is concerned, post-war movement, far from embracing a cross-section of all industry, has been highly selective of the country's biggest, most rapidly expanding and most export orientated firms.' (Keeble, p 25–26).

Detection of and special treatment for those projects where relocation is a possibility remains extremely important[14]. In recent years the emphasis has moved away from the mobile firm and towards indigenous established industry. In part this is an attempt to escape from the constraint provided by the fact that the amount of mobile industry is limited. The desire to discover other sources of employment growth is understandable, but there is little indication that the introduction of a non-selective wage subsidy provided an effective solution.

There is a strong presumption that the firm long established in a Development Area will expand there rather than in another region. The displacement effect is not likely to be important[15] in the case of established industry; assistance may encourage additions to employment, but only as a result of the acceleration effect. The REP adds to the number of firms receiving assistance, but has only a marginal effect on the cost of expansion. Assistance is spread thin rather than concentrated on reducing costs for those interested in growth. A subsidy which is sensitive to, or is allocated according to, additions to employment, output or investment is more likely to encourage response. Such a subsidy could notably reduce the cost of expansion and raise the rate of return on additional investment. If the criticism that capital incentives introduce the wrong type of industry is regarded as important, the logical alternative is to introduce a wage subsidy concentrated on mobile firms[16]. An alternative solution is to provide wage subsidies for new and established firms, but to relate the subsidy to increases in employment rather than pay according to numbers employed. According to an OECD study (OECD 1970, p18), it was originally intended to make REP more sensitive to changes in employment, but practical difficulties ruled out the more effective approach.

A substantial proportion of a non-selective subsidy will go to declining firms. Even when firms are making an accounting loss there may be an economic case for regional subsidisation. Where unemployment is high and men find it difficult to find alternative employment, the wage costs are likely to exceed the real or opportunity cost of employing labour. The great disadvantage of subsidising firms that cannot meet competition unaided is that it is a short-term palliative rather than a long term cure. There is frequently little indication that the relative position of those firms (or industries) in difficulty will improve. Indeed in many instances there is every sign

[12]It could be called a creation effect – the reduction in costs may make previously uneconomic projects worthwhile.

[13]A third effect is important, the multiplier resulting from any initial employment created, but any addition to employment would have a multiplier effect and the essential distinction is between acceleration and displacement.

[14]Including certain parts of the service sector. A high proportion of service industry employment is determined by the need to service local markets and expansion is a natural response to growth of local population or income. Assistance would appear more appropriate where service employment is dependant on national or even international demand. In such circumstances there may be a range of possible economic locations and there are strong economic arguments for using regional policy to encourage location in areas of high unemployment. The argument has been accepted in theory for public sector employment (nationalised industries, government departments etc), but no consistent policy has been pursued.

[15]There may be a modified displacement effect when a firm has plants in Development Areas and other parts of the country. Incentives may encourage firms to expand in the Development Area rather than the alternative location.

[16]Such a subsidy could be gradually reduced.

239

that increasing assistance will be required to maintain employment. In three, five or ten years time there will be the same problem of finding jobs in industries which are economically viable. It is possible to conceive of circumstances where assistance given to firms in difficulty reverses the trend[17], but aid to declining industry is often an expensive way to buy time. More important than the preservation of manpower in unprofitable concerns is the introduction and expansion of growth industries.

According to the Expenditure Committee Report, Public Money in the Private Sector, 'There must be few areas of Government expenditure in which so much is spent but so little known about the success of the policy.' (HC 347 of 1971–72 para 172). The Committee exaggerates. There are still 'significant areas of obscurity' (HC 85 of 1973–74 para 170) and there is a need for more research, but in this, as in other applied economic situations there will always be an element of uncertainty. As economists have consistently emphasised, economics provides imperfect and imprecise relationships rather than iron laws, an engine for discovery rather than 'a body of concrete truth'. (Keynes, 1933, p208). Given that this is so, economic prediction is likely to be extremely difficult, and identifying what might have happened if regional policy had not altered, a form of reverse prediction, must be an inexact and approximate exercise. In this paper the problems of detection have been emphasised. The statistics are imperfect, the sheer Volume of change in regional leglislation complicates analysis, the areas assisted alter, the regional economies are open to outside influence, the time-lag remains a major irritation. In spite of these difficulties the overall picture remains surprisingly clear.

Without the incentives and controls of regional policy, the level of employment in the Development Areas would now be considerably lower. There is sufficient evidence to indicate that there was an important and obvious response to the intensification of regional policy in the early sixties. The success of the coalfield areas confirms that pump-priming has an obvious effect on the location decision.

The attempt to provide a radical, rapid solution to the regional problem by providing a labour subsidy to all Development Area firms has not been notably successful. The search for one simple, obvious, neat answer to the regional problem is likely to prove unproductive.

The nature of 'the problem' varies between and within Development Areas; non selective, 'blanket' measures ignore the differences. It may be possible to encourage firms established in the Development Areas to grow and prosper, but it requires a much more selective and sophisticated approach than has, as yet, been devised.

In an apparently inevitable progression the areas given assistance have been continually extended[18] while the general trend has been towards equal and automatic subsidy rights for all firms. A recent CBI report (1972, p13) suggests that it is logical to give established firms (service and manufacturing) treatment equal to that received by the new because there are more people employed in established industry than in mobile firms. Against this, however, it is wasteful to spend funds when returns will be low and the economic, as distinct from the political, case for assistance depends on response, on an increase in number employed rather than existing levels of employment. Before a convenient, but ineffective, and illogical policy of equal assistance to all is adopted, the case for greater selectivity must be reconsidered.

A previous Minister for Industry admitted that 'REP has been disappointing in the effect it has had in raising the prosperity of the Development Areas and we shall be looking for something more effective to put in its place.' (Trade and Industry, 1971, p500). The search for alternatives is important, but more effective than any monetary substitute would be growth and a lower level of national unemployment. As

[17]A non-selective wage subsidy is not the most effective way to achieve this reversal.

[18]As unemployment has risen the opportunity to give effective help to any assisted area has been reduced, but the assisted areas have been steadily extended. Assisted areas of one type or another, SDA's, Development Areas, Intermediate Areas and derelict land clearance areas, now account for approximately half of the UK population.

Hoover stresses 'We cannot expect any satisfactory solution to the problems of regional unemployment except in the context of a prosperous national economy.' (Hoover, 1969, p346).

Bibliography

Board of Trade, *The Movement of Manufacturing Industry in the United Kingdom.* Ed R S Howard. 1968.

Borschette, A *Regional Policy in the European Community.* Not published. 1972.

Brown A J *The Framework of Regional Economics in the United Kingdom.* 1972.

Department of Economic Affairs, *The Development Areas. A Proposal for a Regional Employment Premium.* HMSO The Green Paper. (1967a).

Department of Economic Affairs, *The Development Areas. Regional Employment Premium.* HMSO Cmnd 3310. *The White Paper.* (1967b)

EFTA, *Industrial Mobility.* (1971).

Expenditure Committee. *Public Money in the Private Sector.* H C 347 of 1971–72.

Expenditure Committee, *Regional Development Incentives.* 85, 85–1 and 327 of 1972–73.

Hoover E *Backward Areas in Advanced Countries.* ed AEG Robinson.

Keeble D *Employment Mobility in Britain – from Spatial Policy Problems of the British Economy.* Ed M Chisholm and G Manners.

Keynes J M *Essays in Biography*

MacKay D I 'Industrial Structure and Regional Growth: A Methodological Problem. *Scottish Journal of Political Economy* 1968.

MacKay, R R 'Evaluating the Effects of British Regional Policy – A Comment.' *Economic Journal* 1974.

Moore B and Rhodes D 'Evaluating the Effects of British Regional Policy. *Economic Journal* 1973 and A Reply. Economic Journal 1974.

McCrone G *Regional Policy in Britain.* 1969.

North West Industrial Development Association Memorandum to the Minister of Technology. Not published. 1969.

OECD *Manpower Policy in the UK* 1970.

Scottish Council (Development and Industry) *Regional Employment Premium.* 1967.

Trade and Industry, p500, Dec 9, 1971.

Wilson T *Finance for Regional Development. Three Banks Review.* Sept No 75, pp3–23. 1967.

Wilson T *Policies for Regional Development.* University of Glasgow Social and Economic Studies. Occasional Papers No 3. 1964.

The Impact of the Regional Employment Premium
R R MACKAY

[1] B C Moore and J Rhodes, *Economic Journal* / June 1974. A Reply to a comment by R R MacKay.

Comments by B C Moore and J Rhodes

After a long introduction, in which the reader is treated to a collection of views of people who are on the whole anti-REP, Mr. MacKay's paper then proceeds to examine some evidence on the effects of regional policy. The indicators chosen are on the whole useful ones for assessing the effects of policy in the sense that regional policy should, on a priori grounds, influence movements in these indicators. The three indicators selected for analysis are:

1 IDC approval share (in terms of expected associated employment)
2 Estimates of employment associated with industrial movement.
3 Actual and expected employment in manufacturing using a shift-share technique.

We offer brief comments on the analysis of each of these indicators to say why an REP effect has not been identified.

1 IDC approval share

(i) On the data side a number of points require clarification – in particular how far the data have been adjusted to allow for changes in the regional and industrial coverage of IDC controls and for changes in exemption limits. Moreover no adjustment is made to allow for regional differences in industrial structure. For instance the inclusion of the steel industry, which is dominant in some Development Areas, had a big impact on IDC approvals in the early 1960s and a much reduced impact in the later 1960s.

(ii) The IDC approval share, as an indicator of the effects of REP, is not sufficiently comprehensive in scope in that it represents only one form of job creation (that associated with new buildings) whereas REP could have influenced expansion of employment in indigenous firms within existing factories and the avoidance of contraction and closures. Moreover Mr MacKay's analysis is not able to identify any impact of REP on the proportion of IDC approvals which actually materialise.

(iii) Our third criticism relates to the equation used to test for the effects of REP No allowance is made for the changing strength of non-REP regional policy between 1967 and 1971 nor for the fall in the real value of REP over the same period. Moreover the 'share' formulation of the dependent variable unnecessarily restricts the relationship between national and regional IDC approvals granted. And, as we have shown elsewhere, the equation is not sufficiently sensitive as to be able to isolate quite a large simulated REP effect[1].

2 Employment associated with industrial movement

Although we agree that the employment associated with movement to Development Areas in the period 1966 to 1971 was substantially below that in the period 1960 to 1966 the entire difference can be accounted for by the once-for-all move of the motor industry to Merseyside and Scotland. It is misleading to accept this as evidence for a zero REP effect as the 41,000 jobs in the car industry in the earlier period, whilst being specifically associated with regional policy, could not be expected to be repeated in the later REP period. Indeed in terms of the number of firms moving to Development Areas there were many more in the REP period.

3 Actual and expected employment in manufacturing

Although we do not regard the period 1959 to 1963 as a really adequate passive policy alternative position we are in broad agreement with these results. Indeed we are encouraged by the fact that a disaggregated approach results in an overall policy effect similar to that derived from our own less disaggregated analysis.

We do not agree with the interpretation of Table 6 in two respects. Firstly Mr MacKay claims that 'investment incentives had no influence on native firms in Development Areas' but this conclusion cannot be drawn from Table 6 without information relating to the passive policy period. For example in row 3 the figure of – 27,000 might be an improvement on a higher negative figure in the 1950s. Secondly it is possible to conclude from Table 6 that a significant REP effect is discernible. From a combination of figures presented in Column 1, rows 3, 6 and 7 of Table 6, it is possible to conclude that REP increased employment in native firms by an amount up to 19,000 jobs, quite apart from any contribution REP might have made to firm movement or second phase expansion of pre-1966 moves.

Finally we would like to put on record our complete agreement with three points made in the MacKay paper. First that the major area of success has been the mobile firms. Secondly the ability of regional policy to revitalise the competitive position of the indigenous (native) manufacturing sector of Development Areas has been disappointing. Thirdly it is unfortunate that regional policy has had to operate in conditions where the British economy as a whole has grown slowly and found it increasingly difficult to compete in both home and export markets.

The econometric assessment of the impact of investment incentives

P J LUND

[1] Fisher (1971), p243. The four papers were Hall and Jorgenson (1971), Bischoff (1971), Coen (1971) and Klein and Taubman (1971)

[2] A detailed description of the post-war development of the investment incentives available in the UK for manufacturing industry is conveniently provided in the background paper by Melliss and Richardson (1975)

'The four analyses are all marked by high quality. Each applies sophisticated econometric tools to the empirical and theoretical analysis of an important problem; each does so in a professional and convincing manner; each sheds light where before there was darkness. If it were not for the inconvenient fact that the four analyses happen to concern the same problem and happen to contradict each others findings, there would be little to discuss'[1].

So began the first discussant of a set of four papers presented at a previous (US Brookings Institution) conference of experts held under the title of 'Tax Incentives and Capital Spending'. The precise nature of the determinants of investment and their quantitative impact have long been a source of controversy amongst economists (and others), and perhaps it should not be too surprising that differing assessments extend also to the impact of fiscal investment incentives. Other papers and discussion at this conference may consider both the theoretical and other cases for and against the use of such fiscal incentives, and the frameworks within which the costs and benefits of such incentives may be compared. The role of this paper is limited to discussing how the effects of investment incentives may be assessed. Do variations or differences in rates of grant or tax depreciation provisions affect firms' investment expenditure and, if so, by how much and when?

The scope of the paper is limited in another way. The availability and rates of investment incentives (accelerated tax allowances and grants) have in the UK varied not only over time, but also at many points in time between industries, types of asset, and location of investment[2]. This paper is primarily concerned with intertemporal variations, which variations are presumed to be motivated by policy considerations of short-run cyclical stabilisation and long-run growth. The basic layout of the paper is as follows. Sections III and IV are respectively concerned with the exposition and criticism of a theoretical framework that has in recent years been much used for explaining the time-path of fixed investment and for assessing the effects of non-discriminatory incentive systems. Section II is concerned with interview and questionnaire studies and in particular with their role vis-a-vis that of econometric studies, the results of which are briefly (for the USA) and more comprehensively (for the UK) discussed in sections V and VI. Section VII concludes the discussion.

I Methods of analysis – a preliminary warning

Although the sophisticated analyses presented at the US conference 'Tax Incentives and Capital Spending' did not yield consistent and unambiguous results this does not provide a valid excuse for an immediate resort to the simplistic approaches beloved by some commentators. The editor of the published volume of the conference proceedings repeated the point made by the discussant, but wrote: 'Merely relating changes in tax rates or depreciation allowances to changes in the ratio of investment to gross national product . . . is inadequate for evaluating incentives in a world in which many influences impinge directly and indirectly on capital outlays'[3]. Two-variable analysis, with or without formal rules for establishing line or goodness of fit, cannot hope to correctly isolate and quantify any relationship which exists between investment incentives and investment expenditure. The relationship between the two variables can only be estimated, subject to deficiencies in data and estimation methods, within the context of an appropriately (but necessarily approximately) specified set of functional relationships or model of actual behaviour. Not only may specific fiscal incentives be only a relatively minor determinant of investment expenditure but the analysis is complicated both by lags in the investment process and by any whole-system consequences such as multiplier effects.

[3]Fromm (1971), p1

[4]The possibilities of 'experimental economics' are here ignored.

II Interview – questionnaire studies

Faced with the difficulties of the model-building or econometric approach, to which we shall return, some have sought illumination through contact with those actually responsible for investment decisions. The motivations and justifications for interview – questionnaire studies are indeed legion: a desire to observe the 'real' world and get the 'feel' of the practices of actual businessmen; to avoid the 'mechanistic' view of the world sometimes (wrongly) ascribed to the model-building approach; to try to avoid the problems inherent in that approach; to obtain additional statistical information; and to employ at least one research strategy when no other alternative appears to exist. Unfortunately these research methods have their own limitations, as discussed more fully by White (1956) and Eisner (1957). Some of these limitations, such as unrepresentative sample selection, inadequate sample size, or a failure to correctly weight the replies of individual respondents, may be avoided by careful research practice; others such as low response rate, by a combination of authoritative sponsorship, persuasion and good fortune; whilst others such as the importance of the precise wordings of questions and the choice of person to whom the questions are addressed, appear to be virtually inherent in this type of study. Of particular importance in this context are the difficulties of requiring firms to isolate the effects of individual factors which affected past decisions, of quantifying those effects, and of translating findings at individual firm level into macro-economic terms. Policy variables such as investment incentives (and also interest rates) constitute part of the decision-taking environment of all firms and their effects, which may seem small to individual firms, do not cancel out upon aggregation. On the other hand the factors which may seem to individual firms to be of greatest importance tend to be more specific ones (such as particular technological developments or gains in market share at the expense of competitors) which perhaps tend to explain the allocation of aggregate investment between firms or narrowly-defined industries rather than its total. Moreover even if interview-questionnaire studies successfully relate what percentage of firms, and also what proportion of aggregate investment, has been influenced by changes in investment incentives they cannot assess the quantitative effect of those changes on aggregate investment. Even if questions required respondents to report whether they were 'never' or 'much' influenced, quantification would be barely possible because the interpretation of such classifications is necessarily highly subjective. A satisfactory basis for quantitative prediction can only be sought through methods which allow the previous quantitative effects of incentives and other investment determining variables to be isolated and measured[4].

This is not however to argue that the results of interview-questionnaire studies do not have any role to play in the specification, estimation, or assessment of econometric relationships. Firstly, despite the above qualifications, it is possible that the results of interview/questionnaire studies may yield some indication of the relative importance of investment incentives in the determination of investment

246

[5] The studies here referred to are those by FBI (1960), Hart and Prussman (1964), NEDC (1965) and Corner and Williams (1965).

[6] It is not wholly clear whether this term was meant in its specific or its general sense, though investment allowances were then and had for some years been quantitatively more important than initial allowances.

[7] The use of different methods of project appraisal has been explored by Mackintosh (1963), Neild (1964), NEDC (1965), Corner (1967), George (1968), Taylor Nelson Investment Services (1970) and in the unpublished 1965 and 1970 studies conducted by the CBI and the Ministry of Technology. The above statements are broadly based on the combined evidence of these separate studies. The CBI found that in the case of large expansionary investment projects, 40 per cent of the larger investing companies (annual fixed investment> £½m) undertook DCF calculations. This percentage was lower in the case of companies with lower annual investment and with reference to smaller or replacement investment projects.

expenditure. A succession of such (UK) studies published in the 1960s indicated that the investment decisions of only a minority (usually around a quarter) of the responding firms had been in some way affected by the investment – initial allowance incentive regime[5]. Rather more widespread allowance for and sensitivity to fiscal incentives was suggested by George (1968) and two unpublished studies conducted by the CBI (1965) and the Ministry of Technology (1970). Of the 84 participants (84 per cent response rate) in the questionnaire study of large retailing firms conducted by George, 35 (42 per cent) said that their investment decisions had been significantly affected by the system of investment and initial allowances (though only seven quoted instances in response to a request to do so). Most of the firms attributed the influence of the allowances to their effect on the available supply of funds, though 12 of them took account of the allowances in their post tax rate-of-return calculations. In the CBI study completed questionnaires were received from 438 companies and subsidiaries which had accounted for almost half of the gross fixed investment of manufacturing industry in 1962 to 1964. Two-thirds of the respondents claimed to take account of the capital allowances in their cash flow calculations, the percentage doing so being 93 in the case of the respondents with annual investment of over £½m. Over a quarter of the respondents, accounting for over half of the investment covered by the survey, stated that the existence of – or changes in – the level of the investment allowances[6] had made a significant difference to their investment decisions.

The Ministry of Technology study, originally intended as a pilot survey, comprised both questionnaire and interview parts. A stratified random sample of 300 companies was obtained by taking one manufacturing company in five with net assets of over £5m, one in ten with assets of between £5m and £500,000 and a smaller sample of companies in the non-manufacturing sectors of industry. These 300 firms received a postal questionnaire and a response rate of about 40 per cent was achieved. A representative selection of some 45 of the firms which had or had not replied were later interviewed together with a smaller number of other firms. Combining the results of these separate approaches it may be broadly said that about a third and over two-thirds of the firms (accounting for over a half and over four-fifths of their overall investment respectively) took account of the capital allowances and investment grants in their appraisals of projects. Moreover the interview study suggested that firms undertaking 94 per cent of the investment of the firms in that part of the study were in some way and to some extent sensitive to changes in some types of incentive. Most firms were considered to be sensitive to both grants and allowances and the percentages of investment attributable to firms primarily influenced through the effects of the incentives on profitability and liquidity were respectively 62 and 32. The proportions of investment due to firms describable as 'slightly', 'fairly' or 'very' sensitive to changes in incentives were approximately two-fifths, two-fifths, and one-sixth respectively.

In interpreting all these findings it is of course necessary to take particular account not only of the response rates and the precise wordings of the questions but also of the timing of the surveys and the nature of the researching organisation. Certainly the sceptic might find grounds for arguing that some of the above quoted results overstate the proportion of total manufacturing investment typically sensitive to government fiscal incentives.

A second result of interview/questionnaire studies which is relevant to at least the interpretation, if not the specification of econometric relationships, is that relating to the methods of project appraisal applied by firms. Common to almost all econometric assessments of the impact of investment incentives is a prior evaluation of the relative values of different elements in a grant-tax allowance package according to some discounting procedure. Interview and questionnaire studies[7] have revealed that the use of discounting procedures is far from universal amongst UK firms, though the use of such procedures may have increased during the past two decades and may be greater amongst larger firms and with respect to larger projects. The Ministry of Technology study found that over three-quarters of the responding firms, accounting for about 90 per cent of their combined investment, appraise at least some investment by making specific calculations of profitability, the percentage of an individual firm's expenditure being so appraised usually being between 60 and 100. However although about three-quarters of investment therefore appeared to be quantitatively appraised, only 40 per cent was appraised by the DCF method – the only one of the three stated alternatives involving discounting. Moreover since some firms were found to use more than one of the three (DCF, payback period, undiscounted rate of return) suggested alternatives the proportion of investment for which DCF was the sole or most important method of appraisal was inevitably rather less. To the extent that the use of discounting procedures based on expected post-tax and incentive cash flows is less than universal the specification of most econometric relationships incorporating fiscal incentives must be interpreted as an 'as if' rather than actual description of the determination of investment, and the results interpreted accordingly.

Some interview/questionnaire studies have attempted to explore firms' preferences between alternative incentive systems. Questions of this nature were asked in the 1965 CBI and 1970 Ministry of Technology studies. Firms might prefer one incentive package to another either because (on the assumption of certain receipt) it appeared the more valuable at the firm's own discount rate, or because it had lower risk of delay or non-receipt, or because of other less easily quantifiable reasons (ease of management, 'illogical' preferences etc). Unfortunately the questions asked do not allow the reasons for firms' stated preferences to be identified[8]. Ideally one would like to know first a firm's own discount rate and then the combinations of incentive instruments between which at that discount rate it was indifferent. This could allow the econometric investigator to weight the value of different types of incentive according to firms' stated preferences at given discount rates and then calculate the overall value of a package according to firms' own discount rate[9]. Another topic apparently relatively unexplored in interview/questionnaire studies is the rate of tax which UK firms themselves consider relevant in appraising projects – that on retentions alone, that on the shareholder interest (with or without allowance for capital gains tax), or some weighted average of these? Some evidence on this was provided by the Ministry of Technology study. Very few of the respondents to the questionnaire said that they made allowance for the income tax payable on distributed profits or for the capital gains tax paid by shareholders when appraising investment projects by their sole or most important method, though a small number of the larger investing firms participating in the interview study said that they did so.

One aspect of the investment process upon which questionnaire studies have undoubtedly thrown considerable light is the lag distribution associated with the gestation process. Although there has been no such study conducted with respect to the UK[10], the work of Mayer (1958, 1960) has frequently been cited as a benchmark with which the results of econometric analysis in this respect may be compared. Mayer's questionnaire study of US companies investing in industrial plants, electric power plants or plant additions revealed an investment weighted mean lag of 38 months from start of consideration to completion, including one of 21 months from final decision to completion. Allowance for lags is clearly vital and it is to econometric studies in which such allowance is specifically made to which we now turn our attention.

8 In both studies the set of alternatives posed by the researchers were considered by them to be of equal DCF value. However since firms' own implicit discount rate may differ from that adopted by the researchers it is unclear whether firms' preferences are attributable to such a difference or to other reasons. In both studies 'free depreciation' was the first preference of far more firms than any of the alternative allowance, grant, or tax credit based systems. However the difference between the preferences for free depreciation and two alternatives was far less in the case of the Ministry of Technology interview survey in which (in contrast to the questionnaire survey) participating firms were told of the intended DCF equivalence of the three alternatives. Nevertheless firms may value the 'freedom' of true 'free depreciation', a view substantiated by the pressure from firms for its introduction even after the granting of 'first-year' depreciation. In the absence of expectations of large rises in corporate taxes, and also of rules restricting tax-allowable depreciation when the full first-year offset cannot be claimed, such a preference would be inconsistent with DCF evaluation.

9 It can of course be argued that a search procedure can be employed by the econometrician to find that weighting of the separate types of incentive which minimises the residual sum of squares provided by his model. Such an argument can also be employed with reference to a long list of other relevant factors – including time discount rate and impact of taxation – and some prior knowledge therefore helps to reduce the burden of searching and/or to provide a means of discrimination between alternative best-fitting formulations.

10 Other fairly direct evidence on gestation lags has however been provided for the UK through the analysis of engineering industry order – delivery statistics: see Bispham (1970), Trivedi (1970) and Lund and Miner (1973). The evidence suggests a wide lag distribution extending up to two years, a strong cyclical shift in the distribution, and a mean order – delivery lag usually between six months and a year.

III The neoclassical framework

The econometric analysis of investment behaviour has in the past decade swung from the previously employed *ad hoc* approaches associated with the 'accelerated' or 'liquidity' propositions and towards the type of neoclassical formulation associated with Jorgenson. The extent of this swing should not be exaggerated in that reference to neoclassical theory had previously been employed to justify the inclusion of such variables as the rate of interest and the factor price ratio in a list of possible determinants of investment expenditures. However the specification and estimation of investment demand relationships specifically derived from neoclassical theory, the combination of such relationships with distributed lag analysis, and most particularly the examination of investment incentives within such a framework all owe much to the lead of Jorgenson[11].

The Jorgenson formulation starts from the proposition that firms aim to maximise their present value, this being defined as the integral of their future net receipts. For simplicity the model is developed with reference to a production process with a single output, a single variable input, and a single capital input. Another important simplifying assumption is that of perfect competition in product, factor, and capital markets such that the prices of output, variable inputs, investment goods, and the cost of capital, respectively denoted by p, w, q, and r are all exogenous to the firm. Denoting quantities of output, variable input, and investment in capital goods by Q, L and I respectively, each firm's objective (in a world without taxes or incentives) is then the maximisation of

$$W = \int_0^\infty e^{-rt} [pQ - wL - qI] \, dt \tag{1}$$

this maximisation being conducted subject to two constraints. Levels of output and factor inputs are constrained by a production function

$$F(Q, L, K) = O \tag{2}$$

which is assumed to be twice-differentiable with positive marginal rates of substitution between inputs and positive marginal productivities of both inputs. The second constraint is that the flow of capital services is assumed to be proportional to the capital stock, the change in which is net investment. Net investment is the difference between gross investment and replacement investment, the latter being assumed proportional to the existing capital stock:

$$\dot{K} = I - \delta K \tag{3}$$

Combination of the necessary maximisation conditions for output, gross investment and capital stock then yields[12]

$$\frac{\delta Q}{\delta K} = \frac{q(r + \delta - \dot{q})}{p} = \frac{c}{p} \tag{4}$$

where

$$c = (r + \delta) - \dot{q} \tag{5}$$

The expression c defines the implicit rental value of capital services supplied by the firm to itself, the 'user cost of capital' in the Jorgenson terminology[13]. A particular assumption of the Jorgenson formulation of the neoclassical theory is that production technology may be described by a Cobb-Douglas production function;

$$Q = A K^\alpha L^\beta \tag{6}$$

Given this, the marginal product of capital is

$$\frac{\delta Q}{\delta K} = a \frac{Q}{K} \tag{7}$$

combination of which with (4) yields

$$K = a \frac{pQ}{c} \tag{8}$$

[11] The existence of this swing does not of course mean that the '*ad hoc*' approach is now redundant; it is merely less dominant. Some readers aware of the problems associated with the 'optimising' type of theory may, like Klein (1974), feel that the more *ad hoc* type of approach is still defensible.

[12] For derivation see Jorgenson (1967), pp140 – 143

[13] Although this section is concerned with the exposition rather than the criticism of the Jorgenson neoclassical framework the author cannot refrain from quoting the wit of Tobin: 'The idea that depreciation depends on intensity of use as well as on passage of time is so outmoded that the term 'user cost' has been appropriated to mean a cost that does not depend on use at all but only on time', Tobin (1967), p53. This criticism has been developed more formally and extensively by Taubman and Wilkinson (1970) and by Feldstein and Rothschild (1974)

249

Jorgenson interprets (8) as defining the desired stock of capital K^*_t for given output and prices, and constructs a formulation for gross investment by linking on to the above model an allowance for gestation lags and a theory for replacement investment. Net (expansionary) investment projects are assumed to be initiated in each period until the backlog of such uncompleted projects is equal to the difference between the desired and actual capital stock, from which it follows (under the assumption of a constant lag distribution) that:

$$I_t^E = I_t - I_{t.} = \mu(\theta)[K_t^* - K_{t-1}^*] \tag{9}$$

where I^E and I^R respectively denote expansionary and replacement investment. The assumption that replacement investment is a constant proportion δ of the existing capital stock, then yields:

$$I_t = \mu(\theta)[K_t^* - K_{t-1}^*] + \delta K_{t-1} \tag{10}$$

Equation (10) is estimated on the basis of some assumed general form for $\mu(\theta)$ and substitution for K^* from (8), with δ being either imposed or subject to estimation. An increase (reduction) in desired capital stock results in net investment (or disinvestment) which eventually brings capital stock up (or down) to its new desired level. If there are no subsequent changes in desired capital stock, net investment eventually drops to zero, but the initial change continues to affect gross investment through the replacement of a permanently larger (or smaller) capital stock. In addition it should be noticed that the effects on desired capital stock of its separate determinants are not independent: a reduction in the user cost of capital results in higher (lower) levels of net and gross investment consequent upon any conemporaneous or subsequent increase (reduction) in output.

It is through the substitution for K^* that taxation and investment incentives, which have so far been ignored, play a role in the determination of gross investment expenditure as portrayed by the Jorgenson model. Both affect the user cost of capital, and through it the desired capital stock. For example, assuming that the prices of new investment goods are expected to remain unchanged,[14] and that the cost of capital is unaffected by taxation and wholly chargeable against taxable income the user cost of capital is given by:

$$c = \frac{q\,[[(1-u)r + \delta]]1 - A]}{1 - u} \tag{11}$$

where u is the constant proportionate rate of tax on business income and A is the discounted value of the tax savings (or grants) which are expected to follow from one unit value of fixed investment.

This framework has been utilised by Hall and Jorgenson (1967, 1971) to investigate the effects of a series of changes in US tax credit and depreciation rules made during 1954 to 1967. Their conclusion is 'that tax policy has been highly effective in changing the level and timing of investment expenditures . . . The adoption of accelerated methods for depreciation and the reduction in depreciation lifetimes for tax purposes increased investment expenditure substantially. They also resulted in a shift in the composition of investment away from equipment toward structures. Limited to equipment, the investment tax credit has been a potent stimulus to the level of investment . . .'[15] Numerical estimates are given of the effects of each of the considered changes on gross and net investment and on capital stock and for each subsequent year, within and outside the sample period, through to 1970. Such quantification is impressive and would appear to supplant 'the belief in the efficiency of tax stimulus (to investment) . . . based on the plausible argument that businessmen in pursuit of gain will find the purchase of capital goods more attractive if they cost less'[16]. However it is to be claimed that the analysis of Hall and Jorgenson – by itself – does no such thing and that their comparisons of the efficiency of different instruments is entirely without validity.

[14] In Jorgenson (1965) this simplifying assumption is given the economic interpretation that all capital gains from changes in the prices of capital equipment are regarded as transitory and do not affect the long-run demand for capital. An alternative assumption is that changes in r and q are exactly offsetting with regard to c, see Jorgenson (1967) pp 147–149. Adoption of this assumption requires use of a constant value of r as in Hall and Jorgenson (1967, 1971).

[15] Hall and Jorgenson (1971), p11.

[16] Hall and Jorgenson (1967) p 391

IV Criticisms of the neoclassical framework

Criticism of the neoclassical framework as presented by Jorgenson is by no means novel or single. In part it has been directed at the unrealism of the associated assumptions about the economic world, characterised by Klein and Taubman as one in which: 'perfect competition exists – implying complete knowledge, perfect capital markets, and prices freely determined by market supply and demand; profit is maximised over the long run; perfect rationality is applied; complete flexibility in term of wages and prices as well as the choice of the means of production is available; the economic depreciation rate is constant; the production function is of the Cobb-Douglas form'[17]. However whilst the realism of each of these assumptions may be contested and the effects of their relaxation explored, it is noteworthy that the Jorgenson framework has been criticised even within its own terms of reference. Coen (1969, 1971) in particular has observed that in empirical application Jorgenson has treated output Q as exogenous and not endogenous, which at the micro-level is hardly consistent with the assumption of perfect competition. The combination of the maximisation conditions and the Cobb-Douglas marginal products leads to decision rules for Q, L and K (and hence I); either all these are determined jointly or one is treated as given and the other two determined within that further constraint. If all these are determined jointly the reduced form factor demand functions do not include output as an argument; however they do include both factor prices, and the elasticity of K^* with respect to c is not -1 but $-(1-\beta)/(1-\alpha-\beta)$[18] (Desired output is of course unbounded if $\alpha + \beta \geq 1$). If on the other hand ouput really is exogenous (and not equal to desired output) the exercise becomes one of cost minimisation and the appropriate decision rule is that of employing factors until their (declining) marginal products are proportional (but not equal) to their prices[19]. In either case there is an implicit assumption that both factors can be adjusted instantaneously. To the extent that capital cannot and this is implicitly recognised by Jorgenson,[20] either labour is employed beyond the point of its profitability or there is a short-fall in output. In the interim period of adjustment the firm could of course continue to aim at the desired level of capital stock, but the use in empirical work of actual output data implies an aim at a target depressed by the constraint on the rate of capital accumulation. This problem, which is not of course unique to Jorgenson's formulation, has been analysed by Gould (1969). He showed that 'if throughout the estimation period actual capital stock is fairly close to desired capital stock . . . the estimates of the parameters may be fairly accurate and the model may "fit" the data quite well . . (whereas) if during the prediction period there is some significant change in the exogenous variables . . substantial prediction errors can result'[21]. As he wrote: 'it is precisely in such periods of major change in the economic environment that policy-makers will need reasonably accurate forecasts to guide their decisions'[22].

This leads on to the criticism by Nerlove (1972) that Jorgenson, correctly recognising the lags in the investment process, has merely superimposed them onto what is essentially a static theory. No adjustment costs or even anticipated lags are incorporated into the model and hence firms, which are assumed to be highly rational and far seeing in a static context, have no need for other than stationary expectations with respect to prices, costs, and output. This feature Nerlove contrasts with the 'new' micro-economics which tries to develop 'aggregate dynamic relations from models of rational optimising behaviour . . . in a world where information flows are imperfect, the future is uncertain and transactions and changes of all sorts are costly and disruptive'[23]. Examples of the latter approach with respect to fixed investment are provided by the work of Eisner and Strotz (1963, pp 64-87), Lucas (1967), and Treadway (1969), papers which on the assumption of stationary expectations provide a theoretical basis for distributed lag models as linear approximations to optimal capital stock accumulation paths. However Gould (1968) has shown that when price expectations are non-stationary adjustment costs make

[17] Klein and Taubman (1971) pp 199–200.

[18] For derivation see Coen (1969) pp 375–378.

[19] Jorgenson's formulation and empirical application together place his analysis in a curious hybrid position. To put it at its most critical he derives his profit maximising conditions holding L constant and then treats Q as exogenous, but still excluding w from his estimating equations. Moreover when advancing his model, (Jorgenson (1965) p 53), Jorgenson incorporated the assumption of $\alpha + \beta > 1$ whereas Hall and Jorgenson in their reply to Coen have claimed that 'since empirical evidence generally supports constant returns to scale Coen's method has serious shortcomings', (Hall and Jorgenson (1969), p 394)

[20] Both by the explicit allowance for gestation lags and more subtly in the description of 'a kind of iterative process' in Jorgenson (1963) p 249.

[21] Gould (1969) p 598.

[22] ibid, pp 598-599

[23] Nerlove (1972) p 228

251

optimal input paths dependent upon the entire future course of prices. Rather *ad hoc* allowance for partial and hence delayed adjustment has of course previously been made with respect to both investment and employment functions but perhaps mention should here be made of two fairly recent and somewhat associated developments. These are the joint specification and/or estimation of two factor demand functions and the distinction between the stocks and rates of utilisation of both labour and capital factors. Examples of these developments which can yield indirect estimates of the parameters of the assumed production functions and separate response patterns for factor stocks and rates of utilisation are provided by the papers of Nadiri and Rosen (1969), Coen and Hickman (1970), and Nadiri (1972).

Perhaps the most discussed aspect of the Jorgenson formulation is its reliance on the Cobb-Douglas production function. A major property of this production function is that in a two-factor situation it implies a constant and unitary elasticity of substitution; a given proportionate change in relative factor prices will always cause a profit-maximising firm to make an equivalent but opposite proportionate change in the factor inputs used to produce a given output. Thus Hall and Jorgenson, in their analysis of tax effects, do not estimate the sensitivity of firms' desired capital stocks to changes in factor prices, they impose it by assumption. Escape from this particular straightjacket is only achieved if the economist adopts some other representation of technology. Leaving aside the Leontief fixed-proportion production function

$$Q = \min(aK, bL) \tag{12}$$

which underlies input-output models, allows no influence for relative factor prices, and leads to the simple accelerator theory of investment, many recent investigators have favoured the CES production function first popularised by Arrow, Chenery, Minhas and Solow (1961). In its constant-returns to scale form this may be written as

$$Q = \gamma [\delta K^{-\rho} + (1-\delta) L^{-\rho}]^{-\frac{1}{\rho}} \tag{13}$$

which for given output has the profit-maximising condition

$$\frac{K}{L} = \left[\frac{\delta}{1-\delta}\right]^{\frac{1}{1+\rho}} \left(\frac{w}{c}\right)^{\frac{1}{1+\rho}} \tag{14}$$

where the elasticity of substitution, $\sigma = 1/(1+\rho)$, is a constant. Adoption of such a production function allows a critical parameter to be estimated rather than imposed. Unfortunately the estimation of this parameter is both fraught with theoretical difficulties and has in practice led to such a diversity of results that the various protagonists in the debate have been able to justify their own preconceptions without too much self-deception[24]. For a survey of the problems and some of the earlier (US) evidence the reader may consult Nerlove (1967) and the ensuing discussion; for more recent evidence particularly related to investment functions the exchanges of Eisner and Nadiri (1968), Coen (1969), Hall and Jorgenson (1969), Bischoff (1969), Jorgenson and Stephenson (1969), Eisner and Nadiri (1970) and Eisner (1970).

Adoption of a CES production function leads to the replacement of (8) in the Jorgenson formulation by

$$K = \gamma^{\frac{-\rho}{1+\rho}} \delta^{\frac{1}{1+\rho}} \left(\frac{p}{c}\right)^{\frac{1}{1+\rho}} Q \tag{15}$$

By respectively separately estimating the coefficients of (p/c) and Q and by searching for a value of σ to maximise the explanatory power of $\left(\frac{p}{c}\right) Q$ first Eisner and Nadiri and then Coen obtained estimates of σ much closer to zero than unity. The later

[24] To quote Nerlove (1967), p 58: 'The major finding of this survey is the diversity of results: even slight variations in the period or concepts tend to produce drastically different estimates of the elasticity'.

exchanges in this series debated the validity of these results and compared them with other evidence. However probably the most important development associated with these exchanges is Bischoff's adoption of a putty-clay rather than a putty-putty description of factor malleability[25]. This modification, developed in Bischoff (1971), implies that changes in prices $\left(\frac{p}{c}\right)$ affect investment expenditures more slowly than do changes in output Q. Indeed on the assumption that replacement is exponential, his formulation provides for no 'accelerator' effect with respect to relative prices; shorter-run responses are always less than longer-run responses.

However whatever the elasticity of substitution there is a further and perhaps even more pertinent assumption underlying the analyses of Hall and Jorgenson – and also of some other workers in this field (both US and UK). This assumption is that businessmen equally perceive, evaluate, and react to each and every variable, and hence separate instrument of tax incentive policy, which affects $\frac{p}{c}$ (or in some cases $\frac{w}{c}$ or even $\frac{p}{c}$ Q). Surely however the question of whether or not this is so should be an objective (secondary if not primary) of research rather than a matter of assumption. The problem is that to the extent that all the variables supposed to affect the user cost of capital, and through it net investment, are incorporated into a single composite variable, the significance and explanatory strength of this composite is necessarily attributed to each of its separate components[26]. This problem is at its most marked in the Hall-Jorgenson case in which the effect of output might be carrying the composite $\frac{p}{c}$ Q and leading to an estimated investment incentive effect where none, or at least only a smaller one, exists[27]. A small number of other US researchers have on the other hand made allowance for, or attempted to test, firms' differential reactions to separate components of 'user cost'. For example Bischoff (1971) and Klein and Taubman (1971) allowed for the apparently sluggish adoption of the 1954 US acceleration in depreciation, and Eisner (1969) attempted to isolate the specific additional explanatory power due to the 1954 and 1962 changes in depreciation rules and found an insignificant one of 'incorrect' sign[28].

There is at least one other point upon which many readers may find a marked dissatisfaction with the Jorgenson framework, namely its exclusion of any 'profit' or 'liquidity' effects. This exclusion arises from the assumption of perfect competition in the capital market, which assumption equates the costs of borrowing and lending funds and makes them invariant to the magnitude of lending or borrowing. However in practice the capital market is not perfect, borrowing and lending rates are typically different and functions of scale of transaction, and firms – for variety of reasons – have a distinct preference for using internal funds. Moreover taxation systems often favour internal financing and fixed interest borrowing as opposed to the raising of equity capital. Thus many studies, especially of the more '*ad hoc*' type, have employed some measure of profits or the availability of internal funds as a possible determinant of investment[29]. Whilst the justification for the use of such variables has been wider than 'financing' arguments alone they do provide a channel for the so-called 'liquidity' influence of investment incentives[30].

The availability of internal finance might enter a properly specified investment function either as a determinant of the cost of capital or as a determinant of the speed of adjustment of desired to actual capital stock. The first role is usually that implicit or explicit in most studies employing such variables; the second has been examined in more recent years by a number of researchers including Coen (1971). However one possibly overlooked problem in the latter specification is the effect of a positive correlation between high aggregate profits and a high pressure of demand on the capital goods industries combined with any positive correlation between the latter and the order-expenditure gestation lag. Such correlations, the first of which

25 For the benefit of the uninitiated a putty-clay model of production is one in which factor proportions are variable *ex ante* before capital has been committed to a particular form of production and becomes 'clay'. A putty-putty model is one which assumes equal ease of factor substitution, both *ex ante* and *ex post*. A clay-clay model is one in which the producer has no choice of factor proportions within the constraints of known technology. Clearly the real world contains elements of each form. It is important to note that the choice between a putty-clay and a putty-putty assumption is to some extent independent of the choice of production function; eg either a putty-putty or a putty-clay but not a clay-clay assumption can be combined with either a Cobb-Douglas or a CES production function.

26 This point has perhaps been made most strongly by Fisher (1971), pp 244–245.

27 An invalid adoption of the assumption $\sigma = 1$ would appear to impart a downward bias to the estimates of the output elasticity. Eisner and Nadiri (1968) quote in support of this the result of Jorgenson and Stephenson (1967) which show an estimate of 0.06 for US manufacturing as a whole and 14 out of 16 industry estimates below 0.1 Harberger (1971) however argues in favour of using the composite variable $\left(\frac{p}{c}\right)$ Q because otherwise, he alleges, the relatively higher errors of measurement in the user cost variable (which in the composite variables are swamped by the larger actual variations in output) will apart a large downward bias to estimated user cost elasticity. The present author rejects this argument because of the implicit assumption of $\sigma = 1$ and the advantages of separating two variables subject to different degrees of simultaneity with the dependent variable.

28 Eisner's analysis was however rather peculiar in that he introduced into his equation user cost variables based both on tax rules and on tax statistics reflecting an amalgam of current and previous rules and practices. The latter type of variable was in fact used in a number of the earlier studies not specifically concerned with the effects of tax policy, eg Jorgenson (1965).

29 The role of profits or internal finance in the determination of investment is itself a matter of no little debate Jorgenson (1971) surveying a large number of US econometric studies concluded (p 1133) 'that where internal finance variables appear as significant determinants of desired capital, they represent the level of output. Where both output and cash flow are included as possible determinants, only one is a significant determinant. The preponderance of evidence clearly favours output over cash flow'. Whilst this position is fairly conventional, and not easily challenged on the basis of existing UK evidence, few would argue that the availability of internal finance may never be a constraint on aggregate investment.

30 Some caution needs to be exercised at this point with respect to the possibility of double-counting. Three separate types of analysis might be distinguished: the collection of evidence on how firms respond to incentives; the evaluation of incentives on some type of DCF basis, as in the paper by Melliss and Richardson; and the econometric investigation of their effects. The danger of double-counting is perhaps greatest with respect to the second of these; reference to the 'liquidity' benefit of a package (except in the short-term following its introduction) implies the use of an incorrect discount rate in the assessment of its 'profitability' benefit. In the short-term the two may be validly considered separately since the benefits of the package may be received with respect to investment goods in the pipeline. This possibility can be allowed for in econometric studies which – if properly specified – can by apportioning the effects between 'liquidity' and 'profitability' influences avoid the possibility of double-counting.

is implicit in the postulate and the second evidenced by recent analysis of variable-weight lag distributions, might tend to hide any correlation between profits and desired rate of adjustment since the common use of expenditure data in investment functions effectively convolutes the separate decision and gestation lags. Nevertheless Coen, on the basis of his empirical analysis, considered that (cash flow) variable adjustment speed models were more satisfactory than alternative constant adjustment speed models in several respects.

Before turning to an assessment of the results of USA and UK single-equation econometric studies specifically bearing on the impact of investment incentives, brief mention must be made of four remaining aspects of the Jorgenson (and other) frameworks for such investigations. These are the treatment of replacement investment; the generation of expectations; the lag pattern of response; and the nature of the stochastic assumptions. Jorgenson's treatment of replacement essentially equates 'depreciation' and replacement. He justifies an assumption that replacement is geometric, which implies that replacement is a constant proportion of the (net) capital stock, with reference to a result of renewal theory relating to a capital stock growing at a constant exponential rate[31]. This justification is obviously inconsistent with his repeated use of the overall framework to explain the fluctuations over time of net and gross investment. Jorgenson's theory is in fact intuitively odd, implying as it does that an initial investment is 'replaced' in the subsequent period by the first and largest of an infinite stream of individual replacements; were this the case the unit value of a single act of replacement would tend to zero. The theory obviously excludes the possibility of 'echo' effects reflecting past variations in gross investment and requires that replacement be an automatic and perfectly foreseen event independent of factor prices. For an excellent critique of the Jorgenson replacement function the reader should refer to Feldstein and Rothschild (1974). These authors identify the highly restrictive assumptions implicit in the function, the lack of evidence justifying them, and the potential sensitivity of replacement investment to both investment incentives and the availability of internal finance. In particular fiscal incentives may affect both the optimum *ex ante* choice of asset life (if value of incentives is related to asset life) and the *ex post* timing of optimum replacement. Moreover to the extent that the rate of investment is constrained by supply of liquidity considerations, variations in replacement (which has less effect on potential output) may be used to smooth out those in net investment. To the extent that some simplistic replacement function need be adopted in empirical work it should only be justified on grounds of convenience and simplicity.

The treatment of replacement is but one aspect of 'dynamic specification' which title also covers the three remaining questions. As already mentioned the Jorgenson framework adopts the assumption of 'static expectations' with regard to the levels of the relevant variables. The inability to successfully measure expectations is a a fundamental problem in economics but less restrictive procedures than Jorgenson's are to base expectations about the future values of a single variable on its own (or other variables') past history, to make use of the results of regular business attitude and trends surveys which include forward-looking questions, or to use additional variables (such as stock market prices) to separately reflect expectations. Of particular importance is the possible difference between the ways in which firms' expectations about fiscal instruments and the other elements of user cost (and output) are determined. Suffice it to say at this point that the framework should be sufficiently flexible to permit a distinction between incentive systems announced to be temporary and all others.

31 See for example Jorgenson (1965), p51.

The past decade has seen a great extension in the range of both the alternative lag distributions and stochastic assumptions employed and explored by econometricians. This is not the place to review this vast literature, but a number of distinct points may be made. Firstly an answer to the question 'what has been the effect of incentives on investment' requires a time-dimension; short-run effects are likely to be different from long-run effects and the time pattern of response is especially important if the incentives are employed as an instrument of counter-cyclical policy. Secondly the recent expansion in the employment of lag and error techniques carries its own dangers. Just as alternative combinations of independent variables may provide equally good explanations of a dependent variable so may alternative combinations of lag and error structures and the choice between the latter is sometimes less readily made on *a priori* grounds. Although direct evidence on lags, such as was provided by Mayer, may be of considerable use in this respect extraneous evidence more typically relates to only part of the lag distribution (eg that between order and delivery). Thirdly the present author is convinced that the prevailing sophistication of much of current lag and error analysis is disproportionate to the validity of its underlying assumption of constancy. Evidence has been presented with respect to both the USA and the UK which suggests that investment expenditure lag distributions vary both cyclically and perhaps also over time[32].

This evidence argues in favour of the use of variable rather than fixed weight lag distributions and if possible the separation of the lag process into a succession of identifiable stages. The possibility should not be overlooked that constraints in the supply of capital goods will result in a flow of actual investment which is smoother than that of desired investment and hence impart a downward bias to the estimated elasticities. Finally there is the familiar statement that error specification is an integral part of complete model specification. All too frequently we implicitly treat a model as if it were an exact representation of behaviour and then tack on some simplistic stochastic assumption. Unfortunately as Lund and Miner (1975) have shown integral error specification results in some rather horrific reduced forms in even the simplest of lag models.

V US econometric studies

Having reached this stage in a somewhat hurried examination of some of the more important research issues, we may turn to an examination of published econometric studies of the effects of incentives. It should now be clear that the 'results' of empirical studies are a product both of the analysed data and of the assumptions and precise specification embodied in the model. Considering first the four USA studies presented at the Brookings conference,[33] it is indeed difficult to imagine how Hall and Jorgenson could have reached a conclusion different from that quoted on p 250. More interest lies in the results of Bischoff who, more realistically and permitting the data to do more of the work, adopted a putty-clay CES representation of production, allowed for the generation of expectations through lag mechanisms, and experimented with alternative measures of the cost of capital. It is therefore noteworthy that his generalised neoclassical model, which outperformed both the 'standard' model and a flexible accelerator in a sample period comparison, yielded a long-run elasticity with regard to user cost of approximately unity. The main distinguishing features of Coen's model were an allowance for a dual role of incentives in determining both desired capital stock and the rate of adjustment, separate adjustment and expectations lags but with the latter being simply geometric, and no explicit production function though the inclusion of $\left(\frac{c}{w}\right)$ as an explanatory variable. His results favoured the variable adjustment speed models, but his estimates of the overall effects of the incentives were less than those of the preceding authors; not surprisingly (due to collinearity) equations allowing for a variable adjustment speed attributed a lower elasticity to $\left(\frac{c}{w}\right)$.

[32] The UK evidence was quoted in footnote 10.

[33] The author is aware that there have been more recent studies of USA investment expenditure which have allowed for the effects of incentives. This discussion of USA studies seeks to be illustrative; that of the UK studies to be comprehensive.

255

The paper by Klein and Taubman was the most distinctive of the four presented at the Brookings conference in that it included not only a lengthy critique of the neo-classical framework but also the only investigation of the effects of the incentives within a multi-equation (Wharton – EFU) macro-model. Unfortunately the treatment of the investigated tax changes does not seem very satisfactory in its single (investment) equation context; the tax changes were evaluated in terms of their effect on rates of return which changes were then imposed on interest rates variables included in a distinctly *ad hoc* investment equation. The other equations which were assumed to be influenced by the changes in tax incentives were the corporate tax function and book-value depreciation equations. The presented results related only to the complete system solution and did not allow the separate sources of influence to be identified and quantified.

VI UK econometric studies

We may now turn our attention to published econometric studies of UK investment which have specifically allowed for the influence of investment incentives. Eleven such studies have been identified; those by Balapoulos (1967), Agarwala and Goodson (1969), Burman (1970), Nobay (1970), Westlake (1971), Feldstein and Flemming (1971), Rowley (1972), King (1972), Boatwright and Eaton (1972), Lund and Miner (1973) and Sumner (1974)[34]. These will be discussed in approximately the order that they resemble the Jorgenson neoclassical framework.

The closest resemblance to the neoclassical framework is probably provided by the analysis of Rowley. The time span of this quarterly analysis was limited to 1957 to 1965; post-war controls at one end and the introduction of Corporation Tax (with its retention-shareholder distinction), the increased regional selectivity associated with investment grants, and the 'shock' to the system provided by these and other (eg SET) changes at the other end, providing the boundaries. Distinguishing but questionable features of this study were (i) an implicit equation of replacement investment and Blue Book 'capital consumption', (ii) use of the dividend yield on industrial ordinary shares as a measure of the cost of capital, (iii) two alternative 'user cost' variables including and excluding the annual allowances (neither appeared to allow for the feature distinguishing investment and initial allowances) and (iv) no allowance for tax payment lags. Nevertheless perhaps almost inevitably he found that 'the theory of optimal capital accumulation does provide an explanation of the pattern of British investment during the specific post-war period under review'[35] and hence that 'capital allowances and the corporate tax-rate may be effective instruments for the control of investment expenditures'[36]. It is however noteworthy that Rowley added several qualifications and in particular one to the above: '...provided sufficient attention is given to the contemporaneous influence of relative prices and the cost of capital'[37]. His experimentation with alternative rational lag functions led to a preference for one with a minimum lag of three-quarters and a mean lag of five to six-quarters (both with respect to net investment.)

The study by Boatwright and Eaton was particularly directed towards measuring the impact of investment incentives. Its data base was that of investment in plant and machinery by manufacturing industry, quarterly and spanning 1959 to 1970. Each of the separate instruments – investment grants and the three types of allowances – appeared to have been reasonably combined on a DCF basis (according to the dividend yield on ordinary shares), though no account was taken of the different regional rates. During the latter half of the period the 'tax rate' was that of Corporation Tax alone. The general framework of the study was that of Jorgenson but the

[84] This provides what the author hopes is an extensive list of research studies in which investment incentives were included in at least some of the preferred equations. The author is aware of only one study in which the possible role of incentives was considered and dismissed: this is that by Wall, Preston, Bray and Peston (1975).

[85] Rowley (1972), p 187

[86] ibid, p187

[87] ibid, p187–188

authors attempted to estimate rather than impose the elasticity of substitution. A search procedure for σ was conducted in conjunction with another selection between three alternative lag generating mechanisms. Of these the Almon technique and the Gamma distribution yielded similar results both of the lag pattern (peaking at 8-12-quarters) and of the elasticity of substitution (in the range 0.4 to 0.7). The Almon equation was then used in a simulation exercise to illustrate the estimated impact of three alternative incentive systems over the period 1967 to 1970.

The least restrictive application of the general neoclassical framework to UK data was certainly the study by Feldstein and Flemming of investment in manufacturing, construction, and distribution and other services; quarterly 1954 to 1967. Their framework differed from Jorgenson's in two fundamental respects; it made explicit allowance for expectations and it allowed for separate estimation of the elasticity of desired capital with respect to each component of user cost. Expectations were introduced not because of gestation lags but through dropping the assumptions of capital malleability and a perfect market in capital goods. Investment determining output was based on current output grossed-up according to its recent short-run growth, and each of the variables affecting the user cost of capital was allowed to be either a single variable or a short distributed lag. The ratio of product price p to user cost of capital as defined in (11) was split into components (p/q), $(r+\delta)$, $(1-u)$ and $(1-A)$, where r is now the post-tax cost of capital, and separate elasticities were estimated with respect to each. The variable r was measured by a weighted average of equity and debenture yields; the tax rate u was that borne by a company with an average dividend pay-out ratio; and the tax allowance variable $(1-A)$ was a weighted average over different asset classes, each based on investment, initial and annual allowances evaluated at a constant 10 per cent discount rate. Moreover the influence of internal finance was allowed to enter through alternative additional determinants of user cost: a measure θ of the differential tax treatment of distributions and retentions,[38] and a measure of internal funds. The adjustment lag distribution was assumed to be in the Pascal class though the special Koyck $(r=1)$ case gave similar results to more general cases. This was a sophisticated study, and one which did not fail to yield surprising results. Constraining the separate $\left(\frac{p}{c}\right)$ or user cost elasticities to be equal yielded overall elasticities of about 0.2 to 0.5 (sign here ignored); relaxing this constraint yielded an elasticity of around – 1.4 for the allowance variable (around – 1.7 prior to an arbitary modification), a small elasticity with respect to the differential tax parameter, but no reasonable (correct sign) or significant elasticities with respect to the other components of user cost. Feldstein and Flemming alleged that 'the constrained "pure" neoclassical function estimates understate the effect of investment allowances'[39]. Simulations showed that by the end of the period (1967) the actual capital stock was already almost 30 per cent higher than it would have been if the allowance variable had remained at its 1952 level, and that in some of the later years gross investment was more than double its otherwise level.

In considering these results Feldstein and Flemming made two important observations which merit quotation in full:[40]

'First, higher allowances increased the flow of internally available funds which may have had an independent positive effect on investment. Second, the frequent changes of the allowance rate may have induced firms to try to concentrate investment expenditures on periods in which rates were high by accelerating investment allowance rates were raised and postponing when they were expected to rise in the future. The estimates of approximately — 1.4 may therefore reflect the timing of government policy; more frequent changes, and particularly more decreases, might have resulted in an even greater responsiveness'.

The second of these observations is both controversial and important. As the authors observed it is exactly opposite to the much stated view that varying the

[38] The variable θ measures the opportunity cost of retained earnings in terms of net dividends foregone; that is, the amount of net dividends shareholders could have received if one extra unit of retained earnings had been distributed.

[39] Feldstein and Flemming (1971), p431

[40] ibid, p 427

incentives reduces their effectiveness[41]. In considering this question it is useful to distinguish between two objectives with respect to which the incentives have been used – short-run stabilisation and long-run growth – and hence between the responses of firms to (implicitly) temporary and permanent changes in the allowances. As Feldstein and Flemming noted their estimates indicate 'the way firms responded to the actual variation in the explanatory variables and not the way they might respond to a very different time pattern of exogenous variable changes.'[42] Use of the incentives as an instrument in achieving short-run stabilisation might cause firms to time their investment expenditure on projects with relatively short gestation lags to coincide with periods of especially advantageous incentives and hence perhaps lead to estimated (stabilisation) elasticities in excess of the long-run (growth) responses. Hence the use of the incentives as a stabilisation instrument may lead both to an over-estimate of their long-run growth effects and to a reduction of the latter effects. A completely specified model would include as determinants of the desired capital stock both expectations about capital goods' prices and incentive arrangements at the time of (future) expenditure and expectations about their then subsequent rates of change. In terms of the neoclassical framework, with suitable allowance for expectations, the variable $(1-A)$ could be linked with q (at least where the latter appears as a rate of change) and the influence of this composite rate of change not so readily dismissed. Unfortunately except in the special case of pre-announced changes in instruments expectations about rates of change are probably more difficult to proxy than those about levels and the author has no new suggestions to offer on this score. Moreover we might at this stage observe one of those oddities which make empirical research so tantalising. This is the contrary case to the Feldstein – Flemming argument: if a short-run stabilisation objective is wholly directed towards fluctuations in investment, always applied and wholly successful, no estimation will be possible. Not only will the incentives and the other determinants (each with their own particular lag distributions) be wholly collinear but there will be no variation in the dependent variable. A data period spanning the use or non-use of the instrument, a more complex objective function, or some degree of 'failure' are alternative necessary conditions for any estimation to be undertaken.

The papers by Burman and Nobay tested Jorgenson-type specifications or variables as one amongst a number of alternatives. Burman compared three alternative investment functions: a distributed-lag accelerator mechanism; a similarly lagged combination of output change and financial variables; and a Jorgenson-type formulation. Each formulation was estimated on the basis of both quarterly manufacturing industry data 1956 to 1967 and quarterly industrial and commercial company (in manufacturing, construction, distribution) data 1957 to 1968. The dependent variable was defined both inclusive and exclusive of the present value of tax allowances and grants, with modification where necessary being made to the neoclassical user cost variable. The neoclassical framework, in which alternative interest rate variables were used, failed to yield as satisfactory results as the simpler accelerator formulation, most particularly with respect to the estimated lag distribution. That the discounted value of the incentives did not have a significant coefficient of correct sign in equations in which gross investment was the dependent variable suggests that the 'real cost' of investment equations (which imply a moderate elasticity of gross investment with respect to $I-A$) were mis-specified. However leaving those equations aside the equation for I & C company investment in plant, machinery and vehicles did include a significant cash flow variable and hence provide another possible route for the influence of incentives.

The main distinguishing feature of the paper by Nobay was an attempt to allow for fluctuations on the supply side by including a 'capital goods waiting time' variable. This was based on 'first-in first-out' analysis of orders and deliveries for engineering goods and of starts and completions of industrial buildings, and its

[41] Some indication of the views of firms is provided by the replies to a question in the CBI (1965) survey which offered five specific alternative reasons why firms' investment decisions may not have been significantly affected by the existence of, or changes in, investment allowances. That 'the level of benefits has been changed at frequent intervals' was the least ticked 'most important factor'.

[42] Feldstein and Flemming (1971), p 427, fn 2.

[43] This result will seem surprising to those who expect the effects of incentives to show 'diminishing returns'. The explanation is that the given increase in grants results in a larger percentage reduction in net price in the former than in the latter case. This feature applies to several other studies in which (1–A) appears as a variable in a logarithmic formulation.

[44] It is arguable that King did likewise through his use of a constant rate to discount the incentives and his inclusion of the post-tax return in the constant term.

[45] On this point King (1974b) distinguished between *ex ante* and *ex post* asset life, and referred in support of a short *ex ante* asset lifetime to the results of survey evidence on 'pay-back' periods and the results of Mizon (1974) who fitted a vintage production model to UK data.

[46] Sumner (1974) p 190

inclusion represented an *ad hoc* allowance for variable lags. The above analysis also led the author to impose a single five-quarter lag on all the independent variables. The most successful of these in explaining quarterly manufacturing industry investment in 1959 to 1966 (alternatively total, plant and machinery only, excluding chemicals and steel) were capacity utilisation, change in output, and the waiting-time variable. The sign and significance of the user cost, and an alternative 'net interest payments' variable which also incorporated the incentives was not consistent between equations and a liquidity variable only proved significant for the restricted industrial coverage.

The papers by King and Sumner presented empirical analysis based on an explicitly cost-minimising model in which a vintage (putty-clay; *ex ante* Cobb-Douglas) production function was employed. The choice variables for the firm were the proportions of exogenous output to be produced by new and old equipment and the factor intensity of the latter. King calculated the discounted value of investment grants (allowing for regional variation) and the various tax allowances according to four alternative discount rates (5, 10, $18\frac{1}{3}$ and 25) and a 'first-year benefit only' criteria. Six alternative prices of new investment goods variables were then constructed; a basic capital goods price index and that adjusted by each of the above incentive valuations. King's data base was annual investment in plant and machinery by manufacturing industry, 1948 to 1968. A one year decision lag and a geometric gestation lag were specified. The most satisfactory results were obtained with the higher discount rates (the first year benefit equation was best of all) and all equations including the effects of incentives outperformed that excluding them. The estimated sensitivity of investment expenditure to the incentives was such that increases of investment grant of 5 per cent from 25 per cent to 30 per cent and from 0 to 5 per cent were calculated to yield long-run increases in investment of 4.4 per cent and 3.3 per cent respectively[43].

King also attempted to incorporate and estimate a 'long-run' tax shifting parameter, this reflecting the extent to which firms adjusted their required post-tax rate of profit in accordance with changes in company taxation, the latter being measured according to alternative 'managerial shareholder', and 'mixed' viewpoints. The results proved to be highly sensitive to the inclusion and rate of discounting of the incentives, though 'full-tax shifting' (firms maintain their desired post-tax rate of profit and alter investment plans accordingly) was evidenced by the most favoured equation. In his analysis Sumner imposed this by assumption[44] and made two other modifications to King's model – cost-minimisation over the anticipated asset lifetime and money wage expectations based on recent experience. On the basis of these he was able to derive by estimation the anticipated lifetime of assets and did so using two different data-sets; King's aggregate data and an indicator of investment decisions (machine tool new orders) which largely avoids the possible biases due to supply constraints. His results for the latter indicated a lower discount rate (10 per cent not 25 per cent) and a higher anticipated asset life[45]. However it is noteworthy that as in King's analysis the estimated effects of incentives were not highly dependent on the discount rate and that Sumner's estimates were very similar to those of King. Nevertheless the choice of discount rate does affect the estimated sensitivity of investment to the various types of incentive. Sumner queried 'the size of the discrepancy between the discount rate (25 per cent) apparently used in investment appraisal and observed market rates', recognised that since 'the incentives were frequently altered . . . some adjustment for uncertainty would not be surprising', but pointed out that 'uncertainty about the incentives does not compound (since the annual allowances have been the most stable element of the fiscal system and the occasional alterations have all been upward'[46]. To the extent that discounting is an acceptable correction for uncertainty, the present author suggests there is a case (with regard to these earlier systems) for using a higher year-to-year discount rate for the earlier than the latter parts of the benefit stream. King's 'first-year benefit only' result together with the comparative constancy of the annual allowances would appear to bear this out.

Sumner's use of machine tool new orders as a dependent variable followed that of Lund and Miner (1973). Their framework was essentially Keynesian in that they specified various possible determinants of marginal investment and marginal cost of funds schedules. Given that the latter was considered to be upward sloping, at least after the point where a firm's depreciation allowances plus 'normal' retention of profits were exhausted, no formal reduced form was easily derivable. The authors also appealed to the problems of aggregation in justifying their modestly *ad hoc* approach. Amongst significant determinants of machine tool new orders (home plus a proxy measure of import ones) were an 'expectational' share price variable, an overall company tax rate (that on retentions plus 'normal' net dividends), and – marginally so – the discounted value of the various types of investment incentives. No role could be attributed to liquidity or interest rate variables. A unitary (point of means) elasticity with respect to the incentive variable was indicated by the preferred equation and a higher one with respect to the 'overall' company tax variable. However the authors would not wish to place too much emphasis on this distinction (because of the use of the same tax rate in both variables in the Corporation Tax period) or to extrapolate too readily from these results (based on machine tool new orders) to other definitions of investment. If two alternative 'dependent' variables are related to the same set of 'explanatory' variables the one with the greater (non-random) variations is likely to yield the higher estimated elasticities. For evidence on the cyclical variations in machine tool new orders and deliveries and on these of both other engineering industries and aggregate components of GDP see Lund (1974).

The paper by Agarwala and Goodson also used as dependent variable an *ex ante* measure of investment – one based on investment intentions as indicated by the published results of the Board of Trade surveys. Their framework was unusual in that it contained no measure of output or capacity utilisation. The only variables were a measure of cash flow deflated by the price of investment goods and an expected rate of return variable; it was through these that the 'liquidity' and 'profitability' aspects of incentives separately operated. Both variables proved significant in an annual analysis spanning only 1958 to 1966 and simulations indicated some considerable total effect. However as Feldstein and Flemming commented 'a change in the rate of return would have the same absolute effect . . . regardless of the scale of output, (and) the cash flow variable is the only one that reflects the scale of the economy; it would therefore have a positive coefficient even if internal availability of funds as such had no economic effect'[47].

The two remaining studies were conducted as parts of more general studies of the UK tax system. In his study of the UK fiscal system Balapoulos included a gross productive private investment function in which past and previous levels of real GNP (net of current public expenditure) and a weighted average of investment and initial allowances were explanatory variables. The data was annual 1949 to 1960, the estimation method two-stage least-squares, the allowance for lags minimal. 'Taken at . . . face value' his results showed that, with respect to 1960 values, 'by abolishing initial and investment allowances we can decrease gross private productive capital formation by 8.5 per cent . . . or by increasing (them) by 100 per cent we can increase the proportion of GNP devoted to productive investment by a little less than 1 per cent'[48]. The study by Westlake used a similar accelerator type formulation in which contemporaneous and one period lagged values of the investment and initial allowances were included separately. The equation was separately estimated for plant and machinery and new building work in eight manufacturing industries using annual data for 1950 to 1966. In only one equation were the allowance variables significant – and even there they appeared to have the wrong sign.

[47] Feldstein and Flemming (1971) p 416

[48] Balapoulos (1967) p 194

260

VII   Concluding thoughts

It is in the nature of empirical research that the results of a succession of separate studies do not yield an easily summarised result. Perhaps the most that can be claimed in this particular case is that the above discussed studies (certainly with the support of the interview-questionnaire studies examined in section II) do not support any allegation that the incentives have been wholly ineffective. It is difficult to go much further.

It might seem to some that each of the studies discussed has some particular merit and that a study combining their best features would provide a clearer indication of the effects of incentives. However whilst there is room for a greater combination of 'best practices' it seems inevitable the 'ideal' study will remain illusive. Quite apart from the question of the ability of any individual researcher to provide all the requisite skills – or of a team to combine to do so – there are at least three fundamental problems. At the start of any empirical inquiry there is the question of how much theoretical prior specification is desirable. Its advocates allege that a rigorous theoretical model reduces the number of possible formulations that might be tested in a search for best fit, that it reduces the risk of 'chance' and 'meaningless' correlations, and that it provides a basis for evaluating the 'a priori' reasonableness of the estimated parameters. Its critics retort that (with aggregation biases and other estimation problems) the latter is but a vain hope, and that a rigorous model may impose rather than estimate the parameters of interest. This is the chief criticism which we have made of the Jorgenson framework.

The two remaining problems become more acute the more prior restrictions are removed. The first of these is that a wide variety of alternative hypotheses may provide very similar explanations of the same body of data; some may even yield the same (reduced-form) equation for estimation. A by-product of the recent increase in sophistication with regard to lag and error structures has been a magnification of this problem. Finally there is the question of the availability of appropriate time series data; will there ever be a period during which underlying structural parameters remain sufficiently stable for all of them to be successfully and independently estimated? The less restrictive a formulation becomes, and in particular the more it allows for the various inter-dependencies between the variables in the real world, the greater this problem becomes. Some degree of inadequacy is inevitable in our sub-utopian world and it is the art of econometrics to identify those areas in which inadequate specification is least crucial.

Having dismissed the concept of an 'ideal' study, the author feels constrained to offer some views about the areas of specification and estimation requiring attention – at least with regard to answering the questions posed by policy-makers. Policy-makers are interested in the choice of 'incentive' instruments, in whether the use of an instrument in a short-run stabilisation context prejudices its longer-run 'growth' effectiveness, and in whether for short-run purposes changes in instruments should be announced as operative for a finite period or left open-ended. Very little guidance on these important questions has been provided by the above discussed investigations. To some extent this is inevitable. The econometrician is constrained by the available data and the comparative regularity of changes in rates on the one hand and a solitary completed experience[49] on the other, respectively make it difficult for him to answer the second and third of these questions. With regard to the first question there could be room for a further study to compare the different types of incentive either by combining interview/questionnaire and econometric analysis as suggested on page 248 or by using only the latter.

One important question relating to the specification of an 'investment' function is the choice of dependent variable. The available UK data takes a variety of forms:

[49] The solitary completed experience at aggregate level was the temporary raising of investment grants by 5 per cent for expenditure on new plant and machinery incurred by manufacturing industry in 1967-68. The announcement of increased initial allowances for industrial buildings in the 1970 budget and for a limited two year period was superseded by subsequent announcements removing the closing date. Also and similarly superseded was the raising of the first-year allowance for plant and machinery for a two year period beginning in July 1971. However with respect to particular industries one might note the provisions for financial assistance for hotel development under the Development of Tourism Act 1969 and with respect to geographical areas the provisions for expenditure on building works in Derelict Land Clearance Areas as specified under the Industry Act 1972.

measures of expected authorisations (more/some/less comparison- type replies to the CBI quarterly surveys); intentions (with respect to a stated calendar year as collected by this Department); new orders and deliveries (of engineering industry products); new orders and work done, and for earlier years starts and completions, (for various types of buildings); and the conventional national income 'expenditure' figures. Which of these is chosen by the investigator will necessarily affect his results – not least with respect to at least the second and third of the above questions. Expenditure is the most common choice, but one certainly subject to problems. The observed cyclical shifts in order-delivery lag distributions reflect a smoothing process, the ultimate limit to which is a delivery (and perhaps hence an expenditure) series which does not reflect any induced short-run variations in new orders. On the other hand there is at least one situation in which expenditure data may 'over-record' the effects of incentives. This is if the announcement of (or rumours of) changes in incentive rates leads to a change in the delivery/work done – expenditure lag. The official adjustments to the investment expenditure figures for 1968-69 to allow for the bringing forward of expenditure into 1968 to benefit from the temporarily (1967-68) higher rate of grant may largely reflect such an effect.

The author strongly favours the separation of the investment process into a number of distinct sequential stages, with data recording the flow of projects past specific points within the total decision to expenditure boundaries. (This viewpoint is not unique–witness the disproportionate study of the machine tool industry!). Whilst an investment equation may be specified in which attention is given both to the determinants of the investment decision and to the lag part of the supply response, estimation is eased if those aspects can be separated. Separation of the investment process into sequential stages also pinpoints certain issues of simultaneity which may be overlooked if a single investment equation, with all variables lagged, is specified. Gehrels and Wiggins (1957) observed that a one period lag on the price of capital goods in an investment expenditure equation is not a sufficient condition for non-simultaneity since if current investment reflects last period's new orders, price and new orders may then have been simultaneously determined.

The issue of simultaneity is in fact one which is generally ignored in the econometric study of investment. Most studies have only a single equation and where more than one equation is considered the others are usually sequential, have imposed parameters, or constitute part of a macro-model which does not elsewhere explain the most important simultaneously determined variables or estimate equations simultaneously. The price of capital goods, 'the' cost of capital, the retention of profits, and output are probably all to some degree dependent on investment – however measured. If so, the consequence of not specifying the whole set of relevant relationships and where appropriate estimating them by simultaneous-equation techniques is that the econometrician obtains parameter estimates reflecting an amalgam of investment demand and other responses rather than the former alone. Such estimates do not provide a sound basis for considering the effects of an exogenously determined change in one of the independent variables.

Even if the various independent variables really are determined independently of the 'dependent' variable they may not be independent of one another. For example whilst the short-run supply of capital goods (perhaps in terms of new orders accepted) may be infinitely elastic (at least over a finite range) changes in the levels of investment incentive might occasion changes in quoted supply prices. Failure to allow for such an inter-relationship would lead to an overstating of the effectiveness of incentives, either at the estimation stage (if the variables are included separately) or in interpretation (if they are included in a composite). Similar inter-dependencies might occur between output and the other 'independent' variables and also with respect to the 'cost of capital' or the 'required rate of return'. This latter variable has indeed been subject to a variety of treatments in the empirical literature. Thus

262

in some of his analyses Jorgenson imposed a constant pre-tax cost of capital; Sumner (1974) imposed a constant post-tax cost; others have used dividend yields or yields on government debt; whilst some authors have effectively treated investment incentive flows and the remainder of cash flow differentially, discounting the former at a constant rate and the latter according to a particular market rate. In practice the source and cost of marginal funds are likely to be functions both of the amount of investment being undertaken and of taxation arrangements. The latter of those relationships is considered by King (1974a) who concludes that the cost of capital is much more complex than its representation in the neoclassical investment model – even in a world in which there is a unique interest rate.

This paper has tried to set out some of the problems involved in assessing the effectiveness of investment incentives as instruments for stabilising or encouraging investment. It has hopefully indicated that the problems are great, but perhaps not insuperable. However it must be stressed that its concern has only been with a simplified world in which there is no differentiation with respect to incentives between assets, industries, or regions. Where such differences exist they have been avoided in aggregate empirical analysis – either by focusing on a particular (asset/industry) classification or by averaging (over regions/assets). Such avoidance is not of course complete, particularly if differentiation with respect to incentives affects other variables such as output or replacement demand. The neoclassical framework discussed in sections III and IV is indeed lacking where differentiation exists. With respect to differentiation between types of assets its extension to three-factors follows the two-factor case in suggesting that (even differential) subsidies to both factors cannot reduce the employment of either factor. However modification to a factor substitution form hardly helps with respect to an analysis of the effectiveness of UK regional differentials since capital receives the greater subsidy the more employment is required. The treatment of output as endogenous and the recent extension of regular regional statistics to cover fixed investment are both requirements for the continuing study of the regional allocation of fixed investment. Other problems affecting the study of that particular allocation arise from the diversity of instruments and the element of administrative discretion.

Bibliography

Agarwala, R and G C Goodson (1969), 'An Analysis of the Effects of Investment Incentives on Investment Behaviour in the British Economy', *Economica*, 36, pp377-388.

Arrow, K J, H Chenery, B Minhas, and R Solow (1961), 'Capital-Labor Substitution and Economic Efficiency' *Review of Economics and Statistics*, 63, pp225-250.

Balapoulos, E T (1967), *Fiscal Policy Models of the British Economy*. North-Holland, Amsterdam.

Bischoff, C W (1969) 'Hypothesis Testing and the Demand for Capital Goods', *Review of Economics and Statistics*, 51, pp354-368.

Bischoff, C W (1971), 'The Effect of Alternative Lag Distributions', pp61-130 in G Fromm (ed) (1971).

Bispham, J A (1970), 'The Use of Engineering Orders for Forecasting', *National Institute Economic Review*, 53, pp38-53.

Boatwright, B D and J R Eaton (1972) 'The Estimation of Investment Functions for Manufacturing Industry in the United Kingdom', *Economica*, 39, pp403-418.

Brown, M (ed), (1967), The Theory and Empirical Analysis of Production, *Conference of Research in Income and Wealth Studies*, Vol 131. National Bureau of Economic Research, New York.

Burman, J P (1970) 'Capacity Utilisation and Determination of Fixed Investment', pp 185-202 in K Hilton and D F Heathfield (eds), *The Econometric Study of the United Kingdom*, Macmillan, London and Basingstoke.

Coen, R M (1969), 'Tax Policy and Investment Behaviour: Comment', *American Economic Review*, 59, pp370-379.

Coen, R M (1971), 'The Effect of Cash Flow on the Speed of Adjustment', pp131-196 in G Fromm (ed), (1971).

Coen, R M and B G Hickman (1970), 'Constrained Joint Estimation of Factor Demand and Production Functions', *Review of Economics and Statistics*, 53, pp287-300.

Confederation of British Industries (1965), *CBI Investment Incentives Survey*, Unpublished.

Corner, D C and A Williams (1965), 'The Sensitivity of Business to Initial and Investment Allowances', *Economica*, 32, pp32-47.

Corner, D C (1967), *Financial Incentives in the Smaller Business*. Occasional Papers in Social and Economic Administration, No. 5, Edutext Publications.

Eisner, R (1957), 'Interview and Other Survey Techniques and the Study of Investment', pp 513-584 in National Bureau of Economic Research Studies in Income and Wealth, Vol 19, *Problems of Capital Formation*, Princeton University Press.

Eisner, R (1969), 'Tax Policy and Investment Behaviour: Comment', *American Economic Review*, 59, pp379-388.

Eisner, R (1970) 'Tax Policy and Investment Behaviour: Further Comment', *American Economic Review*, 60, pp746-752.

Eisner, R and M I Nadiri (1968), 'On Investment Behaviour and Neoclassical Theory', *Review of Economics and Statistics*, 50, pp369-382.

Eisner, R and M I Nadiri (1970), 'Neoclassical Theory of Investment Behaviour: A Comment', *Review of Economics and Statistics*, 52, pp 216-222.

Eisner, R and R H Strotz (1963), 'Determinants of Business Investment', pp 59-337 in Commission on Money and Credit, *Impacts of Monetary Policy*, Prentice Hall, Englewood Cliffs, N J.

Federation of British Industries (1960), Memoranda of Evidence Submitted to the Committee on the Working of the Monetary System, *Memoranda*, Vol 2, pp114-128. HMSO, London.

Feldstein, M S and J Flemming (1971), 'Tax Policy, Corporate Saving and Investment Behaviour,' *Review of Economic Studies*, 38, pp415-434.

Feldstein, M S and M Rothschild (1974), 'Towards an Economic Theory of Replacement Investment', *Econometrica* 42, pp393-423.

Fisher, F M (1971) 'Discussion', pp245-255 in G Fromm (ed) (1971).

Fromm, G (1971), 'Introduction', pp1–8 in G Fromm (ed) 1971.

Fromm, G (ed) (1971), *Tax Incentives and Capital Spending, Studies of Government Finance*, Brookings Institution, Washington.

Gehrels, F and S Wiggins (1957), 'Interest Rates and Manufacturers' Fixed Investments', *American Economic Review*, 47, pp79–92.

George, K in collaboration with P V Hills, (1968), *Productivity andCapital Expenditure in Retailing*, Cambridge University Press.

Gould, J P (1968), 'Adjustment Costs in the Theory of Investment of the Firm', *Review of Economic Studies*, 35, pp47–56.

Gould, J P (1969), 'The Use of Endogenous Variables in Dynamic Models of Investment', *Quarterly Journal of Economics*, 83, pp580–599.

Hall, R E and D W Jorgenson (1967), 'Tax Policy and Investment Behaviour', *American Economic Review*, 57, pp391–414.

Hall, R E and D W Jorgenson (1969), 'Tax Policy and Investment Behaviour: Reply and Further Results', *American Economic Review*, 59, pp388–401.

Hall, R E and D W Jorgenson (1971), 'Application of the Theory of Optimal Capital Accumulation', pp9–60 in G Fromm (ed), (1971).

Harberger, A C (1971), 'Discussion', pp256–269 in G Fromm (ed) 1971.

Hart, H and D Prussman (1964), 'A Report of a Survey of Management Accounting Techniques in the SE Hants Coastal Region'. Unpublished (but the results have been published in part in *Accountants Journal*, January 1964, and *Scientific Business*, November 1964).

Jorgenson, D W (1963), 'Capital Theory and Investment Behaviour', *American Economic Review*, 53, pp247-259.

Jorgenson, D W (1965), 'Anticipations and Investment Behaviour', pp35-92, in J S Duesenberry, G Fromm, L R Klein and E Kuh (eds), *The Brookings Quarterly Model of the United States, North Holland, Amsterdam*.

Jorgenson, D W (1967), 'The Theory of Investment Behaviour', pp129-155 in R Ferber (ed), *Determinants of Investment Behaviour: A conference of the Universities – National Bureau Committee for Economic Research*. National Bueau of Economic Research, New York.

Jorgenson, D W (1971), 'Econometric Studies of Investment Behaviour: A Survey', *Journal of Economic Literature*, 9, pp1111-1142.

Jorgenson, D W and J A Stephenson, (1967), 'Investment Behaviour in US Manufacturing, 1947-1960', *Econometrica*, 35, pp169-220.

Jorgenson, D W and J A Stephenson (1969), 'Issues in the Development of the Neo-Classical Theory of Investment Behaviour', *Review of Economics and Statistics*, 51, pp346-353.

King, M A (1972), 'Taxation and Investment Incentives in a Vintage Investment Model', *Journal of Public Economics*, 1, pp121-147.

King, M A (1974a), 'Taxation and the Cost of Capital', *Review of Economic Studies*, 125, pp21-35.

King, M A (1974b), 'Taxation and Investment Incentives in a Vintage Investment Model: Reply', *Journal of Public Economics*, 3, pp195-199.

Klein, L R and P Taubman (1971), 'Estimating Effects within a Complete Econometric Model', pp197-242 in G Fromm (ed) (1971).

Klein, L R (1974), 'Issues in Econometric Studies of Investment Behaviour', *Journal of Economic Literature*, 12, pp43-50.

Lucas, R E (1967), 'Optimal Investment Policy and the Flexible Accelerator'[7] *International Economic Review*, 8, pp78-85.

Lund, P J (1974), 'A Cyclical Analysis of New Orders and Deliveries in the United Kingdom Engineering Industries, 1958-1971', *Economic Trends*, April 1974, pp xxxii-xl.

Lund, P J and D A Miner, (1973), An 'Econometric Study of the Machine Tool Industry', *Government Economic Service Occasional Papers 4*, HMSO, London.

Lund, P J and D A Miner (1975), 'The Nature of the Error Term in Distributed Lag Models', *Applied Economics*, 7, pp185-194.

Mackintosh, A S (1963), *The Development of Firms*, Cambridge University Press.

Mayer, T (1958), 'The Inflexibility of Monetary Policy', *Review of Economics and Statistics*, 40, pp358-374.

Mayer, T (1969), 'Plant and Equipment Lead Times', *Journal of Business*, 33, pp127-132.

Melliss, C L and P W Richardson (1976), 'Value of Investment Incentives for Manufacturing Industry 1946 to 1974', in *The economics of industrial subsidies*, Ed. A. Whiting, HMSO, London.

Ministry of Technology (1970), *Investment Incentives Survey*. Unpublished, but results summarised in Hansard, 14 Dec 1970, Written answers, cols 238-241.

Mizon, G E (1974), 'The Estimation of Non-Linear Econometric Equations: An Application to the Specification and Estimation of an Aggregate Putty-Clay Relation for the UK', *Review of Economic Studies*, 127, pp353-369.

Nadiri, M I (1972), 'An Alternative Model of Business Investment Spending', *Brookings Papers on Economic Activity*, pp547-578.

Nadiri, M I and S Rosen (1969) 'Inter-related Factor Demand Functions', *American Economic Review*, 59, pp457-471.

National Economic Development Council, (1965), *Investment in Machine Tools*, HMSO, London.

Neild, R R (1964), 'Replacement Policy', *National Institute Economic Review*, 30, pp30-43.

Nerlove, M (1967), 'Recent Empirical Studies of the CES and Related Production Functions', pp55-122 in M Brown (ed), (1967).

Nerlove, M (1972), 'Lags in Economic Behaviour', *Econometrica*, 40, pp221-251.

Nobay, A R (1970), 'Forecasting Manufacturing Investment – Some Preliminary Results', *National Institute Economic Review*, 52, pp58-66.

Rowley, J C R (1972), 'Fixed Capital Formation in the British Economy 1956-1965', *Economica*, 39, pp177-189.

Sumner, M T (1974), 'Taxation and Investment Incentives in a Vintage Investment Model: Comment', *Journal of Public Economics*, 3, pp185-194.

Taubman, P and M Wilkinson (1970), 'User Cost, Capital Utilisation and Investment Theory', *International Economic Review*, 11, pp209-215.

Taylor Nelson Investment Services (1970), 'The Why and the How of Company Investment', *The Director*, Nov 1970, pp334-339.

Tobin, J (1967), 'Comment' in M Brown (ed) (1967), pp50-53.

Treadway, A B (1969), 'On Rational Entrepreneurial Behaviour and the Demand for Investment', *Review of Economic Studies*, 36, pp227-239.

Trivedi, P K (1970), 'The Relation Between the Order-Delivery Lag and the Rate of Capacity Utilisation in the Engineering Industry in the United Kingdom, 1958-67', *Economica*, 37, pp54-67.

Wall, K D, A J Preston, J W Bray and M H Peston (1975), 'Estimates for a Simple Control Model of the UK Economy', in G A Renton (ed), *Modelling the Economy*, Heinemann.

Westlake, M J (1971), 'British Company Taxation and Automatic Stabilisation', *Applied Economics*, 3, pp257-274.

White, W H (1956), 'Interest Inelasticity of Demand – the Case from Business Attitude Surveys Re-examined', *American Economic Review*, 46, pp565-587.

The econometric assessment of the impact of investment incentives

P J LUND

Comments by M T Sumner

Readers of Dr Lund's comprehensive and perceptive survey may find his conclusion depressing, since it suggests a very low rate of return on the considerable intellectual resources devoted to studies of investment behaviour in general and of its sensitivity to fiscal influences in particular. 'That the incentives have been wholly ineffective' was denied, though more positively, by Matthews (1968) on the basis of an inspection of the time series of manufacturing output, investment and profit rates. The elaborate neoclassical formulation, in any of its variants, appears to have added nothing to the conclusions reached by earlier investigators, typified by Balopoulos (1967), who reported a positive coefficient on the capital allowance variable in his investment function, but whose estimates of the magnitude of that coefficient differed, in alternative formualtions, by a factor of two. Such conclusions are of little value to the policy-maker, or to the next generation of econometricians who, inspired by the present diversity,[1] pursue the ideal study. The burden of this comment is that Lund displays excessive caution in his statement of conclusions. The existing literature is much richer than he suggests, though it must be admitted that an uncomfortably large proportion of this intellectual wealth consists of intermediate output, in the form of implicit guidance on mistakes which need not be repeated. Nevertheless, even negative conclusions are better than nothing.

Without disputing Lund's view that the ideal study will remain illusive, it is instructive to identify the sources of the present diversity, and to appraise the prospects for progress in the individual areas of ignorance. The direct effect on investment of a change in fiscal policy may be viewed as a three-stage process, consisting of a relation between the fiscal instrument and the implicit rental price of capital services, the response of the optimal capital stock to the change in the rental, and the response of investment to a change in the discrepancy between the actual and optimal capital stocks. The value of this classification depends on differences in the degree of disagreement and in the possibilities of resolution at each stage.

The first link in this chain involves theoretical issues as well as empirical questions. A minor theoretical controversy concerns the specification of the discount rate used in the implicit rental: for the purposes of analysing the effects of a *ceteris paribus* change in the corporate tax rate, should the before – or after-tax rate of discount be held constant? Since the corporate income tax is very different in its coverage from the perfectly general income tax of the textbooks, most analysts have assumed that the post-tax discount rate, used by the firm to evaluate net-of-tax cash flows, will be constant. Hall and Jorgenson (1971) attempt to defend the alternative view[2] by appealing to econometric studies which suggest that the corporate income tax is not shifted in the short run, but this defence simply confuses short – and long – run tax shifting. It does not seem unduly optimistic to suppose that differences of this kind in the formulation of the rental could be resolved before estimation begins.

[1] Compare Hall and Jorgenson's (1971) result that the US corporate tax cut in 1964 depressed equipment purchases in the following two years by $801m, with Bischoff's (1971) estimates that the same measure increased the same aggregate by $218 m in the same period.

[2] Their assumption that the pre-tax discount rate is constant, together with the excess of tax-allowable depreciation over estimated economic depreciation, accounts for their result that the corporate tax cut reduced investment spending.

While such agreement would seem most desirable, not merely because it would reduce the range of estimated policy effects, it would leave unanswered questions as as to the legitimacy of partial equilibrium analysis. As Lund points out, the *ceteris paribus* assumption may yield incorrect results, because of interdependence among the components of the implicit rental. For example, a change in the corporate tax rate might have indirect effects on the net discount rate resulting from an induced change in the relative size of the corporate sector. To construct a model large enough to encompass all possible interactions would be an impossible task, and some imprecision will have to be tolerated as the price of producing an approximate answer rather than none at all.

A more immediate problem is posed by measurement error. That the problem is serious is strongly suggested by Feldstein and Flemming's (1971) finding that the individual components of the implicit rental entered with very different coefficients when the usual constraint was not imposed; indeed, only the allowance component $(1 - A)$ attained statistical significance. To some extent measurement error is inevitable, since unobservable variables like the discount rate, the physical depreciation rate and, for consistency with the theory, the expected inflation rate, appear in the rental formula. In consequence, the case for entering output and the rental as a composite variable cannot be dismissed as summarily as Lund attempts to do[3]; on the other hand, there is no case for imposing a specific form on the composite variable when there exists the alternative of applying a search procedure, as used for example by Boatwright and Eaton (1972) to obtain the best-fitting value of the substitution elasticity. In addition to being studied by this capital intensive technique, the constituents of the rental are also being subjected to closer theoretical scrutiny, though with results that do not always augur well for the future of Jorgenson's formulation, especially in its treatment of depreciation as radio-active decay at a constant rate (eg Nickell (1975)). This particular area of enquiry is highly controversial at a variety of levels, since it involves issues like the treatment of technical progress and the possibilities of factor substitution *ex ante* and *ex post*.

Not all problems of measurement raise such thorny conceptual questions, nor is error inevitable; yet many investigators have displayed conspicuous disregard of fact or theory in their selection of independent variables. Rowley's (1972) eccentric treatment of the allowances is noted in the paper. A more common source of diversity is the tax rate: most investigators have decided to include, or in a few cases to exclude, the additional tax imposed on dividends on the basis of some unstated criterion; yet *a priori* reasoning and empirical evidence presented by King (1972) both indicate that the appropriate tax rate is that levied on a company with a zero pay-out. Even the measurement of the corporate tax rate is problematic, as it is fixed in arrears, yet corporations have frequently been credited, albeit implicitly, with perfect foresight. The problem is not confined to fiscal variables. Apart from Boatwright and Eaton (1972), the UK studies which adopt Jorgenson's framework use gross capital stock rather than the appropriate net measure. Improved vintages of the neoclassical model, incorporating the most sophisticated technical advances economic theory can offer, will yield an unnecessarily low rate of return if new errors are introduced at the implementation stage. There is such abundant scope for improved measurement of the implicit rental and its relation with fiscal instruments that a belief in the possibility of progress is not too difficult to sustain.

The second-stage relationship between the implicit rental and the optimal capital stock requires less discussion. The crucial parameter involved here is the elasticity of substitution. While disagreement certainly exists, it appears to stem largely from a difference in time-horizons, reflected in the difference between the cross-section and time-series estimates of the substitution elasticity. In terms of the framework suggested above, the existing controversy concerns the third rather than the second stage: the ultimate effects of a change in the rental on the optimal capital stock depend on the long-run value of the elasticity of substitution, though in discussions of stabilisation policy a lower, short-run estimate would be more appropriate. A clearer identification of the questions at issue seems a precondition for progress at this stage. At a higher level of abstraction, the connection between this problem and the question of substitution *ex post* as well as *ex ante* is readily apparent.

The most intractable econometric problems arise at the third stage, in determining the distributed lag between a change in the optimal capital stock and the resulting flow of investment. A cursory glance at any comparative study of alternative estimates of the lag distribution is enough to indicate that the results exhibit extreme diversity. Since few prior restrictions can be invoked, there is little alternative to experimentation.

As Lund points out, one way of circumventing this stage is to adopt as the dependent variable one of the available measures of new orders for capital goods, rather than realised investment spending. The general case he presents for making this substitution is strengthened by a specific illustration of the misleading inferences which may be drawn from studies of investment spending. Such an example is provided by Feldstein and Flemming's (1971) statement that, when initial allowances were replaced by investment allowances in 1954,

'... some firms failed to recognise that the investment allowance was more valuable or were very slow to respond to the change'.

This conclusion was based on the systematic prediction errors produced by their initial equation during the currency of the investment allowance; these errors were eliminated when the calculated present value of allowances was replaced by a linear interpolation between the lower values which prevailed before and after this interlude. Yet their inference seems quite implausible; on the contrary, contemporary business and academic commentators exaggerated the difference between the investment and initial allowances by characterising them as a gift and a loan respectively. A sample of business opinion is reported, *inter alia*, in the case studies of Carter and Williams (1957). A representative academic discussion by Hudson (1954) implies an alternative and more cogent explanation for Feldstein and Flemming's problems with their error structure, in his observation that the introduction of the investment allowance,

'... at a time when specialised industrial machinery is about the only commodity of any importance still in short supply ... would appear ... to be rather odd'.

In other words, the curious results at the beginning of their sample period are a reflection not of perversities in the demand for investment but of supply constraints.

Despite the practical advantages of separating the investment process into sequential stages in order to isolate the effect of incentives on investment demand, the problem of lag structure is not thereby eliminated. Recent developments in the theory of the firm, summarised for example by Brechling (1975), provide a strong theoretical case for the existence of lags in ordering new capital goods, because of internal adjustment costs; the empirical significance of these developments is an as yet unexplored area. Moreover, the policy-maker requires information on the timing of investment responses to fiscal or other stimuli, as well as an estimate of their ultimate effects on the capital stock; hence the technical problems of estimating distributed lags must be faced in one form or another.

While the evidence on this question is, as noted above, remarkable only for its variety, the relevant studies have one common feature, viz. a long distributed lag in the response of investment to a change in the optimal capital stock, typically involving an initial delay of one or two quarters: Boatwright and Eaton (1972) have produced one of the few British studies particularly directed to this question; Evans (1969) presents a convenient graphical summary of American work. These results

⁴The relative merits of this and an alternative prescription for fiscal neutrality have been considered in Sumner (1975).

cannot be discussed fully here, but some perspective is provided by a rule of thumb suggested by Phillips (1962), that contracyclical policies will probably do more harm than good unless half their full effects on demand are realised within six months of the disturbance they are designed to offset. In the light of the available evidence, it seems clear that contracyclical manipulation of investment incentives could be consistent with this requirement only if policy changes were based on longer-term and more accurate forecasts than hitherto. This conclusion is strengthened when it is recalled that most investigations have not distinguished between the possible sources of change in the optimal capital stock when analysing the time-path of the investment response; the estimated lag structure is likely to be dominated by changes in output, but the putty-clay model of technology suggests a slower response of investment to a change in the implicit rental, a prediction which is confirmed by Bischoff's results. Apart from explicitly temporary changes in the rate of investment grants in 1967-68 and in the rate of the first-year allowance in 1971, contracyclical variations in investment incentives have not been employed for more than a decade. These latest episodes raise new issues which have not yet been satisfactorily analysed, but it is worth noting that the second of these experiments was overtaken by events, when the present approximation to free depreciation was introduced in 1972; at the same time, the Chancellor stated an intention to leave this system unchanged until at least 1978. Whether his intention will in fact be fulfilled remains to be seen, but, in view of the econometric evidence and casual empiricism applied to the experience of the 1950s and early1960s, there is a *prima facie* case for such a self-denying ordinance.

This negative recommendation in turn raises the question of the objectives to which investment incentives should be directed, pending the accumulation of more reliable econometric evidence as predicted optimistically above. One possibility would be to deploy the fiscal system so as to raise the proportion of investment in total output, in an attempt to raise the growth rate. Even if the objective were as manifestly desirable as proponents of such a policy implicitly suppose, the efficacy of the method would be questionable. Empirical studies have not revealed any simple, dominant association between growth rates and investment rates; *a priori* reasoning suggests that a permanent increase in the investment rate would produce a temporary increase in the growth rate, during the transition to a permanently higher level of output per head than would otherwise have prevailed. Sargent (1968) attributes an increase in the growth rate since 1953 to a contemporaneous rise in the investment rate, produced by 'an artificial stimulus to investment', and concludes that

'the strains which the economy has experienced in the process, and the limited rewards, must lead one to question the wisdom of forcing the economy through it again'.

This case against pursuing growth through fiscal investment incentives has not been challenged.

At this late stage of the argument, investment incentives may appear to be an instrument in search of a policy objective. This unusual state of affairs is nothing more than a reflection of the low priority accorded to economic efficiency, or the avoidance of excess burden to use the terminology of public finance, in discussions of investment incentives. Indeed, the phrase itself is instructive: the tax-deductibility of the wage bill is seldom described as an employment incentive. Without entering into the debate about the definition of a subsidy, symmetry considerations would suggest that the natural base from which to measure investment incentives is not a zero deduction, as implied by the calculation of the present value of grants and allowances, but treatment comparable to that of labour costs; this could be achieved most easily by free depreciation for all types of investment, together with the abolition of interest deductibility⁴. Semantics aside, a firm's input decisions would then be unaffected by the tax system; and, apart from transitional problems, an administratively costly system of inflation accounting would be otiose. These advantages of fiscal neutrality are considerable; in the present state of empirical knowlege, the case for permanent or cyclical departures from neutrality is far from clear.

Bibliography

Balopoulos, E T (1967), *Fiscal Policy Models of the British Economy*, North-Holland, Amsterdam.

Bischoff, C W (1971). 'The Effect of Alternative Lag Distributions', in G Fromm (ed) (1971).

Boatwright, B D, and J R Eaton (1972). 'The Estimation of Investment Functions for Manufacturing Industry in the United Kingdom', *Economica* NS 39.

Brechling, F (1975), *Investment and Employment Decisions*, Manchester University Press.

Carter, C F, and B R Williams (1957), *Industry and Technical Progress*, Oxford University Press.

Evans, M K (1969), *Macroeconomic Activity*, Harper and Row, New York.

Feldstein, M S, and J Flemming (1971), 'Tax Policy, Corporate Saving and Investment Behaviour', *Review of Economic Studies* 38.

Fromm, G (ed) (1971), *Taxation Incentives and Capital Spending*, Brookings Institution, Washington.

Hall, R E, and D W Jorgenson (1971), 'Application of the Theory of Optimal Capital Accumulation'; in G Fromm (ed) (1971).

Hudson, H (1954), 'The Investment Allowance', *Economic Journal* 64.

King, M A (1972). 'Taxation and Investment Incentives in a Vintage Investment Model', *Journal of Public Economics* 1.

Matthews, R C O (1968). 'Why Has Britain Had Full Employment Since the War?', Economic Journal 78.

Nickell, S (1975), 'A Closer Look at Replacement Investment', *Journal of Economic Theory* 10.

Phillips, A W (1962), 'Employment, Inflation and Growth', *Economica* NS 29.

Rowley, J C R (1972), 'Fixed Capital Formation in the British Economy 1956- to 1965', *Economica* NS 39.

Sargent, J R (1968), 'Recent Growth Experience in the Economy of the United Kingdom' *Economic Journal* 78

Sumner, M T (1975), 'Neutrality Of Corporate Taxation, or On Not Accounting for Inflation', *Manchester School* 43.

Printed in England for Her Majesty's Stationery Office by Burrup, Mathieson & Co., Ltd., London SE1 0NX.
S/908789/w Dd. 289840 K32 12/75